Freedom without Justice

INTERSECTIONS

Asian and Pacific American Transcultural Studies

RUSSELL C. LEONG
DAVID K. YOO
Series Editors

Freedom without Justice

The Prison Memoirs of Chol Soo Lee

Chol Soo Lee

Edited by Richard S. Kim

University of Hawai'i Press
Honolulu
In Association with
UCLA Asian American Studies Center, Los Angeles

22 21 20 19 18 17   6 5 4 3 2 1

Library of Congress Cataloging-in-Publication Data

Names: Lee, Chol Soo, 1952–2014, author. | Kim, Richard S.

Title: Freedom without justice : the prison memoirs of Chol Soo Lee /
    Chol Soo Lee ; edited by Richard S. Kim.

Other titles: Intersections (Honolulu, Hawaii)

Description: Honolulu : University of Hawai'i Press in Association
    with UCLA Asian American Studies Center, Los Angeles, [2017] |
    Series: Intersections: Asian and Pacific American transcultural
    studies | Includes bibliographical references.

Identifiers: LCCN 2016055631| ISBN 9780824857912 (cloth ; alk.
    paper) | ISBN 9780824872885 (pbk. ; alk. paper)

Subjects: LCSH: Lee, Chol Soo, 1952–2014—Imprisonment. |
    Prisoners—California—Biography. | False imprisonment—
    California. | Judicial error—California. | LCGFT: Autobiographies.

Classification: LCC HV9468 .L44 2017 | DDC 365/.6092 [B]—dc23
    LC record available at https://lccn.loc.gov/2016055631

For all those who selflessly gave to Chol Soo Lee

Contents

Acknowledgments

As a COMMUNITY-ENGAGED PROJECT, many people contributed to the publication of *Freedom without Justice*. First and foremost, I would like to thank Chol Soo Lee. Sadly, he is no longer with us, but he has left this brilliant and poignant memoir that illuminates obscured aspects of his remarkable story and a significant, yet largely forgotten, chapter in the history of the Asian American movement. I am extremely fortunate to have had the opportunity to work closely with Chol Soo on this important project. I am grateful for his trust in me as he opened up his life with incredible candor and honesty. I am indebted to K. W. Lee for introducing me to Chol Soo in 2005. Since I first met K. W. Lee in 2001, he has been a source of great inspiration and support for me.

While *Freedom without Justice* is a personal memoir authored by Chol Soo Lee, the long and arduous path to publication has been a collective project involving the generous efforts of many people. Upon Chol Soo's completion of the original manuscript, a dedicated group of undergraduates at the University of California, Davis (UC Davis) laboriously transcribed his 600-page handwritten manuscript into a word processor so that we could begin the editing process. I would like to give special thanks to former students Su K. Lee, Anna Kim, Bo Kim, Jiwon Kim, Daryl Suyat, and Simon Bin for their considerable time and efforts. Rodolfo-Jose Quiambao, a graduate student at San Francisco State University, also skillfully transcribed hours of supplemental oral narratives tape-recorded by Chol Soo Lee.

Emily Han Zimmerman provided expert editorial assistance. Emily helped organize and refine the original manuscript into the powerful, lucid, and coherent book presented here. She has been an indispensable part of the editorial process, providing astute analyses, feedback, and suggestions that improved the manuscript in immeasurable ways. I deeply appreciate and admire Emily's dedication to the project.

Many others have also contributed to this project throughout the years. I would like to recognize the following individuals in particular for their valuable assistance: Jeff Adachi, Eiichiro Azuma, Alfredo A. Bismonte, Tom Byun, Art Chen, Jack Chin, Chris Chow, Grant Din, Warren Furutani, Sandra Gin, Stuart Hanlon, Yoshinori Himel, Bill Hing, Tomo Hirai, David Kakishiba, Do Kim, Elaine Kim, Grace and Luke Kim, Kyu Hyun Kim, Emory Lee, Margie Lee, Stephen Lee, Russell Leong, Derrick Lim, David Michalski, Tom Nakashima, David Rue, Peggy Saika, Dayeon Shin, Brenda Sunoo, Gail Whang, Jai Lee Wong, K. Scott Wong, Ranko Yamada, Doris Yamasaki, Eugene Yi, David Yoo, and Grace Yoo. I am thankful for all their generosity, support, and encouragement. Julie Ha meticulously read the entire manuscript several times, offering valuable insights and suggestions each time. She has been a source of tireless enthusiasm and encouragement. Do Kim and the K.W. Lee Center for Leadership; Arnold Pan, Mary Kao, and Marjorie Lee at the University of California, Los Angeles (UCLA) Asian American Studies Center; and the staff at the Department of Special Collections at UC Davis Shields Library provided important assistance and support during the editing process. I am also grateful to the UC Davis Office of Research and the Dean's office in the Division of Humanities, Arts and Cultural Studies for their timely assistance. Many thanks as well to my faculty colleagues and students at UC Davis for their feedback and support.

I am indebted to Masako Ikeda and David Yoo, editors of the Intersections: Asian and Pacific American Transcultural Studies Series at the University of Hawai'i Press and the UCLA Asian American Studies Center. I thank their enthusiastic support for this project from the very start of our initial discussions. In the months before his untimely death in 2014, Chol Soo was very elated and hopeful to know that his memoir would finally be published for a wide audience after a long journey to publication. I am also grateful to the two anonymous reviewers for the University of Hawai'i Press. Their closely engaged feedback and thoughtful criticism of the manuscript helped me to tighten the narrative and sharpen my conceptualization of the memoir as a whole. Many of their insights are reflected in the published memoir. I am also grateful for the professional expertise provided by production editor Brian Ostrander and copyeditor Sue Sakai.

I want to thank my family, Sylvia, Olivia, and Darius, for their continual support, patience, and understanding while I worked on this project over the years. Lastly, special thanks to all those who selflessly gave to Chol Soo Lee throughout his life. He was profoundly inspired and forever grateful for the genuine care, compassion, and concern for him as a human being. This book is dedicated to all of you.

Richard S. Kim

Editor's Introduction

Chol Soo Lee's memoir, *Freedom without Justice* (FWJ), is a captivating and unique story of one man's wrongful incarceration for murder, and the actions he took to survive for ten years while political activists fought to win his retrial and freedom. As a book with both popular appeal and scholarly importance, Chol Soo Lee's story has great historical and contemporary significance that speaks to multiple and diverse audiences. It is at once a gripping chronicle of his conviction and incarceration for a crime he did not commit, a trenchant description of how prisons produce the non-normativity they purport to punish and prevent, and a poignant remembrance of an important, though now largely forgotten, chapter in the history of the Asian American movement. Lee's story thus provides valuable contributions to our understandings of post-1965 Asian American history, political and social movements, prison and carceral studies, and comparative ethnic studies.

Chol Soo Lee became a rallying point for a historic pan–Asian American movement in the late 1970s and early 1980s. Born in South Jeolla Province, South Korea, on August 15, 1952, he was raised by his aunt and uncle before immigrating to San Francisco in 1964 to live with his mother. In June 1973, he was arrested for murdering a Chinese gang leader in San Francisco's Chinatown. Despite his claim of innocence and the weakness of the evidence, Chol Soo Lee, then only twenty-one years old, was convicted of first-degree murder and sentenced to life imprisonment by the Sacramento County Superior Court on June 19, 1974. He was sent to serve his life sentence at Deuel Vocational Institution (DVI) in Tracy, California, during one of the most violent eras of prison gang warfare in the state's history. While imprisoned at DVI, Lee fatally stabbed a neo-Nazi inmate, Morrison Needham, in a prison yard altercation in October 1977. Although Lee claimed the stabbing was an act of self-defense, the prosecution accused him of carrying out a contract killing as a part of the prison's racial gang wars. Despite evidence to the contrary, Lee was convicted of first-degree murder. Because of his prior murder conviction, he was sentenced to death and transferred to San Quentin's Death Row.

Initially after his arrest in 1973, Chol Soo Lee received very little support from the Korean community; only a few sympathetic family members, friends, and acquaintances independently attempted to help with his legal case, but with no success. One of these early supporters was Ranko Yamada, a Sansei (third-generation Japanese American) college student who was personally acquainted with Chol Soo. Yamada tried to generate support among young people at local college campuses in the Bay Area. An American-born Korean community organizer, Tom Kim, also tried to raise awareness of the case within the small but growing local Korean community that was predominately made up of recent immigrants from South Korea, many of whom were college-educated professionals. While both Yamada and Kim encountered little success at the time, their continual support for Lee would be instrumental in his eventual release from prison.[1]

Mass support for Chol Soo Lee did not begin until 1977, when K. W. Lee, a Korean immigrant and a *Sacramento Union* reporter, visited and interviewed Chol Soo Lee at DVI. In January 1978, K. W. Lee published a two-part investigative report in the *Sacramento Union* called "Lost in a Strange Culture" and the "Alice-in-Chinatown Murder Case." In his investigative report, K. W. Lee questioned the verdict of the first trial, bringing to light a highly problematic police investigation and subsequent trial. The articles specifically criticized the ignorance, indifference, and racial bias of the California criminal justice system in its treatment of Asian Americans.

K. W. Lee's articles generated strong public support for Chol Soo Lee, leading to the formation of the Chol Soo Lee Defense Committee, a national pan-Asian network of support. Davis, California, residents Grace Kim and her husband, Dr. Luke Kim, and Jay Yoo, a UC Davis law student, established the first Chol Soo Lee Defense Committee in Sacramento, which eventually branched out to the San Francisco Bay Area, Los Angeles, New York, and other cities throughout the nation.

Based on suppression of material evidence and other irregularities in the first Chinatown trial, Chol Soo Lee's defense team filed a writ of habeas corpus with the Sacramento County Superior Court under Judge Lawrence Karlton in July 1978, setting into motion a bizarre, twisted journey through the California criminal justice system. Following the habeas corpus petition, the Chol Soo Lee Defense Committee, with funds raised from its supporters, hired renowned Chicago Seven defense attorney, Leonard Weinglass. In the fall of 1978, shortly before the DVI murder trial was to commence, the Sacramento County Superior Court began hearings for the habeas corpus petition, which, if successfully obtained, would overturn the San Francisco conviction. Aware that such an outcome would substantially alter the DVI trial by disallowing the death penalty and eliminating its death-qualified jury, the prosecution for the DVI trial, presided by Judge Chris Papas, proceeded with its case on January 19, 1979, while the hearing on the writ of habeas corpus was still in progress. Several months later, on May 14, the prosecution in the DVI trial succeeded in convicting Chol Soo Lee of first-degree murder and imposing a death sentence. During the course of the trial, however, Judge Karlton of the Sacramento County Superior Court granted Lee's defense team their petition for a writ of habeas corpus on February 2, 1979, and ordered that the Chinatown conviction be overturned. Yet the prosecution in the DVI trial maneuvered to have the habeas corpus ruling set aside as San Francisco prosecutors successfully moved to appeal it, allowing the DVI trial to continue and, ultimately, secure a death-sentence verdict.

In yet another surprising twist, on March 21, 1980, the Sacramento District Court of Appeals upheld the writ of habeas corpus ruling in the Chinatown case and ordered the conviction for that case to be set aside. Although ordered to be freed by the court, the San Francisco District Attorney's Office decided to retry Chol Soo Lee for the San Francisco killing rather than allowing him to go free. On August 11, 1982, the retrial of the first Chinatown case commenced in San Francisco. For the retrial, the Chol Soo Lee Defense Committee decided to replace Leonard Weinglass with well-known local defense attorneys Stuart Hanlon and J. Tony Serra. On September 3, 1982, a jury acquitted Lee of the Chinatown killing, and its foreman, Scott Johnson, joined the Chol Soo Lee Defense Committee. Despite this ruling, Lee remained on death row due to the first-degree murder conviction for the DVI killing.

On January 14, 1983, however, California's Third District Court of Appeals nullified Chol Soo Lee's death-sentence conviction for the DVI case, citing trial judge Chris Papas' misinstructions to the jury and allowing hearsay testimony in the death penalty phase of the trial. One month later, on February 28, the State Supreme Court rejected the prosecution's appeal against the appeal court's nullification of the prison murder conviction. In turn, the prosecution began preparations for a retrial of the DVI killing. Faced with the prospect of high legal expenses and the uncertainty of yet another retrial, Lee agreed to a downgraded second-degree murder charge without admission of guilt and was released from San Quentin State Prison on March 28, 1983, based on time served. Had it not been for the Free Chol Soo Lee movement, Chol Soo Lee would have likely never been released from prison with his life ending in execution.

Chol Soo Lee's life and saga occurred against the backdrop of great historical change in Asian American communities following the passage of the 1965 Immigration Act. At the age of twelve, Lee immigrated to the United States from South Korea in the mid-1960s to reunite with his mother, who had arrived earlier as a military bride. Consequently, Chol Soo Lee's life was both a transnational product of war and empire, and an uneven yet thoroughly racialized class system in the United States. Centrally located within these daily realities of post–1965 Asian America, Lee's experiences highlight the poignant realities of race and class inequalities in the United States that are still relevant today, serving as a powerful rejoinder to prevalent model minority stereotypes.

FWJ also provides a rare and valuable glimpse into a pivotal moment in Asian American history when the Asian American movement united around one of its first major political campaigns. A significant challenge confronting the Asian American movement in the 1970s was how to work with new immigrants from Asia, many of whom were different economically and politically from younger American-born Asian activists. The Chol Soo Lee case brought together immigrant and American-born Asian Americans in a common cause of justice and freedom for Chol Soo Lee. This historic alliance of supporters included student activists, elderly immigrants, religious organizations, small business owners, white-collar professionals, social workers, lawyers, legal assistance organizations, and left-wing communist groups from across the United States. The movement even generated transnational support from abroad in South Korea. Ultimately, the united front that mobilized to attain social and legal justice for Chol Soo Lee was an extraordinary coalition of people from a broad spectrum of social backgrounds.

The pan-Asian social movement emerging from Chol Soo Lee's legal case provides a generative way of rethinking the identity politics of race-based social movements, invoking George Lipsitz's call for more capacious models of political formation that base *identities on politics* rather than basing *politics on identities*.[2] The former conceptualizes identity as constantly open and contestable in its meanings and political use rather than proceeding from a presumption of a uniform political identity based on a specific racial, ethnic, or cultural identity that is central to the latter model. Accordingly, a common identity does not invariably lead to political consensus but rather a common political analysis and critique provide the basis for unified, progressive, and fluid conceptions of identity.[3] Indeed, the Chol Soo Lee movement represented the emergence of a diverse grassroots coalition founded on a shared understanding of social justice rather than a particular cultural or nationalist identity, in which people of different classes, ethnicities, religions, levels of education, generational histories, political affiliations, and geographical locations came together in a common political cause. As George Lipsitz argues, "The panethnic concept of 'Asian American' identity offers the quintessential model for interethnic antiracism in both activism and scholarship."[4] In these ways, the Free Chol Soo Lee movement holds great relevance for contemporary coalition building and social movement mobilization.

The Chol Soo Lee movement also highlights the politicization and empowerment of young people, who formed the backbone of the movement. Many of the young activists involved in the grassroots movement named in *FWJ*, such as Jeff Adachi, Art Chen, Sooknam Choo, Grant Din, Gary Eto, Warren Furutani, David Kakishiba, Tom Kim, Susan Lew, Jeff Mori, Charlie Park, Peggy Saika, Brenda Sunoo, Mike Suzuki, Don Tamaki, Gail Whang, Jai Lee Wong, Ranko Yamada, Jay Yoo, Frank Yoon, and numerous others went on to distinguished public service careers as community and political leaders. Chol Soo Lee's case helped forge a new political consciousness among many young Asian Americans, opening their eyes to the social inequalities and workings of institutional power in US society. The collective grassroots organizing of the Free Chol Soo Lee movement produced an enduring vision of social change and social justice that profoundly shaped the pursuit of lifetime careers in social and public service for many of the young people who participated in the movement.[5]

As it unfolded, Chol Soo Lee's case received extensive media coverage. The high drama inherent in his story even prompted Hollywood to produce *True Believer*, a fictionalized adaptation of the case starring James Wood as the celebrity lawyer (Tony Serra in real life). Lee's story was also featured on the television news program *20/20*, and popularized as a comic book series and a stage play in South Korea.[6] While his case inspired newspaper headlines, television specials, and even a Hollywood movie, until now the full story has never been heard from the protagonist's point of view. As a chronicle of the life of a youth at risk who was wrongfully incarcerated during a time when Asian American inmates were scarce, and Korean Americans even scarcer, Chol Soo Lee's story, told in his own voice, draws readers into a variety of social worlds—war-torn Korea, the streets of San Francisco, the urban public education system, the criminal justice system, prison gang politics, and death row. Chol Soo's narration of his experiences and struggles in these different arenas provides incisive commentaries on the social realities of race and class in America.

As subjective, first-person life accounts, memoirs offer a unique window into the inner life of the thoughts, feelings, and emotions of historical actors. In *FWJ*, Chol Soo Lee immerses readers in his mind-set, whereby he provides his reasoning and justifications for his choices, decisions, and actions. In doing so, he gives cognitive and emotional texture to his narrative, which helps bring his dramatic story and sense of humanity to life. Memoirs such as *FWJ* can thus enrich our historical understanding in valuable and distinctive ways in their elusive ability to capture the complexities, nuances, and contradictions of agency, choice, and lived experience that few other historical sources or texts can illuminate.[7]

While the narrative arc of Chol Soo Lee's memoir follows the trajectory from false accusation through incarceration and eventual release from prison, the bulk of his story occurs inside carceral institutions. As the civil rights–inspired campaign for justice unfolded on the streets and in the courtrooms outside the prison gates, the "inside" story of Chol Soo Lee has been left incomplete in the historical record. *FWJ* presents a view of the race and class dimensions of the criminal justice system from the perspective of convicts who fiercely refuse to be victims. While serving as the defense committee's rallying symbol of racial justice, Lee fought for personal survival for ten years in a parallel world almost completely invisible to his supporters outside of prison. On the one hand, justice triumphs when the defense committee makes history by succeeding in freeing Chol Soo Lee. On the other hand, it is obvious to the reader that the principled struggle for legal justice has occurred in tandem with a strikingly different order of moral complexity, defined by a hypermasculine prison code that dictates an ever-ready willingness and capacity to use unrestrained violence against fellow prisoners—especially when your manhood is challenged—and acting as if you do not mind hurting or even killing them to secure your standing and power within a prison system that is designed to dehumanize and break men of their will.[8]

FWJ invites readers into a step-by-step journey of character development under the extreme duress of life in prison. Chol Soo Lee recounts a series of intense life-threatening scenarios and reveals blow-by-blow details of his internal responses and decisions to act (or refrain from acting) for self-preservation. Readers are led inexorably to an understanding of how someone innocent of murder—someone we can identify with—becomes, by gradual increments, capable of justifying murder. Wrongfully incarcerated for life during one of California's most violent eras of prison gang warfare, Chol Soo Lee offers an insider's view of the California state prison system where racial rivalries are incited and exploited by prison officials. He assiduously narrates a long chain of events, accidents, and actions that place him in ever-increasing jeopardy, showing us how people with little margin for error find themselves entangled in circumstances that allow them no good choices. In the process, Lee provides a searing description of a carceral system designed almost exclusively for punishment and where talk of rehabilitation is futile. Without romanticizing or excusing criminality, *FWJ* shows the penal system to be a crucible for the production of brutal and inhumane actions, challenging the dichotomous constructions of the lawful and lawless prevalent in American public policy and popular culture.[9]

At the same time, *FWJ* is not just simply a story of physical survival. In a steady voice of direct exposition in which he seems to be speaking right to us, Chol Soo Lee narrates in great detail how he acted consistently in ways to elevate his status and power within prison society, where the standards and norms for succeeding are set by the strongest convicts who assess all others in terms of whether they can stand up for themselves or not. He tells us, for instance, how he tried to throw a bomb in another inmate's cell, an act that clearly improved his standing among other inmates. His fatal stabbing of Morrison Needham helped to render him a feared and respected convict among inmates. In San Quentin, he describes not only the attempts on his life, but his own plots to stab other inmates. As leader of the yard on Death Row, he explains how it is necessary to be prepared to kill or order others to kill, to maintain his position in the social order. Lee goes to a lot of trouble to explain as clearly as he can the rules and norms inside prison to be learned and followed by any prisoner who is expected to be there for a long time and needs to "fit in." He describes his constant struggle to maintain his pride and character within prison society by rising to the top of that world. In doing so, he shows an unapologetic willingness to tell us the truth to the extent he can.

With an entrancing sense of innocence and gentleness, Chol Soo Lee draws readers into this alternate moral order that is divergent with what those on the outside, or what he dubs "free" or "normal" society, believe to be right and wrong. Ultimately, the moral framework that guides his actions and decisions in prison is deeply at odds with the defense committee, whose members seek to bring light to the truth of his innocence in a wrongful murder conviction. But they have little notion of the truth of what his life has become in prison. Therefore, *FWJ* is all the more powerful and authentic in presenting a more complete version of the truth, in all its shades of darkness. Reading the memoir gives us pause to reflect upon and analyze our own lives and humanity as Chol Soo Lee shows us a life full of complexity, moral ambiguity, and contradictions, as is the case in most of our own lives.

FWJ also offers readers a humane, vivid, and even humorous inside view of quotidian facets of prison society, including daily activities, friendships, and resourceful living. Chol Soo Lee writes about people such as Johnny Spain and Stanley Tookie Williams, who are familiar to readers of prison literature.[10] He describes the lives and experiences of his fellow inmates without sensationalism or sentimentalism. At the same time, he tells a unique and compelling story that has not been presented before because he is not black, Latino, Native American, or white.[11] As such, *FWJ* makes an important contribution to a rich body of prison literature.[12] As in so many areas of American life, the experience of Asian Americans provides an optic on the US racial order not available from the perspective of any other group. Focusing on a particular Asian American experience, *FWJ* connects the microsocial conditions of Chol Soo Lee's experiences to an array of macropolitical contexts in the chronicling of his life in Korea and California, the racial order of the California prison system, and the role played by the defense committee in generating a historic Asian American movement.

Despite the unprecedented success of the Free Chol Soo Lee movement that helped secure his freedom from prison and the death sentence, Chol Soo's life after prison was anything but joyous; instead, it was continually marred by great difficulties and disappointment as he struggled to adjust to life outside of prison walls. Upon his release in 1983, there were no reentry programs waiting for him. Even after his release, Lee felt he remained imprisoned, admitting that he did not realize how "institutionalized" he was in trying to learn "how to live in a free society as a free man."[13] In my 2005 interview with him, he further explained how prison had fundamentally traumatized him as he faced seemingly insurmountable daily challenges in life outside of prison. He stated he was "not able to adjust to society . . . after living almost like a caged animal where violence is rampant and [there is] a code of conduct that is totally different from normal society. I lived in that for ten years, where life in that struggle is an everyday matter." Humbly confessing he felt like "just a baby starting over, all over again" at the age of fifty-three, he explained that life after prison was "the most difficult experience that I have experienced."[14]

Lonely and depressed, Chol Soo Lee developed a severe cocaine addiction and returned to prison in 1990, serving eighteen months for a drug possession charge. Released in 1991, he became involved in Chinatown gangs in San Francisco. While working for a Hong Kong organized crime triad that same year, he was nearly killed in a failed arson attempt. As a result, he suffered third-degree burns to over 85 percent of his body, leaving his face and body permanently disfigured and causing him multiple health issues for the rest of his life. Following the incident, Lee spent several years living under three different aliases as part of the FBI's witness protection program after surrendering information about the Chinese gang he worked for that allowed him to avoid prison time. Chol Soo Lee's tragic postincarceration experiences thus raise difficult questions, now more relevant than ever, about the lack of support for prisoner reentry, increases in at-risk Asian American youth entering the criminal justice system, and class-based divisions within Asian American communities.[15]

FWJ builds upon the 2005 *Amerasia Journal* interview that I conducted with Chol Soo Lee and Pulitzer Prize–nominated journalist K. W. Lee. During the interview, Chol Soo informed me that he was almost finished writing a memoir that he began in 2003. Since the publication of the interview, I steadfastly worked with Chol Soo to transcribe and edit his original 600-page manuscript, which he had laboriously handwritten with his heavily scarred and damaged fingers. I, along with a group of dedicated undergraduate students at UC Davis, painstakingly transcribed this lengthy, and often difficult to decipher, handwritten manuscript. While we were transcribing the manuscript, Chol Soo, no longer able to physically write for long periods of time, augmented his written memoir with hours and hours of tape-recorded oral accounts, which were also subsequently transcribed.

With the skilled assistance of independent scholar and writer Emily Han Zimmerman, we merged and edited this voluminous body of written and oral materials into its currently published form while working in close consultation with Chol Soo throughout the process until his untimely passing. Together, we arranged the written and oral source materials into a more lucid organizational structure that gives the overall narrative a stronger sense of unity and flow. While Chol Soo Lee composed the original draft of the memoir, we extensively edited for greater clarity, coherency, consistency, and readability while striving to maintain the integrity and authenticity of his authorial voice. In *FWJ*, one can almost hear Chol Soo Lee with his distinctive intonation and diction, speaking to us through the pages.

Anyone who knew Chol Soo Lee can attest to his photographic-like memory, evinced in his ability to recall minute details about people, places, and events throughout his life. He could also remember word-for-word conversations that occurred decades ago, as amply demonstrated in *FWJ*. Chol Soo's memory was remarkably accurate. His facts and details aligned with other available forms of evidence, including court records, newspaper articles, secondary sources, and other people's accounts. We have made the best effort to be as accurate as possible with personal names. When the real name was either unknown or needed to be kept confidential, we substituted names.

Besides his extraordinary memory, Chol Soo had a special ability to extemporaneously organize and articulate his memories into eloquent and compelling narratives. As a master storyteller, Chol Soo intuitively employed elements of fiction—setting, character, and dialogue—that give his narration in *FWJ* a dramatic cinematographic quality, engrossing the reader from start to end. His vivid descriptions effortlessly carry us to the numerous scenes that he recounts throughout *FWJ*.

In December 2014, Chol Soo Lee sadly passed away. He was sixty-two years old. In the months before his death, he had undergone an intensive series of surgeries to address multiple ongoing medical complications arising from his burns suffered in 1991. The cumulative effect of these surgeries left him emotionally and physically drained. In late November 2014, he refused to have yet another surgery and passed away at 4 a.m. on December 2. Although Chol Soo was in poor health in the last years of his life, he remained so strong and resilient. His entire life had been one of endless struggle and pain, but he never gave up. In an interview shortly after his death, Ranko Yamada expressed her sorrow and shock at his sudden passing, recalling that there were so many times she thought Chol Soo should have died, but he just "kept getting back up, back up."[16]

When I contacted former defense committee members to inform them of Chol Soo Lee's unexpected passing, Brendo Sunoo helped make sense of his untimely and seemingly avoidable death. Brenda knew Chol Soo quite well, first as a defense committee member and then as a close friend during his trials and tribulations in his postincarceration years.

Brenda explained that Chol Soo was always very stubborn about his medical care and in control of what medical advice he chose to take or not. In the end, she believed he had decided that he had enough and passed after making his own choices. In this respect, she felt he died in character. Brenda admitted that in many ways, she was relieved that Chol Soo had passed away quietly in a hospital on his own terms and not by coming in harm's way like he did so many times in his life, narrowly escaping death each time. Echoing Ranko Yamada's remembrances, Brenda recalled how the nurses in the hospital's burn unit kept saying that he should have died as a result of his horrific burns from his failed arson attempt, but his body just kept fighting and surviving out of habit because his whole life has been such a struggle. Perhaps now, Chol Soo will finally find the peace and solace that so eluded him throughout his life.

Although Chol Soo Lee left us before seeing the publication of his memoir, he was heartened to know in the months before his death that its publication was imminent. In working closely with Chol Soo on *FWJ* over the years, I got to know his intelligence, charisma, warmth, humor, compassion, hopes, joys, and resiliency. But I also came to know his deep pain, sadness, regrets, anger, doubts, loneliness, and disappointments. He was a complicated man and his life story was a complicated one, all of which makes his story so genuine, compelling, and human.

In 1978, the Chol Soo Lee Defense Committee produced and released a 45 rpm single entitled "The Ballad of Chol Soo Lee" to raise funds for, and increase awareness about, his case. The lyrics of the song poignantly capture the essence of Chol Soo's life and story documented in *FWJ*.

This is a story about a man named Chol Soo Lee
His case is not uncommon; it reflects on you and me.

Chol Soo Lee came to this country to walk the streets of gold
All he found were broken glass alleys where the gangs were pushin'
    dope
He tried to find an honest job to try to make ends meet
Do you sell your soul tryin' to earn that gold?
Do you hustle in the streets?

Strange ways in a foreign land made it difficult to belong
The Chinatown scene for a Korean man was a dream that had gone
    wrong

A captured bird in a gilded ghetto
What did he hope to be?
What did he hope to see?

Chorus:
He's not the only one
Nor does he stand alone
Joined by us all
His Spirit will carry on

There are things to see, truths to hear, there is life to be sung.

But a shot rang out in the alley
A man was lying cold dead
Witnesses—three out-of-town tourists—barely recollected
He kind of looked like this one, but they look alike you see
Cops in a hurry want to close the case so they handcuffed Chol Soo
    Lee.

The courts convicted Chol Soo on a hot Sacramento day
By a frosty white judge and a stone-cold D.A.
He's been in jail since '73 a soul on ice
Can you call it blind justice? You better start thinking twice.

This is a story of a prisoner and a man
Though a prisoner may be chained down, the spirit will always stand
There are captured birds behind barbed wire
The cage may stop their wings, but a voice will always sing

Chorus:
He's not the only one
Nor does he stand alone
Joined by us all
His Spirit will carry on

There is work to be done.

Chol Soo Lee's life and spirit touched so many people in deep and profound ways. He remains very much alive in our memories and in his words printed in the pages of *FWJ*. In my 2005 interview, I asked Chol Soo why it is important for people to know about his story. With his characteristic eloquence and thoughtfulness, he responded:

I feel that the greatest message that could be given from the Chol Soo Lee movement is that, as Mr. K. W. Lee said, the purity, the unselfishness, the integrity of people, giving to a stranger. And I think that message needs to be brought back to the Asian [American] community. I think we live in a world of selfishness. All the past movements, the civil rights to gain the right to attend schools and so forth, and now that education is being used for "everything is for me." We have no room to share with others. I think that if [my] story could be told, yes there is small room there. There are still deprived people, even more deprived people than in the past. The need to give today is far greater than in my own time.[17]

Indeed, there is work to be done. Chol Soo Lee's life shows us the worst and best in humanity. In telling his story in *FWJ*, we hope to carry on with the work that needs to be done.

Notes

1. Warren Furutani, "Chol Soo Lee: Freedom without Justice?" *Amerasia Journal* 10, no. 2 (1983): 73–88.
2. George Lipsitz, *American Studies in a Moment of Danger* (Minneapolis: University of Minnesota Press, 2001), 285–286.
3. Lisa Lowe, "Epistemological Shifts: National Ontology and the New Asian Immigrant," in *Orientations: Mapping Studies in the Asian Diaspora,* ed. Kandice Chuh and Karen Shimakawa (Durham, NC: Duke University Press, 2001), 274. George Lipsitz, "'To Tell the Truth and Not Get Trapped': Why Interethnic Antiracism Matters Now," in *Orientations: Mapping Studies in the Asian Diaspora,* 296–309.
4. Lipsitz, "'To Tell the Truth and Not Get Trapped,'" 305.
5. Grace J. Yoo, Mitchel Wu, Emily Han Zimmerman, and Leigh Saito, "Twenty-Five Years Later: Lessons Learned from the Free Chol Soo Lee Movement," *Harvard Journal of Asian American Policy Review* 19 (2010): 73–84, and Richard S. Kim, "In Search of Freedom and Justice: Thirty Years after the Free Chol Soo Lee Movement," *Amerasia Journal* 39, no. 3 (2013): 1–56.
6. Private investigator Josiah "Tink" Thompson also recounts his experiences with the case in his unique memoir, *Gumshoe: Reflections in a Private Eye* (Boston: Little, Brown, 1988).
7. Jennifer Jensen Wallach, *"Closer to the Truth than Any Fact": Memoir, Memory, and Jim Crow* (Athens: University of Georgia Press, 2008).

See also Marcus Billson, "The Memoir: New Perspectives on a Forgotten Genre," *Genre* 10, no. 2 (1977): 259–282; Paul Hoggett and Simon Thompson, *Politics and the Emotions: The Affective Turn in Contemporary Political Studies* (New York: Continuum, 2012); Jacquelyn Dowd Hall, "'You Must Remember This': Autobiography as Social Critique," *Journal of American History* 85, no. 2 (1998): 439–465; and Paul Thompson, *The Voice of the Past: Oral History* (New York: Oxford University Press, 2000).

8. Don Sabo, Terry A. Kupers, and Willie London, eds., *Prison Masculinities* (Philadelphia: Temple University Press, 2001), and Stephen D. Cox, *The Big House: Image and Reality of the American Prison* (New Haven, CT: Yale University Press, 2009).

9. See also Michelle Alexander, *The New Jim Crow: Mass Incarceration in the Age of Colorblindness* (New York: New Press, 2010); Lisa Marie Cacho, *Social Death: Racialized Rightlessness and the Criminalization of the Unprotected* (New York: New York University Press, 2012); Peter Caster, *Prisons, Race, and Masculinity in Twentieth-Century U.S. Literature and Film* (Columbus: Ohio State University Press, 2008); Ted Conover, *Newjack: Guarding Sing Sing* (New York: Random House, 2000); Cox, *The Big House*; Angela Y. Davis, *Are Prisons Obsolete?* (New York: Seven Stories, 2003); Ruth Wilson Gilmore, *Golden Gulag: Prisons, Surplus, Crisis, and Opposition in Globalizing California* (Berkeley: University of California Press, 2007); Caleb Smith, *The Prison and the American Imagination* (New Haven, CT: Yale University Press, 2009); and Bryan Stevenson, *Just Mercy: A Story of Justice and Redemption* (New York: Spiegel & Grau, 2014).

10. Lori Andrews, *Black Panther, White Blood: The Life and Times of Johnny Spain* (New York: Pantheon Books, 1996), and Stanley Tookie Wilson, *Blue Rage, Black Redemption: A Memoir* (New York: Simon & Schuster, 2007).

11. One notable exception that provides some consideration of Asian American experiences within the US prison system is Dylan Rodriguez's *Forced Passages: Imprisoned Radical Intellectuals and the U.S. Prison Regime* (Minneapolis: University of Minnesota Press, 2006), which incisively analyzes the words and writings of imprisoned political prisoners Viet Mike Ngo and Eddy Zheng in delineating what Rodriguez calls a "radical prison praxis." See also Dylan Rodriguez, "Asian-American Studies in the Age of the Prison Industrial Complex: Departures and Renarrations," *Review of Education, Pedagogy, and Cultural Studies* 27, no. 3 (2005): 241–263; Eddie Zheng and Asian Prisoner Support

Committee, comps., *Other: An Asian & Pacific Islander Prisoners' Anthology* (San Leandro, CA: Dakota Press, 2007); Johnny Thach, "Incarceration: Asian and Pacific Islanders" (Community Engagement Project, State University of New York at Binghamton, 2011); and Tamara K. Nopper, "Asian Americans, Deviance, Crime, and the Model Minority Myth," in *Color Behind Bars: Racism in the US Prison System,* vol. 1, ed. Scott Wm. Bowman (Santa Barbara, CA: Praeger, 2014), 207–243.

12. This body of literature includes works such as Jack Henry Abbott, *In the Belly of the Beast: Letters from Prison* (New York: Random House, 1981); Mumia Abu-Jamal, *Live from Death Row* (Reading, MA: Addison-Wesley, 1995); Lori Andrews, *Black Panther, White Blood: The Life and Times of Johnny Spain* (New York: Pantheon Books, 1996); Reginald Dwayne Betts, *A Question of Freedom: A Memoir of Survival, Learning, and Coming of Age in Prison* (New York: Avery, 2009); Edward Bunker, *Education of a Felon: A Memoir* (New York: St. Martin's Griffin, 2000); Eldridge Cleaver, *Soul on Ice* (New York: McGraw-Hill, 1968); Angela Y. Davis, ed., *If They Come in the Morning: Voices of Resistance* (New York: Third Press, 1971); Martha D. Escobar, *Captivity beyond Prisons: Criminalization Experiences of Latina (Im)migrants* (Austin: University of Texas Press, 2016); Kenneth E. Hartman, *Mother California: A Story of Redemption behind Bars* (New York: Atlas & Co., 2009); George Jackson, *Soledad Brother: The Prison Letters of George Jackson* (Chicago: Lawrence Hill Books, 1994); Ernie Lopez and Rafael Perez-Torres, *To Alcatraz and Back: Memories of an East L.A. Outlaw* (Austin: University of Texas Press, 2005); Susan Nagelsen, ed., *Exiled Voices, Portals of Discovery: Prose, Poetry, and Drama by Thirteen Imprisoned Writers* (Lebanon, NH: University Press of New England, 2008); Victor F. Nelson, *Prison Days and Nights* (Boston: Little, Brown, 1933); Jack Olson, *Last Man Standing: The Tragedy and Triumph of Geronimo Pratt* (New York: Doubleday, 2000); Leonard Peltier, *Prison Writings: My Life Is My Sun Dance* (New York: St. Martin's Press, 1999); Roberto Rodriguez, *Justice: A Question of Race* (Tempe, AZ: Bilingual Press, 1997); and Stanley Tookie Wilson, *Blue Rage, Black Redemption: A Memoir* (New York: Simon & Schuster, 2007).

13. Alice Kim, "A Story of Wrongful Conviction: An Interview with Chol Soo Lee," *The New Abolitionist* 40 (September 2006).

14. Richard S. Kim, "A Conversation with Chol Soo Lee and K.W. Lee," *Amerasia Journal* 31, no. 3 (2005): 88–89.

15. Grace J. Yoo et al., "Twenty-Five Years Later: Lessons Learned from the Free Chol Soo Lee Movement," *Harvard Journal of Asian American Policy Review* 19 (2010): 73–74. See also Johnny Thach, "Incarceration: Asian and Pacific Islanders."

16. Julie Ha, "Free, Free Chol Soo Lee," *KoreaAm Journal* 25, no. 10 (December 2014/January 2015): 31.

17. Richard S. Kim, "A Conversation with Chol Soo Lee and K.W. Lee," *Amerasia Journal* 31, no. 3 (2005): 102–105.

Freedom without Justice

Prologue

In the late 1960s, a new gang called the Wah Ching emerged in San Francisco's Chinatown and clashed with a rival group called the Joe Fong gang, also known as the Joe Boys. Most Wah Ching members were born overseas and were "fresh off the boat" (FOB) young men from Hong Kong, while the Joe Fong gang included both FOBs and "American-born Chinese" (ABCs). The two gangs formed competing centers of local power, and like two lightning bolts crashing over Chinatown, they clashed over which would prevail as the new organization in charge of Chinatown. The ultimate prize was power, and the goal was control of the streets—that is, control of all the normal activities of organized crime, such as extortion of gambling halls and stores, sale of firecrackers, and loan sharking.

Gang violence was not new to San Francisco Chinatown. The two youth gangs in the late 1960s and early 1970s—with members in their teens and early twenties—were caught and tried for cold-blooded executions carried out in broad daylight in Chinatown, including the murders of some tourists whose bodies were found on San Bruno Mountain. There had always been yelling and fighting between groups in Chinatown now and then, but this new struggle between the Wah Ching and the Joe Boys—with intensive violent killings aimed at total control of Chinatown—was new even to the Chinese.

By 1973, the Wah Ching gained the upper hand after false testimony by Wah Ching members sent Joe Fong and some of his officers to prison. But the Joe Fong gang continued to strike against its rival enemy, with each gang looking for a final assault that would decide the ultimate victor of their bitter struggle. Each gang, made up of sworn blood brothers bonded in life and death, devised new plans for deaths in the streets.

Meanwhile, people living in Chinatown, their souls filled with terror and disbelief at the new level of violence, witnessed the executions in silence. The Six Companies' elders, who traditionally wielded power in Chinatown, as well as the ordinary people of Chinatown, were all well aware of the identities of the members of the clashing gangs. Yet Chinatown residents stood by quietly as the death count rose and almost twenty youthful warriors—sons, relatives, and friends—lost their lives to intergang warfare. Even when a killing in the streets occurred right before their eyes, only a few feet away, the people of Chinatown upheld a code of silence: see nothing, hear nothing, and say nothing. Moreover, the San Francisco Police Department was doing nothing to solve the killings. White police officers were known to be "on the take," accepting bribes from Chinatown gambling halls while the killings and other street violence went unsolved.

In May of 1973, the Wah Ching's founder and leader, Anton Wong, was gunned down on the streets. His funeral took place on Grant Avenue, the main street of Chinatown. Leading the grand procession, a band played a loud rolling drum march to alert all onlookers. Unlike the ever-present tourists, for whose enjoyment both sides of Grant Avenue were lined with shops and restaurants, residents of Chinatown knew whose funeral was approaching. In front with the band, a Cadillac hearse displayed a giant picture of Anton Wong. This was followed by a long line of limousines holding family members, elders, and top lieutenants of the Wah Ching, as well as every member of the Wah Ching, their allies, and associates. Meanwhile, friends passing through Grant Avenue stopped at the spot where Anton Wong was killed and burned incense at the site. Gangster funeral processions had become a fairly routine event, honoring deaths on both sides of the war, but Anton Wong's funeral procession was the grandest and longest anyone had ever seen. All members of the Wah Ching, high and low, attended the funeral—with one exception. Noticeably missing was Anton Wong's close friend and advisor, a man named Yip Yee Tak.

In response to the unexpected death of Anton Wong, new leadership of the Wah Ching quickly reestablished itself and retained firm control over Chinatown. After Anton Wong's funeral ended, the top lieutenant called a meeting with the new leadership to raise the questions: Where was Yip Yee Tak? Where was the money entrusted to Yip Yee Tak for Anton Wong's legal defense fund? And as a matter of honor, why didn't Yip Yee Tak show up at Anton Wong's funeral? Yip Yee Tak's disrespectful absence raised more questions than answers for the Wah Ching leadership. They all agreed the only solution was to find Yip Yee Tak and have him killed on sight.

On Tuesday, June 3, 1973, at about 7 p.m., the weather in San Francisco's Chinatown was perfect for thousands of people to be out walking around. Tourists on holiday shopped for souvenirs and looked for good restaurants while the locals did their last runs for supplies. It was the best place to buy fresh items for that night's dinner or just wander about in any direction. Meanwhile, the Chinatown gangs were starting to get ready for the night's take.

Pacific and Grant Avenues were usually so crowded that most people in Chinatown were used to bumping into each other. This most crowded neighborhood in San Francisco was just a block from Broadway, the borderline separating Chinatown from North Beach and Little Italy. Besides the nightclubs on Broadway, upper Grant Avenue was famed for its sourdough bread bakeries, where a loaf bought at five or six in the morning was still hot out of the oven, as fresh as bread can be. Often, tourists on Grant Avenue headed into North Beach after eating, shopping, and gawking right and left at all the wonders of Chinatown and feeling the thrill of tension in the air that is unlike any other part of San Francisco.

That particular evening, a man in his midthirties walked alone through a somewhat less crowded area near Kearny and Pacific Streets. Moving toward Pacific, he passed hundreds of people—the usual out-of-town tourists, visiting locals from other San Francisco neighborhoods, and Chinese residents of Chinatown—all heading toward whatever their intended destinations might be. The man walked past the Ping Yuen Grocery and then crossed past one end of Beckett Alley between Kearny and Pacific. Just as he reached a distance of about fifty feet from the intersection of Grant and Pacific, a gunshot rang out over all the street noises of cars and hundreds of people. The man felt a bullet tear through him. He tried walking faster to escape the shooter but then fell facedown on the sidewalk on Pacific Avenue.

A young man in his late teens, with a clean-shaven face, approached from behind and leaned over. Cupping a gun between both hands, the young man fired two more shots—one into the fallen man's back and a final death shot to the back of the head. Then the gunman ran a few yards up the street to Beckett Alley, and as he ran, he tossed the gun into the alley. Perhaps he ran through Becket Alley to reach Jackson Street. Wherever he went, the shooter was leaving the scene in very fast motion.

Meanwhile, hundreds of people thronging the streets at all four corners of the Pacific and Grant intersection reacted as if in slow motion, turning around to see the source of the unusual noise, which sounded a bit louder than a firecracker. What had just happened? Perhaps they didn't believe what they'd heard—a gunshot followed by two more. Among those close enough to see a gunman execute a downed man in the back of the head, some stood frozen in place, shocked by the violence happening before their eyes and unable to accept that they'd just witnessed a murder.

The dead man's identity was known to some Chinese in the crowd. He was Yip Yee Tak, advisor to the Wah Ching. Now a pool of blood spilled all around the body of Yip Yee Tak, especially around his head, as he lay in view of hundreds of people. Some Chinese knew it was time to leave the shooting area before the police arrived while many tourists and other Chinese stood around still in shock. No one took any steps toward the victim to see whether he had any life left in him or any last dying words.

Only a few seconds passed between the first shot and the shot to the back of his head. In the few minutes until the police arrived, some people stirred out of their slow-motion minds, to think about what had just taken place in front of them. When the police started asking questions, many Chinese people left the area, but some white tourists remained and gave statements about what they had just witnessed.

The next day, on June 4, both the *San Francisco Chronicle* and the *Examiner* newspapers ran the story at the top of the front page. This murder got much more exposure than any past news coverage of Chinatown gangland killings, with quotes from the San Francisco mayor vowing that the murder must be solved at all costs. This June 3 murder seemed to suddenly shake some sense into politicians. There had been fifteen or sixteen previous Chinatown gang murders in the past four or five years that did not count or had been tolerable. Now, everyone from the mayor to every street cop promised to make sure Yip Yee Tak's murderer would be caught.

Chapter 1
San Francisco

John Louie's Gang

I, Chol Soo Lee, started hanging around Chinatown in the late 1960s, especially between 1971 and 1973. I had some family there—my nine-year-old half sister Margie and her Chinese American father, Frank Lee, who was like a stepfather to me. But I still felt like the lone Korean in Chinatown.

During those few years, I hung around Jackson Street, a main hangout for Wah Ching members, and at Mike's pool hall, which, unknown to me, was a regular Joe Boys' hangout. Larry, the owner of Mike's pool hall, and Gin, an older Korean guy, both took a liking to me. Gin was from Hawai'i and had a scar down one side of his face. I often hung around the pool hall late at night or else on Jackson Street, so both the Joe Boys and the Wah Ching saw me around. I believe both gangs viewed me as a loner who minded my own business and avoided associating closely with either gang. In the years when I lived in Chinatown, I was not bothered even once by any gang members during the war between the Wah Ching and Joe Boys. I had a quiet personality, which was the best kind to have when hanging around daily in areas where there were gang members and activities. Maybe my quiet personality was the reason I never got picked on. Even though I lived right in the middle of both gangs' neighborhood, I witnessed none of their gang activities, nor did I ask questions when Chinatown gangland murders made front-page news and continued to go unsolved. I was totally in the dark about gang activities. I was streetwise, but not in the ways of Chinatown.

My only contacts with gang members were very short conversations in passing. Gang members usually hung out in groups of nine or ten. I showed no desire to join any gang, but somewhere along the line, both the Wah Ching and Joe Boys must have gained some trust in me since they allowed me to hang around their main haunts. Perhaps they noticed that whatever I might see or overhear, I kept to myself. In addition, I had done my share of selling firecrackers during the Fourth of July season, buying from the Ping Yuen Boys without getting permission or paying protection money to the gangs, as some others did. So I must have been seen as a loner.

On May 2, 1973, I met John Louie by chance. John was the younger brother of Robert Louie, who was in jail. Robert had organized a small gang of mostly teenager ABCs, who called themselves the United Brotherhood. They operated out of Daly City and were better known as the Ski Mask gang for wearing masks while doing robberies. The Ski Mask gang had no ties to the Wah Ching or the Joe Boys.

I was sitting on the bench in front of Lucky M pool hall, across the street from International Hotel on Kearny Street between Jackson and Washington, where a lot of older Filipinos lived and hung out. John Louie came over and sat next to me, and we started getting to know each other, talking casually for over an hour. I had no idea he was leader of his older brother Robert's gang since John didn't impress me as a leader, much less a gang leader. John Louie was about sixteen years old, while I was nineteen. I saw him as just a teenager who wanted someone to talk to that day. But toward the end of the conversation, John informed me that he had a group under him. He said he was impressed with the way I expressed my thoughts and asked me to join him as his advisor.

John was physically small but carried himself in a manner older than his age. I think he might have known some of the Wah Ching as well as the Joe Boys. We were sitting just around the corner off the block of Jackson Street between Grant and Kearny, which even to this day is the main nerve center for whichever gang controls Chinatown. In 1972, the Wah Ching could be seen sitting in restaurants or hanging around the sidewalks of that block. It is possible that John Louie got some information about me from Wah Ching members before he approached me.

Though I accepted John Louie's offer to be his advisor, I was involved with him for only a short time. From time to time, I went to his house in Daly City, where he lived with his parents. During our meetings, we usually didn't talk about any criminal activities at first. He once got a tip about a house that was supposedly a good target for daytime burglary, but the burglary was a flop because we didn't find any money or valuables. Another time, John asked me to come over to his house. I went over, and we just sat around for seven days doing nothing.

Then one day, John told me we were going on a trip. There were five of us—me, John, John's sister, and two guys I'd never met before. One guy was a houseguest of John's, a fresh-faced ABC whose eyes were still inexperienced with survival on the street. He was the youngest among us and sat between me and John's sister in the backseat. The other guy was a member of John's gang, an ABC about my age, who sat in the front passenger seat while John drove. Even though it was my first time seeing that guy, we were not introduced to each other. I later found out his name was Ronald Fong. He was about 5'5" and 135 pounds with a look of streetwise confidence with hard-looking eyes set in a silent face.

The car was a blue four-door midsized working man's car, only a few years old, which did not stand out among other cars. We brought two handguns, which I advised John to keep in the trunk, in case we were stopped by police. Our destination was unknown to me until we were on the road, when John announced we were heading for Reno, Nevada. He didn't explain and I didn't ask any questions. Whatever my involvement would be, I decided to wait for John to inform me and to be ready for whatever action lay ahead.

We left Daly City at 10 p.m. in full darkness. There was near silence while John drove the car. John drove at a slow pace, staying away from the main freeway. We got to Reno at about ten or eleven the next morning, and John parked in front of a small casino, leaving the handguns in the trunk. John handed me a couple hundred dollars. He also gave some cash to his sister and the fresh-faced guy and told us to split up. The fresh-faced ABC would go with me into the casino, while John, Ronald Fong, and John's sister would go in a different direction. Strangely, John never explained why we were in Reno or what business we were about to take care of. I didn't ask any questions, and everyone else was silent. John didn't even mention when and where to meet up again.

Being uninformed, I guessed we were there to have some fun in the casino. The fresh-faced ABC went ahead of me into the casino. As I entered the casino, I lost sight of him even though the casino was fairly empty; it was still early in the day for gambling. I stood there, still wondering why we were there. I started looking to play the slot machines when I felt something on my back, like a large gun. Before I could turn around, a voice said, "Stay still!" I was then handcuffed behind my back as I saw a middle-aged police officer putting away his bully club, which he had used on my back like a gun. The police officer spoke in a relaxed voice instructing me to remain calm while another police officer joined him. As I was escorted outside to a squad car, I didn't see any of the others who came with me to Reno.

I was taken to the Reno city jail, where, much to my surprise, I was booked on a bank robbery charge. I knew nothing about any bank robberies. As the new guy, I had no information about John's gang's activities so I thought nothing of the charge. The cash I got from John was confiscated, along with the rest of my personal property, except for a few dollars that an inmate is allowed to have for buying things like smokes and candy bars from the jail commissary. Then I was placed in a cell tank with a few other guys. Being in Reno, the city jail had a few decks of used casino cards for passing the time. I kept to myself and waited to be let out since the bank robbery charge had nothing to do with me.

I remembered reading in the newspapers about a few bank robberies on the corner of Stockton and Kearny in the previous week or two. One of the robbers shot out a camera lens at a Bank of America about one hundred feet from the front entrance, just after the camera took one picture of a man wearing a nylon mask. He must have been a good shot to hit the bull's-eye target of a round camera lens. Later I found out the shooter was Ronald Fong, and I realized he was probably set up to get arrested in Reno. There may have been reward money for his arrest, especially after he shot the camera at the Bank of America. But at the time, I was unaware of Ronald Fong's role in anything, and even though we rode together to Reno, I didn't even know his name.

During this arrest, I was never informed of my Miranda rights. On the first two days, I was led into a room where a hard-nosed cop identified himself as an FBI agent and started threatening me with a tough-guy act as if to intimidate me. He asked me what I knew about the bank robberies, but I had nothing to say. The FBI agent told me the bills the Reno police had confiscated were marked money. On the third day, I was released, but the FBI kept the couple hundred dollars as evidence. The releasing police officer informed me that the girl would be released with me, along with the car that brought us to Reno. He said John Louie and the young ABC, who were both minors, were going to San Francisco Juvenile Hall. As for Ronald Fong, there was no mention of him. John Louie's sister drove me back to San Francisco, and I received no contact from John Louie or that young ABC guy again.

Garden of Eve

In early 1973, I was doing some work for the Garden of Eve, a strip club on Broadway Street, across from Big Al's between Columbus and Kearny Streets. I had met the owner, Bob, when he asked me to pass out flyers on Broadway. I did better than passing out flyers by bringing small groups of people into the Garden of Eve. Bob then tried to teach me to drive his Plymouth Road Runner, which had a sign on top advertising the Garden of Eve, but I didn't take to driving too well. Anyway, he paid me twenty dollars for a few hours of drawing in customers, and now and then he'd lay out twenty or thirty dollars as an extra bonus, or he'd give me twenty dollars when I occasionally asked when I was short on money. I also got to know Bob's manager, John, and during one of our short conversations, John said he'd gotten out of San Quentin penitentiary "not too long ago." I thought John must have known Bob for a long time to get hired as manager of the Garden of Eve.

Sometimes, just after the club closed, I would stop by to see Bob for my nightly pay, and I often saw an older African American janitor there. The janitor looked to be in his forties and didn't say much or show any emotions, not even a smile. He had the eyes and set face of someone used to being around the streets for a long time. One time, I got there just after 2:00 a.m. when everyone else had left, and I saw the janitor taking money from the cash registers. Apparently, he was in charge of the night's take since he counted and handled the money, even when Bob and John were around. I found this unusual, as if Bob didn't really own the Garden of Eve. Maybe Bob was just a front person for the real owner.

One night, near the end of May, after the Garden of Eve closed, I was hanging around with John and Bob and the janitor when John said to me, "Hey, Lee! Let me show you something."

"What?"

"Hey, what you think about this?" John brought out a gun, a .357.

It was the first time I'd held a gun in my hand. I said, "Man. This is a sharp-looking gun. A cool gun."

"Yeah. This is real pretty, isn't it?"

"Yeah."

Then I asked John, "Can I borrow the gun for a few days?" even though I did not know John that well.

"For what?"

"Well, I don't know. I am thinking about pulling a robbery or something." This was just an excuse. I didn't really have much thought about what I would do. Basically, I just wanted to look at the gun and see what it feels like to have a gun.

John said, "Okay. Just make sure you return it back to me. And if you use the gun for anything, make sure you let me know."

Arrest

At the time, I lived in a hotel on Broadway just above Mr. Dee's night-club. It was just one room I rented for thirty-five dollars a week, a few blocks from the Garden of Eve. The day after I borrowed the gun from John, my girlfriend, Sandy, came over to spend the night at my place. During the night, I started showing off the gun. Sandy was nervous to see me with the gun, as I was playing with it by pulling the trigger back while it was loaded. I was inexperienced with a gun, and the gun shot off accidentally. After that, Sandy got really scared. I was worried the cops would show up, since it was late at night and the shot sounded loud enough for anyone to hear inside and outside the hotel. However, neither the hotel manager nor the cops came, so Sandy and I continued to stay in my place for the night.

Two days later, I heard a knock on my door.

"Who is it?"

"Police officer."

I still had the gun hidden in a drawer. I opened the door and saw a lone, middle-aged, uniformed police officer, who politely asked about the gunshot reported two days ago.

I said, "Friend of mine visited that night, and his gun went off accidentally."

"Who was visiting you?"

"Guy named Fong." Fong was just the first name that came to my mind.

"Who's Fong?"

"I don't really know Fong too well." I think the cop knew I was lying.

"Show me where the bullet went," the cop said.

I showed him the hole in the window.

"Okay." The cop pulled out a short notepad and wrote something down. The interview lasted only a few minutes.

On the afternoon of June 3, 1973, I received another knock on my door. When I opened the door, an old Filipino man who lived in the same hotel, informed me, "Someone's calling you on the phone."

At the public phone in the hallway, the caller was Sandy. "Pick me up at the Fairmont Hotel, at the employee entrance," she said.

Sandy's grandmother worked at the Fairmont, the most expensive hotel in San Francisco, high above Chinatown overlooking the city and bay. I left my place, walked through Chinatown on Stockton, turned onto Sacramento, and walked uphill to the hotel side entrance. It was about 7:30 p.m. When I knocked, an elderly Chinese lady opened the door with Sandy standing behind her. Even though I had never met Sandy's grandmother, I guessed that was her. The grandmother had a firmly set face and spoke no words as Sandy said "bye," squeezing past her to meet me outside.

Sandy was nineteen years old, and I was twenty. Neither of us had any plans, so we walked downhill on Sacramento to Stockton, passing through Chinatown on an indirect route to Broadway in North Beach. Then we walked through a few blocks of nightclubs and strip joints on Broadway, where the nightlife was just starting to sparkle and come alive. At the time, I was taking some speed in pill form. Sandy was not into drugs, but now and then she would take a little bit of speed with me. That day, I had a few speed pills, and after we returned to my place, both of us got high. After an hour or two, Sandy got very paranoid about the gun, which I'd taken out of the dresser. I was not touching or playing with the gun, but Sandy kept pushing the gun under the bed, and I kept bringing it back out without realizing how mad Sandy was getting. After we argued twice about where the gun should be, Sandy said she wanted to leave. I wanted her to stay. I tried to keep Sandy at my place until she calmed down, but she got worse, to the point where we were knocking over the old furniture in the room and making a lot of noise. This happened at around 9:00 p.m.

Finally, Sandy got out of the room and ran fast down the stairs to get out of my place. The hotel manager's apartment was located about ten feet from the stairwell, and as I reached the top of the stairs to follow Sandy, I saw the manager's apartment door was open. She was standing and watching us, and must have heard the noise of our argument through the walls. Seeing the manager, I returned to my room thinking, "The manager will call the police because of the noise we made. With the gun in my room, the last thing I want is a visit from the police." So I took the gun and left my place.

After I was on the street, I decided to go to Joanna's house. Joanna, whom I was seeing from time to time, was a few years older than me. She always welcomed me to her rented house on Anza at Masonic, which she shared with a few friends. I took the bus to Joanna's house and stayed there for two days until June 6. That day, she and her roommate said they were going to visit Chinatown, so I decided to go with them. After we got to Chinatown, I told Joanna I was going back to my place. As I walked along Broadway, I thought of returning the .357 to John, but when I stopped by the Garden of Eve, the bartender said John was not around. So I kept the gun and walked the few blocks to my place on Broadway.

I opened the front door with my key. As I closed the door behind me with my hand still on the doorknob, all in one motion the door swung open suddenly and someone had his foot against my lower stomach. The hallway was only three feet wide, and some white man was pinning me against the wall with his right leg, bracing his back against the opposite wall. He pointed a gun at my face and howled up the stairs. "I got him!"

Another white man came downstairs, with his gun drawn and aimed at me. Both of these guys seemed to be in their late twenties, and by their actions I guessed they were plainclothes police officers. I had the .357 tucked in the waistband of my pants, and the first cop's foot, pinning me by the stomach, was right over the gun, so when his partner did the pat-down search, he missed the gun. I figured the cops were there because of the argument between me and Sandy, and there was no way I could get rid of the gun, so I said, "I have a gun on me." This took both of them by surprise. After I told them where the gun was, one of them removed it and then handcuffed me behind my back. I was told I was charged with murder.

I was very much surprised since I had no knowledge of any murder. I had never committed a crime anything near to murder. I was placed in the backseat of an unmarked car with one cop sitting beside me while the other cop drove. No one questioned me about anything during the ride. The ride to the Hall of Justice, which took about fifteen minutes, was a time of total silence while I wondered, what murder? I knew it was just a misunderstanding that would be quickly cleared up. I didn't think much about the murder charge because I was more concerned about the gun charge I was sure to face, as I rode handcuffed toward 850 Bryant Street.

Hall of Justice

The Hall of Justice was a light gray, seven-story building that served as headquarters for the San Francisco Police Department (SFPD), as well as the location for the municipal and superior courts. The city prison on the sixth floor received all incoming prisoners in custody of the police department. On the seventh floor, the San Francisco County Jail held prisoners going to court or awaiting trial.

The car pulled into an underground garage. I was taken from there to an office area with desks and a few rooms. The first room to my right had light-colored walls, a wooden table in the middle, and four metal chairs with padded seats, two on each side of the table.

Pretty soon, two plainclothes officers entered the room. Both of them were white men, and I don't recall much about the taller and older of the two, but the younger officer I remember clearly. He was about 5′11″ and 180 pounds, well built, with a roundish body and round face, and a short haircut. He introduced himself as Inspector Frank Falzon. Both cops sat down, ready with a small tape recorder and legal pad. Inspector Falzon read me my Miranda rights and asked if I understood those rights. I said I understood. Falzon then asked if I was willing to answer some questions. Was I voluntarily answering the questions of my own free will? I hesitated but said yes. Did I mind being tape recorded? I consented.

Knowing I'd been arrested for murder and knowing nothing about a murder, only one thought came to my mind—something must have happened to Sandy. I was nervous about the questions these cops had for me. The taller older cop started the questioning, while Falzon, even with the tape recorder on, wrote on a legal pad with fierce concentration, as if his life depended on it. The initial line of questioning focused on the accidental gunshot in my apartment.

"Where did you get the gun?"

"Borrow from friend at nightclub on Broadway," I said, giving a false name.

"And the bullets?" I had been carrying a small pouch of .38 bullets, which matched the bullets in the .357.

"Bullets was in gun when I borrow it. Day or two later, I purchase bullets from gun store in Richmond neighborhood, San Francisco," I said.

"On what dates did you borrow the gun and buy the bullets?"

"I don't keep track my daily activities, not sure exact dates. I think I borrow gun late May."

Then the questioning shifted. "What were you doing in the past ten days?"

I answered those questions as best as I could recall. The only bit of difficulty I had was in trying to remember the last three to five days.

"What were you doing on June 3rd?"

"A man in hotel come to door, say I have phone call," I replied. "My girlfriend Sandy ask to pick her up Fairmont Hotel where grandmother works. Then me and Sandy return my place on Broadway." I did not mention that Sandy and I took speed and had a loud argument at my place. "Then I go spend couple days Joanna's place, then return my place, where cops wait to arrest me."

This question-and-answer session took about an hour and was conducted in a normal tone of voice. At the time, I was asked no questions about the shooting death of Yip Yee Tak or about Chinatown gangs. Then the two cops escorted me to the city prison on the sixth floor, where I was booked on a murder charge. After having my fingerprints and pictures taken, I was allowed to make two phone calls. First I called Sandy but got no answer. Then I called Bob at the Garden of Eve. I told him I was charged with murder. It made no sense for me to call Bob for help with a murder charge when I only worked for him now and then, but no one else came to mind that might help me.

"Can you help me find an attorney?" I asked.

"OK, I'll try to help," Bob responded with no conviction in his voice.

Still, I believed the police would investigate my responses to their questions as well as investigate the murder case itself. I was thinking, "Whatever this case is about, I have no ties to it, so the murder charge against me will be dropped. It's just a mistake. How can I be charged with killing someone when I have no knowledge of the killing?"

I was like an innocent man being taken up the steps of the gallows to be hanged, while still certain that truth would prevail—the police would see their mistake and an innocent man would be cleared. I had the simpleminded thinking of a not-guilty person, so I took the murder charge against me very lightly. An innocent man getting hanged? That just did not happen. As a twenty-year-old high school dropout, I had never heard of anyone getting framed for murder. I had faith in the United States' justice system. Perhaps most people in the same circumstance would think this way, disbelieving the seriousness of being charged with murder.

After the fingerprinting, phone calls, and some medical shots, I was given a tin cup, a spoon, and two blankets. In the San Francisco city prison, inmates are allowed to wear the personal clothing they had on at the time of arrest. I was treated like any other prisoner and led to a light green–colored cell, one of four, twelve-man cells in the back tank. Thin mattresses rested on steel-frame beds, consisting of six lower bunks and six higher bunks. There was a gray toilet and sink in each cell. Outside the twelve-man cells, in the middle of the tank, were long stainless steel benches where the prisoners usually ate. There was also a shower and toilet. I was placed in the first cell to the left and found a green lower bunk in the back. In each of the twelve-man cells, everything happened out in the open, even using the toilet, so the only privacy came from invisible walls within each prisoner's mind. The one similar thought in our private minds was, "When will I be free? What's next toward being free?"

I was the only Asian in the tank among a mix of races. There were a majority of African Americans along with a few whites and Latinos. Eighteen was the youngest age for being held in the city prison, so most prisoners were older than me. The charge against each prisoner could be anything from a misdemeanor to first-degree murder. Prisoners rarely talked about the cases against them, however. Many were older—in their midthirties—and had already experienced jail before. Some were undergoing withdrawal from heroin addiction. Most had already adjusted to being there and kept to themselves, passing the time by lying on their bunks or having quiet short conversations in normal voices. It was as if they were all tired out from whatever they had been doing on the outside, and being in the city prison was a time for taking a break and resting.

Every day at around 7:00 a.m., your cell was opened for breakfast and warm cereal with two or three slices of bread was placed on your tin plate and coffee was poured in your tin cup. The cell stayed open until about 4:00 p.m., when it was closed for the SFPD prison guards to conduct a prisoner count. I soon learned you were allowed to smoke. If you had the money, you could buy smokes and candy bars from the commissary man, who stopped daily in front of each tank (the city prison had about ten tanks) with his rolling cart and sold items through the bars. Also, each morning and afternoon, prison guards came around calling out names of those scheduled for court appearances that day. Throughout the day, the loudest noise you heard was guards calling prisoners' names, usually for visitors. For a personal visit, you used a booth behind a glass panel and talked to your visitor through an old telephone. Attorney visits took place face-to-face in a small room.

On June 7, 1973, the day after my arrest, I heard my name called for an attorney visit. I was escorted to the room, where a heavyset middle-aged man with a full beard introduced himself as Clifford Gould of the San Francisco public defender's office. He said he had just gotten my case file and would be representing me as my attorney.

In 2005, thirty-two years later, Mr. Gould recalled this first interview, and how we were unable to communicate fully due to my poor English. I was still speaking broken English, after living in the United States for eight years. He remembered trying to find out if I had any friends or family who could help me as a support network and reached the conclusion that I was totally alone. He could see I was concerned about what was happening to me. I asked him if he would be my permanent attorney. Mr. Gould said yes, he would represent me. Then he informed me that the next day I would stand in a police lineup to be viewed by witnesses to the murder. I believe I was searching for security from Mr. Gould, for someone to protect me. Even when I seemed to take the murder charge lightly, I must have been worried.

The next day, I was taken to a lineup alongside five other Asians, all Chinese. Later I learned the names of three of them. One was John Louie's older brother Robert (founder of the Ski Mask gang). Also in the lineup were the Leng brothers, John and Jerry, who were Wah Ching members and FOBs. There was another Chinese ABC, who seemed to know me from John Louie's gang. Then there was one other guy I can't recall. None of us looked anything alike. Even the Leng brothers looked different from each other. At the time, I wore a mustache, which no one else in the lineup had. The police lineup was supposed to consist of people who resembled each other, so that no one person stood out from the others.

Each of us was given a large number covering our chests. We stood with bright lights in our faces, while some unknown witnesses, police officers, the D.A. (district attorney), and the public defender viewed us from behind darkness. We were asked to look straight ahead, turn sideways, and pose in shooting position as if holding a handgun. The lineup may have taken about ten minutes.

Strange Visitor
On the same day as the lineup, I received a strange visitor. I was called out by the prison guard and led to the attorney visiting room. Sitting there was a lean guy about thirty years old with distress and anger showing on his face. I could see he was Korean, from Korea. Very coldly, he informed me that he came from the Korean consulate's office in San Francisco. He didn't bother to show me any identification or even a business card, and right from the start of the conversation, in a voice louder than normal, he started demanding that I should confess to the crime of murder. When I tried to inform him I had nothing to do with the murder, he continued talking as if he did not even hear me. He kept insisting, "You must confess to the crime!"

I kept trying to tell him I was innocent of the murder charge against me, and I needed help. However, he continued demanding that I make a full confession to the police. I was a bit shocked and shaken up by this. Here was a man who represented the consulate, the Korean government. I felt confused as to why the consulate had taken an interest in my case, as well as totally surprised by his visit. After about ten minutes of angry insistence that I confess, he walked out of the visiting room, looking very disgusted with me.

I sat there, baffled. Here was this man from the Korean consulate, to whom I had briefly hoped I could explain my innocence and even seek help to prove it. Why did he demand I confess to the crime? What reasons did he have without even listening to one word of what I was trying to say? I left the room feeling more emptied of hope than ever, feeling that I stood alone in facing the false murder charge.

I started taking the charge against me more seriously.

Justice versus Justice System

The morning of the third day after my arrest, I was called out to go to court. I was placed in a large holding cell with about twenty others awaiting arraignment. Upon entering the court, I was asked to state my name, and the judge read off two charges against me: murder in the first degree and ex-felon with a gun. It was just a routine court appearance that was over in a few minutes.

In retrospect, it seems strange that there was no news coverage of my arrest, considering I was the only person ever charged with murder after a string of sixteen unsolved murder cases involving Chinatown gang warfare. Numerous gang members had committed murder on the streets of Chinatown, and there had been much news coverage of the unsolved murders, especially after Yip Yee Tak's murder when the mayor publicly demanded that the case be solved and a special Chinatown gang task force was formed. Yet the San Francisco media was totally in the dark and silent about my arrest.

Since I was brought up in Korea's traditional Confucian society, I respected the judges, as well as the law enforcement officers, and assumed they were all honorable people. I firmly believed that mistaken identification led to my arrest on a murder charge, and it would be cleared up in due time. As a twenty-year-old facing a life sentence for a murder charge, I can't imagine what my state of mind would have been like without that belief. I would have felt totally overwhelmed. I knew the case against me was a reality, but I had to think justice would prevail to keep my personal spirits up in facing the false charge against me.

I tried to seek support from Jeff Mori and a few other people I knew from the Japanese Community Youth Council, where Jeff was the executive director. I had known Jeff for two years, and I felt great friendship toward him. Jeff visited me after my arrest, as did Tom Kim, the Korean Community Service Center's director, whom I had met a few times in Chinatown. Both were community activists. Neither was able to draw the attention of Asian American communities to my case, however. They knew I was innocent of the murder charge, but people seemed to view my case as falling outside the civil rights struggles of Asian American communities, especially since it related to Chinatown's ongoing gang violence. This circumstance seemed to prevent them from speaking out on my behalf, even though I was wrongly facing a murder charge. Thirty-two years later, retired public defender Clifford Gould said, "What I remember most is that the case against you was so neatly put together, it seemed like a CIA plot."

Frame-up

I have to admit that I had no clue at the time what it meant to go through the legal system. I was not a lawyer. I recall being taken to the municipal court for pre-preliminary hearing motions, and then, two months after my arrest, returning for the preliminary hearing, which lasted less than a day. At the hearing, the three main witnesses against me were all white American men—out-of-state tourists who visited Chinatown that day. One was a young man in his early twenties, serving in the US Navy, and the other two were his friends, a young man training with the US Olympic ski team and an older man in his thirties who used to work as a counselor at San Francisco's Juvenile Hall. I believe this older witness may have convinced the other two eyewitnesses to turn against me since he had seen me before at Juvenile Hall. He had been working there in 1969 when a few other teenagers and I escaped by forcing open a door. Some months after breaking out of Juvenile Hall, I had been arrested again, and even though I was under eighteen, I was not returned to Juvenile Hall but instead held in the San Francisco County Jail. That is how my teenage face ended up in the mug shot book of Asian adults.

Now at the preliminary hearing, all three witnesses stated that they had picked me out of that mug shot book from when I was sixteen or seventeen years old. My face looked totally different then, rounder with a bit of baby fat and no mustache. The witnesses also said they recognized me at the lineup as the shooter of Yip Yee Tak on the afternoon of June 3, 1973, though my face now was leaner and had a mustache compared to the mug shot book out of which they supposedly picked me out. These three witnesses had stood twenty-five to thirty feet from the shooting, which took place in a span of five or six seconds on a crowded street. How had they witnessed it? At first, their initial statements to police right after the murder had claimed a clean view of the shooter and described him as being 5'7" to 5'9", with a medium build, and weighing around 140 to 150 pounds. There was no way anyone could describe me that way. I was of slender build, 5'4", and at the time of my arrest I weighed about 125 pounds. Also, the witnesses made no mention of a mustache. To anyone catching a first glimpse of my face, my mustache could be clearly seen, as it was not common for many Asian men. During the hearing, my attorney Clifford Gould did good legal work by having the three witnesses describe the shooter on the record as having a medium build and weight, and being between 5'7" and 5'9" in height.

A few other witnesses then testified, including a ballistics expert, the crime scene officer, and the San Francisco County coroner. The ballistics expert testified about a .38 bullet extracted from the wall of my apartment, after I accidentally shot the .357 in my apartment a few days prior to the murder. Evidence retrieved from the crime scene included bullets and a .38 caliber handgun. As with most preliminary hearings, the prosecutor aimed to present enough evidence to prove the defendant's guilt, and the defense witnesses were saved for the trial itself. After hearing only the prosecution's side of the story, the judge found there was enough evidence against me to send the case to superior court for trial on the charge of murder in the first degree.

Hearing evidence against me that was totally unjust, I started fuming with anger. Still fuming after the hearing, I was escorted down the city prison hallway. Just as I passed the booking desk, I saw a white city prison guard sitting on a tall stool, looking at me very coldly. Four or five feet from him, with anger exploding within me, I looked at him and said, "What the fuck you looking at?"

As I expected, he responded angrily. San Francisco guards took no shit from any prisoner. In a hurry, he got off his stool and came toward me, "What did you say, asshole?" He tried to grab me, and I resisted his physical attack. Next thing I knew, five or six prison guards had gotten hold of me and pushed me to the floor, where I was punched and kicked. While struggling, I may have gotten in a few light punches against the guards, but I was overwhelmed by them. They then placed me in a nearby eight-by-eight-foot padded isolation cell, with a hole in the floor for a toilet. To let some anger off, I'd confronted a prison guard, knowing what would happen. Luckily, I'd gotten off with a light ass kicking by all those feisty prison guards and then thrown into isolation to cool off my anger. At the time of this altercation, I think the police knew I had just been bonded over to superior court for the murder charge.

After a preliminary hearing, you can wait a day or two before being taken up to the seventh-floor county jail to await trial, but I got lucky. Instead of being kept in isolation for days, I was let out within a few hours, and a sheriff deputy took me upstairs to the San Francisco County Jail, which was under the control of the sheriff's department. I was surprised that nothing more was said about my incident with the guard just a few hours earlier, nor was I given any further punishment for it. I was charged with a misdemeanor for assaulting the guard, however. Later, when I appeared in court to answer this charge, I was offered ninety days in the county jail, and since I knew I would be in jail for longer than ninety days while awaiting trial for the murder charge, I pled guilty to the misdemeanor.

County Jail

At the San Francisco County Jail, I was rebooked and underwent more fingerprinting and mug shots. Next, my clothing was exchanged for jail clothing—blue jeans and a shirt—and I was given a small metal tin cup, a spoon, and blankets. Then I was showered and sprayed with disinfectant to kill any possible lice. Afterward, the sheriff deputies escorted me into the mainline of the San Francisco City and County Jail, where there were sixteen, fourteen-man cell tanks, eight tanks lined up on either side of a wide main hallway. The whole county jail was painted with fading gray color, and even the cell bars were that same gray color. Like in the city prison, there were lower and higher steel bunk beds. Three-inch-thick cotton mattresses, faded white with thin blue stripes, were flattened from years of use, as were the pillows. I was placed in the first tank on the right. The cell tank was divided in two parts. On one side were all the bunk beds, an open small sink, and toilet in the back. On the other side, a long stainless steel bench and table were bolted to the floor.

What is daily life like inside a fourteen-man cell tank twenty-four hours a day? The sliding cell door opened at about 6:30 a.m. and stayed open until about 4:00 p.m. Then it was closed for the afternoon count, when each prisoner was expected to be found lying on his bed. After the count, the door reopened so you could line up to receive dinner in the same way that you got breakfast and lunch. From a cart, the prison trustee handed your tray of food through a small open slot of eighteen by fourteen inches. It was up to the trustee to give normal portions or a little extra if you knew him.

After dinner, at about 5:30 or 6:00 p.m., the cell door between the day room and back area of the tank was closed, and a tank trustee in the day room turned the TV channel to whatever the majority of prisoners wanted to see. Since the back area was small, about twelve by thirty feet, there was not much movement in the crowded space. Some prisoners watched TV, while others read paperback books from the county jail library or books that got passed around for months or years by prisoners awaiting trial or plea bargaining. Some played games provided by prison recreation—cards, checkers, or chess. Even in such crowded conditions, the setting was fairly quiet. Only rarely did an argument or fist-fight break out. It was more like people were waiting for the outcome of their day.

The highlight of our day was when the commissary wagon arrived. Every day, the prison trustees carted in newspapers, cigarettes, candy bars, a few pastries, orange juice, and milk for those prisoners who placed orders the day before. Payment was taken out of whatever funds prisoners might have among their personal property kept by the county jail staff. Deliveries of mail would also be placed on the "cell tank bus" by the sheriff deputy. Also, there were visiting hours, when prisoners could talk through a phone while seeing visitors through a Plexiglas window. The visiting room was well lit and painted white with visiting time lasting about one and a half hours. Attorney visits took place in small rooms furnished with a gray table and chairs, where prisoner and attorney could meet for as long as needed to discuss their case.

Conditions at the county jail were a great improvement over the city prison. Since a prisoner's stay in the county jail was usually longer than short stays at the city prison, the system was better organized for longer terms of imprisonment, from a few weeks to a year or more for those unable to raise bail from outside sources. The longer stays resulted in prisoners' feeling more interactive and mindful toward other prisoners.

At the county jail, I soon encountered three of the Chinese guys who had been in the lineup with me, the two Leng brothers, John and Jerry, who were lieutenants in the Wah Ching, plus Robert Louie, the older brother of John Louie, whom I had known from the streets. Even though Robert Louie had started his own small "Ski Mask" gang outside of Chinatown, he seemed to be in line with the Leng brothers. I was not Chinese, but all of us were FOBs. Jerry, John, and Robert all knew I had come from San Francisco Chinatown and was fighting a murder case involving the Wah Ching. So I was welcomed by all three Chinese gang members. They all knew I was being framed.

Jerry Leng was in the cell tank next to mine, and we had short quiet conversations through the bars. We didn't talk about Wah Ching gang activities since I knew nothing about the Wah Ching. I had seen numerous Wah Ching members on Jackson Street, but most of them knew I was a Korean, not involved with Chinatown. However, whatever information Jerry Leng had received about me from the street seemed to have gained me his confidence. Within a few days, he told me the name of the Wah Ching member who killed Yip Yee Tak. I told him I needed legal support to fight the false murder charge, and Jerry said he would try to help, but I sensed he spoke without conviction or commitment. Telling me the name of the real killer was the best he could do for me. Since I was well aware of keeping the code of silence, I did not disclose the killer's name to anyone, not even to my attorney, Clifford Gould.

John and Jerry Leng did give me some support by sharing their commodities and making life a bit easier, whereas Robert Louie seemed to keep a distance from me. One benefit in knowing Jerry and John was that they were Chinatown insiders. A Chinese deputy who worked at night would wrap take-out Chinese food containers in newspaper and pass them through the bars to John and Jerry, who in turn would share the food with me and Robert. As most Asians do, we kept our business to ourselves as quietly as possible. The Leng brothers shared their food with me and Robert almost every night for a month until the time came when John and Jerry and Robert were sentenced to state prison and removed from the county jail. I too was soon about to join them in state prison, not for the murder charge but for an eighteen-month sentence for probation violation.

While I was still at the San Francisco County Jail, a private investigator for the public defender, a former police officer about fifty years old, came to the jail to interview me. I told him that the investigation of my case, if there was any, had so far turned up nothing to support my innocence. A second public defender, a young Japanese American, was brought in to work with Mr. Gould. Between them, their main efforts focused on getting a change of venue to another county for my trial. They believed the massive publicity for Chinatown gang warfare in the past five or six years—all the news articles could make a four- or five-inch-thick pile—would make it difficult to get a fair trial in San Francisco.

Years later, Mr. Gould explained to me that the change of venue might have been a mistake. Even though I had no support at first to prove my innocence, new support might have come to light if the trial had remained in San Francisco. After all, it was a known fact in Chinatown—and to the police—that I was innocent. Doubts might have surfaced. People on the outside may have been watching my case more closely than I realized. As it was, taking the case out of San Francisco caused a geographic break from support I could have received from people who knew I was innocent.

Ranko Yamada

In September of 1973, while I was still in the San Francisco County Jail, the *San Francisco Chronicle* ran a Sunday news article about Chinatown gang warfare. Near the end of the article, my name was mentioned almost in passing, as the man awaiting trial for Yip Yee Tak's murder. At least one person who read the article took great interest in my arrest—Ranko Yamada, a twenty-three-year-old Japanese American.

Ranko was the younger sister of Reiko Yamada, whom I used to date between 1971 and 1972, until Reiko got married to a Japanese man and moved to Japan. Reiko used to work in San Francisco's Japantown in a cultured pearl jewelry store. By chance one afternoon when I was visiting Reiko, Ranko happened to be there, and Reiko introduced us. Ranko was on her way to Chinatown, where she worked at another jewelry store on Grant Street, and since I was returning to Chinatown, I took the bus with Ranko. I had nothing else planned for the day, so I asked Ranko whether she minded if I hung around the store with her while she worked by herself from 3:00 to 9:00 p.m. I sensed she felt at ease with me. Unknown to Ranko, I had taken a liking to her during the few hours I spent at the jewelry store with her, and I would have liked to spend the whole evening there. But after a few hours, I thought I'd hung around long enough, so I made off into the night into Chinatown.

After meeting Ranko, I felt engrossed with her. She seemed like a very sincere and good person, but no other opportunity arose to see her.

I think I stopped by the store once more to see her again, but she was busy with a customer so it was just a short hello. I didn't see her again before my arrest in June of 1973.

Therefore, I was very surprised to receive a short letter from Ranko during my stay in the San Francisco County Jail. It was like a gift from heaven. Ranko wrote to say she was aware of my innocence and would try to help me in any way she could. She knew about the frame-up murder charge against me through her friends in Chinatown. It may have been a single spider's silk thread, but Ranko's letter gave me enormous hope because I felt connected to someone on the outside who knew I was innocent, and this connection gave light to my darkness.

I took Ranko's gift of support very personally. Reading her letter, I felt my spirits rise high. Here was a woman I had only met once, who not only believed in my innocence but wished to help prove it. My spirits must have gone to heaven. What may have started out as a thin silken thread of connection between me and Ranko in September 1973 soon turned into a bright and permanent attachment.

Probation Violation

Meanwhile a strange thing happened while I was in the county jail. One day, a young black prisoner was placed in the cell tank. As soon as he entered the tank, he tried to get close to me, saying he knew people in Chinatown. He was trying to get me to talk about my case. As a matter of common sense, I figured he was working for the D.A. or the police. For two or three days, he continued trying to talk to me, but I just walked away to another part of the cell tank. One afternoon, I took a nap, and when I woke up, he was gone. Without question, he must have been planted to help the D.A. or police.

My case moved to the San Francisco Superior Court, where Clifford Gould and the other public defender moved to change the trial venue. The judge granted their motion in September 1973. Given a choice of three counties—I think two were east of San Francisco and one might have been Los Angeles or Orange County—it was agreed to move the case to Sacramento.

At the same time, the S.F. District Attorney, James Lassart, sought to have my probation revoked because I had been arrested. Here's a strange thing about the legal system: if a person, who is on probation, is arrested while on probation, simply being arrested is enough cause for a probation violation, even if the person has not been proven guilty or innocent of the charges for which he was arrested. So although I was innocent of the crime for which I was arrested, I was found in violation of probation just for being arrested. When my probation was revoked, I was sentenced to eighteen months' time in the California Department of Corrections. By this time, my feelings about my experience in the judicial system were starting to go numb.

Along with two other prisoners in their midtwenties, I was taken, wearing leg irons and a waist chain, in the S.F. sheriff's van with two sheriffs driving to the Northern California receiving center of Vacaville Prison. It was a quiet trip. All three prisoners said nothing to each other, but we looked out the window as if it might be our last time seeing the view. I wondered what awaited us. I believe the other two were also facing prison sentences for the first time in their lives.

The deputy had the radio playing at low volume, and there were two songs I remember hearing during the drive—"It's Too Late" by Carole King and "You're Still a Young Man" by Tower of Power. I felt those songs affecting me in different ways. It's as if I were leaving everything in the free world behind me. I felt very old, as if life were closing in on me at age twenty-one. We arrived in Vacaville at around midday.

Chapter 2

Vacaville

Gateway

At the Vacaville Receiving and Release (R&R) Center, the expected transitional stay for a prisoner was sixty to ninety days before assignment by the administration to a prison in California. The decision about where to send a prisoner was based on his age, background, medical condition, and the contents of his central file.

We happened to arrive at a time when the whole prison system was going through one of the most violent phases in the history of California. The major prison gangs—Nuestra Familia (NF), the Mexican Mafia (La Eme), the Black Guerilla Family (BGF), and the Aryan Brotherhood (AB)—were all engaged in gang warfare for control of the prison population. In the early 1970s, prisoners were getting killed in the highest numbers, and the three prisons with the most intense violence were San Quentin, Deuel Vocational Institution (DVI), and Soledad. The NFs, who were mostly Northern Californian Latinos, were allied with the BGF's African Americans, while La Eme's Latino members, mostly from Southern California, were allied with the AB's whites. Since the NF fought La Eme and the BGF fought the AB, these alliances seemed natural.

Gang violence within the prison system was out of control. The California Department of Corrections (CDC) officials could not stop the killings and stabbings within the system, or perhaps they just allowed the violence to continue as a method for dividing and conquering the prisoners. The prison guards were unable to prevent outbreaks of gang violence, and at the time of my arrival, the guards were on full alert in response to recent incidents of attacks on guards. In 1972, several prison guards had been killed during a confrontation when inmate George Jackson, founder of the BGF, tried to escape and was killed just before his trial. In the California system, even the prison guards were not safe, let alone new and inexperienced young prisoners.

44

We could feel the tight tension within ourselves as we prepared to enter into the heart of darkness and the insane world of a very violent prison system. How were we to stay alive and survive a system we were unprepared for? Even while feeling afraid, I followed the first rule of survival in any prison system—to not let my fear show. I tried to bury my personal fears deep within myself. With this maddening tension in the air, we three new arrivals were led into the sickening, unfeeling, and wounded embrace of the CDC. With our legs in irons and hands shackled to waist chains, we passed through the main gates. Nearby, a gun tower stood as a silent deadly warning and reminder that we were now on the grounds of the CDC.

After entering the main gates, we were taken through a thick green door and into a large room where there were a few guards in khaki uniforms and a racially mixed group of prisoners, who wore blue shirts and jeans, working in the new prisoner receiving area. After a formal transfer of documents by the San Francisco deputies to the CDC guards, the deputies removed the leg irons and waist chains, and the guards ordered us to sit on a long bench while they looked over the court documents committing us to CDC.

We sat on the bench for half an hour while they handled the paperwork. The worker-prisoners or prison trustees looked over at us from time to time. Finally, a prison guard called us over and instructed us as a group about our personal property and clothing. Any personal items held for us by the county jail had already been turned over to the CDC. Any money would be placed in a prison trust account for our use at the prison commissary (better known as the canteen). As for the rest of our personal property and clothing, we had the choice of discarding it or else mailing it to our family or friends. "But you have to pay for the shipping and mailing cost," the prison guard told us. He made it sound as though he wanted us to discard our things to save him the extra work. All of us decided to go ahead and discard our personal property.

Then all our clothing was removed, and each of us in turn was strip-searched. They looked in our mouths and behind our ears, had us raise our arms to check under the armpits, lifted our balls, then made us bend over for an asshole check. This was all just a routine search for contraband. After the strip search, we were ordered to take a shower in an open area where showerheads were lined along a wall. After that, one of the prison workers came over with a spray pump and sprayed each of us with white powder from head to toe and gave us each a pair of white boxer underwear to put on. Next they gave us a short haircut and a shave. It was a standard rule for prisoners to have no facial hair. After the haircut, each of us was fingerprinted and our faces were photographed with our prisoner numbers. For the rest of the time I was imprisoned, I would be identified by that CDC identification number. The number was designated to remain in my central file in Sacramento for the rest of my life.

Then we were given three sets of green clothing with a jacket of the same color. The color identified us as newly received prisoners, better known among prisoners as "fish," a nickname for incoming inmates who do not yet know the ways and rules of prison life. We were escorted to the new arrival section, which for all of Northern California was the point of entry to the jungle of the whole prison system. Holding our clothing and bedding, we were taken to our units and each assigned to a cell. A single cell was about eight by six feet, with a metal bed, and a toilet and sink against the wall. The prison cell was about the size of a person's home bathroom with a bed in place of a bathtub.

As newly arrived prisoners, our green pants and green pullover shirts distinguished us from mainline Vacaville prisoners, who wore blue shirts, jeans, and jackets. The mainline prisoners and new arrivals were kept separated. However, some mainline prisoners taught the orientation class that new arrivals were expected to attend in the mornings. A docket slipped under your cell door told the time and place of the class. In those classes, we were told the dos and don'ts of adjusting to the world of prison. For example, they taught us to watch out for "nice" convicts. If another convict started acting overly nice—say by offering you a pack or carton of cigarettes or other prison commodities, you had the choice to turn down the offers. You needed to assess the convict because he might be trying to put you in his debt or feeling you out to see if you were too weak to stand up for yourself. Those "nice" convicts might want to make a punk out you (use you for sex), and if you didn't show yourself to be strong in the firmest terms, you'd be viewed as weak.

Other things they taught us: it was better not to gamble or get yourself in debt. The convicts played mind games better than anyone, so you always had to be on guard and watch your words and actions. If you needed to fight to defend yourself, then it was advised to get some kind of prison-made weapon, even a bar of soap in a sock. If any convict came onto you like you were a punk, you should fight like you intended to really kill him. A punk was the second lowest form of convict. The lowest of the low was a rat, an informer. If you had a rat tag over your head in the streets or in court, without a doubt, you'd get assigned to be killed as soon as other convicts found out you were a rat.

The highest-ranking convicts were those doing time for murder. Armed robbers were next, and so on down to the lowest convicts, child molesters or child killers, whom other convicts would try to kill or make into punks. But in reality, members of prison gangs were respected and feared the most within the convict world, and were ranked highest. Even though Vacaville was supposed to be neutral territory, it was declared so by agreement among the prison gangs, and from time to time, gang violence broke the peace.

Asian Inmates

On my first day in Vacaville, when my cell was opened for dinner, or "chow time," I met up with Jerry and John Leng, as well as Robert Louie—the Chinese guys I knew from the San Francisco County Jail. I was very glad to see them, and for that matter, I would have been glad to meet just about any Asian. Seeing some guys I already knew, I felt more secure being at Vacaville.

Since it was September, there was night yard while daylight lasted, so we went onto the yard. The Leng brothers and Robert Louie seemed to act like it made no difference to them to see me again. Robert must have been on the low end of his funds or just tight, but John and Jerry brought out some packs of smokes and a few other items for me—a bit of food, soap, and toothpaste—without being asked. They knew that even if I had friends in prison, which I didn't, it would be a week or two before new prisoners would be allowed to go to the canteen.

We talked a little bit during the night yard. There was not much news to catch up on as the Leng brothers and Robert Louie had left the county jail only two or three weeks before me. It seemed a bit strange that Robert knew I had some brief contacts with his brother John Louie on the outside, but Robert acted as if he didn't know me. During the six weeks we were together at Vacaville, however, I noticed Robert did all he could to get close to the Leng brothers.

Whenever your unit was called, you went to chow time for three daily meals in the large dining room. The tables seated four prisoners and were made of wood with steel plating underneath to bolt them firmly to the floor. You entered the dining room in single file. As the chow line prison guard watched, you picked up your spoon, fork, and knife (the knife blade was cut to half the length of a regular knife). Then you picked up a metal tray and pushed it forward for food items you wanted. Afterward, you walked to your table following the prisoner ahead of you, so if you wanted to eat with someone you knew, you got in line next to each other to sit at the same eating table. After you were done eating, you threw away uneaten food and set the tray on a stack of other trays, then showed the prison guard your spoon, fork, and knife before placing them in a large shallow bin.

I found the tension level at the Vacaville Receiving Center was just about the same as at the county jail. It was fairly calm, with most prisoners trying to get a feeling for which prison we might be transferred to. The yard was about the size of a baseball field with three or four guard towers and a double fence topped with razor wire. There were not many activities out in the yard; it was mostly hanging around and talking to the guys you knew. If you wanted, you could return back to your unit and watch TV in the dayroom with other prisoners, or go to your cell during the times when the guards unlocked the cell doors in all three tiers.

Each unit housed about one hundred fifty prisoners. Since I was not in the same unit as the Leng brothers or Robert Louie, we mostly met in the yard. I didn't speak to the Leng brothers about getting legal support from the Wah Ching on the outside, as they were Wah Ching themselves. Jerry Leng explained that there was nothing he or John could do, nor was anyone willing to die on my behalf, even though it was a Wah Ching murder case I was charged and framed up with. So we went about a daily routine of meeting in the yard, and when commissary day came, John and Jerry—more John than Jerry—would kick down with smokes and a few items without my asking for them. I think John Leng wanted to help me out much more than he was able to. One day, he pulled me aside and explained to me that he was supporting me as far as he could within his limits. He said he understood the ordeal I was enduring better than the others. That was as far as John got in helping me.

We didn't speak much about the widespread violence within the California prison system, or which prison we might get transferred to because the tension level seemed no different from the county jail, and we hadn't yet seen any evidence of lethal violence. Then we did witness something after about a month at Vacaville. First, we heard the general alarm go off on our side of the prison where both receiving units and the mainline were located. The alarm came from inside the mainline "Hole," the solitary confinement unit. We gathered in the hallway where we were ordered to stand against the wall while a group of guards rushed to the

Hole, and unit guards stood overlooking the housing units. A few minutes later, we saw a prisoner being rushed out on a gurney. He lay still with his head bleeding badly. We never found out what happened to him. In a serious way, Jerry said something like, "Maybe he dropped a weight on his own head as an act of trying to commit suicide?" This goes to show how ignorant we were about the California prison system. As I watched the prisoner lying unconscious on the gurney, I felt nothing much, other than awareness that an unusual event was passing by. Maybe if I had seen or known what actually happened to the convict, I might have felt differently.

Soon after this incident, the Leng brothers and Robert Louie were all transferred out on the same day. Since none of us knew when we would be transferred, we didn't get a chance to say any parting words. About two weeks later, I was told to pack up my property because I was being transferred to the mainline in Vacaville. If the receiving side got overcrowded, they sometimes moved prisoners who were soon to leave Vacaville into transfer units in the mainline. So I turned in my fish's green clothing for a convict's blue clothing.

Mainline Transfer Unit

I noticed most convicts on the mainline had prison tattoos and wore more serious looks in their eyes and faces as they went about their daily routines. I noticed some were signing up to be paid for wearing a medical patch to test the effects of medications on humans. An outside pharmaceutical company preferred to use only the convicts at Vacaville prison. As to what those tests were, I never found out. As I found out, the Vacaville prison was considered the medical center for the whole CDC system, and the mainline housed some prisoners who had ill health or mental disabilities. Some transvestites even had breasts implanted there.

I did see some transvestites with breasts, acting like women. I took no interest in them. To me they were like any other convicts, and I had no interest in punks. However, one day as I returned from the yard, just inside of the hallway door I saw a convict and a transvestite kissing tongue to tongue as if a man were kissing a real woman. As I walked by, I couldn't help staring at them. At the time, I was unable to comprehend two men kissing each other in such a way, like a man and woman. I couldn't believe what I was seeing as I and other convicts passed by without being paid any notice.

I didn't get a chance to get to know any of the mainline convicts, unlike the newly arrived prisoners in my transfer unit. In the transfer unit, there was a mix of races among the prisoners, but no other Asian except me. Word would normally get around to any Asians in a given population as soon as a new Asian was placed among them. In a brotherly way, they would come around to school you on what was happening as well as help you out with smokes or other daily need items. Instead, in the transfer unit, there were about a dozen Latino prisoners, all in my age range. A few of the Latinos were friendly toward me, so I ended up being friendly with those guys. By now, all prisoners were taking prison life more seriously, so there was not much horse playing or joking. Young as we were, we tried to look serious like the older convicts in the mainline.

There was a small dayroom with benches for watching TV, and one room with a table that prisoners could use for letter writing and playing cards or games like checkers or chess. This room was always open, so when we were bored, three to five of us would go into the room and close the door and try to sing some oldies. I tried to sing with them but had no singing voice whatsoever. However, no one laughed at my attempts to sing because they sang just as badly as I did.

Once a week during the day, a movie was shown in a large auditorium on Saturdays for the mainline and Sundays for the receiving center. During the screening, if a visitor arrived for any convict, he would see a small sign on the bottom of the movie screen displaying his prisoner number. Once during a movie I saw my B number show up at the bottom of the screen. I thought, "Maybe Ranko has come to Vacaville to visit me?" With my hopes and emotions at high tide, I reported to the visiting guard, only to be told the B number was for another prisoner.

As I returned to the movie auditorium, I felt a deep sense of loneliness, and the distraction of the movie did not relieve my aching hollowness inside. It wasn't reasonable to expect that Ranko would want to visit me. We had just exchanged two or three letters in a friendly way, and Ranko never visited me while I was in the San Francisco County Jail. But my personal emotions were riding high on seeking the comfort of a woman friend from outside.

Speaking of movies, one weekend when I was still on the receiving side of Vacaville, a movie called *Last House on the Left* was shown to the receiving side prisoners. One prisoner pointed out to me that some convicts in the Vacaville mainline were there for the kinds of crimes we saw in *Last House on the Left,* which showed people's body parts getting cut off during very bloody killings. Most convicts didn't talk much about themselves or the crime that landed them in prison. Therefore, it was better to know something about a convict before talking to him because the use of one wrong word might end up getting you killed if you had no idea who they were.

Here is an example of how looks can deceive. There was an inmate I'll call "Juan," who was due to go to state prison. While still in the Los Angeles County Jail, he somehow disrespected another inmate who happened to be a high-ranking La Eme prison gang member, a fact Juan probably did not know. The high-ranking La Eme member asked Juan, who was about to be shipped out to Folsom, to carry a coded written message addressed to some homeboys in Folsom. Juan agreed, and upon his arrival at Folsom, he got in touch with some La Eme members and passed on the message. La Eme in return gave him a small welfare package, including basic needs like smokes, coffee, toothpaste, soap, and food items. They welcomed him as their homeboy and told him to let them know if he needed anything else.

Their warm greetings were deceptive. In the Vacaville orientation, we were told by experienced convicts to accept nothing from strangers. However, if you were a prison gang member, a basic custom was that the gang would greet your arrival to prison with a welfare package. This custom was kept for gang members, or even for friends of gang members, so there was no need to fear receiving this goodwill offering from your own gang, or from people you knew from outside, or from convicts who knew you through their friends or who knew you from another prison. You just didn't want to accept it from strangers.

Anyway, Juan felt free to be welcomed by La Eme even though he was not a La Eme member but just a messenger. Unfortunately, the message he carried from the high-ranking La Eme was to "hit" the messenger. Soon after his arrival at Folsom, he was killed without even knowing that the message he had carefully passed on was his own death sentence.

As for my own experience in the Vacaville mainline transfer unit, one day an older convict stopped by to talk to a guy who acted like the leader of the Latinos in the transfer unit. The older convict dropped off a package containing smokes and commissary food to be shared with the Latinos. When the Latinos received their items, I was also given an equal share. I was informed by the older convict that since the holidays were coming up, he was asking for the names and B numbers of the Latinos so that people on the outside could send in holiday packages or greetings from the streets. He asked for my full name and number, which I gave him, thinking I was going along for a free ride. However, he was using this method to gather information for the prison gang by collecting full names and numbers of new prisoners. I did receive a holiday card from an unknown woman about a month later, to which I responded with a short letter, but then I never received a response back.

A little short of two months in Vacaville, I was told to turn in all my personal property to R&R (Receiving and Release) because the time had come for my transfer to a prison decided upon by the prison administration. The next day, I reported to R&R in the same large room where I had first arrived. We were told to sit on the concrete benches and one by one remove all our clothing for a strip search. Then we were given gray overalls, placed in leg chains and waist chains, and loaded on a transfer bus, which the convicts had nicknamed the "Gray Goose." On the bus, each convict was given a brown bag lunch with a peanut butter and jelly sandwich and a piece of fruit.

I didn't mind the uncomfortable bus ride too much because I had a chance to see the outside free world through the barred bus windows, although my mind was heavy with wondering which prison I was going to. On the bus were three prison guards, the driver, plus a guard each in front and back of us in an enclosed cage, carrying side arms and shotguns. The guards knew of instances where convicts had used their waist chains and leg chains to kill enemy gang members on the bus. They weren't taking any chances.

Chapter 3
Tracy

Gladiator School

After about an hour and a half, the bus made its first stop at a prison called Deuel Vocational Institution, or DVI, which was better known as Tracy due to the nearby town of Tracy in the San Joaquin Valley. At the time, the other two major state prisons were San Quentin and Folsom. Both had high walls surrounding the whole prison. The rest of the prisons were called luxury prisons. If you were lucky and had a clean record and a short sentence, after two years or less you might be sent to a camp where there were no walls or razor wire fence and inmates lived in a dorm with totally free movement within the prison camp. You were trained how to fight forest fires in California alongside regular fire fighters. Since the camp had fewer than one hundred prisoners, the food was much better than in most other prisons. If you wanted, you could escape by just walking away and wouldn't be noticed as missing until count time by the camp prison guard. However, it was rare for any prisoner to try escaping the prison camp.

DVI was definitely not a low-security prison camp. After the "Gray Goose" bus entered a square fenced-in area, the Tracy prison guards checked all outside surfaces of the bus, using mirrors to check underneath. All incoming and outgoing vehicles were checked with this same routine. After inspection, the bus drove into R&R. My name was called out, along with the names of some other prisoners. Before getting off the bus, we had our names, prison numbers, and pictures all checked by the prison guard.

I arrived at DVI in June 1973. As I entered the R&R building, I felt tension within me rising as we were ordered to sit on the bench and then, one by one, had our leg and waist chains removed. We underwent another routine strip search, received boxer shorts to wear, and continued to sit on the bench while the prison guards reviewed our paperwork and central files. After about an hour, we were issued prison clothing—blue jeans, shirt, and jacket—plus a set of blankets and sheets, toiletry articles, and a bag of tobacco. I just pushed everything down my pillowcase as other prisoners were doing. Then we were ordered to follow the prison guard, whom we were instructed to address as "officer," to our living unit.

The R&R door opened into the hallway, and I stepped through it. Within a few steps, before I got a chance to view anything around me, I felt a powerful invisible force of tension running through every part of my mind and body. The level of tension hitting me was unbelievable, and my very first thought was, "I am in a real prison." All the things I'd seen in newspaper articles or heard about—stabbings, killings, and rapes—were all realities on the ground where I was taking my first steps.

Before me, I saw an orange-colored thick wire fence in an exercise yard about half the size of a football field. The two, three-story buildings on either side of the yard were known as the East and West Halls. I later found out the East and West Halls were used as segregation lockup units for prisoners in transition between the Hole and the mainline. In the yard, there was a cement wall used as a handball court, a basketball court, and a weight-lifting corner with weights on the ground and thin benches. To my left, I saw a grass lawn enclosed by a thick wire fence and a one-story extension of the R&R center to my right.

As I walked, I noticed a window where prison yard guards sat watching. Some of the convicts in the yard also watched us as we moved past them. At the yard guards' office, we turned right, passed through the screen gate in the fence, and walked down to the mainline. The hallway to my left led to the G, J, and K unit wings, which were also lockup units like the East and West Halls. The C, D, E, and F unit wings were to my right. As I walked down the mainline hall, I tried to look straight ahead, but I couldn't help glancing around to see the faces all looking at the newly arriving fish.

Tracy was known as a "gladiator school" because of all the violence. It housed mostly younger convicts from eighteen years old and up, and gang violence had been ongoing there for a number of years. Tracy had one of the highest numbers of stabbings and killings in all the California state prisons. I can't recall how many others were dropped off at Tracy with me, maybe four or five. We were yet to be turned into hardcore convicts. When we arrived, the prison was in a state of high tension, and the mainline hallways were clear due to a general lockdown of the whole prison that was imposed after a recent fatal stabbing of a prison guard on one of the mainline tiers.

All newly arrived prisoners were sent to C Wing and assigned a cell. My cell was on the second floor and was about the same size as in Vacaville. It was painted pale blue and had a small window in the green cell door. To the left of the door was a metal toilet and sink. There was also a metal bed with a spring mattress, a small metal table with a seat that slid out from under it, and a two-by-four-inch window with a steel-framed glass panel instead of iron bars.

After placing my bedding, clothing, and other prison-issue items on the cell bed, I looked out the window, which gave a view of D building about fifty feet across the way. It was a light tan–colored building with neat flat-trimmed lawns between C and D buildings. I went about cleaning my cell, making the bed, and rolling cigarettes from the prison-issue tobacco.

It was cold and quiet in the cell block building. The tension I felt when I came out of the R&R building felt much colder than any month of December. I tried to think more keenly about what I needed to do to survive in this violent world of prison. Many thoughts came and went, but an overall feeling of being alone in this unhealthy place remained constant. I thought to myself, "I'll just check out how other convicts go about their business and take each day step-by-step to adjust to this new prison."

Even though the world I'd come from was a little rough and I was no angel, the way I'd ended up in Tracy angered me. I was there for violating probation by getting arrested, and I was arrested for a murder caused by gang warfare that didn't involve me in any way. Even though the Chinatown murder trial still lay ahead of me, my foremost thoughts focused on survival since I was now in the very core of one of the most violent prisons in California. Personal survival had to come first, pushing aside bitter feelings about the murder case. As I was thinking these thoughts, the prison guard called out, "Chow time."

Joe Fong's Group

One by one, all the cell doors were opened. As I cautiously stepped out, I saw other convicts leaving their cells, some in a rush and others taking their time. As I entered the mainline hallway, I saw two organized lines reaching from one end to the other of the hallway to make it easier for guards to supervise convicts going to and from chow. Convicts were not allowed to walk in the middle where the prison guards stood, and I noticed the guards were very alert as they surveyed the movements of convicts.

As I walked in step with the other convicts toward the chow hall, I saw a mix of races—Latinos, African Americans, and whites. Then I noticed four Asians coming toward me. I didn't know their names, but I thought two faces looked familiar to me from Mike's pool hall. I soon learned their names were David Wong and Richard Lee. Joe Fong and Chico Wong were with them. Chico Wong was a gang lord from Los Angeles, serving two life sentences for first-degree murder convictions. He was the youngest man ever to be sentenced to state prison, having been charged, tried, and sentenced at the age of sixteen.

Just seeing these welcoming faces provided very great relief to the tight tension within me. Somehow they all knew my name and knew I'd come from San Francisco Chinatown as they welcomed me into their ranks. Each of the Chinese gang members introduced themselves. Joe Fong went first. He was about the same height as me, but I could sense the confidence he carried inside himself. David Wong, who was two or three inches taller than me, seemed a more happy-go-lucky type of person, and Richard Lee, who was the tallest at about 5'8" smiled, but I could sense his reserve. Chico Wong was about two inches shorter than me and his youthful face was friendly, but he had a more serious look in his eyes than the others. Even though all of them may have been imprisoned for two or three years, none had the very serious hard-core eyes of prisoners who were involved in prison gang warfare.

Just seeing these guys and being welcomed to their group, I felt I was going to be okay. I was not standing alone in Tracy, and this was most important to me as just a fish. Moreover, I had arrived just when a prison guard had been killed a few weeks prior, and there was extra tension in the Tracy mainline. Without my having done any state prison time, their warm welcome and embracing me almost as a new brother was far different from the attitude of the Leng brothers and Robert Louie, who had kept up some wall of distance and treated me somewhat as an outsider.

As we walked toward the chow hall and stood in the line, Joe Fong did the most talking, letting me know that he and the others knew I faced false murder charges. He said he felt for me and would see what support he might give me for my trial. Even though Joe Fong was speaking casually (walking to the chow hall was not the time for serious conversation), I felt he was sincere, and I believed him.

Joe Fong was an unusual man. He had a small round face with a bright smile. He didn't show the full seriousness of his inner self, but I could see in his eyes he was a serious man who shouldn't be taken for granted from his easy manner of conversation, nor should his strength or intelligence be underestimated. His eyes looked right into me. David, Richard, and Chico didn't interrupt our conversation out of respect for Joe.

While waiting in the chow line, Joe said, "Did you know we went to Galileo High School at same time? I remember seeing you at Galileo."

I did attend Galileo in 1968 and 1969, but I said, "No, I don't remember."

"Okay, forget about it."

There were not as many prison guards watching for movement in the dining room as there were in other parts of the prison. Even though high windows overlooked the whole dining room, there were no gun tower guards at the windows. The prison guards were armed only with small tear gas tube guns, handcuffs, and whistle chains at their shoulders for sounding the alarm in case of any trouble. The dining rooms, of which Tracy had three, were the last places the guards wanted any problems. The dining room had the greatest concentration of convicts in one area. If a prison riot was brewing, the dining room was the most likely place a riot would start. Armed only with tear gas guns and whistles, the prison guards were defenseless against the convicts' prison-made weapons of knives or clubs, and the guards were fully aware of how defenseless they would be if attacked.

Much of the time the guards stood around trying to show how confident they were, but they must have felt fear of violence against them at the very core of their beings while working anywhere within the prison walls. This is the reason why the convicts ruled the prison, even though every convict received a copy of the official prison rules upon arrival. Another code of conduct existed—a code made by the convicts—and violation of the convicts' code was punishable by death.

Each table seated four, so Joe, David, Richard, Chico, and I sat at two tables next to each other. Since there were no Asians sitting at the tables with us, we ate mostly in silence. After the meal, David and Richard laid some smokes on me as we walked in the mainline hallway. Joe and Chico didn't smoke. Before we parted, the guys promised to bring me more smokes and some stamps and envelopes next time we met during chow time.

However, it was difficult to meet them during chow time since I was in C wing and they were in the workers' E wing, and each wing was released at different times for chow, especially while the whole prison was on lockdown status. All of them had made a special effort to meet me on my first day at Tracy, but after that, I sometimes passed them at chow time in the hallway, going in opposite directions. I don't remember being able to meet those Chinatown guys again during my first ten days at Tracy. After ten days, I received a docket to appear before the main classification committee.

Classification

The prison docket told you the time and place you needed to appear. Because of the prison lockdown, only convicts who were needed, like kitchen workers, were allowed out of their cells, so the corridors were empty when I went to answer the docket. On my way, I passed by the central station, which had windows overlooking broad views of the general mainline housing units. The center view looked down the corridor of the dining rooms as well as overseeing the doors to the yard, and the further-off doors to the prison industries where convicts worked. To the right was the prison administration, and to the left were the prison laundry room and classrooms. From the central station, all guards had a full view of all movement within the main corridors. Whenever the prison alarm sounded, you would also see blinking and flickering lights in front of the central station.

After I passed the central station, I stopped at a bar gate, where I gave my docket to the guards. They pat searched me before opening the bar gate and allowing me inside a hallway where five or six plastic chairs lined a wall, and a few other convicts sat waiting to meet with the classification committee. Since I had only been in Tracy for a short time, I'd heard only that the classification committee decided work assignments for convicts, so I prepared myself for a kind of job interview. I saw myself as a short-timer in prison, doing eighteen months for probation violation, and I expected my still-upcoming trial would prove me innocent. As I sat in a plastic chair, waiting for my name to be called, I recalled my experience as a short-order cook and thought I could ask the classification committee for work as a cook in the staff dining room, where the best food in the prison system was served to prison staff. I felt confident that whatever kind of work the committee decided I should do, I could face whatever was expected.

I heard my name called, and I entered a mid-sized office with a large table. Five or six men wearing neckties sat stone-faced in front of me as if they were looking at an empty chair on my side of the table. I have no idea if the prison warden was present or who these men were in the prison administration system. No one introduced himself or his position. Most were looking at me, while the man seated in the middle leafed through my thin central file. He asked, "What do you look forward to doing while here at DVI?"

"I used to work as a short-order cook. Maybe I be allow to work as short-order cook at the staff dining room?"

Before I could finish answering his question, he looked at me and said, "In your record, it says you have an assault on a police officer in San Francisco. Well! We can't have that kind of behavior here."

The other men at the table, trying to look important, started applauding. As the man in the middle spoke, a few others muttered among themselves, using some kind of prison administration lingo I was unable to understand. Before I had a chance to say anything about my mistake in the assault on a police officer five months earlier, a prison guard entered the room and ordered me to step outside the classification room.

The Hole

Once outside, the guard ordered me to put my hands against the wall to be pat searched. Then he placed my arms behind my back to be handcuffed and led me into the mainline corridor, holding onto the handcuffs. As he led me along, I wondered where we were going. He took me to an area called K wing, the solitary confinement unit also known as the "Hole." K wing was where the prison gang members who engaged in gang warfare, including stabbing and killing other prisoners, were all locked up together in one cell block.

The place looked crammed, and I could feel high tension in the air. I was led into the Hole and placed in a three-by-three-foot holding cell. I was being reclassified and placed in the Hole because of the assault misdemeanor charge against the San Francisco city prison guard. However light that incident may have been, the Tracy administration was up in arms because a Tracy prison guard was killed just a month prior to my arrival. I thought to myself, "What I feel about this reclassification does not matter. The only important issue is how I will adjust to whatever unknowns lie ahead, as best as I can. Without the benefit of any real experience of prison convict mentality, I must survive any way I can." These were my first thoughts in the quiet holding cell of K wing.

The Hole was a building within a building, a prison within a prison. After half an hour, a prison guard came to the holding cell and ordered me to turn over all I had with me, including my clothes and shoes. Being strip-searched meant they ran a hand through your hair, opened your mouth, turned you side to side, looked behind your ears, lifted your arms to check your armpits, lifted your balls, made you bend over for opening your ass, and lifted one foot at a time. It was a routine strip search that quickly looked at every part of you before you could pass through the first locked gate. This was the standard procedure for all Holes in the California prison system. After the strip search, another set of prison blue clothing was handed to me without a belt for the jeans. The guard held a pillowcase full of prison-issue sheets, matches, tobacco, under-wear, socks, and a toothbrush cut in half.

I was once again handcuffed behind my back. I looked to my left into a well-lit office about eight by twelve feet in size. This was the main office for the Hole where pictures on the wall indicated where all con-victs in the Hole were housed. I was led through another locked gate up to the second floor where the floor guard unlocked two bar gates to let me and the escort guard through. As I looked down the halls of the sec-ond tier, I noticed the tier itself was dark even during the daytime as if it were a forbidden place to enter for convicts who were new or inexperi-enced with prison. As the gloom descended upon me, I became filled with a darkening tension that reached into my mind and soul.

The first thing I noticed was that the cell bars were covered over by prison-issue blankets, and there were no lights on inside the cells. I couldn't see where the convicts were in their cells, but I felt them watch-ing my every movement, every step I took. To avoid showing any weak-ness, I kept my head up and looked straight ahead until I reached my cell, which was the seventh from the front. The guard opened the cell, which had a sally port with two doors. After I entered the cell, the guard ordered me to put my hands through the food tray slot and then he un-locked and removed my handcuffs.

I placed my prison items on the mattress. The cell was brown in color and the same size as cells in the mainline. There was a sink and toilet against the back wall with a single lightbulb that could be turned on and off with a piece of string. I went about rolling a cigarette of prison-issue tobacco. I tried to escape the reality of the Hole. It was be-yond my comprehension. One of my first thoughts was, "Why do all the convicts' cells have blankets up over their bars to cover the cell in dark-ness? What kind of convicts are in the Hole?" I felt no fear but rather a darkness of mind at not being able to understand the place and situation I was in. My instincts told me to be very, very careful as I was in a very dangerous place. Unlike other convicts, however, I didn't put my blanket on the bars to conceal myself in the darkness of my cell.

The bed was made of a flat, one-inch thick, metal frame. Parts of the bed, sink, and toilet had been cut out. It was easy to guess that the cut-out metal parts were used to make prison knives. All cut-out metal parts were sprayed an orange color so that any new pieces cut from metal in the cell would be noticed by the guards. As I recall, I felt no loneliness as I was used to feeling alone for most of my life. But I wanted to know how to adjust to the Hole. The answer started to come by itself when I heard someone in the cell next to me bang on the wall softly, and I heard a voice saying, "Hey, homeboy. Come to the wall near the hole."

There were two holes above my bed. In the past, holes had been drilled to hold another bunk bed, and when they turned the cell into a single, they left holes through the wall from my cell to his cell. The holes were about one inch around.

Like a fish just entering the prison system, I went to the little hole in the wall and said, "What happening?"

He sounded like a Latino convict as he asked me in a low voice, "What your name?" I pressed my ear to the wall to hear his voice.

"Lee."

"Where you from?"

"S.F."

"Why you in the Hole?"

"I had assault charge on a cop while I was in S.F. city prison."

"How long you been here in Tracy?"

"Just two weeks."

"You need anything?"

"No, I am all right."

"All right, I get back to you later."

This is where the short conversation ended even though there were lots of questions I wanted to ask him. The questions he asked were trying to feel me out and get information—to check out if I was an enemy, a friend, or a nobody.

I didn't realize at the time how dangerous it was to talk to some convict in the next cell through a hole in the wall, pressing my ear there or trying to look through the hole. If he had thought I was a gang enemy, he could have stabbed me with a thinly made pole, a prison-made knife, or a prison-made zip gun to take out my eye or ear without my being aware such things could happen. Another weapon he could have used was a long pole with a "piece" (knife) made of tightly rolled newspaper, tied with a strip of bedsheet and bound to the end of the pole. This was one reason convicts in the Hole covered their cell bars with blankets. If your enemy came close enough to your cell, you could use a knife pole or zip gun to kill or hurt him. Such incidents took place within the Hole.

One way an enemy might fight you was by trying to set you up when you were in the hallway passing by his cell. He would leave the blanket off the bars and the lights turned on so you could see him clearly, which gave you a false sense of security. He would call you over as if wanting to talk to you while he knew a gang member in the next cell was hiding, pressed against the wall, holding a spear. If you fell for the false sense of security and came near to his cell bars for a moment, just as you turned to continue on your way, a spear would fly out of the next cell, aimed at your neck vein or artery.

There definitely had been incidents where convicts got lured into this trap and were stabbed or killed by a spear, and once even by a zip gun. More experienced convicts in the Hole stayed alert and on guard whenever called over to a convict's cell to talk and stayed a distance of three or four feet away to view both neighboring cells. The way the trap worked, your enemy tried to get closer to you gradually without your realizing he was your enemy. He might talk to you a few times in a friendly way while you were in the hallway going to shower or walking up and down during your twenty minutes' exercise time. The idea was to build up trust to set you up for the kill. Also, if you were known to be sleeping during the day or night, your enemy could try to spear you through the bars while you slept or otherwise catch you off guard when you were in your cell.

There was no gun rail in K wing so there was nothing to stop a convict from trying to spear another convict to death in his cell. The tier guard watched the convicts' movements through the sally port bars, and if a convict was spotted spearing someone, a guard blew his whistle to sound the alarm but would not come onto the tier as long as the convict still had the weapon. The guard waited for backup, only entering the tier with a mass of other guards who could make sure to disarm the convict.

For the guards, it wasn't worth taking a chance of getting stabbed or killed while trying to stop convicts from killing other convicts. Guards were there to do their eight hours and not to play some kind of hero role. They were trained not to approach the scene of an attempted killing. Instead, it was up to guards in the gun towers or gun rails to stop fights.

A convict may have his own personal courage, integrity, and humanity burning deep within him, but his own personal survival guides his actions as he is slowly transformed by institutionalization. As the prison system exerts control over the convict, he must let the institution become a part of him through his interactions with other convicts and through his struggle against the prison system to remain an unbroken man and guard his personal survival. The convict deeply involved in a prison gang is even more institutionalized than most gang members on the outside. For prison gang members, their whole world is prison.

I was more relaxed than other convicts in the Hole due to being a fish while all around me were live sharks. But as far as I was concerned, I was not a threat to anyone. I didn't know anyone on the tier, and my cell was on the end. No one took any interest in knowing me, so I kept to myself. If by some chance I were set up or attacked, I would not have known how to defend myself while I was out on the tier or in my cell. This is what I mean by being a fish.

It was well known that Asian convicts did not get involved in any of the power struggles within the prison system. We kept to ourselves when problems arose. Other convicts respected the way Asians conducted themselves and were aware that Chinese prisoners were involved in Chinatown gang warfare and were doing long sentences. Asians had the will to fight back against anyone if we were forced into that position. As for the other convicts who engaged in gang warfare and struggles for power to control the prison, they kept the tension level high at all times. It was as if all convicts were involved in combat every hour of every day for personal survival.

In the Hole, the convicts were issued some writing paper and a pencil cut in half. The soft plastic toothbrush was also cut in half. Your next-door convict could give you a few books to pass the time. My day in the Hole started with breakfast served on a tray with a plate and teaspoon. Since I didn't have a cup, I used a leftover milk carton as my cup for the coffee served with every meal. Every day, at around 11:00 a.m. or noon, lunch was passed through a three-by-ten-inch slot into my cell. At about 4 or 5 p.m., I was given dinner. By the time I received my meals, the food was cold but edible. During the day, I sat or lay on the bed and watched for convicts passing by.

In 1973, there was no exercise yard for convicts in the Hole. One at a time, each convict was allowed twenty minutes a day to come out of his cell for exercise or to take a shower. The small shower room was at the front of all the cells, and there were twenty-five cells per tier, so the twenty-minute shower-and-exercise time slots continued throughout the day and into the evening. The tier guard sat by the locked gates watching the lone convict moving on the tier. Cell doors were opened by a pulley system. When I heard a clicking sound in my cell door, I knew my cell gate was open. Then I slid the cell door to go onto the tier to take a shower, which used up most of the twenty minutes.

I don't think I had addresses for Ranko in San Francisco or for my mother, who had moved from San Francisco to San Jose. At that time, my mother owned and cooked for a Korean restaurant, and my younger American sister, Mary, worked there as a waitress. Also, by then, my uncle and aunt, who raised me in Korea, had arrived in the US and were helping out at the restaurant and living in a room above the restaurant. My mom had an apartment, but she only allowed my uncle and auntie (my mother's older sister) to use it for taking baths. This seemed unusual, as the Korean way was normally for the whole family to live together in the same place. My uncle and auntie must have been unhappy as they waited for their sons to come to America, but eventually their family was reunited, and they moved in with their sons. Their oldest, who was a daughter, lived with her husband and children in San Francisco, and I believe she later moved to Los Angeles to start a business and did very well.

So I passed my days in the Hole thinking of my family and Ranko, each day hoping for a letter from my mother, and more especially, from Ranko. My feeling of loneliness hurt most whenever a guard walked down the tier passing out letters to convicts. Six days a week, I felt hopeful I might receive a letter, so I felt especially alone during the passing out of letters. Even as I learned to not expect a letter, I still felt a big letdown each time, as I am sure many convicts felt when receiving no letter. During the times when the guards walked down the tier with mail, there was total silence in the Hole.

Weapons Manufacture

During my first night in the Hole, late at night at about 11 p.m. or midnight, I heard what sounded like a .22 gunshot, followed by some laughter, as if some convicts were letting off some steam. Hearing this sharp sound had me totally puzzled. I thought, "Is there some convict who has a small gun in the Hole? What is going on with the gunshot? Why is no prison guard coming onto the tier to investigate?" Nothing happened. I saw no movements by the guards. I learned later that the gunshot sound must have been a prison-made zip gun going off.

While I was in the K wing hole, I made no weapons, but later on, I learned how to make a zip gun. This is the way it is made: First, you wrap eight to ten sheets of writing paper around a pencil, then tightly wrap that with wet strips of bedsheet. After it dries, you fold one end of the paper tube, and tear it off, then pull out the pencil and pack the back of the tube with dry toilet paper. Next you crush match heads. You may need forty to fifty books of match heads to get enough powder without letting any match paper get into the powder. Then you pour the powder into the tube, and pack it down with a pencil. For the bullet, you put in bits of metal, like staples or any other little bits of metal. Again, you use a pencil to pack the metal to the back, in front of the powder. Next you stuff in a small amount of toilet paper, not tightly, to hold the powder and bits of metal in place. Then you use a nail taken from your prison-issue shoes, and drill a small hole through to where your match powder is. Lastly, use thin cigarette rolling paper mixed with match powder to make a fuse to install in the drilled hole. At this point, you are ready to fire a prison-made zip gun, which most of the time is not very effective. You aim for the eyes of your target. There was one case where a small solid piece of metal was used as a bullet in a zip gun, and this bullet had enough power to penetrate a convict's heart and kill him. This was the only case I'd ever heard of where a zip gun was used to actually kill another convict while he was on the tier in the Hole.

Here is how you make a prison-made knife—or in prison terms, a "shank" or "piece." First, you try to find a piece of sharp metal, such as a nail from your prison-issue shoes. Once you have the metal nail, you light some matches to melt it to your plastic toothbrush to attach a handle to the nail. Then you sharpen an edge using the cement floor. Next, select a piece of metal to cut, such as your metal bed, sink, or toilet. Cut a scratch in the metal, outlining the piece you want to cut out, by using the sharp pointed nail. Then just keep cutting the metal in the same direction. It may take you one to three days before you can cut out a long enough piece of metal to be used as a knife. Just as only a diamond can cut another diamond, so metal can cut metal. Lastly, you use the cement floor to put a knife-edge on the steel. Since the Hole is so quiet, you can be sure the convicts near your cell can hear your scraping noise, and they know you are making a knife.

Even a hard bar of soap in a sock can be used as a weapon. If an experienced convict wants to make a weapon, some kind of weapon can be made from just about anything that at first may seem like nothing. Rolling writing paper around the end of your toothbrush or pencil extends its length for use like a normal toothbrush or pencil. In a similar way, if you have a few inches of metal, you can add paper to extend the end of your weapon, tying it down tightly with part of a bedsheet or T-shirt to make a firm handle on your prison-made knife. Then you sharpen the metal on the cement floor. You can also take a magazine, roll it tightly, tie it with string and wrap it with wet strips of bedsheet or T-shirt. When the wet cloth dries, you have a club for a weapon. It might not be as hard as a wooden club, but it's nearly as good as a wooden club to have a ten- or twelve-inch magazine club. I learned how to make these prison-made weapons later on, not during my first visit to the Hole.

During my first few days in the Hole, when my cell door opened, I stepped out to take a shower and then returned to my cell and closed the door. However, on the fourth day, I heard my cell door click open, and then I heard the clicking sound of someone else's cell door opening. All the convicts on the tiers heard the sound of two cells clicking open at the same time, and before I could slide open my cell door, many convicts in the Hole started shouting out, "Setup! Setup! Setup!"

I stepped out of my cell, aware of what the term "setup" meant, but unsure what was going on. Just as I stepped out of my cell, I saw a white convict also stepping out of his cell, as the shouts of "Setup!" continued. The prison guard hollered down the tier for both of us go back into our cells, which I obeyed. Had we been enemies, one of us might have tried to kill the other, and for that reason, convicts on the tiers were shouting, "Setup!"

Even the convicts on the first and third floor were shouting, which goes to show how alert the convicts were to any sounds made on the tier. These so-called accidental openings of two cell doors at the same time took place whenever the guards wanted to set up a convict to be hit. Since it was my turn to shower, my cell door opened again, so I came back out to take my shower, then returned to my cell as if nothing had happened, but I was learning how unsafe I was. The danger came not only from other convicts but from the guards as well.

One night, as the guard on the lower tier was making his rounds, a convict called out, "Hey, officer."

In a bored and tired voice, the guard responded, "What?"

The convict asked, "Where is Joe?"

The guard responded, "Joe your mama," and then the convict busted out laughing along with many other convicts on all three tiers. The guard didn't even respond to the trap joke but went on making his rounds. Even I smiled in my cell at the joke played on the guard. Even though the joke was not too funny, hearing some of the convicts laugh felt like a release of the convicts' tension, like the sound you heard almost every night of zip guns going off. Before I was aware that those sharp sounds were made by zip guns, I concluded that those shots didn't trouble anyone during the night. A zip gun shot around midnight was like a night bell telling convicts it was time to go to sleep.

After I had been in the Hole about ten days, a guard came to my cell to inform me I was going to classification, and he ordered me to undergo a strip search. After I placed my boxers back on, I was told to turn around and put my hands out the food port, where I was handcuffed behind my back. Then I was ordered to walk ahead of him to the sally port, to pass through two gates. The guard opened the gates one at a time. Then we went downstairs to an office I had noticed when I first arrived in K wing. The office had a six-by-three-foot table in the center of the room, which was sometimes used as the K wing classification room and other times as the officers' room.

There were only three people in the classification committee—one person in civilian clothing, who was in charge of K wing, and two uniformed guards, a lieutenant and a sergeant, who reviewed my central file. No one said anything while my central file was reviewed. Within a few minutes, a prison administrator in civilian clothing told me I would be transferred out of K wing to West Hall. Then I was led back to my cell.

That afternoon, I went through yet another strip search. Any time a convict came out of his cell, he was strip-searched and handcuffed before the cell door opened. This protected the guards, as the Hole held the most violent gang members who had been involved in prison stabbings or killings. As I was led out of K wing into an empty corner of the mainline, I headed toward the buildings that I first saw upon my arrival to Tracy. I had no idea what going to the West Hall meant, but I was glad to get out of the darkened K wing as I walked handcuffed toward West Hall.

West Hall

As I was escorted out the last gate of the mainline, on my left was a small yard guard office, and on my right a wing called East Hall. Between East and West Halls, there was a concrete exercise yard for both halls. Upon arrival to West Hall, I passed through a steel-plated door.

West Hall was well lit with three tiers and a stairway in the middle. To my left, was an office for the guards, and a kitchen with a dining room; on my right, was the door to the yard. In the middle, a small surveillance room jutted out to give gun guards a good view of all the movements of convicts coming and going from their cells to the yard, the dining room, and showers. The open shower room had about ten showerheads on light-colored tile, and I was placed in a cell on the same side as the shower room. The steel cell doors each had a small three-by-five-inch window, and the cell I entered was about five by eight feet. There was a mattress and pillow on a steel-plated bed near the window, and a sink and toilet made of one piece of stainless steel. There was also a split window, shared with a neighboring cell. I could open a portion of the window about three or four inches and look into the exercise yard.

On my first afternoon in West Hall, I was in my cell when the East Hall convicts were in the yard. Word of any new arrivals must have gotten around real fast, because someone in the yard came right up to my window and said, "Hey, Lee."

When I saw who it was, I was filled with relief and gladness. It was Gilbert Wong, a friend I knew from the streets, who was half Chinese and half Latino. Gilbert seemed the same as I knew him from the street—easygoing with an easy smile, just like when he used to hang around Powell and Market in front of Woolworths with a few guys in the early 1970s.

Gilbert said, "I heard you just got here, how you doing?"

"I am all right," I said.

"Okay, you need anything?"

"I could use some smokes and stamps, envelopes, or anything else you could throw my way."

"I don't smoke, but I'll try putting things together along with some tobacco as soon as I can," said Gilbert. "We have to use an officer since we are not allowed to pass anything through the windows, and East and West gangs are not allowed contacts with each other."

"All right, thanks! What been happening, Gilbert?"

"Nothing much. I am waiting for a transfer to Soledad to be with my brothers Ellis and Johnny. The transfer should take place any day now."

I knew both of his brothers from the street. I couldn't help wishing I were in Soledad to do time with them, as I knew them better as friends than any members of either gang in San Francisco Chinatown. Gilbert and I talked a bit more. Then Gilbert said, "I am going to introduce you to a friend of mine named B.B., who is also from San Francisco. After I am transferred, he will look out for you." This meant B.B. would school me on how to conduct myself. Gilbert brought B.B. over to my cell window and said in a friendly way, "That's my homeboy, Lee, from San Francisco. Look out for him if you can."

B.B. and I exchanged, "What's happening?" And then it was time for their yard recall. I saw a great deal of contrast between Gilbert and B.B. While B.B. had a very serious attitude, Gilbert was easygoing. Among 350 hard-core convicts in West and East Halls, Gilbert was a good uplift for my spirits. Knowing Gilbert also opened small doors to communicate with a few others in the yard. Otherwise, I was alone. I walked around the yard or stood around just checking things out, but the fact was, I was a lone Asian, and whatever might come down, I would have to stand on my own.

At night for about four hours, a prison radio played music. The music varied by racial theme nights. On certain nights, the radio played oldies preferred by Latinos, or country music for whites, or jazz and soul music for blacks. West Hall was a segregated lockup unit like K wing, but it allowed much more freedom than in the Hole, which made me feel less darkened in my mind. What I didn't realize was that most West and East Hall inmates were involved with prison gangs, especially Nuestra Familia (NF) and Black Guerilla Family (BGF). The dominance of gang members made these areas an ongoing battleground.

Like me, most West Hall convicts had been transferred there after spending time in the K wing Hole, but unlike me, these convicts were much more experienced. I knew prison gangs existed, but I learned nothing about them in K wing, and I was not about to start asking questions. The best policy for a convict was to mind his own business and keep his mouth shut. Talking a lot of BS or asking dumb questions could lead to getting killed. I didn't have time to think much about the Chinatown case because my full attention focused on personal survival in prison. I didn't know it at the time, but the prison administration had thrown me into a lions' den before I had any understanding of the convicts' code of conduct.

Even though the West and East Halls housed members or close associates of NF and BGF, plus maybe some Mexican Mafia (La Eme) and Aryan Brotherhood (AB) members, I had yet to even learn the names of these prison gangs. I could only guess that these convicts I shared the yard time with were very serious people. As they walked, they talked in mostly low tones with a lot of brass in their voices. In their firm faces, their eyes glinted like steel, forever on the alert, accepting life in the man-made jungle.

There had been quite a lot of stabbing and killing in the yard for West and East Halls, as well as inside the units. While I had not yet witnessed any stabbings, I found it strange that this was known to be one of the most violent yards in California, for West and East Halls did not have a prison guard tower to cover violence in the yard. Inside, each unit had six prison guard gun tower rooms, one for each tier, and those rooms were kept very dark, so you couldn't see which gun tower was shooting. There was usually only one prison guard inside a gun tower room, and other guards roamed around to different gun towers, depending on tier movement. But for the yard, there was only one yard guard, sitting inside a darkened office, looking for any signs of violence in the yard through a thick wire orange-colored mesh fence. In comparison, in the less violent mainline, about five gun towers covered the yard in case of any violence.

Since it was winter, most prisoners wore the prison-issue black jacket and black wool cap. Many prisoners had personal sweatshirts mailed to them from friends and family outside. Each convict was allowed to receive three personal packages for Christmas, and one special package on his birthday with a fifty-pound weight limit for each package. Since we were in the semi-Hole adjustment center (AC), any items in personal packages that came in glass or metal containers were poured into paper bags, plastic containers, or pouches obtained from the canteen, and the glass and metal were confiscated.

After a few times in the yard, I saw a young white convict who stood by himself by the weight-lifting area drinking coffee from a plastic cup about the size of a medium fast-food cup. I decided to stand around with him and start a small personal conversation. He was about nineteen years old, with a shy smile, and none of that hardened convict's look of experience, so I thought he must be new to prison, as I was. I saw no serious tension in him. I asked him, "What's your name?"

"Danny."

"Why are you in prison?"

"I'm doing two life sentences for double murder," he said with a shy and gentle smile.

During our short conversations, one time I asked to drink some of his coffee. He looked a little bit surprised, but with a shy smile, he handed over his coffee, and we shared the cup back and forth a few times. Since

Danny was the only convict I saw standing around alone in the yard, during the next few yard times I met up with him and shared his coffee.

One day as I was walking around the yard, one of the Latinos started walking with me. I didn't know him well but had just met him in the yard within the first week. (Later, I learned he was an NF member.) During this short walk, he said, just before walking away, "Danny with the cup you're drinking from—he's a punk." This was advice to me, and a warning that sharing the same cup and drinking coffee with a punk was not acceptable to all convicts.

I was surprised to hear Danny was a punk. He must have gotten raped and made into a punk, which was the lowest level in the convicts' hierarchy. Here was a guy doing two life sentences for double murder, yet he was weak and had accepted his role as a punk. I felt sad for him that he was doing hard time on two life sentences. He seemed like a nice guy who had gotten trapped in the jungle of life in prison. But each convict had to do his time on his own, for there was no one who could do the prison time for him. As to the warning I received, the convicts who observed me were saying, "Even though you're new to the prison system, we know who you are. We may be willing to accept you, but don't make mistakes like sharing a cup with some punk."

Maybe Gilbert passed down word about me to B.B., who passed on the information to NF as well as BGF that I should be left alone, and no one should make a move against me, but that I should be allowed a fair chance to gain experience as a convict. If so, then having a friend, like Gilbert, who could put in a good word for you in such a hard gang battleground as West and East Halls made a world of difference. If I had continued to associate with Danny, I would have been looked down upon as weak. If I were tested for associating with Danny, I could have been put in the position of fighting for my life to prove I was not weak. When I received the warning about Danny, I appreciated the warning and listened—I disassociated myself from Danny.

Though I still saw Danny in the yard, he and I might just say "hi" to each other but that was as close contact as I would allow. When Danny saw I had distanced myself from him, he looked a bit sadder and a little more alone. Even though I was also alone, I had to put myself at a different level than Danny according to the convict code of conduct. Here was a young man with two life sentences, who would be abused through the long hard years ahead of him. Seeing him in such a light, I couldn't help wanting to feel my own humanity arise, to care about his plight.

However, part of the unfairness of the prison system was to force those of us who wanted to survive to suppress our humanity. Instead, I felt a bit more bitter and angry toward the prison system, as well as toward some other convicts, for not accepting someone who was young but not strong enough to coexist with the rest of the convicts. It was part of minding your own business and doing your own time, to take aggressive control, and never let any feelings of insecurity show. This was especially true for a new convict, who didn't know other convicts and didn't know all the pitfalls I still needed to learn.

Those gang members of West and East Hall were watching for signs of weakness in how I carried myself and watching to see how I would grow into the convict experience with every passing day. It was a trial I needed to pass, even with so little experience of state prison time and with few or no friends or allies within the walls of the segregation unit. If I failed the trial, I could end up like Danny. One fact I had firmly set my mind on was this: I would be no one's punk. I would fight back, even if fighting back led to my death—for if I attacked one gang member, it could be viewed as an attack on the whole gang, and I stood no chance against the prison gangs.

If I didn't learn to stand on my own, knowing Gilbert, B.B., Joe Fong, and the other Chinese in the mainline did not mean anything. No convict wanted to associate with a weak convict. The able or strong convict did not want to place himself in the position of standing up for a weak convict. This is what I mean when I say prisoners got more institutionalized with more experience. Most prisoners learned this basic lesson on their very first day in battle-hardened prisons such as Tracy, San Quentin, Folsom, and Soledad.

The yard time lasted about three hours, and when our time was up, we entered back into our unit. A line of six or seven prison guards stood about two or three feet apart, and we each had to go before one of the guards and hand over all our clothing for a strip search, and then carry our clothing back to our cell door.

Cell Time

Back in my cell, I felt less tension than in the yard. It was time to relax a little, even though I still felt the tension of being trapped in warfare twenty-four hours a day. The tension was ever-present, like an invisible mist over the whole prison, especially in the segregation units. Although I could see the West and East Hall yard from my window, there was not much to see, and there were no convict visitors stopping by my window for conversation since I didn't know anyone other than B.B. in East Hall. So I tried to relax and read some easy-to-read books.

Some convicts loaned me books. My English was not so good but just by reading, I improved my reading level greatly. I read a lot of different writers such as Danielle Steele, James Michener, and James Clavell. I was more interested in adventure novels, but I read whatever books happened to be available to borrow from other convicts. Asking other convicts what books were good to read also helped open up some communication. There was a small prison library by the dining room, but there was no system for checking out and returning books, so convicts kept most of the good books in their cells and loaned the books to convicts they knew.

There was a small metal desk in the cell with a stool attached. At the time, I just had Ranko, Reiko, and my mother to write to, so I wrote letters to all three of them, once or twice a month, sometimes more often. I wrote to Ranko the most and thought about her a lot. Reiko was married, so my letters to Ranko were more personal than my letters to Reiko, even though Reiko was closer to me and had greater feelings toward me than did Ranko, who was more interested as a friend in finding ways to help my legal battle on the Chinatown case.

Ranko at the time was attending college full-time as well as working part-time. Years later, I heard from Reiko that while Ranko was in college, she tried to organize a dance party as a legal fund-raiser on my behalf. People had a good time at the dance, but the fund-raiser was a failure. However, Ranko's commitment to support me and to prove my innocence on the Chinatown case was unlimited, and I felt very fortunate to have such strong friends.

Ranko and Reiko's friendship truly made a great difference—the difference between total darkness and light. Ranko and Reiko may not have realized it, but their friendship and letters were all I felt I had in this world, which kept my spirits and hopes up. Their friendship helped me through the total darkness of being alone. I feel unconditional gratitude to Ranko and Reiko for all of my life. They gave me personal support during my darkest hours in prison without asking for anything in return. I had nothing to return but my friendship.

In a way, I was selfish for continuing to pursue Ranko by showing interest in a personal relationship in my letters to her. She never responded to my personal feelings but continued to write me back in less-than-one-page letters. I received a letter from Ranko every two or three months (and from my mother every six or seven months). I believe Ranko was well aware of my situation, of needing to release personal feelings to a female because she continued to receive my letters, and in return wrote nonpersonal letters back. During all my years of imprisonment, I never had any negative thoughts toward Ranko for her nonresponsiveness to my approach, but I felt positivity toward her for the friendship she gave me. It may not have been a personal relationship, but Ranko's friendship was pure light in my darkened world.

Bird Bath

On days when we didn't go into the yard, we were allowed to shower. A group of about fifteen convicts were allowed out for showering, even though there were only ten showerheads in the open area. The guards turned the shower on for about ten minutes. As soon as the water started flowing, the first group got wet, then stepped out of the shower to soap down while the others stepped in to get wet and then stepped out so the soaped group could rinse themselves, and so on.

During my first shower time, I had gotten back under the shower after soaping myself from the face on down, but before I could rinse off, the guards shut off the water. I was the only one left in the shower full of soap, so I asked the guard, "Can I get a minute to rinse off the soap?"

He firmly told me, "No, rinse off in your cell."

I returned to my cell and used the water from the sink to rinse off, which convicts called a "bird bath." Most convicts, especially on hot days or nonshower days, would take bird baths in their cells. I told myself, "I won't get caught in the same situation again during shower time." In future showers, I was able to quickly soak, soap, and rinse.

After a few times showering with groups of Latinos, I noticed they all only showered from the neck down, which made me wonder why those guys didn't take full showers. Sometime later when I got to know some of the Latinos better, I asked them about this. It was a rule among NF members not to get soap on their faces because soap could blind your eyes or make you unable to see clearly. It was a self-defense tactic to stay on guard while showering in case you were attacked or someone else got stabbed in the shower. If you had soap in your eyes, you wouldn't be able to defend yourself or get out of the way of a stabbing. Within all groups, there are set rules that each member is expected to follow. If a member breaks one of his gang's rules, he will be disciplined or even killed by his own prison gang members, which happens often enough to set an example to the rest of the gang members so they fall into strict line with the prison gang rules.

In my own cell, besides reading or writing letters, I set up a little workout program for myself, doing push-ups, twenty-five reps of four sets, and the same amount of sit-ups. As my muscle tone started to build, I increased the number of push-ups and sit-ups. Reading books improved my reading of English, and I tried to improve my spelling through use of a dictionary, but made very little improvement in spelling.

Since I was in a segregated unit, there was no prison program for us, just lots of cell time and some yard time, so whatever self-improvement program I wanted, I had to set up on my own. With about forty-five hours out of every forty-eight locked inside the cell, I found it very difficult to fill all the cell time with worthwhile activities. The cell was equal in size to a bathroom—five by eight feet, with a three-by-six-foot bed taking up most of the space. Even though there was so little space, I paced back and forth and did my push-ups and sit-ups. I found the best time to write letters was at night when the prison system radio was playing, especially when the convicts running the radio room played mostly love songs or mellow music. Then my thoughts might be taken over with daydreaming about what I would like to be doing if I were free. By the time the radio stopped playing, at about 11 p.m. or midnight, I would fall asleep still filled with dreaming thoughts.

Yard Time

Each day was mostly about going through my own routines. During yard time, I started lifting weights on my own, just light weights, which I started using for curls, then bench presses and back-arms. Since weight lifting was new to me, I watched how other convicts did it and followed their example. Since I didn't know the rest of the convicts in the yard, I set my own pace of weight lifting.

Most convicts were members of NF or BGF and under tight leadership. After being watched by the rest of the convicts for a few weeks, some easygoing convicts started to socialize with me, making small conversations, nothing of importance. What was important, however, was my slow acceptance by other convicts. I got invited to play basketball, which was more like football. Being 5'4", I was one of the shortest guys and worst basketball players, but no one seemed to mind. If by chance I got knocked on the ground by accident, I would just get back up and play as hard as I could by pushing and shoving.

The basketball game usually involved a mix of Latinos and blacks, and no one tried to push or shove purposefully to knock someone down. Most African Americans were more interested in basketball or lifting weights, and Latinos mostly played handball. A few Latinos who played a lot of handball started inviting me to learn how to play. The handball was small, about half the size of a baseball, and made out of hard rubber. Most of the convicts used a band to wrap the palm of their hand to play handball. This protected your palm and gave your palm more flat surface to hit the ball. To this day, I enjoy this game the best. When I first started to play handball, the ball stung my hand in cold winter weather, especially if I hit it wrong with my fingers. It stung my fingers until they turned blue. But I enjoyed both handball and basketball, and these games released lots of tension.

Conversation with other convicts was light, nothing serious. They might tell me where they were from, but nothing about their background, as if their past and how much time they were doing did not exist. As far as discussing topics like their gang membership or gang activities or rival gang activities with anyone outside their prison gang—that could get them killed.

During the start of my association with other convicts in the yard, I met an African American, a member of BGF who used to belong to the Crips in Los Angeles. His name was Jo-Mo. He was short—only two or three inches taller than me—but he had a natural big-hearted smile, compared to most others who tried to keep a serious look on their faces. He was easy to get along with, and we became as close to being friends as friendship was possible in prison. We were usually housed in different segregation units, though. When I first met Jo-Mo, I didn't know he was a BGF hard-hitter who carried out a lot of stabbings.

During the light conversations with others in the yard, I tried to tell two or three guys about the false murder charge against me. In return, I got no response, just a blank look, as if they were saying, "Why are you telling me about some BS false murder? There's nothing I can do for you." Wanting some kind of sympathy for my personal problem of falsely being charged with murder was another one of those mistakes that showed weakness. I stopped complaining about my personal problems. I am sure numerous convicts were in prison for murder, and many were serving murder sentences for killing someone in prison. For prison killings, convicts usually pled guilty to second-degree murder, which carried a sentence of five years to life and made them eligible for parole after five years. Back in 1974, if you were sentenced to life for first-degree murder, you were eligible for parole after seven years, and if you had a clean prison behavior record, as well as no gang ties, you could be paroled after ten or twelve years.

Despite my mistakes, I related well with convicts in the yard, and my acceptance by most of the guys eased a little of my inner tension, even though I was still feeling very low about prison life. At this time, I was still new to the prison system and was not receiving any schooling about convict life, nor did I have any insight into prison gangs and gang warfare. The reader can in no way imagine the full tension of a new and inexperienced prisoner, housed with top-level gangsters responsible for killings and stabbings within the prisons. The lesser gang members were in the mainline, not the segregation unit, and here I was in the segregation unit, standing on my own, trying to put my fear aside and stand as well I could, saying I am just as strong just as I am. This was one of the hardest mental adjustments I was faced with daily.

One time I saw Jo-Mo had a tattoo on his forearm—"Crip"—so I asked him what that tattoo was about. Jo-Mo gave me one of his big smiles and put his hand into a C sign with his thumb and first finger, with the rest of his fingers folded in (the hand sign for "Crip") and said nothing else. I also noticed many Latinos had prison tattoos. Almost all the tattoos were a dark blue color—the darker the blue, the older the tattoo. Even though they had many different tattoos and patterns, almost all the Latinos displayed the initials "NF" in old gothic lettering on their left elbow. At first, I was not aware of the meaning of "NF," but I eventually figured out that it stood for membership in a Latino prison gang.

One unwritten rule for convicts was to avoid friendliness with any prison guards, which I followed. All the guards of West and East Hall were white, and a few prison guards were friendly with a few prisoners. I believe consent was given to certain convicts by their gang leader to try to win the guards' trust in order to get information or contraband from them. I noticed the guards treated African American convicts as lesser than the Latinos. I saw no guards act friendly with any African American. The undercurrent of racism—or right up-front racism—ran deep within the prison guards and civilian administrators working within the system.

Every day consisted of yet more routine—the yard, chow, shower, and the rest of the time in my cell, but the tension of prison became part of my being. I had first felt that invisible tension hitting me, piercing through my mind when I first passed through the R&R and walked through the door into the heart of the prison. It was as if I had entered into Hell itself. I never talked to anyone about how I felt when I first walked down the corridor, seeing West and East Hall right in front of me. Was it only me who felt that way, or did other new prisoners also feel the same powerful tension as I did? In order to not show any weakness, I never asked other new prisoners how they felt, but I will never forget that feeling of my first entry into the Tracy prison grounds.

I felt the undercurrent of tension in the yard the most, and by natural instinct, I allowed for my eyes to be my ears and my ears to be my eyes, as if just by watching the movements of convicts in the yard and by listening closely to the voices around me, I could guess the level of tension in the yard and around me, and second-guess how to survive it.

Court Date

I had been at West Hall for two or three months when my cell opened one day. After stepping out, I was informed by the guard that I was going to court. After the strip search, I was handcuffed behind my back and escorted by two prison guards to R&R where I was ordered to wait in a caged area. Since I was taken away from the segregation unit, the handcuffs remained on. After a short time, the R&R guard called me over and asked for my name and prison number. The guard held up a five-by-eight-inch card with my name, picture, and B-number, and after matching my picture with the number, turned to two white deputies from Sacramento County and said, "He's all yours."

With the deputies in the R&R room, I underwent another strip search and was issued a fresh set of prison blue jeans and a shirt, along with underwear and new shoes. Issuing all new clothing was a security measure to make sure nothing could be smuggled out. The Sacramento deputy put me in a waist chain with handcuffs, one on each side near to my right and left pants pockets, and then leg chains. It was standard to be chained up during transportation. I was led out the front of the R&R room and into an unmarked police car. I got into the backseat with the deputies in front. There was no shield or window between the front and backseat. The deputies drove the car to an enclosed caged area, overseen by a gun tower. Some guards checked the deputies' paperwork and checked under the car with a mirror on an extended pole. After all these formalities, the exit gate opened. I was not going to freedom; I was going, in chains, to face the corrupt murder charge against me.

I did like the feeling of being out of Tracy and enjoyed the view of the landscape as the car sped north toward Sacramento for a nearly two-hour drive. As I sat in the backseat, I thought about the unfairness of the justice system; I would be tried for a murder I had no connection with whatsoever. I also felt confident I would be cleared of the murder charge. I was sure I'd be found not guilty in the trial. I knew the first thing I needed to do when I arrived in Sacramento was to contact Ranko to see if anything new had turned up to help the case against me. During my first few months at Tracy, my contact with Ranko was very limited, and I had no legal contact with any attorney. This was my first jury trial in my life, but all my questions had to wait until I arrived in Sacramento to meet with an attorney. I hoped I could even see Ranko. With many thoughts going through my mind regarding my case and the process of going to trial, I arrived in the state capital of California for the first time during my nine years in America.

The Sacramento County Jail was downtown. I was led inside shackled in chains and taken to the booking area, where I underwent the routine booking process. I was allowed to make two phone calls, but they had to be collect calls since the calls were from Sacramento. I first called Ranko, who assured me she was doing all she could to gather support for my case but was finding it very difficult to get support. She said a Chinese guy named Wayne Yee, who knew lots of people in Chinatown, was willing to help out. Later I found out Wayne was one of Joe Fong's advisors and was in the top leadership of the Joe Boys, which I was glad to hear.

I made a short call to my mother to let her know I was in Sacramento for the trial of the Chinatown case. I asked her to mail me some money as soon as she could, which she did. I did not often ask her for money, and when I did ask, she sometimes mailed me twenty dollars, which was enough to buy things you needed for a month, such as tobacco to roll your own smokes, stamps, envelopes, and a few food items like candy bars, chips, or cookies.

After the booking, phone calls, and strip search, I was given county jail prison clothing and blankets, and I was taken to the second floor without any restraints to a ten-man cell tank built in the same model as the San Francisco County Jail. Most prisoners there were white, plus one or two Latinos. The window to the street was about three feet from the cell bars, so that when the panel window was open, you could see a bit of the outside and hear the sounds of passing cars. Sometimes if you hollered loudly enough, you could exchange a few words with people outside on the street, especially at night.

I had no trouble adjusting to the Sacramento County Jail as most of the guys were short timers and mostly passive. The bunk area had beds made of metal bolted to the wall. There was a dayroom with a long stainless steel table and a shower, toilet, and sink, but unlike in San Francisco County Jail, the door between the dayroom and bunk area stayed open. The only times guards came to the tier was to serve our meals or to take prisoners to court in the morning and afternoon. Around 4 p.m., all prisoners were supposed to be seated on the dayroom bench for the guard to count us through the bars. Once a week, we could buy commissary items from the canteen if we placed orders the day before. There were some paperback books to read. I was glad the charge against me did not mean I had to be placed in a single cell. I didn't mind at all living and communicating with nine others guys, especially after my experience of living in the Hole and the segregation units in Tracy. In jail, I felt some relief from the tension of prison.

After the guys in the tank knew I came from the state prison and was on trial for a gang killing, I had no problem with anyone in the tank and got along well with the rest of the prisoners. I played checkers, chess, and cards, and also kept up my daily push-up and sit-ups. Within a few days of my arrival, I was called out for court. I was transferred to an unmarked car with a waist chain and leg irons, which was always the procedure when transferring to or from the court building. The ride took less than ten minutes, but I always enjoyed any ride simply for being out of jail, even if just for ten minutes. I felt some sensation of being free during those rides.

Hamilton Hintz

After being transported to the court buildings, I was placed in a cell with a door leading out to the courtroom. While I waited, a middle-aged man came into the cell and introduced himself as Hamilton Hintz, my court-appointed attorney. Mr. Hintz informed me I would soon be in court, but we would have a lot of time to discuss the case, as I would be held in the county jail until my trial was over. He tried hard to impress me with how good a lawyer he was, saying that he expected soon to be appointed as a judge.

A short time after Mr. Hintz left the holding cell, the door to the courtroom opened. The court deputy held the door open as I entered the Sacramento County Superior Court. Before the superior court judge, the court clerk read off the charges of first-degree murder and use of a gun during the commission of a felony. The judge asked me, "Do you understand the charges?"

I answered, "Yes."

Then he proceeded to appoint Hamilton Hintz as my attorney. The court proceeding took only a few minutes. Then I was transferred back to the county jail.

When I think back on my first meeting with Mr. Hintz, he seemed to me more like a fast-talking used car salesman than a lawyer. I didn't know if I had any say in whether to accept him as my attorney. I should have asked around, but being young and new to the process of going to court, I didn't think I had a choice in the matter. With a different attorney, especially an Asian American attorney who might understand my case much better than a white attorney, the outcome might have been very different. Maybe I could have asked Ranko if she knew of any good attorneys. However, like many prisoners, I just accepted what the court said without knowledge of legal matters and gave my full trust to the police department and the court-appointed lawyer to look out for my best interests.

I now believe the most important part of going through court proceedings is to have the right attorney to represent you from the start. Choosing a good attorney is the most important decision a prisoner can make to influence the outcome of the case. You may have a solid evidentiary case, but without a good lawyer to put your case before the jury, you may easily lose.

Just as I learned only later that the S.F. public defender put most of their efforts into getting my case moved out of San Francisco but did almost no investigative work on the case, I didn't understand the situation I now faced in Sacramento. With a good attorney and good investigative work, I should have had a solid case to put before the jury. At the time, I thought Hintz was just as good as any other attorney. Yet the only times I saw Hintz were short meetings in the courtroom holding cell before each court appearance. I don't remember him ever visiting me at the county jail's attorney room or explaining to me how he was preparing for trial.

Since I was innocent, I felt it was just a simple matter of presenting my case to Hintz and asking him to investigate the truth. For example, I told Hintz that the bullet retrieved from the wall of the house next to my rooming house was fired out of a .357, not a .38 as claimed by the D.A. and the SFPD ballistics expert. I told Hintz about getting a phone call at about the time Yip Yee Tak was murdered and going to pick up Sandy that evening, walking through Chinatown to meet her at her auntie's workplace. Yet Hintz just picked up where the S.F. public defender left off, taking no trouble to investigate. Although I informed Hintz of these issues, I didn't realize he wasn't doing anything to check out my story or have the bullet retested. Basically, he did nothing to aid in proving my innocence.

I believe that after Hintz reviewed the case and talked to the San Francisco District Attorney, James Lassart, Hintz viewed me as guilty. It seemed to me Hintz was almost working with the D.A. to get me convicted. The truth of his attitude came out at the trial.

Hintz asked for an investigator to be appointed two or three days before trial. The investigator, a white woman, did not consult with me about my case but only met with me the day before the trial. She informed me that she had gone to Grant and Pacific Streets in Chinatown and asked around about whether any people had witnessed the murder on June 3, 1973. I couldn't believe what I was hearing. A white woman with an investigator's badge asking Chinese people about a cold-blooded gangland murder in the heart of Chinatown when she had no contacts or connections in Chinatown? People she asked must have thought she was crazy. She was lucky she didn't get suckered into getting hurt for being so stupid.

How do we mistakenly believe something even when the contrary reality is written right in front of our eyes in big letters? We want so badly to believe in the false beliefs we create in our minds. No matter how painfully the reality is hurting us, we have our reasons for refusing to see it clearly. It was my choice to believe in the purity and greatness of justice in America in order to give myself hope. Meanwhile, still waiting for the jury trial date to be set, I appeared in court with Hintz representing me for pretrial motions. I had no understanding of legal pretrial motions and no knowledge of law.

While waiting for trial, I contacted Ranko and Wayne, who informed me they were having a very difficult time finding any witnesses willing to testify on my behalf. I thanked them for their efforts. Numerous eyewitnesses to the murder existed, but the real witnesses, living in Chinatown with the Wah Ching running the neighborhood, were too fearful of retaliation if they came forward to testify at the trial. I don't think Ranko or Wayne were in contact with Hintz.

At the county jail, I kept to myself and didn't talk to other prisoners about the case. Ever since my experience with the planted jailhouse rat back in the San Francisco County Jail, I trusted no one. However, no one asked me about my case, so I got along with the other prisoners in the cell tank.

Luna and Friends

One day, a big American-born Latino was placed in the cell tank I was in. He was close to 6′ tall, weighing about 180 pounds. His name was Frank Munoz. The next day, Frank took over the tank by telling other prisoners to clean up the cell tank and keep it neat. He acted like an army officer giving orders. I paid no attention to what he said, but all the other prisoners let him take the role of being in charge. If he'd done something like that in state prison, he would have gotten killed. But he didn't seem to be looking for fights. He was just intimidating other prisoners to keep the cell tank clean.

I was the only one who paid no attention to what he said but sat back and watched him. I knew if he approached me as he did the other prisoners, I would have to fight him. In a way, I had been running the cell tank and was respected by the others because they knew I had come from state prison for my trial. They must have seen whatever little bit of hardness that showed in my eyes from being in the Tracy segregation unit. Even though I only had a few months of convict experience, it reflected in my eyes and actions.

After a few days, Frank Munoz approached me. I was a bit surprised when he started talking to me in a normal, respectful, and friendly way. Frank started with light conversation, and I responded back in a friendly way. He told me he had a Chinese wife and respected Asian people. Since he knew I was not from Sacramento, he asked, "Have you had any visitors?"

"No," I answered.

Much to my surprise, Frank said, "Well, then I'm going to fix you up with visits from my sister Luna and some of her friends as soon as I get out on bail."

In county jail, you heard prisoners promise you lots of things they'd do once they were out of jail, but 99 percent of the time these were just empty promises, so I took lightly Frank's promise to fix me up with his sister and her friends. However, we did become best of buddies for about two weeks before he was bailed out. Just before he left, he gave me his phone number and address.

Within a few days, I was called out for a visitor. I wondered who would be visiting me. The visiting room was a row of phones with stools to sit on while talking through a glass panel. I was really surprised to discover that Frank kept his word, and his sister Luna had come to visit. She was very attractive, twenty-three or twenty-four years old, and tall. Trying to get over my surprise to receive such an attractive woman visitor,

I became very shy as we talked about each other. Luna said she heard a lot of good things about me from her brother Frank and was pleased to meet me. I tried to say some nice words to her, and toward the end of the visit, I asked her to mail her picture to me, which she did mail me.

After my first visit with Luna, almost every visit day I started to receive young female visitors. I think one of the visitors was Luna's younger sister, who brought friends with her. Sometimes I had back-to-back visitors on the same day. I felt really good to be receiving these young women visitors, who were all Latinas. During one visit with two females, near the end of the visit I said "bye" and hung up the phone. Then a good-looking white woman that looked to be in her midtwenties, came over and picked up the visitor phone. I didn't know her, but I had noticed she kept looking my way during the twenty to thirty minutes' visiting time. I had no idea why she was there, but when I picked up the phone, she said, "You look so young to be in the adult jail. Why are you in jail?" I told her my name and age. Her face looked friendly and concerned as if she were interested in getting to know me, but before I could ask for her address, the phone went dead, the sign that visiting hour was over. There was no more time to communicate through the glass panel before all visitors were led out of the visiting room. I didn't see the stranger again, but I kept receiving visits from the young Latino women, including Luna, who visited me a few more times.

Receiving these visitors made a big difference in making me feel good, and it gave me new people to write letters to, as I did with Luna. I have to say, we prisoners are very greedy about corresponding with as many females as possible. It's only natural for men in prison to desire to reach out for the soft touch of a woman through their letters and visits.

Murder Trial

The jury trial finally started in June 1974 about one year after my arrest. At the trial, twelve white Americans were picked for the jury, and there was a white judge, a white police inspector, a white D.A., and a white defense attorney. On the first morning of the trial, I saw Ranko and Wayne sitting in the mostly empty courtroom. The day started with one of three eyewitnesses, a man who had worked at Juvenile Hall back in August of 1969. This man spoke very aggressively in his testimony as if he wanted to leap out of the witness chair to accuse me of being the shooter. After lunch in the holding cell of the court, the same witness was still on the stand, but I noticed Ranko and Wayne were no longer in the courtroom. I guess they had already heard enough to know I was doomed.

The next witness, in his early twenties, was a member of the American Olympic ski team and a friend of the first witness. He testified calmly that he and his friends were standing across the street about thirty feet from the shooting and identified me as the shooter. The third witness, who was in the US Navy and also in his early twenties, testified a bit reluctantly that he was with his Navy buddy about twenty-five to thirty feet from the shooting. He also identified me as the shooter. Then the San Francisco police ballistics expert testified that the bullet recovered from the accidental shooting at my place prior to the murder was an exact match to the .38 gun that had shot the victim in the case. This was impossible. Scientific testing could easily show that the bullets could not match when fired from different guns, but Hintz hadn't done any tests on the guns. The last witness was SFPD inspector Frank Falzon, testifying about his interview of me after my arrest. When it was time for Falzon's cross-examination by Hintz, I said to Hintz, "Ask him how the police could have picked me as a suspect."

With a smile at me, Hintz started the cross-examination. To the disbelief of the whole courtroom as well as myself, Hintz asked Falzon for the reason why I was accused of the murder of Yip Yee Tak. The police detective should never have been asked this question, since up until that point, the D.A. was unable to prove any motive behind the killing of Yip Yee Tak. Hintz, who was an experienced criminal trial lawyer, knew Falzon's testimony could supply the missing motive.

Frank Falzon testified that Yip Yee Tak was a Wah Ching gang advisor, closely related to the Wah Ching leader Anton Wong who was killed a month prior to Yip Yee Tak's murder. Falzon also told the court that Yip Yee Tak didn't pay his respects at Anton Wong's funeral and that Yip Yee Tak supposedly stole the money supposed to be used for Anton Wong's defense. Falzon then testified that I was a member of the Chinese "Ski Mask" gang involved in robberies and that I was a hit man for hire that the Wah Ching asked to borrow from the Ski Mask gang to make the hit on Yip Yee Tak. In this way, my own defense attorney brought out the motive for the murder.

Hintz did not ask any follow-up questions to Falzon's false testimony about me, nor did he even question whether Falzon was aware that I was Korean and not Chinese. This question of ethnic identity was never raised during the trial. The eyewitnesses were never questioned about how much they'd been drinking since they had all testified that they were in S.F. Chinatown for dinner and were drinking during their sight-seeing. No one asked how difficult it might have been for the eye-witnesses to be sure I was the shooter.

Hintz instead asked questions that were damaging to my defense. His cross-examination gave me the impression he was helping the D.A. provide a motive for the murder of Yip Yee Tak. When Hintz put up a few witnesses, there was only one eyewitness for the defense, a Navy buddy of one of the D.A.'s witnesses, who testified that I was not the shooter. The D.A.'s cross-examination implied that this eyewitness had an alcohol problem. For my defense, Hintz never conducted any research into the witnesses' backgrounds or brought in any expert witnesses, such as a bullet expert to refute the false testimony by the D.A.'s ballis-tics expert or an expert who could explain the difficulties of cross-racial identification.

The trial presented only the D.A.'s side of the case with help from my own defense attorney to supply a motive, which Lassart repeated dramatically during his closing argument. The only thing Hintz did in my defense was to establish that the witnesses saw the shooting in fewer than three seconds. Otherwise, he accepted whatever documents Lassart gave him and never tried to reach for the real truth. In fact, whenever the trial broke for lunch or the court day ended, I saw Hintz leave the courtroom together with D.A. Lassart and Inspector Falzon, the three of them all talking together like buddies. Meanwhile, I still hoped justice would prevail, even with all the evidence against me and the very weak defense Hintz put up on my behalf.

After about two weeks of trial proceedings, the case was handed over to the jury. It took the jury three days before they brought back a verdict. I think this suggests that some jurors sensed the frame-up of the case. On the first reading of the jury findings, I thought at first I heard "not guilty." When it was reread a second time, I heard the words de-claring that I had been found guilty of first-degree murder. I felt shocked. How could I be found guilty of a murder I had not committed and knew nothing about? In my state of shock, I lost my faith in the purity of jus-tice and the patience of hope. Something deep inside exploded in rage, and I lunged toward Lassart and Falzon. Before I could get to them, the courtroom deputy got hold of me and carried me out of the court as I shouted, "No, I am innocent! I am innocent!"

I was placed back in the courtroom holding cell. I sat on a concrete bench in the holding tank, feeling insane. Thoughts shouted in my mind, "How could such injustice happen! Why! Why! How could this impossible injustice happen to me?" At the age of twenty-one, or even one hundred, I couldn't comprehend the injustice. You might hear about people being framed for false criminal charges, but until it happens to you, you'll never feel the full impact. I sat in the holding tank in a red-hot state of confusion. About five minutes later, one of the court deputies opened the door and asked me, "Are you all right?"

How could I be all right? But since I had calmed down, I said I was okay. In the darkened light of what had just happened, I tried to convince myself that one day this mistake would be exposed, and I would be set free. It was the only hope that comforted me, but the feelings of bitterness, anger, and sadness all seemed bottomless. I kept all those feelings to myself.

Hintz didn't even come to see me after I was found guilty of a crime that I didn't commit. What kind of self-respect could these people feel as officers of the court, sworn to uphold the full integrity of the law? The honor these people sought and received from their community was a total disgrace. Many people honor law enforcement not just for enforcing the law but for giving a false sense of security that allows only white people to live in safety. There is a long list of innocent people who were framed and made national news headlines, even some who were released from death row based on new evidence, such as DNA tests. Yet some white communities unwittingly continue to believe that all law enforcement officers serve everyone in society honorably. Dishonorable people exist in every part of society, including some in law enforcement who act with license to do as they see fit with total disregard for law. They feel they have become the law, and it's a crime to be a minority. Minorities are most often the victims of injustice. In my case, racism caused my ruin.

When I returned to the county jail, I didn't speak much to other prisoners in the cell tank but continued on with my routine. There was no need to call Ranko to tell her the bad news. I am sure she already guessed the outcome of the trial from that morning she was in court.

About a month later, while I was waiting in the court holding tank for my sentencing, Hintz stopped by. As if covering up a guilty look, he said to me, "My son said thanks for the five-dollar bill he found when I returned your court clothes to him." (Prior to the trial, Hintz had given me a pair of his son's pants and a shirt that fit me.)

"What five-dollar bill?"

A prisoner was not allowed to have cash money, and I surely did not put five dollars into his son's clothes. Here was a man so low that he used his son to cover up his guilt. Most likely he threw the shirt and pants away, especially after I had worn them for over two weeks during the trial without having them cleaned.

When I entered the courtroom, I saw a replacement judge sitting on the bench. Hintz lightheartedly pled for a new trial. The D.A. argued for upholding the verdict. As the judge was about to sentence me, something broke within me. I start to explain, "Your Honor, Your Honor, I didn't kill no one. I didn't kill no one. Please, Your Honor, try to understand I didn't kill no one!" Uncontrollable tears were coming down my face. I tried to look up at the judge to tell him, "Your Honor, I'm innocent! I'm innocent! I didn't kill no one! Please! Please!"

The judge, whose face I was seeing for the first time, looked down at me. He had a very sincere and sympathetic look on his face as if he was trying to tell me that he understood but that he had no choice. I was grateful for the sympathetic way this judge listened to my plea of my innocence. Finally, the judge said, "I hereby sentence you . . ." In legal terms, he sentenced me to life in prison.

Still, with uncontrollable tears spilling from my eyes, I was led out of the courtroom. A few days later, I was transferred back to Tracy. It was still June 1974.

Prison Industrial Complex

I was placed back in West Hall in the third cell toward the front of the second floor with a window overlooking the weight-lifting area in the West and East Hall yard and a corner of the mainline yard. By then, the lockdown on the mainline was over, but my cell was too far away to see any of the Chinese guys in the mainline yard. From West and East Hall yard, you could look through a fence between the handball court and East Hall and see what was going on in the mainline yard, which was bigger than a football field.

Tracy was originally built to house young prisoners, including some California Youth Authority (CYA) inmates who were too difficult to handle in CYA. Besides this group, any inmate over eighteen years old could also be sent to Tracy. Because Tracy housed the youngest prisoners, there was a lot of fighting and stabbing by young convicts trying to prove how tough they were. They were basically convicts in training, which is how Tracy came to be called "gladiator school." Over time, all the CYA inmates were removed from Tracy with the increase in prison gangs, but Tracy continued to hold a good proportion of younger convicts, as did Soledad prison.

Back in 1973 when I was sentenced to state prison, only one S.F. deputy was needed to transfer prisoners from the county jail to state prison once a week. But by 2005, the numbers had increased to two or three busloads of prisoners coming from San Francisco alone to the state prisons. California has more prisons than any other state, with plans to build more. Nowadays, prisons are built by modular design. For a new prison to be built, the parts to build a whole prison are sent to a new prison site and then put together.

In returning to Tracy, I felt greater solitude within myself and kept my feelings to myself. To complain about injustice was a sign of weakness, and many convicts felt some sense of injustice one way or another. Even though I was out at court for less than three weeks, there were already new prisoners in West Hall. I continued to try to get along with all the convicts in the yard, mostly Latinos and African Americans. I continued going through the same routines.

The convict next door to me on the right was a Latino, most likely an NF member. Often a convict would break the corner window of his cell. His next-door neighbor would do the same, and they would use the small prison-issue mirrors. We might talk about lighter things and then cover the window back up with cardboard.

While doing time in the lockup unit, you had just a couple hours every other day for exercise or yard time. All other times you spent in your cell, so you had a lot of time to think. One of the most difficult things about doing time was fighting boredom, trying to pass the time reading, thinking thoughts within your own mind, trying to maintain yourself, and not letting your surroundings get the best of you. One day, waiting in my cell and thinking about things, I started remembering my life in Korea.

Korea

I was born out of wedlock on August 15, 1952, on the anniversary of Korea's liberation from Japanese occupation. I may have been born in Seoul, but nobody is sure. I was possibly born in the city of Mokpo in the southwest province of South Jeolla. Wherever it was, I was born into a Confucian society, so my mother paid a heavy price for having a child out of wedlock. She was disowned by her family and left to live on her own. I only have two memories of my mother from those early child-hood years. I remember one day she took my hand, and we walked along a dusty road on a hot summer day. In the years right after the Korean War, all roads in Korea were unpaved and dusty. We came to a roadside stand and ate lunch. In my second memory, she took me out to eat at a nice Korean restaurant in downtown Seoul.

Those are the only early memories I have of spending time with my mother because I was raised by my auntie and uncle, who had six children. Their oldest was a daughter, followed by five sons, all older than me except for Myung-hak, who was a year younger than me. Their family name was Kim. My auntie and uncle originally came from Mokpo, but my memory starts after we moved to Seoul. My auntie and uncle were very gentle people with a happy marriage and a happy family. My earliest memory of living with them was somewhere downtown in a white house with a very big room where all the family members slept together. During winter, the floor was heated to ward off the cold, and the stones under the floor were cool in the summer, which kept the house cool. Back in those years, there was no plumbing, so every Korean family used an outhouse, but our house had an indoor bathroom, which was kind of a luxury.

My uncle and auntie owned a liquor store, and I would sometimes hang around the store. At the liquor store, my aunt and uncle did some black market transactions, selling American goods, such as candy, liquor, and cigarettes, and exchanging American dollars for Korean currency. Koreans could not legally sell anything that was American, so my aunt and uncle purchased American goods from middlemen who worked at American military bases, or from American GIs. One day, I remember my auntie gave me a candy bar from their liquor store. I think it had caramel on top and milk chocolate underneath. It was the only time in my life in Korea that I remember eating a whole candy bar by myself, and it was the most delicious candy bar I ever ate in my life. No candy bar in America ever compared with the one my uncle and auntie gave me in Korea.

I remember going to kindergarten with my youngest cousin, Myung-hak. All the favoritism, love, and attention my auntie gave to her youn-gest son, she also gave to me. My older cousins all treated me like a younger brother, and I grew up alongside Myung-hak. I always called my auntie and uncle "mother" and "father" because they accepted me and loved me as their son, but somewhere in my child mind I had the idea of my real mother as a mysterious figure who I did not know.

In my next memory of Seoul, we moved to the city outskirts into an old-fashioned house, built of mud brick with a grass roof. Some railroad tracks ran nearby, and just beyond the tracks, was the Hangang, or Han, River. My uncle and auntie owned another liquor store where I stopped by often. While we lived there, my real mother came by one day. I didn't see her, but she left behind a baby girl. My uncle and auntie explained to me that the baby was my half sister, Mary, with the last name Lane. She was the most beautiful baby I had ever seen. I had never seen anyone with blue eyes before, and I was proud to have such a beautiful sister. I never could remember my sister crying. She was always smiling. I must have been maybe seven years old when I first met her. But about a month after she arrived, one day I came home to find out she was gone. It saddened me to know her for such a short time. Somewhere in the back of my mind, I knew she must have returned to live with my mother.

Then about a year later in the late 1950s, my mother asked me to come live with her and Mary in an apartment in downtown Seoul. Along with my sister, my mother, and me, there was also a live-in housekeeper who looked after me and Mary when my mother was not around. Mary would sleep with my mother, and I would sleep with the housekeeper who was a very kind person. Now and then, Mary's father came by and stayed with us. Each time he saw me, he gave me some American money. I would quickly run downstairs to a Korean market or liquor store and exchange the dollars for Korean money. Then I put the money in my piggy bank, which had the shape of a little post office box.

I cannot recall exactly how long I lived at the apartment, but it must not have been for long. I don't remember talking with my mother about anything as mother and son. After maybe a month or two, I missed living with my uncle, auntie, and cousins. One day, without asking my mother, I went back to my auntie and uncle's house. I took the piggy bank, which was full. I don't know how much money was in there. As soon as I saw my auntie, she gave me a big hug and asked, "Chol Soo, what are you doing here?"

"I want to come back and live with the family," I said, and gave her the piggy bank. My auntie was very happy to see me. Since I lived with my mother for such a short time, I never really had a chance to bond with her, whereas my uncle and auntie both treated me like their son. When I was gone, the whole family had missed me.

Several months after my return, one summer evening after dinner my auntie said to me, "Chol Soo, come outside with me." She had a sad and serious look on her face. I went outside and she took me by her hand

and said, "Chol Soo, your mother went to America." That was all she said and left me to think for myself. I stood alone for a few minutes just feeling confused. I was raised by my auntie and uncle all my life, except for a month or two with my mother. Who was my real mother or father? For me, auntie and uncle were my real family. Still, I felt there was something missing in my life but was unable to understand fully what it all meant.

Myung-hak came out to join me to comfort me. We were close to each other as brothers, and we walked in silence and then returned home for dinner. Everyone in the family wanted to comfort me. I may not have understood it, but the older family members understood that I had been abandoned by my real mother. It was a very quiet dinner, but the next day, family life went about its normal ways. I guess my young mind decided to accept the fate that my mother and sister went to America with my mother's American husband. I had no reservations about staying in Korea with my uncle and auntie. I do not recall missing my mother.

Sometime later, my auntie and uncle moved again to an area called Bogwang-dong on the outer edge of Seoul. Once again, it was near the railroad tracks and the Han River, and not far from one of the few old river bridges still standing after the Korean War. While living in Bogwang-dong, I must have been eight or nine years old. Somehow, we must have fallen on hard times, as I remember my auntie telling me one day, "Chol Soo, come to work with me."

The work we did was carrying gravel and placing it on a road. Then a tar truck would spray tar over it, making a paved road. It was summertime, which was very hot and humid in Korea, making the work even harder. My auntie could not endure the work for long, so she quit after a few weeks, and I quit along with her.

My aunt and uncle started over with another liquor store with a room in the back. The new liquor store was much bigger than their first liquor store. On many days when I wasn't in school, I would hang around the liquor store with my uncle and auntie, and we would go home on a bus after they closed the store at night.

Through all my years of living with my auntie and uncle, they were always very kind and gentle. I never heard my aunt and uncle raise their voices or argue. They never disciplined any of us with spankings. Living with my uncle and auntie's family, I grew up as normally as any other child and had a happy life. I did not get into any mischief or cause any problems, and I usually played with Myung-hak. I would say I had a happy childhood.

I recall another auntie and uncle with children who would visit us in the summer. We would take the train to visit them too. Sometimes my cousins and I would also visit some other relatives in Mokpo where my auntie's youngest sister was married to a banker who was living fairly well. The banker's family then moved to Bogwang-dong in Seoul to a house not far from our house, and sometimes we went over there to visit our grandmother who was sick and bedridden. I don't recall my grandmother ever being well. I'm not sure if my grandmother was from my auntie's side or was her husband's mother. Anyway, within a year of their move to Seoul, she passed away.

I started to attend elementary school in Bogwang-dong when I was eight or nine. I went for approximately two years and learned how to read and write a little bit of Korean before I stopped going. Parents had to pay a certain amount for the children to attend the school, so I lasted in school as long as I could.

We spent most of our time playing around the house or at the Han River. In the summer or winter the river was our favorite playground, which was a short distance from our house. At that time, there were only two ferry boats to carry people across the river. On the other side of the river there were no houses; we could only see the sandy beach and swampland beyond the beach. One day my cousins and I went to explore the swamp. During our exploration, I was walking along and suddenly came upon thick mud that kept pulling my legs in deeper no matter which way I tried to walk. Even though my cousins were nearby, I didn't cry out as I knew I was on dangerous ground. I walked very slowly to find some solid footing to get out of the mud, which was almost reaching my knees by now. Somehow I managed to find solid footing and was able to rejoin the rest of my cousins. Another time with my cousins, we were playing near the river and I went too far into the river. I couldn't swim then and was unable to cry out for help because the water was right to my mouth and nose. None of my cousins noticed the danger I was in. Finally, I swam underwater doggie style to reach more shallow water a few feet away. Both of these times I felt the danger of losing my life, but I thought there was a way out of danger without panicking, which would become a pattern in my life.

One summer morning, when I was nine or ten, I woke up way past time to go to school after playing in the river the day before. For some reason, I fell back asleep. For the next ten days, I lay in bed, stricken with "river fever." It was summertime, and I lay next to a window to keep cool. I went in and out of consciousness, and I heard the voices of my uncle or one of my cousins from time to time. They woke me up and tried to get me to eat, but I threw up every time I ate. Many times my uncle came over and said, "Chol Soo, here, try to drink this, try to drink this." He gave me soda or juice, and sometimes I was able to take a few sips. I don't know how close I may have come to death, but I think I was able to survive the river fever because of the care of my family.

In Korea during the early 1960s, it was too expensive to see a Western medical doctor, so my family just had to hope I'd get better. One day, even though I was a fully grown kid, my auntie strapped me to her back like a baby and went up the hill to see a shaman who performed a shamanic ritual. I cannot clearly recall the ritual, but I started eating a little bit on the next day. I cannot be sure that it was the shaman who cured me of the river sickness. I may have already been getting better when my auntie took me to the shaman because I was conscious at the time. But I know my auntie went to great lengths to care for me and seek the best cure possible.

After my recovery, I returned back to my normal self, going back to school and playing war games with my friends and cousins until dinner time. After dinner, if it was in summer and not monsoon season, we would play outside until it got dark. The whole family would also listen to drama stories on the radio. Another one of our favorite pastimes in the evening, especially during the winter months, was to listen to my uncle tell us about Korean freedom fighters, in which he had been a participant. My uncle was a good storyteller. In his gentle voice, he would tell us the exploits of heroic Koreans fighting against the Japanese military occupation of Korea without any help from other nations. The United States even signed a treaty of mutual aid, which America totally disregarded in Japan's conquest of Korea.

I can strongly identify with Korean history. Like in my life, Korea throughout its history has struggled to remain a free country against the powerful nations surrounding it from all sides: China to the west, Russia to the north, and Japan to the east. Whenever I read about the history of World War II, I never read about the Korean people's lone struggle against Japanese colonial occupation. But Korean history shows that no matter how many times Korea was invaded, we always found the inner strength to struggle against the foreign invaders to protect our freedom.

One day in 1962, I was in school when one of my older cousins showed up and talked to the schoolteacher for a minute. Then the teacher called me over, and said, "Chol Soo, go home with your cousin." As we left the school, my cousin said, "Your mother has returned from America. She wants to see you."

It came as a shock to me that my mother was in Korea, and she was waiting for me at the house. At age ten, I had mixed feelings about identifying with my real mother and comparing how I felt about her to my aunt and uncle. When I got home, my mother had a big smile and a big hug for me. She said, "Here's my son, here's my son! My pride and joy!" and stuff like that. She gave me some money. "Chol Soo—here, go buy yourself candy. Have fun!"

I cannot remember any real conversations with my mother about her life in America or my life in Korea. It was just a kind of dramatic reunion scene between me and my mother. The purpose of my mother's return visit to Korea was to start the paperwork for me to immigrate to the United States. My mother stayed for a short time in Korea, perhaps a week or ten days. When she came to my uncle and auntie's house, she stayed in a small side room like a visitor while I still slept in the main room with my uncle, auntie, and cousins. I saw my mother four or five times during her visit, and when she returned to America, she didn't let me know she was going and didn't even say goodbye.

I remained in Korea for the next two years while expecting to go to America. During that time, my uncle came down with a life-threatening stomach illness. I don't know what caused it. He was hospitalized for surgery, and the hospital demanded payment for the full hospital bill before they would release him. In a way, my uncle was held hostage at the hospital. My aunt sold everything they possessed—the liquor store, their house, and all their savings—to bring my uncle back home. After that, it took some time for my uncle to get well, and in the winter of 1963, we had to move to a shack town.

Not too far from Bogwang-dong was one the biggest intersections in Seoul, surrounding a statue of General John Coulter. We lived northeast of there on the hillsides that had numerous small houses built illegally. These were very difficult times, but we made it through the first winter. In 1964, after my uncle got well, he bought a handcart and asked me to work with him. Starting at sunrise every day, we went all over Seoul, collecting scrap metal. At sundown, we took all the metal we had collected throughout the city to a shop where they purchased it. This went on throughout the summer of 1964. It was very, very hard work, pushing the cart all over Seoul, trying to scrape up a living from bits and pieces of metal. Due to my uncle's ill health, he had to stop doing it.

By then, the oldest cousins were living and working outside our home. I believe all three older boys joined the Korean Army to fight in Vietnam. At the time, Korea was going through very difficult economic times, and people were dying of starvation or eating spoiled food to survive. Those who joined the Korean Army to go to Vietnam were promised $400 to $600 of American money per month, which was an enormous sum for Koreans back then.

Meanwhile, my uncle was going out in search of work every day while Myung-hak and I would stay home. We were lucky if we had one small meal a day. I remember one time we didn't eat for over two or three days, and one of the neighbors gave a little bit of rice to my auntie. She cooked the rice, gave it to me and Myung-hak, and only ate a little leftover burned rice for herself. As children, we did not complain. We were still having adventures playing with other kids, but it was a very difficult time for my auntie and uncle.

Sadly, just before the start of winter in 1964, the Korean government decided to tear down the shack town. On the first day they came, all the residents of the shack town protested, and the police officers backed down. But they came back next morning with far greater force and overwhelmed the protesters. Each family and their belongings were placed in a truck and relocated to a housing compound located north of Seoul and near the demilitarized zone (DMZ) that divided South and North Korea. The house was a one-story building. All the buildings were in rows made of cement blocks. Each family was placed into a single small room about thirty by thirty feet without running water or electricity, like most homes in Korea. My auntie and uncle's meager savings had to be spent on heating stones to place under the floor in preparation for winter.

The housing compound was located in a flat area, but there were hills nearby. Within days, my cousin Myung-hak and I started to explore the new area we lived in. At the bottom of the hills, we found streams coming down from the mountains. In the streams, hidden under the rocks, we could find freshwater claw fish. While we went on exploring at the bottom of the hill, we would sometimes see patrols of South Korean army soldiers in the hills. I didn't know exactly how close our house was to the DMZ, but we must have been very near to see the patrolling soldiers. Seoul was also nearby enough to walk to within a day.

Then came the news. A plane ticket had arrived for me. It was time to go to the United States to join my mother. My auntie pleaded with me to ask my mother to send money, so the family could buy food. I promised her I would and told her I would go to work in the US and send them my earnings. In November, my auntie took me to see the banker's wife's auntie. We went shopping, and they bought me a new set of clothes and shoes.

By going to America, I felt that I was my family's greatest hope to give them immediate relief from their hunger and suffering. To me as a young boy, going to America was like a fairytale about a boy who dreamed of going to London, a city so rich that streets were paved with gold, and every tree was adorned with every kind of jewel. Along with the plan to ask my mother for money to support our family in Korea, I would ask her to allow me to return to Korea to rejoin my auntie, uncle, and cousins after I made enough money to be rich. This personal plan seemed so easy that no way could I fail in a country as rich as America.

On the day of my departure, the weather was bitterly cold. My auntie wore her *hanbok,* the one traditional Korean dress she owned. Even though the fabric was thin, she wanted to look her best and so did my uncle. We took the bus together to Kimpo Airport—me, Myung-hak, auntie, and uncle. At the time, the Kimpo Airport was very small. I remember I kept promising to send money to Korea to help my auntie.

When I got on the plane, tears filled my eyes, and I started sobbing. I tried to look out the window to see my auntie, uncle, and Myung-hak, but I couldn't see them. Later I learned that as my plane took off, my auntie fainted at the airport. On the airplane, I was crying quite a bit. Some tourists came by and offered me candy, but I refused to be comforted. Leaving the only family I knew was a shock. It was traumatic. However, hearing about America's riches, I had great dreams that once I got there, I would make money, and my mother would send money to help my auntie and uncle and Myung-hak to eat and survive.

The plane first flew to Japan since there was no direct flight from Korea to the United States. From the plane window, I saw Fuji Mountain with its beautiful snowcap. The layover in Tokyo was about eight hours. A Chinese-Korean man, who worked for the airline and knew I was going to America, greeted me at the airport. "What's your name?"

"My name is Lee, Chol Soo."

He introduced himself and said he was going to keep an eye on me until the plane left for America. "Are you hungry?"

"Yes."

He took me to a Chinese restaurant at the airport. Despite my near-starvation diet in Korea, I only ate small portions of the beef and vegetables over rice that the airline guy ordered. After dinner, he told me to wait in some area of the airport. After about six hours, he finally came back and said, "Your plane is taking off soon, so let's get you on that plane." Before I got on the plane, I saw a double-wing shape on the tail of the plane, perhaps the logo for American Airlines. On the plane, I was seated toward the back. The stewardess tried to talk to me, but I did not speak any English or any Japanese, so she could not understand what I wanted. She brought me a soda, though I kept asking for ice water.

With all my mixed feelings about going to America, it took me quite a while to fall asleep. What would it be like to live with my mother and my American sister? I didn't know them. The only thing I knew about America was the American dream of success. I thought the great, rich country of America was a place where all dreams were possible. I was a twelve-year-old kid not knowing one word of English, and I imagined everyone in America lived in houses like the nicest houses in Korea. I thought everyone would speak Korean as well as English. As I began drifting to sleep on the plane and dreaming of riches in America, I started thinking about my father for some reason.

I never met my father. However, there was one time in 1960 or maybe 1961 when my auntie called me aside and said my father wanted to meet me. She said I should go to a certain Chinese restaurant at noon, and he would recognize me. There was a large field, about twice the size of a football field between the house in Bogwang-dong and the restaurant, so I walked across that wide and empty field. I arrived before noon and stood outside the restaurant, waiting to see my father for the first time. At age nine or ten, my emotions of expectation were hard to describe. I think I was looking very much forward to meeting him. Time passed. Noontime passed and nothing happened.

At one point, I saw a man sitting down by himself. I can't recall whether he was drinking some tea or having a meal, but he was the only person sitting at his table. I was not close enough to see him clearly. He might have been a middle-aged man of normal build. I thought perhaps he was my father, but whatever he was doing—whether eating or drinking tea—he left afterward. I cannot recall whether he glanced over my way or not. I stood almost directly in his line of sight. After waiting for about three hours, I said to myself, "My father did not come to meet me." I returned home feeling disappointed and sad. My auntie saw me enter. She looked as if she understood my feelings about not meeting my biological father, and she comforted me.

These thoughts went through my mind just as I fell asleep on the plane. I don't know how long I slept, but a stewardess shook me awake, saying some words I did not understand. She pointed, and when I looked out the window toward the ground, I saw a big city with a lot of tall buildings. It looked kind of small from up in the air.

America

I arrived in San Francisco on November 14, 1964, at the age of twelve. When I came out of the airplane and walked through the airport, I saw people behind a glass panel, waiting to greet the new arrivals. Then I saw my mother, my little sister Mary, and two other people, all waving at me. My mother's face looked happy. I recognized a lady we called "Auntie Kim," who was a close friend of my mother in Korea. There was also a man I didn't know. After I passed through the walkway, a US Customs official sent me to a room to be X-rayed, which I guessed they were checking for tuberculosis. Shortly after that, I joined my mother and heard her say, "Welcome. I am very glad to see you. You're looking so well."

The unknown man was a friend of Auntie Kim, who was not really my auntie, but just my mother's friend. Her gentleman friend had a car and did the driving to and from the airport. It was about an hour's drive to my mother's apartment where he dropped us off and then left. It was a basement apartment, located on Noe Street at Duboce, right across from a great big hospital. When we entered my mother's apartment, I saw a little baby in a crib, and I asked my mother, "Who is that?"

"Oh, she's your sister Margie."

The baby looked Korean. She was very quiet. Later, I learned that her father was Chinese.

Soon after we arrived, five or six of my mother's friends came to visit. Each brought some kind of small present for me, and they all smiled and shook my hand even though I was a kid and said, "Welcome to America."

I noticed a bunch of bananas on the table and some red apples, and I asked my mother, "Can I eat one of those bananas?" In Korea, tropical fruit was very, very rare. So the first thing that I ate in America was a banana. Later that night, my mother, Auntie Kim, my sister, and I had dinner. My mother prepared T-bone steak, rice, and canned corn, and poured some ketchup over the T-bone steak. It was the first time in my life I'd seen so much beef at one time, much less eaten that much in one sitting. I was very hungry, and I ate the whole steak, the rice, and the corn. It's possible I had not eaten that much beef in all the years I lived in Korea. Most of the time we ate pork mixed with vegetables or pork *kimchi chigae*. Beef was very rare and expensive in Korea, so my first American meal was a happy occasion.

My mother showed me the apartment—it had a kitchen with a gas-burning stove and a bathroom that had a bathtub with hot- and cold-running water, which was something almost impossible to find in Korea. I thought, "How rich my mother must be to have such a great luxury of hot and cold water, a private bath, and a big kitchen to cook in." After I took my first bath on my first day in America, my mother pulled out the couch bed in the living room for me to sleep. My mother, sister, and Auntie Kim slept in another room. I fell asleep quickly, for I must have been pretty tired from the flight from Korea to the United States. But it was a very happy day. The confusion that I had in my mind about seeing my mother seemed to have dissolved, but my auntie was still in my mind, along with uncle and Myung-hak.

On my second day in America, my mother served an American-style breakfast of bacon, eggs, and rice. She said her boyfriend, a Chinese man, was coming over, and I should call him "father," as he would be my step-father. Because I had gone through twelve years of life addressing my uncle as father, I found it very difficult to address a stranger as father. But when he arrived, he told me his name was Frank, and I called him "Father" (*abeoji*) in Korean. He was a big man, about 6′ and 190 pounds. He seemed healthy and drove a very nice car.

There were no cars in Korea, only jeeps left over from the Korean War, so I was amazed to see so many cars. I also noticed for the first time that there were other minorities in America. I thought America would have only white people and Koreans. I didn't know there would be a great mix of different nationalities and races.

Later that night on my second day, I noticed that the baby and the baby's crib were gone. I did not ask my mother anything about it. Seven years would pass before I saw my sister Margie again. Meanwhile, my first few days in America were about exploration, going outside, and looking around. But usually, I just stayed inside watching TV, especially cartoons. Since I'd never seen a cartoon before, I thought, "How could those people act like that?" Everything in America was strange and far from what I thought America was going to be like.

Here I was in a strange country, not knowing any English, but I was determined to help my uncle and auntie in Korea. When I asked my mother about helping my auntie in Korea, she got quite upset. She said, "I have no money to send to them."

"Mother, they are very hungry. They need money."

"No, I don't have money. I have no money! I cannot send them money!" She was very angry. It was customary that I should obey her, so I stopped asking her about sending money to Korea. Instead, I tried to keep in mind that I must find work to make money to send to Korea.

We lived on Noe Street for about five months. One of my mother's friends lived nearby and had a son named Carl, who was full-blooded Korean. His mother had remarried a Japanese man, so his younger brother was half Japanese and half Korean. I usually played with him, his brother, and a couple of other neighborhood kids on the same block.

Because I spoke no English, one of the first priorities was to send me to school. About ten days after my arrival, my mother taught me how to say, "My name is Chol Soo Lee. I am twelve years old." From there, I was taken to elementary school, the same school as my sister Mary, except I also took a bus to another school, maybe for special education. All the children I met were about my age or a year younger. There were some white Americans and African Americans. I cannot recall meeting any Latinos.

At the first school, there were no problems. The day started with the Pledge of Allegiance to the flag. I just tried to say whatever the others seemed to be saying. We sat in classrooms and watched a school movie with nature scenes now and then. Then my mother moved to Japantown on Laguna and Bush Street. It was a great big Victorian house, and we lived on the second floor. Another tenant on the second floor had a separate entrance. The Japanese lady who owned the house lived down on the ground floor. After the move, I went to Lafayette Elementary School and was still trying to learn basic English.

After a short time, maybe four or five months, I graduated and attended Benjamin Franklin Middle School, located on Geary Street, not too far from our house. At the time, the United States was going through serious civil rights litigation, and the school was 99 percent African American. I remember just seeing one other Asian kid there, and I never got a chance to meet him. Whenever somebody made a funny face—like making their eyes slanted or calling me some racial name such as "chink" or "ching-ching-chong"—I got into a minor scuffle. After a few months of getting into these scuffles with other children, I was called into the school principal's office and notified that I would be transferred to another school. I remember the school principal saying, "We're going to send you to school with your own kind."

That school turned out to be Francisco Middle School, located near Fisherman's Wharf not too far from Chinatown. There were many Chinese students as well as white Americans and African Americans, and a few other foreign students. However, since I still had great difficulty speaking English, I was not able to communicate with other kids very well, but I still got into small scuffles with other kids routinely. The school principal was a 6' tall former FBI agent. Pretty soon, the principal sent me home whenever I got into a minor scuffle. I would then get a lashing from my mother.

This went on for several months until one day, a white student passing me in the hall shoulder-bumped me as kids do when they want to pick a fight. I started swinging at him, and he started swinging back. The fight lasted less than a minute when a schoolteacher came by saying, "Hey, break up the fight, break up the fight."

After breaking up the fight, the schoolteacher told the white kid to go to his class but told me to go to the principal's office. I obeyed his orders instead of just going on to my next class, which I believe I could have done without anybody taking notice. I believed in taking orders from authority figures, so I went to the school principal's office and explained to him as best as I could that I had a scuffle with another kid, but it was not my fault this time. Any other time, I never argued or talked back. But the principal still insisted on sending me home. I was afraid of getting another lashing from my mother, so I went to the classroom to get the kid I had the scuffle with and brought him down to the principal's office. I said, "Tell the truth. Tell the truth about the fight. Tell the truth."

The kid pointed at me and said, "He started the fight."

I started shouting to defend myself, "No, no, no! I did not! I did not!"

At this point, the school principal sent the white kid back to his classroom. He informed me that he was calling my mother to send me home. I started arguing more vigorously with the school principal, saying, "I did not start the fight!" Then he tried to grab me. A couple of things got knocked loose. Maybe I was having a mild temper tantrum over the unfairness of being sent home when I did not even try to start the fight. The principal called the police. When the police came, I was charged with assault on a school principal. I must have been 4' tall, weighing maybe 70 pounds. Compared to this ex-FBI agent, who was over 6' and 200 pounds, it was pitiful to say that I assaulted him. This seemed totally unfair. The injustice was outrageous. Why was I getting punished for something I did not start?

The police took me to Juvenile Hall. Throughout my time in the United States, I had not met one Korean-speaking counselor or any type of guidance counselor to help me adjust my behavior or understand the challenges I faced by not speaking English. I spent a couple of days at Juvenile Hall where there was no Korean interpreter or anyone who could communicate with me. After a couple of days, my mother came to court, and I was sent home. After the incident of going to Juvenile Hall, I said to myself, "You're a bad person now." This made sense according to my cultural upbringing in Korea in which problems with law enforcement made you a bad person.

After that, I had a schoolteacher come by the apartment twice a week instead of going to public school. Carl's family moved down the block from where we lived on Laguna Street, and soon I was playing with him again. Though I was a bit older than Carl, his English was much better than mine.

After a while, my mother started working for a cannery, leaving early in the morning while I was left alone at home. I still thought about my auntie and uncle, and asked my mother about money to send them, but she still got highly upset and said she had no money, which she didn't.

Across the street on Bush Street, there was a tropical fish store. I went there one day and asked to see the owner, a Japanese guy named Ernest. Ernest was in his midtwenties, but he was the oldest son managing the store. All the people working for him were middle-aged Japanese people. I asked him for a job, and he hired me to clean the fish tank filters and do small chores. Unfortunately, he paid me only 35¢ an hour, and I worked only two or three hours a day a few times a week. At the time, the minimum wage was $1.25. Since such small money was not enough to send to Korea, I just spent it on candy.

After a while of homeschooling, I was sent to Marina Junior High School when I was thirteen or fourteen. At home, I felt most comfortable staying in my room rather than watching TV with the others, as I felt very unwelcome at home. I had to do all the chores around the house while my white sister, Mary, did no chores. I never saw my mother shout at her or even speak loudly toward her. I felt she was taking her anger out on me, lashing out in bitter disappointment over not finding the American Dream. I'm sure she was trying hard, but she herself was illiterate and unable to get anything started such as a business to make our lives more comfortable. But to this day, I wonder why my mother decided for me to emigrate to America to join her and take me away from my loving uncle and auntie.

Around this time I started to run away from home, basically trying to escape the lashings and the loneliness, and looking for some way to get back to Korea. But I always got caught by the police while I was wandering around at night. I got into this pattern of running away, which only led to more Juvenile Hall arrests for small thefts as I tried to survive on the streets. I was even sent to the Napa State Hospital for a ninety-day evaluation because youth authorities believed I was insane. The team of doctors at Napa State Hospital found me to be a normal smart kid who had trouble speaking English and a difficult home life. I was released after they diagnosed me as sane. But I was sent to a foster home in Hayward instead of to my mother. After about three months, I ran away from the foster home and stole a bike and rode all the way to Livermore before I was caught and returned to San Francisco Juvenile Hall. My probation officer met me there, where he interviewed me and recommended that in my best interest I should be returned to my mother.

But once again I ran away from home and was sentenced to a Juvenile Hall camp that lasted three to four months before I ran away. After that, when I was fourteen and a half, I was sent to CYA (California Youth Authority) for tougher young criminals. I also spent time at a more comfortable place called "Orange Clothes" for kids thirteen to fifteen years old. In total, I did about eighteen months in the juvenile justice system, then came back home and started attending Galileo High School. Once again, I began running away and was returned to CYA for another six months, then returned home, and went back to Galileo. When I was about sixteen, I got arrested for breaking a store window and taking a couple of watches. I was once again sent to CYA for nineteen months to a place called Preston for more hardened CYA kids.

Nowhere in the CYA system did I see any Asian American employees. It was almost all white counselors. Once again, I felt a lack of guidance or direction in my life. When I took English classes at Preston, I progressed well. Then I was sent to learn sheet metal and arc welding as a trade. In 1971, I was released from the CYA and returned home at the age of eighteen. I found the youth jail a safer place than living at home.

Once home, my mother talked to me about joining the army. She knew an army colonel who could possibly get me into the US Army. But at the time, I was hanging around with this group called the J-Town Collective. It was a radical group associated with JCYC (the Japanese Community Youth Council). Jeff Mori, the executive director of JCYC, was only a little older than me, and I got along well with him. Unknown to me at the time, there was also a Korean Community Service Center started by Tom Kim. When I started hanging out with the J-Town Collective, I resisted joining the army since they were against war.

It was at this time that I decided to move out and live on my own. I started living at the International Hotel on Kearny Street near San Francisco Chinatown and went searching for my sister Margie in Chinatown. I knew where Frank Lee, my mother's ex-boyfriend, had his sweatshop in Chinatown, so I went to him to find my sister. Trying to survive on my own, I got on public assistance. Back in 1971, it was easier to receive public assistance. If you walked into a Social Security office, you didn't even need to show identification to be issued a Social Security card. It was a very open and trusting time, but at the same time, the antiwar movement was building against the war in Vietnam, and the civil rights movement had inspired militant movements that spread across the country. However, I was not interested in those movements. I was interested in just trying to survive.

One day I tried to rip off some money from a guy who turned out to be an undercover cop. Before I could take his money, he pulled out his gun and arrested me. I was charged with grand theft and did six months in the San Francisco County Jail. Ranko Yamada's sister, Reiko, used to come by to visit me in jail. When I was released, she picked me up and took me to her place where she lived with a friend and treated me to a nice big steak as a homecoming celebration.

Afterward, I returned to Chinatown where time to time I saw my sister Margie and her father, Frank. By that time, Margie was seven years old and lived with her father upstairs above the garment shop that he owned in Chinatown. Frank continued to be a kind man, maintaining a good relationship with me like a stepfather and encouraging me and Margie to see more of each other. He would ask me to pick her up after school in Chinatown and gave me spending money to take Margie out shopping. One of the first times shopping, I took Margie to Macy's in downtown San Francisco. I tried to buy her girls' clothing, but she refused any girl clothing and cried until I gave up and left her to choose the clothing that she liked, which was a pair of boys' jeans and a jean jacket. Margie was a tomboy through and through. With our time spent together, Margie started feeling closer toward me as her brother.

In 1972, Frank Lee was hospitalized with throat cancer. I went to see him at Chinese Hospital in Chinatown. I saw he had a lump underneath his throat, but I was not aware of the seriousness of his condition at the time. At twenty years old, what does one know about medical conditions? When I saw Margie by chance, I said, "Oh Margie, have you gone to see your Dad yet?"

"No, I don't know where he is at," she said.

"Oh, you don't know he's in the hospital?"

"No."

"Come on, Margie, let's go," I said. "I'll take you to go see him."

For reasons unknown to me, Margie was not informed of her father's condition and didn't know he was in the hospital. We arrived at the hospital just before sunset. But when I tried to take her upstairs to see her father, a nurse stopped us saying, "She's too young to come into the hospital."

I told Margie to wait while I went to get her father. When I found Frank in his hospital room, I thought the lump on his throat looked bigger. "Frank, Margie wants to see you and is waiting downstairs."

Frank's face lit up. "Where? Where?" Joy spread across his face as we went downstairs together. Margie waited just outside the door. She gave a big smile upon seeing her father. Frank gave her a warm hug and held her hand. As he spoke to her in Chinese, I was not able to understand his words, but his voice sounded alive and joyful. He seemed full of happiness throughout the visit, which lasted about twenty minutes. The sun had set and night was coming on. It was starting to get cold outside.

"You better take Margie home," Frank said. He gave Margie one last very loving hug. As I walked him back to his hospital room, Frank said nothing and looked very sad. I returned to Margie who took my hand. Margie was excited to see her father, so I told her, "Listen, we'll see him again very soon." As we walked back to Grant Avenue, it was already dark. I said goodbye and let Margie go home to her grandmother's place because I didn't know where that was.

A few days later, I went back to see Frank and found his room empty. I asked the nurses, "What happened?" They told me that he had passed away. I was very sad to hear that, but I was glad that at least Margie was able to see him one last time. I had no understanding of how fast cancer could take one's life. I'm sure Margie went to Frank's burial. Since I did not know Margie's grandmother or any of Frank's relatives in Chinatown, I was not invited.

By that time in mid-1972, I was working as a short-order cook on the corner of Kearny and Columbus Street (just one block from the site of Yip Yee Tak's murder a year later) at a breakfast and hamburger restaurant that used to be part of Zim's. The manager of Zim's bought the restaurant and changed its name to his name, Jim's. He hired me for the night shift since the restaurant was open twenty-four hours. While I was still working at Jim's, Margie would come by the restaurant from time to time after her father passed away. She wore a happy face when seeing her older brother even though it might be 8 or 9 p.m. I was always very happy to see her. She would sit on the first seat at the countertop near the front where she could see me work. When there were no orders to fill, I would talk to her for a while. Margie would tell me how she was doing. Her visits were usually short, maybe half an hour, or if the restaurant was not busy, a little bit longer.

I would always tell her, "Don't stay out so late." I was concerned about her being out late at night by herself, although sometimes she came by with a friend her age. She would leave reluctantly. As her brother, I felt her loneliness when she had to leave, as I felt the same loneliness seeing her go. We formed a bond, which we did not share with our mother and white sister, Mary. The job at Jim's restaurant lasted for about five months. I quit right in the middle of a work shift after getting into a fight with a drunken customer.

Weight Bench Hit

I heard a soft bang on the wall, bringing me out of my daydream about my life in Korea and in America. My next-door neighbor called my name very softly, "Lee! Lee!"

I went to the window to see what he wanted. There was no need for him to say anything because with the view under my window, I saw three African Americans walking away with another African American lying on the bench press with a sixty-five-pound weight lying across his neck. His arms were down. I may have seen his body shaking and going into death convulsions, but my mind was unable to accept the reality of the brutal killing that occurred almost right in front of my cell window, so I thought he might be resting on the bench, which would have been unusual. I glanced around the rest of the yard where a small number of guys were playing basketball, and some Latinos were playing handball. The image of the yard looked normal, so I just lay back on my bed and went back to reading. I may have fallen asleep before the yard recall.

I was brought back to reality when I heard lot of activity by the guards. By then, the yard was empty of prisoners, but a few guards were around the weight-lifting area where I had seen the African American lying with the weight on top of him, and the guards were taking pictures.

Then I heard some music on the tier, so I looked out through the small window on the cell door. I was a bit shocked to see about five or six African Americans totally naked, not even wearing boxers, handcuffed behind their backs, and being marched down the stairs and out of the unit.

We were on lockdown for a few days and then allowed back in the yard. I learned from one of the Latino convicts that the African American I'd seen dying on the weight bench was doing bench presses when a few other African Americans held him down with the weight he was using. Another hit him on the head with a dumbbell, knocking him unconscious. Then they rolled the weight down on his neck and left him lying there choking to death.

After the guards reopened the yard, I asked one of the Latinos I was getting along well with what had happened. The full information I received from him was very important to me. It was a sign or maybe a warning to keep my mouth shut about whatever I'd seen of the killing. I think the convicts in the yard were starting to accept me more even though I was new and standing on my own and still unschooled in the convicts' code of conduct. I carried myself well enough for someone to tell me about the killing on the weight bench. After being told about it, I asked no more questions but made some light conversation and then went about my usual routine in the yard. However, I did notice the dumbbell was no longer in the weight-lifting area.

Ill-Fitting Suit

About a week or so later, my cell door clicked and opened. When I stepped out, I was informed by the guard, "Pack your things. You're going out to court."

Since I didn't have many things, I hurried and got my stuff. After the strip search, I was handcuffed to my back and escorted by two prison guards. The guards were acting friendly. As if on cue, one guard said to the other guard, "Man, that hit on the weight bench was a good hit."

The other guard responded, "It sure was." Then he turned to me and said, "Didn't the hit happen right in front of your cell?"

I made no response but kept walking toward R&R as if I didn't hear their comments about the hit. I knew the guards were trying to get a reaction from me. Nothing more was said before we reached R&R, where I was ordered to wait in a caged area of the room. Two deputies prepared to transfer me to San Francisco. Once again, I underwent a strip search and was placed in a waist chain and leg chains before being escorted out.

I was transported back to San Francisco County Jail. I enjoyed very much seeing the view of San Francisco during the ride across the Bay Bridge. At the S.F. jail, I was allowed to make two phone calls. I called Wayne and Ranko to let them know where I was. D.A. Lassart had gotten a grand jury indictment against me for illegal possession of a firearm by an ex-felon. As if being sentenced to life imprisonment on framed-up charges was not enough, this additional charge would add a one-to-ten years' sentence to the life sentence I was already serving.

One day, I was called out for a visit and the visitor was Wayne.

Wayne asked, "How are you doing?"

"I am doing OK. Is there anything else you can do to help me out with the Chinatown case?"

"No, there's not much more I can do, but I will keep trying," he said.

This was not a surprise to me, but I found him to be an honest guy who would really have helped if he could. When the fifteen minutes of visiting time was up, Wayne said, "I'll keep trying. Keep yourself well."

"Thank you very much."

While at the county jail, I met Eddie Yuen, who was charged with a different Chinatown gang murder case. We got along well without talking about anything relating to gangs in Chinatown. I also met this white guy who told me about an African American lawyer who took his case for free and was willing to help out any prisoners in county jail. I asked him if this lawyer would take my case, an ex-felon with a gun charge. Within a few days, the lawyer visited and said he would take my case for free. I was elated. I passed this information on to Eddie Yuen, and the lawyer also took Eddie Yuen's murder case for free.

Since I'd gotten a change of venue on the Chinatown murder case, the superior court judge decided I couldn't get a fair trial in San Francisco and transferred the case back to Sacramento. The trial processing went fast, and the trial was somewhat comical. Jury trials do not allow the defendant to wear jail clothes since that may bias the jury, but the only way I could get personal clothing was through my attorney. The lawyer brought me a suit of clothes that was way too big. Two of me could fit in that suit, so I just wore the shirt and pants. D.A. Lassart presented his case, and then my lawyer put me on the stand as his only witness. He asked me about the gun charge, thus having me admit to carrying the gun. With the way he questioned me and the way I was dressed, the jurors were kind of laughing and smiling.

Before the closing arguments, the D.A. reexamined me and asked, "Were you not convicted of first-degree murder?"

I had to answer, "Yes, I was convicted." I tried to explain that I was innocent, but neither the prosecutor nor the judge would allow me to explain my innocence. The judge warned the prosecutor that his question was biased and instructed the jury to disregard the question. I saw no way that the jury could disregard the question about the murder conviction after hearing my testimony on the stand. The D.A. then summarized his case.

Next I watched my attorney try to summarize my case as circumstantial. In his closing remarks, he said something like, "If a person came to your front door, left his shoeprint in the snow and left, when you opened the door, how would you know whose prints were in the snow?" Hearing this, I realized this guy was the worst attorney a person could ever have. Basically, he was just out of law school, had no experience, and was using people who needed attorneys for practice. And I thought to myself, "Oh my God, I have set this lawyer up to fight Eddie Yuen's murder case." I knew I'd doomed any chance of a fair trial for Eddie Yuen.

The jury and the judge seemed to find the trial to be almost a joke. In less than two days, the jury returned with a guilty verdict. They seemed to be in a good mood, and as they left the courtroom, some even waved "bye" to me. After I was sentenced to eighteen months to ten years, I was transported back to Tracy West Hall.

Adapting to Prison Culture

After losing my cases at both court trials, I reflected on life ahead of me. Freedom seemed too far a dream even to think about. My only hope for justice rested in the possibility that my mistaken identity would be discovered. Meanwhile, I continued to adapt to life in prison. For justice ever to prevail, for hope ever to become reality, I knew I must survive the trial of violent prison life. As the saying goes, anger can destroy a man, but anger can also keep him alive. My anger at injustice continued to grow within me, and a theme of "Never give up, never surrender!" continued to keep my hope and fire for justice alive.

Returning to West Hall, this time I was placed on the third tier overlooking the basketball court. My new neighbor to the left was another NF member, Sam. That was not his true name, as all NF members picked a nickname for security reasons. If your enemy found out your real name, they would note it beside your nickname on their hit list, which they checked against the names of newly arrived prisoners. Sam had been stabbed repeatedly at a camp and was partially disabled from his wounds. We broke out the corner window so we could just BS.

In the yard, nothing was said about the guy who was killed on the weight-lifting bench. By now the convicts were getting to know me, and I was treated in a friendly way in the yard. I knew more Latinos than African Americans, but I was still on friendly terms with Jo-Mo. I think racist mistreatment was much worse for African Americans, as when I saw five handcuffed African Americans being escorted totally naked out of West Hall. Racism in California prisons was a tradition passed on from older guards to the next generation of new guards. I knew I was a victim of the administration's racism when I arrived at Tracy. Here I was, knowing nothing about prison, and they threw me into the Hole and then into the adjustment section with all the prison gang members like a piece of raw meat thrown to hungry lions. It would have struck fear in the heart of any prisoner as inexperienced as I was.

Since I was Asian, I was not easily accepted by Latinos or African Americans. It was just my good fortune that I met Gilbert, the one experienced Asian convict in West Hall, who had friends among the Latinos and was able to introduce me to B.B., a hard-core NF member. This connection bought me some time to gain badly needed experience in how to conduct myself as a convict and gave me a chance to get along with those who wished to get along with me. I didn't go after friendships with all the convict gang members in the yard, but accepted the friendliness shown me while trying to get along with everyone.

On a warm day in the yard in 1974, I was playing basketball with a few other convicts when the yard was recalled sooner than usual. In small groups, we reentered West Hall, and each prisoner was strip-searched. The guards examined our arms closely as if looking for needle marks, and looked over the rest of our bodies. I thought someone must have used drugs in the yard, with the way we were searched so carefully. After putting my boxers back on, I carried the rest of my clothes back to my cell.

By then the yard was empty except for a few guards taking pictures of a lone tennis shoe, which lay on the handball court very near where I had just been playing basketball. As I watched the guards talking among themselves and taking numerous pictures, I thought to myself, "These guards must have killed one of the convicts, and as a cover-up they are taking pictures to make it look like the convict was trying to escape."

Later on that evening, I called my next-door neighbor Sam to the window. Since I was getting along well enough with him, I thought it was safe to ask him what had happened in the yard earlier that day. I was totally unprepared for Sam's answer. In a very low voice he said, "Didn't you see the guy got hit right behind you when you were playing basketball?"

I didn't ask for any more details about the hit even though I wanted to ask many more questions. In this kind of situation, the fewer questions you ask, the better for your safety, especially when you're not involved in the prison gangs. So the conversation on that topic came to a stop. I felt shocked that a convict was stabbed to death within a few feet of me. I was totally unaware of the killing. If I had been trusted by the gangs, I would have been warned beforehand that something was coming down so I could stay alert. If I had been forewarned, I would have stood somewhere with my back to the wall and kept close watch on the movement in the yard. But since I was still new, I received no warning. Maybe luck was with me on that day since I was totally involved with the basketball game, and if by chance I had bumped into the guys making the hit, I could have been hit also. No matter which way I turned, danger was nearby for an inexperienced prisoner.

After that, every day brought the same routine for a while. But one hot day in late 1974, the yard seemed calm, yet filled with tension. There was very little action or movement, just some walking around. Although it was hot outside, some African Americans came out with their jackets on. I felt a bit uneasy. Sensing the tension, I stood off by myself in the middle of the weight-lifting area with my back against the fence. I watched some convicts playing basketball. Within about forty minutes, I noticed some commotion by the basketball pole.

One African American grasped hold of the right side of another African American's jacket. The second man tried to loosen the hold on his jacket and started pulling himself toward the middle of the yard. He was about 6' tall and 180 pounds. At the same time, a third younger man in a T-shirt, about 5'7", got hold of the left side of the targeted man and started stabbing him in the back while the first assailant stabbed him in the front. I heard a loud exhaling of breath with each impact, followed by an intake of breath, especially when the victim got stabbed in front. With all the other convicts standing against the wall and watching, all you could hear was the loud exhale of "Huh!" and then a big intake of air. As the stabbing continued, the victim tried to drag himself away without fighting back, as if he were in shock. Seeing this taking place just twenty-five feet in front of me, I was somewhat in a state of shock myself, feeling numb to see such brutality. This was the first time I witnessed a prison stabbing.

Within a minute, the alarm bell sounded, sending many guards toward the West Hall yard. Some brought a "Big Bertha," which could shoot a large canister of tear gas, while other guards had taken out their small tear gas guns. About fifteen or more guards stood outside the fence of West and East Hall yard shouting, "Stop it!"

Even with all those guards standing and watching through the fence and gate, none of the guards fired tear gas into the yard or even opened the gate to enter the yard. After a few minutes of stabbing right in the middle of the yard, both attackers turned and walked away toward the basketball court. As if to give cover to the aggressors, about a dozen convicts started playing basketball. As the aggressors mixed into the basketball game, they dropped their prison-made knives. At that point, all the guards rushed into the yard and ordered all convicts, "Stand where you are!"

I continued to watch the stabbing victim. He walked slowly toward the yard gate where he collapsed. The guards approached the basketball court and ordered the rest of the convicts against the wall. Some guards handcuffed both aggressors, while other guards stood over the prison-made knives with about six guards staying outside the fence to cover the guards in the yard.

It was truly shocking to witness such brutality inflicted by humans on another human being. I had never in my life seen such brutal force. I was also shocked to see so many guards watch the stabbing from outside the yard while none tried to stop it. It was truly an awakening for me to realize that if I were ever a victim of a stabbing, I could never rely on prison guards to help me.

The prison guards had their own rules of personal conduct. One of the first rules was that no convict is worth getting hurt over, so never interfere with a stabbing in progress; that job was up to the guard in the gun tower. After we returned to our cells, I was still in disbelief at what I had just witnessed. I learned that I was truly alone in this violent world of prison life, and I started preparing myself for the need to defend myself if I should ever be someone's intended victim.

Later that evening, with the image of the stabbing still on my mind, I gave a soft knock on the wall of my next-door neighbor Sam. He came to the corner window and responded in a soft voice, "What's up, Lee?"

When talking through the window to next-door neighbors, all convicts talked in a very low voice to make sure no other convicts overheard. There was always the chance someone was listening, trying to pick up information, since gang members didn't trust anyone else, even members of their gang's allies.

I said, "Man, that was some hit."

"Yeah." He spoke in a voice that sounded like he had witnessed many other violent stabbings.

Still in a state of disbelief, I asked a very stupid question, "Were they really trying to kill him?"

"Didn't you see what happened? What you think they were trying to do?" His answer sounded like he was saying, "What kind of dumb question is that?"

"But hey, I heard he survived, and he was hit twenty-four times." Since I thought I could talk to Sam, I asked him, "What happened to you at the camp?"

"Well I'd just gotten to the camp. During the night while I was sleeping, two La Eme members wearing masks made a move to stab me. Since California prison camp is out in the woods, a helicopter came and flew me out to the hospital. One of the wounds left me paralyzed in my left arm, but I was hit eight times so I am lucky to be alive."

Even though I had many more questions about the prisons, as well as about how Sam had gotten involved with NF and about the gangs themselves, I had enough sense to know those kinds of questions could get me killed. After a few more light words, we closed the window back up with cardboard. The NF has very strict rules, so any conversation I had with Sam or any other NF members in the yard might have been written up in a report to the NF leaders in West Hall.

Within less than one year in prison, I had encountered four violent hits. I saw one convict with his head bashed in, lying on a gurney in Vacaville. In Tracy, I witnessed a man dying on the weight bench. Playing basketball, I just missed bumping into a killing that happened just a few feet behind me. And then I saw a convict get stabbed twenty-four times right out in the open. I was getting my experience of prison life, adapting and surviving.

In my routine daily life in West Hall, I tried to pass the time in my cell by reading, and against all odds, I kept hope for justice alive within me. I continued to correspond with Ranko and Reiko about once a month. I didn't say much about the case, since Ranko had not visited since her first letter to me in 1973. My letters to both Ranko and Reiko were personal, more to Ranko than to Reiko. Both were as dear to me as life. In their friendship, I found life and did not feel abandoned and totally alone in prison.

As for my mother and my white half sister, they viewed me as guilty of the murder charge. Every few months, I would write a letter to my mother letting her know I was okay and asking her for some funds. I received twenty dollars from her now and then. Sometimes Ranko also sent twenty dollars. I greatly appreciated these funds, which I used for my daily needs such as tobacco, coffee, soap, and toothpaste.

I didn't exchange bad feelings with anyone in the yard, and both the NF and BGF left me alone on a friendly basis to do my own time. The closest I got into any trouble happened in the yard when a white lieutenant, who seemed on friendly terms with the convicts, was walking along the fence. When I walked by him, the lieutenant stopped me and said, "Shave that mustache off your face."

I responded, "I will." I hadn't shaved in two or three days, and a little bit of mustache could almost be seen. I shaved it off after returning to my cell. It was still a prison rule back in 1974 for all prisoners to be clean shaven with a short haircut at all times.

I was held in West Hall for about nine months, and then once again, I was escorted to K wing for classification. I had a good conduct prison record since my arrival at Tracy, so the classification committee decided to transfer me to East Hall. The system was set up so that after your time in the Hole in K wing, which could be a few weeks to years, you then got transferred to West Hall. After months or years of good conduct in West Hall, you got transferred to East Hall. Again, through good conduct time, you could then transfer back to the mainline into the general population. It was up to the classification committee who reviewed your case every ninety days to decide where you would be housed within the different cell units in Tracy.

Short Fuse
In East Hall, I was placed in a cell on the first floor with a view between the weight-lifting area and the basketball court. Then one day, we received word that the first and second tiers of East Hall would start housing PC (protective custody) inmates. All the convicts on the first and

second tiers had to vacate their cells to make them available to PC. I was moved to the third floor of East Hall.

By now, I had done over a year in lockup units in the Hole and in the ACs of West and now East Halls. I had received no bad conduct reports for breaking any prison rules. A short time after the PCs arrived at East Hall, a guard in charge of prison orderlies asked if I wanted to work as an East Hall orderly. There were about four or five orderlies to keep East Hall clean and to serve food to prisoners on the third tier. It was easy work. Best of all, orderlies could stay out of our cells all day and spend time in the dayroom, which had a nineteen-inch TV mounted on the wall and where we could socialize with other orderlies. I got along well with the other orderlies and felt less tension, as they also seemed relaxed. Out of our small cells, we enjoyed some freedom in the dayroom.

One day, I was sitting by the East Hall door waiting for the yard recall when one of the Latino orderlies dropped a folded towel nearby me, which I thought nothing about. When yard time was over, he came over to get the towel. Since I got along well with him, I said, "Yo, let me help you. I'll get it." As I reached for the folded towel, the convict looked a bit caught off guard. As soon as I picked it up, I felt it was much heavier than a normal towel since it contained prison-made metal knives. By leaving it near the door, the orderly avoided being searched at the time of the yard recall. The weight of the towel surprised me, but I said nothing. Very calmly and carefully, I handed the towel to the orderly. I knew what could happen to me if I betrayed an unwritten convict rule by letting my surprise show, so I passed that small accidental test, and soon a bigger test came my way.

In the dayroom, there was another Latino orderly who was easy to get along with and seemed to have some rank in NF. While we were BS-ing one day, he started to talk about how the NF really wanted to get one particular Latino prisoner in PC. But because he was in protective custody, it was very difficult to get to him in person, so the NF's plan was to get him with a prison-made bomb made of a tobacco can. The NF orderly asked me, "Do you want to take care of business on the PC guy by tossing the bomb under his cell door?"

I felt like I was being tested, so I said, "OK, I'll take care of the business." I thought this was a safe move since the convict was in PC, and I wasn't moving against any prison gangs.

That night at shower time, like everyone else, I came out with a towel, but instead of going to the shower area, I went over to the cell of a white guy who was an associate of NF and asked, "What's happening?"

"All right, here is the bomb," he said. He handed me a flat triangular-shaped metal object. "Notice it has a short fuse. Once you get down to his cell, jam some magazines under his cell door so there is something blocking the opening under his door. Then light the fuse, pull out the magazines, and slide the bomb in as fast as you can. You got that, right?"

"Yes," I answered.

I picked up two magazines and lit a smoke on my way to the second tier. Once I got to his cell, I did what I was told to do. But as soon as I released the bomb from my hand, the bomb went off, and I was stunned by a powerful sting on my third and fourth fingers. Did the bomb tear off both those fingers? I didn't check my hand or fingers but just wrapped my towel around my hand. As I headed back toward the stairs, I heard a guard say, "Knock that shit off!"

I got back to my cell and told my next-door neighbor, who was a BGF member, to bust out my window from his side and to shout out, "Man down!" After several shouts, guards came to my third-floor cell and asked, "What happened?"

"I cut my fingers against the cell window." I showed him my hand still partly wrapped in the towel.

"OK, come out of your cell so you can be taken to the prison hospital."

One of the guards escorted me down the mainline corridor to the prison hospital. He left me there to be examined by the prison doctor, who was an older man. The doctor opened up the towel and asked, "What happened to your hand?"

"I cut myself busting out the window in my cell."

My lower joint on my second finger was a mess, and the inner top part of my third finger was puffed out and cut down to the first joint. As the doctor stitched up my fingers, he asked me in a gentle way, "You want to tell me what really happened?"

I felt I could trust him and replied, "A bomb went off on my fingers."

"I thought so because of the puffing which I need to cut out. But don't worry, I am not going to put what you said in a medical report. After I stitch you up, you need to stay in the hospital overnight."

"Thank you, doctor."

The next day, a guard escorted me back to East Hall. As we walked the mainline corridor, he said, "It sure looks funny how all the window glass landed inside of your cell when you said you cut your hand busting out the window." He laughed.

I did not return any remarks to the guard but continued to walk, holding up my bandaged fingers. After I got back to East Hall, out in the yard around the handball court, the Latino guy who asked me to throw the bomb stopped by to talk with me alone. "You all right, Lee?"

I gave a low laugh. "The fucker fuse was too short, almost took my two fingers off."

Smiling, he said, "You're all right. You got any problems, let me know, and I'll see what I can do."

Afterward, I walked around the yard, saying hi to a few guys that I knew. Jo-Mo saw me and started laughing at me in a friendly way, but no one asked about what happened. In fact, the whole yard, as well as the guys from West Hall, all knew what had happened. After the bombing incident, the rest of the convicts in the yard saw me in a better light and were friendlier to me. "This little Chino got heart," which meant they knew I would stand up for myself. Some had thought I was weak, but after the bombing incident, I got a little bit of respect from the hardcore convicts. That was not my intention, but it worked out in my favor.

Seeing that other convicts were now standing with me erased some of my fears. As the only Korean, let alone Asian, among all those gang members, I did the bombing to show I was as tough as anybody in prison. I had been getting weird looks from some predatory convicts, and I thought this was a way to prove I could stand up for myself. Years later, Ray Contreras, a former NF lieutenant who cooperated with federal prosecutors on racketeering charges against the NF, told investigators that some NF members were thinking about forcing me to become a punk, but after the bombing incident, they saw me as a fighter, so they changed their minds and left me alone. Unknowingly, I had saved myself. If I had been attacked by NF members, I would have fought back, and I would have gotten killed, so I was very lucky that I took that action against the PC who was not hurt by the bombing. I passed the test which may have saved my life and kept my sense of self and dignity intact.

Legal Education
Within a few weeks of the bombing incident, I received a letter from the court of appeals informing me that the court had denied my appeal on the Chinatown murder case for which Hamilton Hintz was my appeal

lawyer. I felt it was a letter of doom, sealing my fate into the violent world of prison forever. Yet I also knew there must be laws that could help me continue the fight to prove my innocence on the Chinatown case.

At the time, Ranko was going to law school, so I wrote to her, asking to send me some law books. Within two weeks, I received a package from Ranko, containing the California Penal Code and a book explaining how to address the law of writ "in a nutshell." As I read these books, I tried to understand how the law applied to re-appeal my case. But no matter how hard I tried, I was unable to comprehend the words written in the law books. This should be understandable since it was the first time in my life ever reading such books. I was having enough difficulty with letter writing. For example, one day I received a letter from Ranko in response to my personal letters to her, in which she wrote, "I don't want to create any illusions for you in regards to our friendship." I had to look up the word "illusion" in a dictionary to find out what it meant. However, this did not stop me from reaching out for Ranko's personal feelings, which I continued to do in all my letters to her. I believe Ranko showed great understanding of my loneliness but kept true to herself and continued our correspondence without ever responding to my expressions of personal affection.

Big Red

For about a month after the bombing incident, my daily routine in the yard was to continue learning handball and to work out a little with weights. In my cell, I also did push-ups and sit-ups, trying to build up my 5'4", 125-pound body.

One day, I came out to the yard and felt deep tension. I kept to myself around the weight area and watched for any movement in the yard. After about forty-five minutes, I heard an African American yell out in a loud voice, "Hey!" and start running toward the gate. He continued to yell to the yard guard who sat in the office, "Get me out of here! Get me out of here!"

Then I noticed Big Red, a BGF member, walking toward the guy. Big Red was almost 7' tall and 200 pounds, with a mean-looking face. He was carrying a prison-made, double-edged knife about a foot long; it looked more like a short sword than a knife. He passed by near me. Just looking at him with the knife, I felt fear going through my whole body. While his target at the gate was screaming for his life, Big Red was calmly and slowly walking over to his intended victim. Since there was no gun tower coverage of the East and West Hall yard, he could easily have gone ahead and stabbed his target. But when the yard guard came out of his office and walked about eight feet toward the guy who was yelling for help, Big Red turned around and walked back toward the basketball court. As I watched the other convicts starting to play basketball, I noticed a white rope dangling out a window from a cell to retrieve the knife, and then I heard the guard asking the convict at the fence gate, "What's the matter?" The guard seemed to have no idea what was happening, but there was only one reason a convict would yell out to get off the yard.

"Man, just get me off the yard!" There was deep fear in his voice and face as the guard let him out of the yard and sounded the alarm button.

By the basketball court, I noticed the leader of BGF and another African American coming down on Big Red for not making the "hit" as he was supposed to. It didn't matter what his excuse was since there was no tower gun coverage in the yard. According to the convicts' code, you made the hit no matter what.

When I first saw Big Red with the big knife, I felt fear just at the sight of him. But when I saw him turn around to retreat toward the basketball court with a shitty grin on his face, I thought to myself, "The guy is just a big bully, who failed to take care of business." He was merely putting on a show, revealing the weakness of his character. Any convict involved with a prison gang who was serious would have made the hit without any regard to getting caught or not. I think most convicts in the yard shared my view of Big Red.

I was not aware at the time that black-on-black hits were caused by internal power struggles within the BGF, which continued throughout my years of imprisonment. As a rule, you didn't ask questions about gangs, so I didn't ask about the BGF's internal conflicts and continued to maintain good relationships with those BGF members I'd gotten to know.

After a few months, my fingers had fully healed (but even to this day, scars on both fingers are visible). Around this time, we were instructed to pack up our personal property because the whole of East Hall was becoming a PC unit. Some of us were transferred to another lockup unit in L wing of the mainline next to the Hole in K wing. L wing had two tiers totally separate from each other, and all the convicts doing lockup time in L wing lived on the third floor.

Getting adjusted to L wing meant eating in your cell, showering within the unit, stepping out fully dressed, then undergoing a pat search with a metal detector passed slowly over the length of your whole body. For daily yard time, you were handcuffed in the back, escorted down to the second floor, and taken through the door and past the yard guard cage. Once in the yard with the gate shut, your handcuffs were removed through a porthole by the guard.

L wing yard was a little smaller than West and East Hall yard, but there seemed to be less tension in L yard since everyone gave space to each other. As an unwritten rule, the convicts of each race kept to themselves in their part of the yard. Latinos stayed on the west side with the handball court. I believe they were all NF members. The east side, with the weights and chin-up bar, was the BGF side. The racial barriers were so high that even though there was no tension between NF and BGF, I saw almost no interactions between the two races. Maybe each race kept to itself to prevent problems. As for me, I was the only Asian in the yard, but I felt accepted by the others because by now I had spent over a year's time in the lockup units. I knew more Latinos than African Americans since my sport activity was more handball than weights. As a result, I stayed mostly on the Latino side.

Each day when yard time was over, we returned to our cells, and dinner was sent to us there. Nights became my worst time. At night, I remembered I was an innocent man convicted and imprisoned just for being Asian. What had I done wrong to deserve such injustice in a free country where I had full faith in the justice system? How could the prosecution and police imprison a man for being Asian? Why was the fact that I was Korean never taken into account? It seemed surreal. Meanwhile, every day I had to watch my every step, every word, and every action if I wanted to survive, especially in the lockup units that were filled with prison gang members who were the most violent of all convicts.

My angry cry for justice was heard only by Ranko. She was my only outlet, as it seemed the rest of the world was blind. Meanwhile, I had to do my best to survive the world of prison. If I was ever to see justice prevail, even if it was a hopeless dream, I needed to keep a flicker of hope lit in my mind. The only other course was madness. So I continued to grow more entrenched as a convict, adapting to my circumstances while fueling an impossible light deep within my mind and soul.

Return to the Mainline

I did about eighteen months in the lockup units of K wing, West and East Halls, and L wing without receiving any disciplinary reports. Then in the summer of 1975, I went before the classification committee once again. They told me, "Mr. Lee, you have done well since your arrival at DVI, and now we are releasing you to the mainline."

I guess my attempted bombing of the PC in East Hall was never reported to prison officials. After the reclassification, I packed my few personal properties and was escorted to C wing of Tracy's mainline population. As I walked toward the chow hall for dinner, I was once again joined by Joe Fong, Richard Lee, David Wong, Chico Wong, and Eddie Yuen. Good feelings were exchanged over my being released back to the mainline. David asked, "What the fuck did you do to get lockdown?"

"I had a fight with a police officer while I was in city prison in San Francisco because I got so pissed off over getting bonded to superior court on the case," I said.

Then Eddie Yuen started talking, "Man, that lawyer you turned me on to in San Francisco County Jail was the most fucked-up lawyer I ever had! Goddamn!"

"Man, I didn't know how bad the lawyer was until my trial in Sacramento on the gun charge, and then I had no way of getting in touch with you about the lawyer," I said.

I have no idea about and never talked to Eddie about what kind of evidence was brought against him, but I was sure Eddie could have gotten a better trial with a different lawyer. That lawyer used me and Eddie and many others to get his criminal trial lawyer experience. He may have meant well, but he was too inexperienced, especially for a big gangland murder case like Eddie's. I felt sorry for introducing the lawyer to Eddie, but after he complained without showing any anger toward me, nothing more was ever said about the lawyer.

Richard and Chico were quiet, but I think all of our moods were high. The group was in good spirits to have me back. After we sat down with our dinner trays, David asked, "How you doing on money?"

"Real bad," I said.

"All right. We know some people who work for the job assessment office, and we're going to get you a job at an industry where you could get better pay than most other prison jobs. Me and Richard work at the prison warehouse. Chico, Eddie, and Ernest work in the laundry room so we can get you fixed up with clothes when you come through the laundry room for exchange of clothing." Ernest was an ABC from Los Angeles, unrelated to S.F. Chinatown.

David went on to say, "Whatever you need, let us know. We will help you out until you get a prison industry job."

Then Joe, who was just listening to everything, spoke, "Whatever you do, stay out of problems and don't try to show off. We had a problem a while back with a Chinese guy who worked in the laundry room. He started to show off like he knew kung fu, and we told him to stop several times, but the guy didn't listen. He ended up getting raped by two black guys in the laundry room, and later he ended up PC-ing. So keep to yourself and don't try to show off." Joe's statement was a warning. If I started acting like a fool, I was not going to receive any help from him or the other Chinese at Tracy.

To be back in the mainline and to be still accepted by the guys from Chinatown sent my spirits high. Just to be with and be seen with other Asians, I no longer felt so alone as I did in the lockup units. It felt good to see these guys. At the end of dinner, David said, "There is a Korean guy named Kim in J wing, you may want to check him out."

"I'll do that soon as possible."

But the way David talked about Kim, it was clear they didn't associate with him at all. Kim was in J wing, which housed prisoners who were going to school or training programs to take up a trade. Joe Fong was also housed in J wing, attending school.

On my second day back in the mainline, I went to the laundry room to pick up my prison-issue clothing and bedding. I went through the line where Chico and Eddie were passing out rolls of clothing. When I saw Chico, he pulled out a special bundle all rolled up in a new towel. We exchanged greetings and said, "See you later at the yard or chow time."

When I returned to my cell, I unrolled my bundle along with the sheets and blankets. Within the clothing roll, I found that everything was new—the pants, boxers, T-shirts, and shirts. Chico and Eddie set aside special rolls for prisoners who wanted new-issue clothing and could pay for it with cartons of cigarettes. But Joe, David, Richard, and I all received new clothing for free. It was just one small way of giving support to each other.

I adjusted well to the mainline and the prisoners in C wing. Within the mainline, there were some NF and BGF members that I knew from East and West Halls and L wing. When I met them in the wing or out in the yard, we exchanged warm greetings. The mainline felt like we were set free from the jail of the AC's lockup units. Some of those guys said to me, "If you need anything, homeboy, let us know." This was their way of saying, "Let's get along out here on the mainline." They were aware I had fallen in line with the guys from Chinatown, and I stood with the Asians. I replied, "I am OK. I am with my homeboys out here."

I didn't get to know BGF members very well other than Jo-Mo, but I knew some of the Latinos well, like B.B. and Tony, another NF member I met in East Hall. I continued to maintain good relations with them and their associates. Tony introduced me to some NF members, and even though I had been in the lockup units for a long time, I was given respect and had no problems with anyone. If a gang member got out of line with me, all I needed to do was talk to the leader who would put the member in check.

I also met Lefty, who was an NF captain in charge of the mainline. He worked as a mainline corridor cleaner, which allowed him access to all the mainline wings. He was about 5′8″ and 160 pounds. It was hard to get to know him because he acted like a loner and said little, always keeping a straight face with an unreadable expression. Day or night, you would sometimes see him sweeping the mainline corridor with a dust mop, walking at a slow pace as if always in deep thought and keeping to himself. Seeing him like this, people kept their distance. He looked like he didn't want anyone to bother him.

Within a week of transferring to the mainline, Chico Wong pulled me aside in the yard to talk about some matters. Chico said, "There is a white punk in your wing, who is under our protection. Whatever money he collects, he turns over to me. His name is Steve on the second floor."

"All right," I said.

I was surprised to hear we had a punk under our protection and were collecting money from him, as none of us Asians ever used punks for sex. We stayed away from associating with punks. To my surprise, Chico was giving this punk protection and collecting money off his earnings as a prostitute. Since I was new among the mainline Asians, I didn't question Chico or ask anyone about the protection fee Chico got from Steve.

In a serious tone, Chico then asked me, "You don't have TV, right?"

"No, I don't," I replied.

"Okay. We got a TV that belongs to us, but we loaned it to Spider, who is leader of the white bikers. Spider transferred out and will be returning sometime in the future, but he didn't return the TV to us when he transferred and instead left it with one of his guys in your wing. We need to collect the TV from the guy, and that can be your TV. I'll be in C wing at two o'clock to talk to the guy, and you should come with me."

"Okay, I'll meet you in C wing when you come over," I said.

That day, I found Steve to tell him I'd be collecting the money for Chico from now on. Steve was in his early twenties, white, and a bit skinny. I could see he was a guy who couldn't stand up for himself. He counted on Chico, which meant all the Asians, for protection from being totally victimized by other convicts. I told Steve, "If you have any problem, come to me and I'll take care of it. Also any money you earn, dockets, or cigarettes, turn over to me daily."

Steve responded, "All right, I'll do as you say. Here is about twenty dollars in dockets and if I have any problem, I'll come by every few days and see you." He handed over the dockets, which were used as a form of money to buy snacks and small commodities in the yard, such as soda, ice cream, chips, and so forth. That ended my conversation with him.

The next day, Chico came to C wing and asked me, "You ready?"

"Yes."

"Don't say anything. I'll do all the talking to the biker, but in case he gives me any problem, be ready to back me up."

"All right."

We met the biker near the front by the guard cage and TV room. The biker was about 5'7" and skinny. He looked worried when talking to Chico. I stepped back about five feet since I had learned in the lockup units the habit of stepping away from conversations whenever gang members talked to each other to give them privacy. But since this involved Chico and me, I stayed nearby enough to hear the conversation, so if any fighting broke out I was ready to assist Chico. Chico was telling the biker, "The TV you got from Spider is mine, and I want the TV back."

"Hey, Spider left the TV to me, so I'll return the TV to Spider when he gets back to Tracy, which will be very soon," the biker said.

"It doesn't matter if Spider is here or not, the TV still belongs to me, and you need to return the TV now."

"I am not going to return the TV until Spider is back."

Chico was speaking in a firm voice, and the biker's responses sounded weak, but Chico didn't sound ready to fight over the TV. Chico looked at me as if he thought I might not back his play because I had stepped back, but he saw me in the wrong light because I would have backed him all the way with whatever needed to be done. Reflecting on this incident, I think Chico wanted us both to get in the biker's face to pressure him. But instead, the conversation ended with the biker's refusal to return the TV until Spider got back. After the confrontation ended, I asked Chico, "Now what we do?"

Chico had an annoyed look on his face. A few months later, Spider, who was the recognized leader of the whites at Tracy, returned. Chico went to talk to him and got the TV back, and then I got to use that TV. Chico didn't show any ill feelings toward me. In fact, within the group of Chinese convicts, I got along best with Chico and David.

One day, we were walking out to the yard together as a group with a relaxed feeling. I was walking with Joe Fong when all of a sudden he stopped and turned to me, asking with a light smile on his face, "Hey, Lee, if you were in a city where you don't know anyone and you needed to find someone, what would you do?"

I turned to him as all the others did and said what came to my mind, "What, look up in a telephone book?"

Joe's face turned sour. I realized his question was aimed at teaching me something new, and I was expected to allow Joe to answer his own question. I made a mistake by trying to answer his question. All the others knew Joe much better than I did and knew I made a mistake. It was a fatal mistake on my part. After that, Joe didn't try to teach me about anything. If I had kept my mouth shut, maybe Joe would have taught me many things about life on the street and survival. I have always viewed Joe with respect, and even to this day, I have respect for Joe's accomplishments after his release from prison.

In my view, Joe Fong set the best example of any Asian, or any prisoner released from prison. Joe stayed out of gang warfare by not returning to the leadership of his Chinatown gang. After ten years of false imprisonment, his followers hoped he would resume leadership of the gang to carry on the struggle against the Wah Ching, which by then controlled Chinatown. However, Joe refused any further involvement, much to the disappointment of many young gang members. Instead, Joe enrolled in a university, earned a PhD, and became a professor of ethnic studies at a California college. This was a shining example of his determination not merely in adjusting to freedom, but in reaching a much higher level than most Asians ever achieve after imprisonment. Sadly, many ex-prisoners return to their former ways. Much to Joe's credit, he set an example for those of us trying to adjust to living in society.

Witness to Gang Rape

David, Chico, Richard, and Eddie normally got off work in time for the afternoon yard at 1 p.m. I usually met them at the handball court. We played handball along with Three-Finger Larry, who was white and had lost two fingers in an industrial accident. Now and then, Joe came around, but he was not much interested in handball. We played handball two to a team, with usually about six of us playing, but when Joe came around, we often stopped playing handball and bought sodas and ice cream, which were sold only at the yard canteen. During those restful moments, no one talked about the streets. We just had light conversation, sitting with our backs against the handball court.

Each of the Chinese guys knew each other well from the streets, and even though I was accepted by them, I was not an insider. None of us talked about our fate of being imprisoned, but we accepted it. Since they showed no interest in my unjust imprisonment, I kept my thoughts to myself. David told me they knew the prisoner who ran the work assignments in the prison administration office and was trying to get Three-Finger Larry and his friends to give me a job assignment as a welder since I had some welding experience from classes I took in CYA.

The daily routine in C wing went something like this: We were locked in our cells until after breakfast when our cells unlocked. We returned to our cells for lunch call, then were let out for work, yard time, or hanging around in the unit until the 4 p.m. count. After the count, we were released unit by unit for dinner. During the summertime, there was a short night yard and all prisoners were locked down for the night at 10 p.m.

After about a month after my release to the mainline C unit, I was just about to go out the front gate to the yard when I saw four African Americans enter the cell of a young African American. I continued on my way, going through my daily yard routine and did not say anything about what I had witnessed. I returned to C unit about two and a half hours later. As I entered, I saw the same four African Americans coming out of the cell they had entered earlier. Apparently, their activity went unnoticed by the unit guard, even when the guard went through the tiers of open cells for the afternoon count.

I didn't know all the African Americans who were leaving the cell, but I knew one of them who was in his early twenties and most likely a BGF member. As he was coming out, I caught his eyes. He looked away with a silly stupid look on his face. From his look and the way the others looked, I realized they had entered the guy's cell not for a gang-related murder but to rape the prisoner. The African American I knew seemed to be a pleasant guy with whom I had some rapport, but I was very disappointed with him now. I felt sad and angry with the prison system where we lived with such inhumanity.

The next day, I saw the prisoner who was gang raped. He was a young African American, about eighteen or nineteen years old. He had two black eyes and looked like he had been beaten up. He had a hopeless saddened look on his face. If the victim decided he would retaliate by killing one of his victimizers, then he would not be victimized again. Even after being raped, if he showed the will to fight back afterward, he would be respected by the hard-core convicts and would not be bothered again. But if he was weak, he would do the rest of his time as a punk.

It could have been me who was victimized, but I carried myself with confidence and hung out with other Asians and escaped victimization. After two years in Tracy, even though I was only twenty-two years old, the other convicts must have viewed me as someone with the will to stand on his own, for no one made any bad moves against me. When you do time with other convicts, the convicts get to know you as well as you get to know yourself because convicts see how you conduct yourself in words and action twenty-four hours a day. If you're weak, especially if you're standing alone, you will be noticed in no time. As in the jungle, only the strong survive and the weak are prey to the strong. This is true for all convicts. Not many of the strong can complete their time without getting some blood on their hands.

Occupations

After waiting for over a month, I got a docket to report to the industry welding shop. David and the other Chinese guys knew the whites who handled job assignments and helped me get an interview with the free man who ran the welding shop. Nonguards employed by the prison were called free men. The free man who interviewed me was an African American of light complexion. He asked me, "What experience do you have in welding?"

"While I was in the California Youth Authority, I did welding in lead and arc welding," I said.

The free man took me in the back where the lead and arc welding was located. "OK—show me your welding skills."

I turned on the gas and oxygen, put on safety glasses, and welded together scraps of sheet metal for a few minutes until the free man stopped me. "Come back tomorrow at 8 a.m. and someone will show you what to do."

After the interview, I was pat searched by the prison guard at the gates of the industry shop. I returned to my unit to tell David I got the job and found him in the yard with the others by the handball court. He said, "All right, we knew it already. Now we are going to have you transferred to the workers' wing."

The workers' wing was E wing, where David and Richard were housed, but not Joe, who was in school and housed in J wing. At 8 a.m. the next day, I started work at the welding shop. Besides welding, the shop had many kinds of metal work. The convict I worked with showed me what needed to be done. He did most of the work, filling up dents in chair parts with lead. Sometimes work was very busy, and other times, slow. Next to our welding area, there was the heliarc (tungsten inert gas welding) workshop where two white guys worked, and in due time, they taught me heliarc welding so I could help them whenever our work was slow or they were overloaded with too much to do. I learned well. Besides heliarc welding, I learned tack welding, and mig (metal inert gas) welding as well.

When we stopped for lunch, the industry shops had their own special dining room and small yard we could use. Four or five guys played poker at lunchtime, with whoever was running the game taking 10 percent of the pot. Because poker was played on credit, each month the person running the game was responsible for collecting money from losers and paying in full to winners. Pretty soon, I ended up running the game.

The work we did at the welding shop paid five or six cents an hour, which came to about forty-five dollars per month and barely enough to buy your personal need items. However, after I started running the poker game, I had saved enough within a few months to buy a TV from the prison commissary. According to prison rules, you could have a twelve-inch TV, either bought in prison or mailed to you by your family. After that, I returned Chico's TV back to him.

After a few weeks, I was transferred to E wing, next door to David and Richard. I'm sure David and Richard put in a fix for me to get that cell. When I moved in, David showed great happiness with lots of jokes and laughter, and I felt the same. Here we were, the only three Asians in E wing, housed in three adjacent cells on the second tier. We felt more united than ever. Although Tracy had only seven Asians in total, Kim and Ernest, who were both from Los Angeles, chose not to stay close to the San Francisco Chinese. I tried to reach out to Kim, but he seemed content doing time without me or other Asians. That left the three San Francisco Chinese—Joe, David, and Richard—plus Chico from Los Angeles and me, the lone Korean among the Chinese. Doing our time together, we kept to ourselves and stayed out of trouble. It was the summer of 1975.

After my move to E wing, I decided to start running my own illegal poker games in the wing to earn extra money. The rest of the Chinese guys made extra money in the laundry room and received some support from their family and friends. By comparison, I had only Ranko and very little support from my mother. A few weeks after I started running nightly poker games, David pulled me aside in the yard one day and said, "Lee, you know gambling is nothing but trouble, so why don't you let loose the poker games."

I responded, "That's my only way to make a little extra money. I have very little support from outside. I'm trying to make the best of my situation."

"Well, do what you got to do, but if any problems come up over the poker games, we are not going to back you."

As I continued to run poker games, I saw an invisible wall start to build between me and the Chinese as they were doing their best to avoid trouble, and they saw gambling as leading to problems.

Most problems arose when someone was unable to pay in full at the end of the month. I didn't take strong action but firmly explained that the credit limit was so much and expected to be paid the full balance next month. I usually had no trouble, except with one Latino who always lost. After he reached the limits on my tables, both at the industry shop's lunchtime table and in E wing, he tried playing poker at Spider's table. When he went into debt, he came and talked to me. "Hey, Lee, I can only pay so much this month, but I am expecting money from my family, so can you wait for the rest until next month when I get it?"

"How much can you pay this month on canteen day?"

"About 50 percent of the money I owe you."

"All right, that cool but be sure to pay the rest next month."

"Thanks, Lee. I'll pay in full next month."

Next month on commissary day, he paid me 50 to 70 percent. I thought as long as he kept talking to me about the money he owed and

I collected thirty to fifty dollars from him every month, I didn't need to pressure the guy for the full amount.

Now and then, when there were not enough poker players in E wing, I sometimes played at Spider's table, or Spider would come over and play at my table. The whole time I was on the mainline, no problems arose during these poker games that required the use of force.

Drinking Soda, Eating Chips

When a stabbing was about to take place in the yard, solid convicts received advance warning so they could stay out of the way. One afternoon when we got to the yard, David said, "I heard from NF something is coming down this afternoon."

We went over to the yard canteen to purchase some sodas and chips, and returned to the handball court. We sat there with our backs to the wall, drinking our sodas and eating chips. In a short while, we saw four NFs attack one guy just beyond the handball court. On each side of the victim, two guys grabbed and held him. A short guy nicknamed Fly climbed on the victim's back and hit him with his fists while the fourth guy in front tried to stab him. We just sat calmly drinking our sodas and eating our chips as if we were in the Roman Coliseum watching gladiator sword fighting.

I don't know how he was able to do it, but the targeted victim got loose from the four guys and started running toward the yard equipment room. This was a fatal mistake. The area he ran into was a blind spot for the gun towers. A pack of attackers zoomed in from all sides. The victim made a mad dash toward the L wing gun tower and the yard entrance. As he ran at full speed, one NF stood near where he was about to pass by. The NF drew back his arm and stabbed with full force. Upon impact, the victim let out a loud scream. Two other NFs quickly joined in stabbing him. Then the alarm sounded, and numerous guards poured into the yard toward the scene.

The stabbing was truly like a nature show on TV, where you see lions take different positions and close in on their prey from all sides. All of us continued to sit and watch the whole stabbing from start to finish without talking or showing any emotion. We watched like it was a routine matter and continued to drink our sodas and eat chips. We all saw what happened, but none of us made any comments, looking on in silence. The victim was carried out of the yard on a gurney. We later learned that he survived.

The guards started looking for the stabbers, who by then had gotten rid of their knives and were walking among other convicts in the yard. As the guards searched the convicts by the equipment room, I saw B.B. come nearby the handball court, lean sideways, push a prison-made knife into the ground so that it was covered by grass, and then go on his way. In a short time, the yard was recalled, and each convict went through a strip search. The guards checked each convict for any scratches.

Almost monthly, someone was killed or stabbed somewhere in the prison at Tracy; it was as if the constant warring and friction soaked the whole prison in blood. There was nowhere in the prison system where prisoners would not stab or kill, not even the prison church. All prisoners were aware of the danger every time they stepped out or even into their cells. It was as if any problem could be solved by killings.

This was the reason David warned me about playing or running poker games. I was lucky that no problem arose from the poker games, which could have led to a killing or stabbing. I should have listened to David's warnings. During this time in the mainline, I still knew many NF and some BGF members from East and West Hall, and continued to stay on friendly terms with them. However, gang members stayed close to their own ranks, as I did with the Asians. Each race imposed order upon itself, keeping social activities within the race.

Meanwhile, alone in my cell, I continued to write to Ranko and Reiko, and received their letters once every month or two. I had given up on writing to Ranko about the Chinatown murder case until one day by chance I read in a San Francisco newspaper about a convicted murderer. He was a white guy who was released from Soledad after Inspector Frank Falzon admitted the guy was wrongfully convicted of murder. Seeing this, my personal hopes soared high, thinking that Falzon's mistake in my case could also come to light. I immediately wrote to Ranko with high hopes of being cleared of the false murder conviction. But Ranko's reply letter said the white guy's lawyer came up with so much evidence of his innocence that Falzon had no choice. To save himself, Falzon was forced to admit his mistake in the white guy's case. But Falzon was unlikely ever to admit to a mistake in my case.

My high hopes for justice were thus short lived. How could I continue to be falsely imprisoned for murder when the whole of Chinatown, as well as some Chinese SFPD officers, were aware of my innocence? How could this injustice ever happen? I continued to be haunted daily by the miscarriage of justice. My hope for justice seemed darker than ever.

Visitors

One night in the summer of 1975, I dreamt in color of four different horses—red, brown, white, and black. They were racing across the sky. I rarely remembered my dreams, but I remembered this dream clearly the next morning when I awoke. I had never in my life dreamed in color, and it was the most beautiful dream I'd ever had in my life. I awoke feeling in high spirits and feeling good about the dream.

That afternoon, my name was called out for a visit. Since I didn't receive visitors, I wondered who came to visit—maybe Ranko? When I entered the visiting room, the officer told me my visitor was waiting for me on the lawn in the outdoor visiting area. To my great surprise, I saw Reiko sitting on the bench. I gave her a big hug of happiness, and she totally embraced me back with kisses. We sat down to talk, holding hands, and I asked her, "How were you able to visit me?" I knew she lived in Kobe, Japan.

With a beautiful smile, Reiko explained, "My parents and brother live in Stockton, and since you were nearby, I decided to visit you."

For the next two hours, Reiko's visit was one of the happiest times ever in my life. Throughout the whole visit, I forgot anything else existed on earth. I kept holding her hand in mine, never wanting to let her go. Toward the end of the visit I said, "Let's take a picture together."

There were convicts working in the visiting room who took instant Polaroids for a few dollars. Reiko paid since convicts were not allowed to have real money in prison. With me embracing Reiko, the cameraman snapped the picture, and Reiko and I watched the picture of our embrace come alive. Even though the visiting hour was just about over, I felt no sadness but only happiness to see Reiko in person and to have a picture to remember the visit by.

As I watched Reiko walk out through the prison visitor gates, I was filled with happiness. I believe she knew how much impact her visit had upon me as she turned to wave a last goodbye with the brightest smile. Reiko and Ranko's friendship always meant a great deal to me, and Reiko's visit in 1975 is one of the most truly happy memories I will always cherish. It is engraved into my soul.

The following year in 1976, I received a visit from my mother. My mother brought with her my auntie, uncle, and their youngest son, Myung-hak. Even though I was very glad to see my auntie and uncle, and especially Myung-hak, the visit was very sad. After eleven years in the US, I no longer remembered how to speak Korean, and they spoke no English, so I talked to my mother while my auntie and uncle sat there uncomfortably. I wanted to address my auntie and uncle as "mother" and "father"—the way I always used to—but I couldn't do so because my real mother was present. I felt very lost in my personal feelings toward the only loving family I ever knew.

Turning to look to my left, I saw Myung-hak sitting with his chin on his hands and silent tears rolling down from his eyes. Myung-hak had just arrived from Korea, and I felt the greatest anguish at not being able to talk with him. It was as if we both silently realized that the closeness of our brotherhood was lost forever. I tried to put up a good face, but Myung-hak's sadness was too great for me to take. He called out to me, "Brother (*hyung*), brother," as his tears continued to fall from his face. The visit ended in less than an hour. I knew as they were leaving the visiting room that I would not see them again so long as I was in prison.

The visit affected me deeply with sadness, for my uncle and auntie were like my father and mother, and Myung-hak, my closest brother. But the tie was cut because I was unable to communicate with them. This pained me the most. They seemed to share the emotions I felt about my childhood years in Korea, feeling I belonged to their close-knit family as one of their children. But I was Americanized now and unable to speak Korean. I felt I had become a lost son and brother to the family who raised me. The separation was too much to bear.

At the same time, with my real mother I always felt a distance too great to relate to her as mother and son. As a result, I was alone during my years in the United States. Even though my auntie, uncle, and Myung-hak desired in their hearts to reach out to reembrace me as family as we once were in Korea, my real mother and the prison walls stood between us. I left the visiting room still thinking about Myung-hak sitting next to me, letting his innermost tears fall in silence for his lost brother. I returned to my cell and stayed there in a state of depression. I feel sadness about this even to this day. There is a word in Korean, *oet'ori,* which translates into English as "alone person" or "outsider." I felt that I was one of those *oet'oris* of this world.

Witness to Smuggling

By 1976, I had been in the Tracy mainline nearly one year and in prison for three years. I remained free of disciplinary actions and was classified as a model inmate. I continued to hang with the guys from Chinatown, and I got along well with other convicts I came in contact with. One day,

I was approached by Art "Fly" Serrato, who I knew from CYA. Art's nickname was "Fly" because he was short, standing about 5' tall, but he was well built. Art asked me for a favor by helping him get a job at the welding shop where I had been working for close to a year. I told Art I'd see what I could do for him.

I talked to Steve, the free man who supervised the metal shop and hired me. He asked for Art's name and prison number. I knew Art was a member of NF, but I guess there was no mention of Art's association with NF in his central file when Steve had Art's prison record checked out. In short time, Art was given a docket for a job interview. I told Steve I would teach Art the welding work I was doing and that another prisoner was needed in the welding area where I worked by myself. Since there was a job opening, Steve hired Art to work under me.

When the shop was very busy and my area was slow, I helped other workers with heliarc, mig, and tack welding. For about a month, Art kept low-key and did his work well under my supervision. Then one day I noticed him taping up some pieces of metal, the six-feet-by-one-inch flat bars that we used in the welding area. I assumed he was smuggling metal for the NF to sharpen into deadly knives, but what Art did was not my business so I kept it to myself. I believe the NF ordered Art to smuggle metal into the nonmetal trash cans so that other NF members who collected the trash could retrieve the metal.

I knew Art was acting to support his gang, but he acted much too openly. I was not in a position to tell Art to stop because that would be like telling NF what to do. So I decided to talk to Lefty, the man in charge of all NF members and activities on the Tracy mainline. Lefty was a very quiet man, but everyone from the prison administration on down knew of his powerful position as NF captain. When I pulled him aside to meet with him, I said, "Hey Lefty, I am having a problem with Art. I know what he is doing, but he is doing it too openly. I'm feeling the heat from the prison guards. Something is about to come down. Will you ask Art to keep low-key the moves he is making at welding shop?"

Lefty listened thoughtfully and then said, "All right, I will look into it, but you know that's part of our NF business. I will tell Art to be low-key in the welding shop. Will you agree to that?"

"That would be cool," I said. I knew Lefty would continue to order Art to smuggle out metal. When I returned to work the next day, I pulled Art aside where no one could hear us. "Whatever you do is your thing, but the way you're going about business is drawing lots of attention from anyone working in the metal shop. Sooner or later, someone is going to snitch on you. Can you stop it for a while to take the heat off you?"

Art responded, "I understand, but you know I got my orders. But I will be much more low-key."

"All right. I just don't want to see you get busted by the man, so be cool for a while."

A few weeks later, I needed to talk to B.B. about something. He was in E wing, and when I stopped by his cell, I noticed he had his cell door window covered. I knocked, telling him it was me. Just as I started talking through the cell door, the unit guard unlocked all the cell doors so prisoners could return to their cells. For whatever reason, B.B. opened his cell door just a little so we could talk. By then, I had the trust of the NF, BGF, and the white biker gang, and was known in the mainline as a trustworthy convict. When B.B. opened his cell door, I noticed he was sweating all over his face and held a metal file in his hand, which he was using to put a point and edge on some prison-made knives. To avoid drawing attention, I cut my conversation short so no other convict could look into his partly open cell. I told B.B., "There's nothing of importance I need to talk to you about, so I catch you later."

As I left, he closed his cell door. I was surprised that the NF, and maybe the BGF as well, possessed metal files. It seemed strange that convicts used metal files to make prison knives but not to escape from prison. Why make knives when the same tools could be used to free themselves from prison? The NF also had all kinds of drugs to sell for cash. Convicts got cash money from their visitors and smuggled it out of the visiting room. The cash value was worth one and a half to two times more in the mainline—the larger the bill, the more inflated its worth. If you had twenty dollars in cash, you could exchange it for thirty dollars' worth of goods from the commissary, and the cash could be used to buy drugs— anything from weed to speed to heroin.

Two weeks after my conversations with Lefty and Art, a sergeant and two other prison guards came into the welding shop and hand-cuffed both me and Art. The sergeant said, "We received information that you guys were making knives back here. You guys got anything to say?"

We both responded, "No."

Even though I had nothing to do with Art's smuggling, I had brought Art into the metal shop. The guards were also aware that I knew many NF members from my time in the AC. Fortunately, I did not receive a highly negative CDC 115 disciplinary report for serious prison rule violations but rather a CDC 128 conduct report, which was an informational write-up that documented my involvement with smuggling metal out of the welding shop according to a reliable source. Regardless, any kind of disciplinary report went into my central file.

Babo and D.R.

Art and I were taken to the Hole in K wing and placed in different tiers. I ended up on a tier that housed mostly NF and BGF members. Since I did not receive a 115 disciplinary report, the less severe 128 report was not enough to keep me in the Hole, so I was transferred to the L wing AC within a month. The guys I knew from a year ago in L wing were no longer there, but I soon met two NF members, Babo and his close associate, a convict named "D.R."

I later found out that Robert "Babo" Sosa was the main force of NF, their founder and supreme commander. Babo was intelligent and powerfully built, with years of experience and a hard-core look on his face. In the California prison system, he had no problem attracting followers to join NF. In fact, Babo was not Mexican but Puerto Rican, and not from Northern California but from Bakersfield.

Joe "D.R." Gonzales was Mexican. I later learned that he was Babo's top captain and the highly intelligent brains behind the NF. D.R. spent time on San Quentin's Death Row for first-degree murder (thus his nickname, "D.R." or "Death Row Joe"). When the California Supreme Court ruled in 1976 that the death penalty was unconstitutional under the US Constitution, D.R. was released from Death Row after his death sentence was changed to a life sentence and hooked up with Babo after being transferred to Tracy. D.R. was a neat man with very bright eyes who looked more like a teacher than a gang leader. He was about 5'6," 150 pounds, and looked like he never got into prison bodybuilding. He lacked the hard face that normally goes with years of prison experience, and he talked softly with an easygoing attitude and without the tough-acting cuss words used by a majority of convicts.

In L wing, I hit it off with Babo and D.R. right away, and we quickly became friends. Both Babo and D.R. seemed to be in their thirties. I was Babo's teammate in handball, dominoes, and workout partner at the pull-up bars. I did feel a bit strange that three or four guys guarded Babo whenever he and I went over to the pull-up bars on the BGF side to work out. This told me that Babo was a high-ranking NF leader. He kept a low profile, but all the NF members seemed to have high respect for him.

Babo also had a very good memory. He told me one story after another, but never spoke about NF.

Sometimes I played chess with D.R. During these chess games, D.R. quietly taught me about how best to survive within the prison system. He even had an NF member mentor me in how to make different prison weapons, teaching me how to cut metal and make zip guns. I believe D.R. had orders from Babo to recruit me to become an NF member. Membership in NF was never mentioned right out but hinted at for me to think about. However, in my mind, I had already decided against joining NF and staying with the Asians.

One day while I was playing chess with D.R., he told me that Kim was trying to organize the new Asian arrivals to Tracy. He asked me, "Once you get back in the mainline, why don't you help Kim with the new arrivals?"

"I'll think about it," I said. I didn't tell him that I didn't get along too well with Kim.

I spent six months in the L wing AC between 1976 and early 1977, and then went before the classification committee again. The committee told me I would be released back to the mainline since I had remained free of disciplinary actions. That day, I packed my personal belongings. Unknown to me, Babo and D.R. also went before the committee that same day, so I was surprised to see them being released to the mainline too, but we were placed in different units, with me returning to C unit on the mainline.

New Asians

Much to my surprise, upon my return, I received a big welcome from Kim and four other Asians, mostly Filipinos who had arrived at Tracy while I was out of the mainline. The new Asians were Andy, Ray, Carlo, and Glenn, but they were all in different units than me.

I believe Kim was working with the NF as leader of the new Asians. That must be the reason why D.R. talked to me about working with Kim. Kim was more of a show-off than I was, but he spoke highly of me to the new Asians and instructed them to look to me for leadership. Kim may have done more time in Tracy, but I had more connections to NF and BGF gang members from doing time with them in the lockup units.

That afternoon, I saw Babo walking with two bodyguards. In the past, I'd seen other NF leaders in the mainline walk to the yard or chow with only one bodyguard. I went up to Babo to say hi, but one of his bodyguards blocked my way. I said to Babo, "Man, get this out of my way. I'm just coming up to you to tell you I am glad to see you."

Babo had a big grin on his face and told the bodyguard, "It's all right; he's all right with me." Babo and I exchanged greetings and walked back to our units with his bodyguards on both sides along with a few other NFs. To me, Babo was my friend, so I paid no attention to his bodyguards.

I received less of a welcome back to the mainline from the Chinese under Joe Fong, who had gotten word of why I went to the Hole. From my own personal experience of adjusting to prison life, I wanted to help out the new Asians, whereas the Chinese wanted nothing to do with them. This was a turning point in my life in prison. My decision to work with the new Asians in the mainline resulted in a permanent split between the mixed Asians and the Chinese, who wanted to do their time among only Chinese. However, I continued to associate myself with the Chinese while in the yard, mostly through playing handball.

Joe and David did not discuss with me why I decided to work with the new Asians rather than staying with them. My thoughts were mixed. I felt a bit low for leaving the Chinese group I had known since my arrival to Tracy. Now I would no longer be seen as part of them. I also think the new Asians split from the Chinese because Kim wanted to be leader of the Asians and show off his status to the rest of the convicts in Tracy. For example, one day Kim was playing handball with some Latinos, and I was walking around with Ray, Glenn, and Andy. As we walked past him, he asked me, "Can you have two of our guys be my bodyguards while I play ball?"

It was like he wanted to show off by imitating the NF general, Babo, who always had two bodyguards any time he was out of his cell. I told Kim, "There are only six of us. How you need two guys for bodyguard and for what reason? We don't have a problem with anyone."

Kim responded, "Well, you know I am leader of the Asians and brought them together while you were in the Hole."

I replied, "Listen, we are not a large organization like the NF, and our members are too few for anyone to have any bodyguards." Then I turned and walked away with the rest of the guys.

After that conversation, Kim tried at every chance to undermine me. None of the guys responded to this since I was teaching them valuable lessons that I learned about survival skills while Kim was merely acting out the role of gang leader. I found Ray and Andy were more streetwise, Glenn was new without much street experience, and Carlo was hardheaded. But they all listened closely to what I told them.

One of the first rules was to give support to each other, but most importantly, we had to do our best to stay out of conflicts since our numbers were so few. If need be, we would fight back twice as hard to show that even with just a few of us, we would show no fear about standing up for ourselves. If forced to defend ourselves, we would fight back with knives and not our fists. More important than being twice as brave as other convicts, we had to be twice as smart and think about our actions to avoid problems.

Within a month after I was back in the mainline, three additional Asians arrived to Tracy—a Filipino named Pinoy and two others who were half white and half Japanese. I went to ask Pinoy how he was doing. Since he was a new arrival, we had already set aside a small bank of personal-need items such as coffee, tobacco, soap, and toothpaste. I asked Ray and Andy to take the care package to Pinoy. Pinoy had some street experience but little prison experience, and after talking to him about Asians supporting each other, he eagerly joined up with us. As to the other two, Stan and Steve, I was unsure if they would go with the whites or the Asians, but after I talked to each one of them, both decided to get in line with the Asians.

Mr. Wong

I noticed a higher level of tension in the mainline after my release from L wing. Before I was sent to the Hole in 1976, you could take a shower in the mainline without concern about getting killed in the shower room. While I was in the Hole, someone might have gotten killed while showering because when I returned in 1977, most prisoners showered with two or three friends standing guard outside the shower room. That kind of action raised the tension level higher than usual. Since I was the lone Asian in C wing, I showered without having anyone on guard. Tony, an NF member I knew from East Hall, was in C wing with me, along with a few other NF or BGF members that I didn't know as well. Since it was standard to have friends on guard while showering, Tony asked me, "Hey Lee, do you want us to watch out while you're showering?"

"Thanks, but I'll be all right," I said.

But now and then, there would be two or three guys outside the shower room when I came out of the shower, who would go on their way after I came out. I would nod to them as a way of saying thanks. Even though I asked no one to guard when I showered, it was their way of showing me their friendship as well as respect, for they knew I had survived my first eighteen months in the Hole and then another six months without seeking support from anyone.

After returning to the mainline, I got a job as a clerk for the prison food manager. At first, I worked with another clerk, but he got transferred to another prison within a month. Soon after that, the food manager retired, and the assistant food manager, a free man, filled in for a short while. As directed by the free man, I typed up the weekly prison menu and handled food supplies. Then a new food manager took over running the kitchen, a Chinese man named Mr. Wong, who treated me favorably. When I asked him if another clerk was needed to replace the clerk who left, Mr. Wong asked me, "Did you know anyone who can work with you?"

I said, "Yes, there is guy I know. He don't have much experience as a clerk, but I will teach him."

"All right. Have the guy come in, and I'll interview him."

I arranged for Glenn to interview with Mr. Wong for the job. Mr. Wong seemed pleased and hired Glenn to work with me. We started work at about six in the morning and were done by noon. With Mr. Wong as food manager, all of us worked well without any tension. Mr. Wong kept the kitchen running smoothly and looked upon me and Glenn favorably. We never asked Mr. Wong for personal favors like outside Chinese food or any other thing.

Since the food manager's office had a locked gate between the main cooking area and the office, my only contact with prisoners working in the kitchen occurred at breakfast and lunch. Sometimes Glenn and I ate in the unused dining room with the kitchen workers, but there wasn't much chance to get to know them well. Now and then, if there was a lunch we didn't like, I'd ask the food preparation guys to give us some meat and vegetables and rice so Glenn and I could cook our own meal. Sometimes I asked one of the African American cooks for some cooked steaks for me to smuggle out of the kitchen and share with the rest of the Asians. Smuggling food out of the kitchen was a common practice, and usually the guard on duty in the kitchen let me pass through the locked gate after a pat search. The guards were more concerned about anything that could be used as a weapon rather than minor food items. Sometimes I just asked the guard, "Hey boss, here is some food I am taking with me for later—is it all right?"

"OK, but put the food away so you won't get busted by the corridor guards."

"Thanks, boss."

Balancing Acts

Kim had a release date of sometime in early 1978, but my relationship with him didn't improve. I could not change his mind about his self-glorification and misuse of the Asian guys as if we were his gang. One day, I saw D.R. in the yard and learned from him that Kim got some schooling from the NF while I was in the L wing Hole. I told D.R., "Kim thinks he is some kind of big shot and is overreacting and out of line with what I am trying to do with the Asians."

D.R. advised me, "Kim never did any hard time in the Hole as you did. He doesn't have the self-control and discipline that you have when he overplays his role. You just have to keep him calm and keep his ego in check. Or, if you want support from us, from NF, we will do the hit. Is that what you want?"

"No, I don't want Kim hit," I said, "but I'll take your advice and try to keep him calm. I think he has never in his life had people look up to him as these new Asians do. My main goal is keeping the Asians together and supporting each other, rather than getting involved in any violence. Well, D.R., thanks. I be seeing you around."

After this conversation, I thought about D.R.'s advice. As for doing a hit on Kim, it was out of the question. If D.R. arranged the hit on Kim, then in return, these few Asian guys, including myself, would come under NF rule. I think that was the plan Babo and D.R. had designed from the start. That is why D.R. schooled me in prison survival skills while I was in L wing with them. Meanwhile, NF was schooling Kim to organize the new Asian arrivals while I was in the Hole. Kim fell into the NF's design due to his own personal power tripping. I had known Kim in the mainline from 1975 to 1976 when he had kept low-key and to himself, but now he wanted to rise like an NF leader—like a fool.

After talking to D.R., I advised the other Asians not to associate with NF members. If any issue came up that required dealing with NF, I'd take care of it. My goal was to protect these guys from being used by NF. Through my personal friendship or a connection to both Babo and D.R., I would resolve any problems with any NF members. I hoped no problem would ever arise, for with just a few Asians, who were mostly untested, we stood no chance if violence erupted. So we kept to ourselves and gave support to each other as Asians and friends, as the Chinese were doing.

One day, Glenn, whom I'd known for only a few months, kind of surprised me. He came up to me and said, "There's a black guy I want to kill."

Glenn was in prison only a few months, and nowhere near the condition of a hard-core convict and already he had the mind-set to kill someone? I said to Glenn, "What the reason you want to kill this guy?"

Glenn explained. "I was coming down the stairs during chow time. I was just behind a few black guys, and one of them turned around with his fist raised as if to hit me. After seeing me, the guy walked on, laughing about it. I took his action as disrespectful to me."

At the time, Glenn had no idea. If any Asians crossed the racial line in stabbing another race, it would start a race war. I explained the race politics to Glenn. At that moment, I wanted to solve this problem to save face for Glenn and the other Asians because what had happened to Glenn was in full view of other convicts.

"Is this guy in your wing?"

"Yes."

"Okay, I'll talk to him about what happen between you and him."

Glenn was in E wing, so that night I went to E wing. There was a group of people called the MAC (Men's Advisory Council), where each member represented his own racial group, and I was the MAC representative for Asians. That's why I was allowed to visit the different wings, which convicts were normally not allowed to do. After I got to E wing, I met with all three Asians in E wing—Glenn, Ray, and Andy—at the front of the wing.

"How you guys doing? Everything all right?" I asked.

"We are doing okay."

"I am here to talk to the guy Glenn had problem with, so watch my back for me but stay distance from me so I can talk to him alone."

Ray responded by saying, "Okay, two of us will be up on the stairways, and one will stay on the first floor stairway."

Ray was short, about 5′5″, but he was smart and conducted himself more skillfully than the others. As I started up the stairs, the blacks caught sight of my movement with the three Asians, so by the time I got to the guy's cell, small groups of blacks waited for us near the stairways on the third, second, and first tiers. I saw the way the blacks positioned themselves to protect the guy I was about to talk to, as if ready to confront any problems from the Asians. So I turned and waved my hand at

Ray on the second-tier stairway and to the others, signaling them to return to the first tier and go back to the TV room because we were drawing too much attention. When the blacks saw all three Asians withdrawing to the first tier, they also came off the tiers, but two remained on the first floor to watch me. I knocked on the guy's cell, and he came to the door.

"What happening?" I said through the door by way of greeting.

"Hey Lee, whassup. Don't you remember we was in West Hall together?" This refreshed my memory that he was a BGF lieutenant. We were speaking to each other through his door, but just then, cell call time started, and the guards opened all the cells for prisoners to come out or go in their cells. So he came out of his cell, and we went over to the second-tier stairway. After exchanging greetings, I explained what the problem was.

"You know, the day when you acted like you was going to hit him, then laugh about it—my guy felt disrespected."

"Lee, your guy was right behind me. I don't know if he was going make a move against me or not."

"No, my guy Glenn is new to the system and didn't know better than to be too close behind someone. I'll talk to him about it." At this point, I had to come up with a face-saving deal for both of these guys, as the BGF member understood this was a serious matter of respect.

"How about we do this," I said. "I'll have my guy apologize to you for coming up too close to you, and you apologize to my guy for raising your fist at him." I knew this BGF lieutenant was a bit hardheaded, but he saw my reasoning was right.

"All right, sounds good to me," he said.

Both of us went to the first floor under the watchful eyes of a few BGF members. I pulled Glenn aside and told him, "You was in the wrong for following too close. When you follow someone that closely, he take that as sign you may try to make move on him. So apologize to him for following too close, and he will also apologize to you for using his fist against you."

I then led Glenn to the BGF guy, and both guys apologized to each other. Afterward, I talked to the BGF. "Listen, you know these guys are bit new, so any problem you or any your guys have with my guys, I will set things right."

"All right, Lee, I know I overreacted, but you know how it goes. From now on, I'll have my guys give your guys room and respect them."

"Thanks, I appreciate you helping look out for my guys."

"It's all right, Lee. I know you way back to West Hall. I know you're good people so don't worry about your guys. Everything is cool."

After that, I told Ray and Andy, "Glenn said everything is all right. I will see you tomorrow."

Such small matters, if not resolved in the right away, have led to race wars. With the convicts, it's all about respect. With life in prison, sometimes you're living on top of ocean waves, never knowing when the next wave you encounter may overwhelm you, or if you'll be strong enough to survive whatever waves may come, small or great.

Free Enterprise

One day, I saw Steve and David with Kim on the grass by the handball court. Steve and David were lying down without tops on, getting sun-tanned. I thought to myself, "These guys are not taking prison life seriously as if they were in summer camp." I went up to them.

"What you guys doing? This is not a beach but a prison. How you guys going to react if something came down in yard, and you guys have to go into action?"

They looked as if they were still on the beach. Kim turned to me and said, "Nothing is going on in the yard, so forget about it."

"Bullshit," I said, "we should always be ready any time or place we are at." I walked away, not wanting a confrontation with Kim over these guys. David would listen to me when not around Kim, but Steve was less likely to learn. Steve's position was tight with Kim after Steve arranged to smuggle in weed through the free man he worked for. The cash raised from selling weed went into Kim's pockets, and the commissary dockets went into a bank for any Asian to use for his needs. Kim was about to be released, but his interest lay in pocketing the cash from Steve's weed. He was just a selfish, self-serving guy. Even though I had a Latino guy in my wing selling the weed, I made sure all takings from weed sales went to our bank. After a while, I started keeping my distance from Kim and Steve, for I saw they were into only self-interest and less concerned about the rest of the Asians.

I regretted teaming up with Kim as well as breaking ties with Joe and the Chinese, but I still felt good about working with the new Asians. All of the new Asians stayed out of problems and remained free of disciplinary action. We empowered ourselves by supporting each other in all situations and planned to help any future Asians coming to Tracy so that no Asian had to stand alone or be victimized by other races in Tracy.

Except for Steve, all the other Asians were learning well from the experience I had gained in Tracy before they arrived.

Two problems came to my attention regarding the sale of weed. One was when my Latino weed seller told me another Latino refused to pay five dollars he owed, arguing the weed was no good. So I went to the guy's cell to talk to him. When I knocked on his door, I saw him through the small window. I thought to myself, "This is going to be trouble—he's one of best boxers in Tracy." But when I said, "What your problem paying for the weed the guy was selling for me?" The guy went pale. I think he knew I was in line with the other Asians and friendly with Babo and D.R.

He said, "Lee, next time I go to the canteen, I will get the dockets to pay you off."

"All right," and I left his cell door.

Another weed buyer was in debt to us for about twenty dollars. He was an African American, and when I went to E wing to talk to him, Ray pointed him out. It turned out he was the young guy who was raped a year earlier in C wing. Since this situation crossed the racial line, I just told him he needed to pay. He took me seriously. Then I went over to J wing to find one of the BGF leaders I knew. I explained that the African American guy needed to pay his debt to us. Would the leader make sure he came through for us to avoid any problems? He agreed to make sure the guy would pay up.

After four years in Tracy, I was taken seriously by each person I talked to. This may have had to do with the way I conducted myself. As a convict, I had spent two and a half years out of four years in the lockup units, and everyone was aware I didn't play games. Though small in number, the six Asians I ran with in the mainline were viewed as solid convicts by the rest of the convicts in Tracy.

Death of B.B.

One night an alarm bell went off in F wing, which housed prisoners who were close to being released, and so it was mostly a problem-free wing. Within minutes, I saw prison guards rush by with a gurney, carrying someone with half his face mashed in. The next day, I talked to Chinese David, who said the victim was B.B. He was killed by NF guys on the third tier and then thrown onto the first tier. Rumors ran that B.B. was trying to organize his own gang, especially with San Francisco guys within the NF, and for that reason, he was killed. (Later I learned that many NF guys from San Francisco turned PC after B.B. was killed.)

A few days later, one of the NFs came up to me. "Did B.B. ever talk to you about anything?"

"No," I said, ending the conversation.

Shortly after B.B. was killed, I heard a rumor that the NF wanted to take over all poker games on the mainline or else wanted a percentage from the poker games. This move was mainly aimed at biker Spider's poker game in E wing, but I decided to shut down my poker game in C wing. Then a couple of NF members approached to ask me, "Why did you close down your poker game?"

I gave an excuse. "There was not enough guys to keep up the poker game."

"We are opening our own poker game, so why don't you come and play in our poker game?"

"No, I am too short on money," I said.

Playing poker with the NF would cause problems, so I shut down my poker game. In fact, when the NF opened their poker game, no one played because the NF members were too serious as convicts. Most likely, D.R. was the brains behind trying to control the poker games. The prison administration's reason for letting Babo and D.R. into the mainline was to keep the violence down, but instead the violence got worse. After B.B. got killed, both Babo and D.R. were transferred out of Tracy. But in the six months that Babo and D.R. were in the mainline, there were two kills, and the NF in the mainline got much better organized than before.

Baseball Bat Attack

With Babo and D.R. back in the Hole and soon to be transferred out of Tracy, the mainline NF continued to tighten their control. They tried to extort money from the main poker game in E wing, run by Spider, the biker leader of the whites. In doing this, the NF underestimated the whites, who were unwilling to cooperate with the NF's demands. One early evening during yard recall, the whites, under Spider's leadership, attacked anyone who looked to be Latino or a member of the NF with baseball bats.

When the attack on the NF took place, I was in C wing and didn't go out for night yard that evening. Alarms sounded throughout the whole prison as if a full riot had broken out. It was more of a race war. I heard gunshots from the yard as the gun tower guards tried to break up the fight between whites and Latinos. One of the NF members in J wing, seeing what was going on in the yard, started stabbing a white prisoner in the wing. For a while, prison guards ran around the mainline corridors without knowing what was taking place. To the guards' credit, the yard and mainline were brought under control within twenty minutes.

The incident took place mainly in one area of the yard. If the whites had attacked all over the prison in the wings and the yard, it would have been a full-scale race riot, and many prisoners would have been killed. The NF was caught totally off guard in underestimating the whites' will to stand up for themselves and not be pressured by the NF. I believe the whites made the right move against the NF by standing up for themselves. The NF overplayed their power, thinking the whites would not fight back.

After the guards brought the prison under control, the mainline went on lockdown. Next morning, I was let out of my cell to go work as the food manager clerk, and Glenn was also allowed out for work. I told Glenn why the whites attacked the NF, and said, "Be very alert, and whenever we go to the kitchen to eat, we go together."

The white and African American kitchen workers were also let out to work in the kitchen. But all Latinos were on total lockdown because the prison administration was fully aware that if both whites and Latinos were let out at the same time, there would be a full bloodbath with many whites getting killed. The NF was too highly organized not to be seeking revenge for the baseball bat attack. When the Latinos came to the chow hall to eat, all the whites were locked up, and the kitchen was locked to protect whites in the kitchen.

For first time in Tracy's history, prison guards covered each of the three dining areas. About five or six sharpshooters with Mini-14's looked down from on high over the dining rooms and through the dining room windows, just in case the NF overpowered the dining room guards and took the keys to open the gate and go after the whites in the kitchen. The prison administration was taking no chances in underestimating what NF would do to retaliate against the whites.

When Glenn and I went into the kitchen for our breakfast and lunch, we got sour looks from some of the whites because they knew my association with many NF members. But since I was equally friendly with Spider and many of the whites, I was not going to let hard looks from the whites intimidate me. I noticed that a few whites who used to greet me in the kitchen no longer said anything to me. Up until now, both whites and blacks used to exchange greetings with me of "What's happening?" and made special meals for me and Glenn to share. But now, even the African Americans seemed to keep a bit of distance from me when they saw the hostile looks from the whites toward me.

At mid-morning on the second day at work, a sergeant and a prison guard came to the food manager's office and ordered me and Glenn out of the office. The sergeant talked to Mr. Wong, and then came over to me.

"I want to warn you," he said. "I received information that the whites want to kill you because of your association with many NF members. I came to get you out of the kitchen, but Mr. Wong assured me you're not having any problems, and he needs you to work at the office. So it's your choice. If you want, you can go back to your unit with me, or take a chance and continue your work with Mr. Wong."

"No, I will stay and continue my work," I said.

"All right, that's your life, not mine." Then the sergeant left. When I returned to the office, Mr. Wong said, "The sergeant wanted to remove you from working in my office, but I told him no. As long as you're willing to work for me, I'll back you up all I can. Do you feel all right to continue working in my office? If not, I understand."

I really appreciated Mr. Wong's regards toward me, backing me up so I wasn't taken away and locked down with the rest in the mainline. But two days later, a lieutenant, sergeant, and two other guards came by the food manager's office at mid-morning. The lieutenant said, "All right, Lee, we are taking you back to your cell. We've received too much information that whites plan to make a hit on you in the kitchen. Also, we found weapons yesterday in the kitchen. We won't take any more chances on your continued work in the kitchen."

Mr. Wong tried to speak up on my behalf. "Lee can continue to work at my office, and the gate between the main kitchen and my office will remain locked at all times."

The lieutenant said, "Mr. Wong, I understand you want to keep Lee as your clerk, and I know he does good work for you, but we received too much information that Lee's working in your office is a danger to Lee's life. My orders came from the warden's office. I am sorry, Mr. Wong."

Mr. Wong looked upset, but with orders coming from high prison officials, there was nothing he could do. It was not in his power to keep me working at his office. I believe Mr. Wong understood that the prison administration was showing racism. The whites were allowed to work in the kitchen, but Latinos were not. And now, even as an Asian, I was not allowed to work. While the administration sorted out the race problem between whites and Latinos, the prison administration could have ordered only African Americans to work, but they chose to show one-sided racism by allowing whites to come out to work while keeping all Latinos locked down.

Since the lieutenant had no orders regarding Glenn, Mr. Wong turned to Glenn and asked him, "Since Lee is not allowed to work in my office, do you still want to work for me by yourself?" I think Mr. Wong's question to Glenn had a deeper meaning. It was a way of warning Glenn that if he worked without me, his close association with me might put his life at risk without two of us to back each other.

Glenn understood the question and said, "If Lee can't work with me, then I don't want to work by myself."

Mr. Wong said, "I understand. You guys be careful." With a bit of anger and disappointment, he told the lieutenant, "Well, you're taking both of my best workers away."

The lieutenant ordered the guards to pat search us, and we were handcuffed behind our backs. With a satisfied look on his face, the lieutenant escorted me and Glenn out the kitchen side door and returned us to our units and cells to be locked down with the general population. When the lieutenant escorted me to my cell, I said to him, "You know I don't have anything to do with NF."

The lieutenant replied, "Well, you've got a choice. Either fall in with the NF or else with protective custody."

I had no intention whatsoever of going into protective custody.

From this point on, I was allowed to go to chow only with Latinos for about a week. The mood among the Latinos was silent. They were the victims of a baseball bat attack, yet whites were allowed to come out to work in the kitchen while all Latinos remained on lockdown. We could see clearly the prison administrators' racism, which is all too common throughout the California prison system.

About four months earlier, someone had written up a 128 conduct report, stating that I was associated with NF. I knew that kind of information could get me killed by the enemies of NF, so I asked an older white convict to help me file a writ requesting that this 128 report be removed from my central file. The older convict, who was a jailhouse lawyer, showed me how to file the writ with the Stockton Superior Court, and I won. The judge stated that the Tracy prison administration showed no proof I had ever been associated with NF. He ordered that the 128 conduct report be removed from my central file with a statement that there was no association between myself and the prison gang.

I won my writ, but the prison administration did as they pleased. About a week after I was removed from the food manager's office, the prison administration decided to move all NF members and their associates or superiors from the mainline to East Hall. At this same time, they decided I should move to East Hall, too, along with a Filipino named Aguila.

Lockdown with NF

When we got to East Hall, we were on total lockdown. We were given brown-bag food three times a day. After more than a week of mistreatment, the NF decided to riot, and non-NF prisoners joined in. The riot mostly involved throwing burning objects through our cell windows out onto the tier and throwing water or whatever else at the prison guards when they came onto the tier wearing riot gear to take convicts to the Hole in K wing. I was one of the many convicts taken to K wing. So many prisoners from East Hall were taken to K wing, the prison administration had to place two convicts in each one-man cell. After a few days of rioting, the guards decided to take some of us back to East Hall due to the overcrowding in K wing. One guard who was friendly toward me told the other guards, "Lee was not one of the guys in the riot." So the guards let me out and returned me, handcuffed, to East Hall.

The prison authorities agreed with the NF's demands to set up the East Hall kitchen for us to eat hot meals and to be allowed to go out to West and East Hall yard. The guard I was friendly with picked me as one of the kitchen workers.

While in the yard, Aguila and I received a message placed inside a handball and thrown over the fence. We saw Ray and Andy through the fence between the mainline yard and West and East Hall yard. We threw messages in the handball a few times back and forth to let each other know that we were all okay.

One day while working in the kitchen, I was pulled aside by Sanchez, an NF guy I knew from C wing. He told me they wanted one of their people to take my job. The way he talked to me was more like a pressure move because I knew Sanchez didn't have any rank in NF, for I knew all the high-ranking NFs in East Hall.

"I'll talk to Carlos about it," I said. I was on good terms with Carlos, who was an NF leader.

"Don't go talk to Carlos. He can't do nothing about it." This no-body in NF was trying to pull rank over Carlos.

I told him, "Bullshit. I'm going to talk to Carlos anyway."

But that afternoon before I had a chance to talk to Carlos, the kitchen guard pulled me aside and told me I was fired for some BS reason. I guess Sanchez went to the kitchen guard, and the guard didn't want any problems, so he fired me. I knew if I had talked to Carlos, he would have taken my side, but since the guard fired me, there was no reason for me to go to Carlos over the job matter.

Since Aguila and I had no bad disciplinary reports in our central files and were not involved in the war between the NF and the whites, we had done nothing that called for being locked down. So we both filed prisoner appeals for being wrongfully locked down with all NF members in East Hall. The Tracy administration turned down our appeals, but our appeals went all the way to Sacramento, and we eventually won our appeals with orders that we be moved out of East Hall.

Chess Moves

After our successful appeals, the classification committee decided to send Aguila and me to the lockup unit of L wing to see how we would adjust there. Though we had done nothing wrong, we were still sent to the lockup unit of L wing, where Spider and the whites who attacked the NF with baseball bats were all housed. Knowing we were moving to L wing, Carlos came over to me. "Just be careful of those bikers." He was concerned for my safety. However, if I chose to stay in East Hall, I would be labeled as an NF or NF associate, so I had no choice but to accept the move to L wing. Also, since I was on friendly terms with Spi-der from playing cards with him, I thought his view toward me would be good. I planned to talk with him as soon as I got to L wing.

As Asians were so few in number, it seemed we always needed to talk to the leaders of other races whenever there were signs of problems for us. We stayed out of all problems as much as we could. We were liv-ing in a jungle where only the strongest survived, and if we Asians showed any weakness, we would perish in the mad world of prison.

When I consented to move to L wing, it was like diving into the perilous waves of the sea. My only hope lay with knowing Spider, who would see through the prison administration's attempt to set me up to be killed by the bikers in L wing. These setups were planned by prison administrators and guards alike. They decided to move me to L wing right after a white prisoner was almost stabbed to death by NF in a corridor on his way to R&R. He was stabbed numerous times and almost died of his wounds. Transferring me to L wing was like giving raw meat to hungry lions bent on revenge.

When we arrived in L wing, Aguila and I were placed on the first floor, along with a third convict, whom I later learned was named Morrison Needham. There were just three of us on the first floor. Needham was a white biker with numerous tattoos on his body symbolizing white power.

After a few days on L wing's first floor, the three of us were transferred to the third floor and housed with the rest of the L wing prisoners. I was in a cell on the east side of L wing and Aguila was on the other side. The next day, we were allowed out to the yard.

In the yard, whites stayed on the west side with the handball court, and African Americans remained on the east side with the weight-lifting equipment. I felt the tension in the yard coming from the whites, who sent hard looks toward me and Aguila. Next to the guard cage, a stainless steel table was located right at the midway border between the whites and blacks. Me and Aguila sat at this table and were soon joined there by an African American. We introduced ourselves, and I was surprised to learn the African American's name was Johnny Spain. He was one of the San Quentin Six, convicted of killing a prison guard during the attempted escape of George Jackson, who was BGF's founder and killed while trying to escape.

Johnny Spain sat at the table every day, where he and I played chess. As I sat at the table, I looked to the white side and saw about twenty-five whites in the yard, along with Spider. I think Johnny Spain sat at the table between the whites and BGF so as not to involve himself with the BGF. On the BGF side, I saw my friend Jo-Mo, along with a few others I knew. On the white side, I saw a few whites I knew from the mainline. After a while, Jo-Mo came over and sat at the table with us. Since Johnny Spain was viewed as a solid convict, especially among African Americans, we didn't have to hide our conversation from him.

Jo-Mo flashed his big smile, "Hey Lee, how you been?"

"I been all right, but these guards keep locking me down."

"I know how that goes. I remember you from the first time they lock you down in West Hall four years ago."

"I spend about total of year and half locked down in the past four years."

"Well, you know, Lee, let me tell you something. Those bikers and whites are going to try and make a move on you. Watch your back.

I want to help you out, but we in BGF are not at war with the bikers. But I will give you my support any way I can."

"Thanks, Jo-Mo, but I hope everything will turn out all right."

"Okay Lee, watch your back. If you need anything, I'll be around." This meant that if I needed a prison-made knife, Jo-Mo would help me out with that.

"Okay, I be seeing you in the yard."

Jo-Mo was sincere in what he said. He was telling me that since I was not NF, which was allied with BGF, they saw my problem with the whites as my own affair. I needed to take a stand on my own, but if I asked the BGF, they would supply me with a knife since many of the BGFs knew and were friendly with me.

I looked toward the white area. It looked like Spider was having a meeting with most of the whites. No one made any eye contact with me. I was in the L wing yard with most of the whites who went after the NF with baseball bats about six months ago. Yet I was removed from my job at the kitchen because the administration and prison guards received so much information about threats to my life by whites. While I worked with Mr. Wong, his office by the kitchen was protected by a locked gate; yet the prison administration said my life was too much in peril to continue working there and transferred me instead out of the mainline and into a locked-down East Hall unit where almost all convicts were NF and associates.

And now the administration had decided it was safer for me to be in a lockup unit with the whites who attacked the NF with baseball bats. It was a stone-cold setup. Had they returned me to the mainline instead of transferring me to East Hall with the NFs, at least there were other Asians in the mainline. Few in number as the Asians were, I stood more of a chance of meeting with whites and settling our differences in the mainline, but the L wing AC was totally different from the mainline.

On the second day in the yard, I called out to Spider and walked alone to meet him at the handball court on the white side of the yard. To put both of us at ease, we sat on the ground. As I talked to Spider, I noticed that a white guy I knew from the mainline stood around nearby, as if he were Spider's bodyguard. Spider started the conversation by asking me, "What do you want to meet me about?"

"Spider, you know me from the mainline. I got nothing to do with NF. Whatever problems you guys have with NF is none of my concern."

"Well you know a lot of NF, and you just came from East Hall, so if you want to stay in the same yard with us, I want you to give us names of all the NFs you know."

"I can't do that," I said. "If things were other way around, I wouldn't be giving up names of you and the guys you're with."

"If you're not going to give up the NF names, you can't stay in the same yard with us," Spider said.

"Spider, you know me and the other Asians well in the mainline. I am not going to get involved with you guys' war with NF. Think about it."

I left the meeting with that statement to Spider. While I was meeting with Spider, the whole yard was watching us, including guards in the yard and gun tower. I returned back to the table where Johnny Spain was sitting and started playing chess with him. I think Johnny Spain guessed what the meeting was about—that I was trying to secure myself in the yard with the whites. I didn't talk with Johnny Spain about my personal problems with whites, and he asked no questions.

I knew the reason Spider was asking for NF names was so the bikers could make up a hit list of NF members. There was no way I was going to get weak and give up NF names. I saw a few of the NF as personal friends.

There were about twenty-five whites in the yard, and I told Aguila to continue staying alert because as soon as they could, the whites would move against us. My chess games were not fully up to my best, for my mind was focused on how to survive in the yard. I wondered when and how the whites would move against me. As long as I stayed in the middle of the yard at the table, the only way whites could move against me would be to come over to the black side, so I had some ground from where I could see the whites' movements.

I have to give Spider credit for being up front with me and not playing games to give me a false sense of security. I think that was due to his knowing me well in the mainline, where we had gotten along very well. Also, he had to tell the rest of the whites why I couldn't be in the same yard with them, so it was a face-saving move for him to be up front with me. He couldn't change the way the other whites viewed me.

Every day, Aguila and I sat at the table with Johnny Spain, playing chess to pass the time. As for the rest of the yard, the whites kept to themselves without getting involved in any activities. It seemed as if the prison guards were waiting for the showdown between me and the whites. Playing chess with Johnny Spain, I didn't make much conversation. Both of us were aware of great tension in the yard, which could explode at any time.

As I played chess with Johnny Spain, I respected him highly for his decision to sit at the same table with me. If anything came down, he would be in the direct line of fire from the gun tower. The gun tower guard could kill him and call it an accident since Johnny Spain was one of the San Quentin Six, who were convicted of killing and wounding prison guards and convicts in the San Quentin AC in 1972. Johnny Spain was aware that prison guards would kill him on any pretext, so he was taking a big chance with his life by spending the whole yard time every day with me and playing chess or having light conversation.

I noticed the whites continued to be less active on their side of the yard, so five days after my first meeting with Spider, I signaled to him for another meeting. Same as before, we spoke on the handball court on the white side. Aguila came with me and stood back about seven or eight feet. The convict acting as Spider's bodyguard held a street-cleaning broom and acted as if he was sweeping around the handball court. He stayed about six or seven feet in front of me, which allowed me to watch him as a protective move. In the second meeting, Spider said the whites would move against me unless I gave them names of the NF I knew. The meeting lasted less than five minutes. Then me and Aguila returned to the table and rejoined Johnny Spain. I was disappointed. I had not come to an understanding with Spider, and my life continued to be in danger while I was in L yard.

End Game

On October 8, 1977, about six days after my last meeting with Spider, our wing was released out to the yard at 10 a.m. It was a hot day, so I wore a tank top. As I came out into the yard, I noticed all twenty-five whites were having some kind of meeting. After half an hour, I noticed seven of the biggest whites were all wearing jackets or sweatshirts. These seven guys started walking toward the black side of the yard and seemed to be going over to lift weights in the weight-lifting area. I was sitting at my usual spot at the table at the border between the white and black sides, playing chess with Johnny Spain. I asked Aguila to watch the movement of the seven white guys and to strike if any of them came toward me and him.

The yard had the very highest tension level since I'd come to L wing. With the tension so high, the white guys walking toward the weight-lifting area seemed to be moving in slow motion as they walked in groups of two and three. I noticed Morrison Needham was last, walking behind the others and closest to me. I made a decision right then to go after Needham before he could join the other whites to regroup and attack me and Aguila. Without looking at Aguila, I went toward Needham, who was about ten feet from me. I moved at a very fast pace, and before Needham could fully see me, I rushed at him.

Instead of fighting back, Needham grabbed my tank top and jerked me toward him with his left hand. I put down my arms to push him off me and felt a hard object on his waist. I knew it was a prison-made knife, tied to a piece of loose rope. Needham reached for the knife at the same time, but was just a fraction slower than me. I pulled the rope, and the knife was in my hand. I made stabbing moves. We were bent over a little. In one stabbing motion, I felt the knife strike deeply. The struggle may have lasted one or two seconds.

I soon heard the gun tower guard shouting down, "Knock it off!" If the gun tower guard had seen any weapon, he would have first fired a shotgun warning. He was armed with a shotgun in his hands, a Mini-14 on his shoulder, and a handgun on his side. But the gun tower guard never fired.

As I heard the tower guard shout, I started walking slowly backward toward my table. Still watching Needham, I prepared for the rest of the whites to rush at me from the weight-lifting area about fifteen feet away. Backing up, I was going to throw the knife toward where the BGFs were standing. But then I noticed Jo-Mo had his arm up, holding Big Red against a fence. Even though Jo-Mo was a foot shorter than Big Red, it looked like Jo-Mo was stabbing Big Red in the lower chest area. Seeing this and not being sure what might happen to the knife I'd taken from Needham if I threw it on the ground, I tossed it onto a low part of the roof of L wing. By then, I felt safe from any whites rushing at me. After I threw away the knife, I saw the yard gates open to let a group of guards in. The gun tower guard told them, "Grab the guy in the tank top!"

Two of the guards pushed me against the fence and handcuffed my hands behind me. They led me out of the yard over to W wing where the prison hospital was located and ordered to undress. One of the hospital doctors examined my body while one of the guards took some pictures of me. During the whole process, my mind was numb in a state of shock from trying to comprehend what had just taken place. I also felt a great sense of relief for having escaped the death trap I had been in for two weeks in L yard.

The guards kept me in the hospital for about half an hour before taking me to the Hole in K wing and placed me in a tiny cell. I waited in the cell for about five or six hours. As I waited, I kept thinking about how bad Needham had been wounded, knowing I was lucky to get out of L wing unhurt. I knew Aguila was all right as I'd seen him standing near the BGFs, but I wondered what happened to him after I was escorted out. I also wondered what would happen to me now. I knew if I tried to explain to the prison officials what happened in the yard, they would not believe me. As I was waiting, I thought, "How long am I going to stay in this small cell where there is not enough room to sit?" I found I could kind of sit by having my full back to the wall and putting my feet up. The cell was too small for me to sit cross-legged. Another possibility was to kneel, which I refused to do. None of the guards said anything to me. Around dinnertime, a food tray was given to me; I ate standing up with the tray propped against my chest and the wall.

Thinking over the altercation between me and Needham, I thought he must have grabbed my tank top to get a good hold on me so he could stab me in the same manner as many stabbings I had witnessed. With my fast reaction, I luckily took the knife from him. Since metal detectors were used on all convicts coming to the yard, he could not have brought the knife with him, but the knife (or knives, since three knives were eventually found) may have been lowered down through a cell window. The white area of the yard was below their cell windows, right under the gun tower and out of view. I thought to myself, "I may have escaped getting stabbed today, but there will surely be future attempts on my life, and I will need to stay alert at all times."

After hours of waiting with only my boxers on, the guard ordered me to put my arms behind me out through the food tray slot to be handcuffed and then led to a conference room where the classification committee for prisoners in lockup units sat at a large table. The five people in the room included a lieutenant, sergeant, prison guard, and two other people in plain clothes, one of whom was a detective from Stockton. The detective read me my rights and said, "You are charged with murder in the first degree and will be facing the death penalty for having a prior first-degree murder conviction. Do you have anything to say?"

I replied, "No."

The charge of first-degree murder and facing the death penalty sent chills through my mind and body because I was not aware until that moment that Needham was dead. I was then taken to a cell on the first floor facing east and noticed Aguila in a cell near me. I guessed he had been brought to the Hole while I was being checked out in the hospital. I wondered if Jo-Mo was also in the Hole or if he had gotten away with stabbing Big Red due to all the confusion between me and Needham. After I was placed in the cell, my next-door neighbor called to me softly, "Hey Lee. You all right?"

"I am okay," I said in a calm voice. He was one of the NFs I knew.

"Hey Lee, you want a smoke?"

This surprised me as we were not allowed to smoke or have personal property in the Hole, and the first tier was only for convicts newly arrived in the Hole.

"Yeah."

Through the bars, he offered me one hand-rolled cigarette and a few matches. I badly needed the smoke. I asked the NF, "What's going on?"

"We had a riot on the second tier," he said. "And they put most of us down here on the first tier. We brought some tobacco with us, and we smoke four times a day to make the smokes last while we are down here. You and your friend will be issued your share whenever we smoke. We should be going back upstairs in four or five days."

"Thanks."

He knew better than to ask me what happened in the L wing yard, so I said nothing about it. The NF possibly knew what happened from the guards working in the Hole.

It felt strange to feel so little about the death of Needham, for I had never stabbed or killed anyone before. I felt guilty for caring so little, but maybe deep within my mind, I had become a changed person from witnessing so much violence in the four years of my imprisonment. I may have no longer felt what I was supposed to feel, like soldiers must do on the battlefield. For convicts, each day was like a battlefield. You struggled to stay alive, and your enemies no longer existed as human beings. If the whites had regrouped themselves to charge me with their knives, I'd have been dead.

Chapter 4

Defense Committee

Nuestra Familia's Loyal Soldiers

In the Hole I felt safe, for I no longer had to think about being attacked in L yard. But I still did feel a constant undercurrent of tension and potential violence since most convicts in the Hole had very violent histories of prison-related killings or stabbings, and some had been there for months or years. But I maintained myself as I had in other lockup units, exercising self-control and keeping my thoughts and business to myself. I avoided having problems with anyone at all costs.

First, I figured out who was on the first tier with me. From prior experiences, I already knew some NF and a few BGF members. The NF tier leader was known as Little Oso (Little Bear). He was in the Hole for stabbing a white prisoner in J wing during the whites' baseball bat attack on NF six months ago. I'd never met the BGF leader before, but we were soon on friendly terms. In a week, all the NF on my tier were slated to move to the second tier of the Hole, where most convicts were NF or BGF. I would be moved with them.

I took note of the only non-NF Latino on the tier, a young man nicknamed Pancho, who was about nineteen. Pancho was in the Hole because he killed Kenko, a Latino who had been in prison for some years and saw himself as a spokesman for Latinos in the mainline. In reality, Kenko had served as a mouthpiece for the prison administration. From time to time, he'd broadcast his views on prison radio, explaining why the mainline was better off without the NF. One day, Pancho got into Kenko's cell and stabbed him to death. Pancho then cleaned up all the blood, pushed Kenko's body under the bed, and let himself out the next time all cell doors were unlocked. It was a clean hit, but a prison snitch must have informed on him. Pancho might have had some connection to NF, but he seemed mentally disabled—very violent and uncontrollable— and for these reasons, the NF did not recruit him. Any member unable to follow the NF's military chain of command would be killed by fellow members, as B.B. was.

As it happened, both of B.B.'s killers, Sanchez and Yuba, were in the Hole on my tier with Sanchez in the cell next to mine. Just prior to transferring to the Hole, Sanchez and Yuba had been housed in F wing, which was the area for inmates preparing for release from prison. After many years of imprisonment, both were so close to freedom—Sanchez had five months left on his sentence and Yuba had fewer than sixty days—when the NF ordered them to kill B.B. and make a public spectacle of B.B.'s killing as a warning to all. Sanchez and Yuba did their duty as NF soldiers, carrying out orders fully. They tossed away their near freedom when they threw B.B. off the tier. Later, they pled guilty to second-degree murder and received new prison sentences of five to life. Although eligible for parole in five years, both knew their involvement with NF meant they'd probably serve many more years before seeing any chance for parole.

I knew Sanchez, who was in his early thirties, from previous times in lockup units at Tracy. One time in the past, I remember Sanchez had recently returned from a brief release on parole, and I talked to him in the yard. We didn't discuss our cases, but I asked him, "How long was you out of prison?"

"I was on the streets five days," he said, "but man, I didn't feel comfortable at all on the streets. I feel I don't belong out there. Man, I am so glad to be back in prison. I don't want to go back out there again."

"Man, what matter with you?"

"Lee, all I known is prison life, and I belong here because I feel so uncomfortable on the outside. I can't never adjust out there."

"Well that's your life. Do what you got to do," I said. Sanchez had fully internalized prison as the only life he knew.

As for Yuba, one night after my shower, I decided to stop by Yuba's cell. He probably used a prison-issue plastic mirror to see me coming, and when I got to his cell, he was standing just a few feet from the bars. Yuba was 6' tall and well built. When I'd known him before in East Hall and the mainline, I'd always seen him wearing the hard eyes and face that are normal for hard-core convicts. But this time, when I saw his eyes and face, they were stone hard, much harder than I'd ever seen.

"Hey, Yuba, how you doing?"

"Okay."

When I looked in his eyes, they were the hardest eyes, filled with so much hate that I sensed a man of deepest sorrow, like a dead man going through the motions of life without hope. The depth of his eyes communicated that he didn't want to be bothered by anyone, and his only aim was just to kill and kill, to strike at his deepest sorrow.

It was time to return to my cell. "All right, Yuba, I see you later."

"Okay, Lee, see you in the yard tomorrow."

In all my years in prison, I never saw another look of so much hate and anger as I saw reflected in Yuba's eyes that day. Yuba was a product of prison, as was Sanchez and thousands of convicts whose lives are so altered by prison that they find it almost impossible to adjust to life in free society when they are released. Prison life can be compared to a combat zone, where you need to be able to fully trust the man next to you, for your very life depends on him. But in prison, you're in the combat zone twenty-four hours a day, seven days a week, and fifty-two weeks a year. Most people take the simple view that if you can endure and survive all those horrible conditions for years of imprisonment, then surviving in free society should be easy. Free society will never be able to live alongside men like Yuba and Sanchez, unless there is some long-term program of readjustment for released convicts.

As hardened convicts, we can endure anything, psychologically, that the prison system imposes on us. We are conditioned to endure the imprisoned way of life by learning specialized survival skills. When freed from prison, however, we may view the whole of society as one large prison with different survival rules. Most freed convicts are unable to adapt to the changed rules for how to succeed. We may have been highly successful as prisoners in terms of surviving within the prison system, but in the free world, we are like babies trying to understand ourselves and how to belong to society.

Ex-prisoners who successfully adjust to free society are usually first-time offenders who have served short prison sentences. They stand the best chance. But those of us with longer-term penalties become so familiar with our positions that we grow afraid to face the great unknown jungle of free society. Many of us were institutionalized since youth through juvenile detention and the world of street gangs in our communities. The prospect of a normal life can seem like a made-up dream world. We have dreams about rejoining free society unable to understand its rules, so we become loners withdrawn into ourselves. After so many years of dreaming about freedom, we don't know how to grasp the reality of the dream.

It should be unacceptable both to free society and to convicts that all are victimized by the way the system is designed to fail for released prisoners. Great change is needed for society to live whole and free.

Leonard Tauman

On October 10, 1977, I received a visit from the public defender of San Joaquin County, Leonard Tauman. Meeting him in the attorney visiting room, I thought he looked about thirty years old. He said he would represent me on the prison murder charge, and then he asked, "What happened?"

I explained the events in the L wing yard. Then I pleaded with Mr. Tauman to look into the Chinatown case. "I'm totally innocent of the Chinatown gang murder charge," I said. "If I was cleared of that wrongful conviction, I would not be facing the death penalty."

We met for about an hour. Finally, Mr. Tauman said, "Yes, I will look into the Chinatown case. At some point, you should expect a visit from the public defender's investigator. I'll do the best I can, but your case seems very complex. It will take time. For now, we need to sort through evidence on the murder charge currently facing you. Tomorrow, you will be taken to court in Stockton to be arraigned, and I'll meet you briefly then. Afterward, I will return in a week to discuss the case in more detail. Is there anything else you want me to know right now?"

"No, I'll see you in court tomorrow," I said, "and I look forward to your future visit and the investigator's."

After Mr. Tauman's visit, I felt a bit uplifted. When he agreed to look at the Chinatown case, I saw a ray of hope that the case might be reopened.

Back in my cell, I wrote to Ranko and my mother about the new murder charge. Ranko's response was slow, but I received a quick reply from my mother and my white sister, Mary. Their letter stated that whatever problems I faced were my own problems, and I should not bother them; they wanted nothing more to do with me. They had taken this same stand on the Chinatown case, so I wasn't really expecting their help, but the letter saddened me anyway. Their tone was so cold. In a time of great need for moral support, I felt sad that my mother and sister felt so far from me. We might as well have been strangers to each other.

Knowing I would receive steady moral support from Ranko and Reiko comforted me greatly. I understood there was nothing Ranko could do for me other than to give me her supportive friendship which I cherished above all else, along with Reiko's. As long as Ranko and Reiko remained my steady friends, I felt I would somehow be okay, and my heart felt lucky that I could continue to stand as a man with dignity in the lonely world of prison. But the world I lived in was so far away from any public understanding. I was just a lone man climbing toward a mountain peak with no other aid than Ranko and Reiko's moral support.

On the day of my court appearance for the arraignment, I underwent the usual routine at my cell—getting strip-searched, wearing only boxers, being handcuffed in back—before my cell door opened. While a guard carried my clothes, I was led to the front gates of the tier. Between each gate, I was stopped for more strip searches. My prison jeans, blue shirt, shoes, and socks were returned to me before I was led out to the yard. Fully clothed again, I was placed in a waist chain with my hands cuffed to the sides. In addition, leg irons were placed on my ankles, limiting my walking to half steps.

We went downstairs, where three other prisoners waited to visit the Stockton court building. Sergeant O'Neill and two other white guards prepared to escort me. I already knew Sergeant O'Neill from the mainline as someone who was on friendly terms with the Chinese. He was in his midthirties, and the other guards, whom I'd never seen before, seemed in their midtwenties. Sergeant O'Neill explained to me, "We will be your escorting guards for your court appearance. Just maintain good conduct, and we will treat you with as much respect as you show us. Any questions?"

"What can I take with me to court? Can I take smokes and books?"

"The only printed materials allowed are legal papers. I'll allow you to take smokes, but any smokes you take out of prison you cannot bring back in. Anything else?"

"No."

I was taken outside to a parked plain car and ordered to sit in back. All three guards sat in front with Sergeant O'Neill driving. After a twenty- to thirty-minute ride, we entered an underground parking garage at the Stockton courthouse. Once inside the courthouse, I was placed in a large holding cell.

Sergeant O'Neill said to me, "I am going to remove your leg irons, but if you start acting up, they'll be back on tight, you understand?"

"I understand," I replied.

With the leg irons off, I waited for an hour before being taken upstairs, where some court guards stood around drinking coffee and BS-
ing. Sergeant O'Neill asked, "Want a cup of coffee?"

"OK," I said. However, before I could finish the coffee, a court official announced that the court was ready for me. Sergeant O'Neill led
me into a mostly empty courtroom, along with two prison guards and
the court deputies. The judge read off the charges and set a preliminary
hearing date two months away. A few paces away, the district attorney
sat next to some other guy in plain clothes, maybe a police inspector.
The D.A. was a small man, about 5'6" and looked to be about thirty years
old. He wore badly fitting clothes and had an agitated expression on his
face. Mr. Tauman, sitting next to me, said quietly, "He's one of the best
D.A.s in San Joaquin County. Don't underestimate him."

A New Kind of Hole

With the leg irons back on, I was placed back in the car for the return trip
to Tracy. I looked out the car window and enjoyed the view, trying not to
allow worst case scenarios about whatever I might face in court to get the
best of me. Bright anger burned deeply within me because of the injustice
I was forced to continue enduring. The police framed me for a murder
I didn't commit, and now the system wanted to impose the highest sentence on me—death—because I defended myself against the white convicts. What an upside-down justice system! But even if I were in the darkest
tunnel of my life, I had to look for the light. Without any hope, the injustice
would kill me sooner than any life or death sentence. As the prison motto
goes, "Never give up, never surrender."

I returned to Tracy once again and went through the routine strip
search before returning to my cell in the Hole. This was a new kind of
Hole, much different from the Hole I had experienced back in December 1973 when I first arrived. Now the prison administration gave each
prisoner a black and white twelve-inch TV and a few hours of yard time
every other day. Two small yards on either side of the tier were empty
of equipment except for a high concrete wall that convicts used for a
handball court, and no other activities, such as weight lifting, were allowed. The yard now had a gun tower. Every other day, each convict was
allowed out of his cell to shower for twenty minutes. Altogether, we stayed
in our cells forty-five out of forty-eight hours.

While the TVs and yard time were much welcomed by the convicts,
I think these recreations were designed by the prison administration to

control our thought processes. Prison administrators were determined to prevent violence against the guards, so everything we were allowed to do served their goal of mental control. The prison administration used the pleasures of TV and yard time as tools for keeping the prisoners passive. Without these kinds of programs, all the convicts in the Hole might feel anger toward the guards and each other. As it was, ever since the convicts received TVs and yard privileges, there had been no violent actions among convicts or any stabbing of guards through the bars. The convicts no longer covered the bars with blankets to hide in the darkness of their cells, and there were no sounds of zip guns at night. The lighting was still dim, but convicts passed the time by reading, studying, watching TV, or writing letters. The tier was very quiet.

However, even in the Hole, the prison gangs still controlled the tiers that they occupied and oversaw the TVs and yard privileges. Nothing was said between the guards and convicts, but an unspoken truce between them was understood by both sides. Convicts would not take any abuse from the guards, and new guards were trained by more experienced guards on how not to take abuse from convicts. In small ways, the convicts still had the upper hand, for the guards' lives were always at risk. Even from our cells, we could make spears and zip guns to hurt or kill the guards, which the guards understood well. They knew they faced possible danger whenever they came close to the convicts, when serving meals, taking counts, or exchanging our clothing.

Convicts also came in close contact with guards during visits to the yard. Before going to the yard, we handed over all clothing to the guard for a strip search, and afterward put our boxers back on. Then we put our hands out of our cells through the food port to be handcuffed behind our backs. Once reaching the gates at the front of the tier, once again we were fully stripped and searched, rehandcuffed, then escorted to the yard where we were unhandcuffed after the yard gate closed. The guards then returned our prison clothes and we dressed in the yard. It was dehumanizing to undergo strip searches and have hard metal detectors passed over our bodies, but it became a matter of expected routine for the convicts. As for the guards, dehumanizing the convicts was also a daily ritual. However, new guards were often surprised to see convicts go through the routines automatically without the guards saying a word.

When the three-hour yard period ended, we were handcuffed in back through the port in the yard fence and then led to a small holding cell by guards holding the few inches of handcuff chains. There we underwent the same routine of handing over our clothes to be searched, undergoing a strip search, putting our boxers back on, and then being rehandcuffed in back and escorted back to our cells, where the guards threw our clothing into the cell and locked the cell before removing the handcuffs.

I don't know how the guards could stand to do their jobs of looking under the prisoners' balls and into their assholes so many times a day. I guess they must have gotten used to carrying out strip searches, just as the convicts got used to undergoing them. However, I think convicts never felt indifferent to the degradation of being strip-searched. We just learned never to show our emotions about it. The degradation, dehumanization, and entrapment within all the rules of the prison jungle built up inside like the fire of hell, seeking release for the anger, but somehow we controlled our emotions. We were very much aware that if we released our inner anger, we might no longer respect ourselves as human beings. Especially in the Hole, we continually kept ourselves in check to endure the passage of time. Within every convict was acceptance of each of us who held his own and stood up to do his own time. This shared way of thinking united the convicts in the Hole, who viewed the guards as standing below us as human beings, even though the guards acted superior to us.

Who Should Be on Trial?

After the first court appearance, Mr. Tauman came to visit me in the attorney's room, and once again we discussed the case. Having thought it over carefully, I said to Mr. Tauman, "The prison system should be put on trial for setting me up to be killed!"

I tried to explain why. First, the jury needed to know that I was a lone Asian wrongly seen as an associate of NF. When the NF tried to move in on the white bikers' poker games, the bikers attacked with baseball bats, starting a race war between Latino and white prison gangs. To prevent NF members from retaliating, the administration moved them to the East Hall lockup unit and decided to move me with the NF, which made me look even more like an associate of NF. Meanwhile, the administration said they had information that my life was endangered by whites who believed I was with NF. Soon after that, the administration transferred me to L wing, knowing full well I would be a target of the whites, the same white bikers who had attacked NF with baseball bats and who outnumbered me twenty-five to one. So anything I did in L wing was in self-defense. I tried to explain to Mr. Tauman how the prison system forced me to act in self-defense.

But Mr. Tauman was not willing to put the prison system on trial. He said the trial would focus only on issues concerning the events in L yard on October 8, 1977. He didn't seem to understand my reasons, based on my first trial experience, for distrusting the legal system. He had agreed to look into the Chinatown case, yet how could he reopen the Chinatown case if he didn't get what I was trying to tell him about the prison system? It troubled me that Mr. Tauman was entrusted with my life, yet seemed positioned for a losing fight. Would I be the victim of injustice once again? I tried to have faith in Mr. Tauman, but I knew the prison trial was set to take place in one of the most racist counties in California. What hope did I have of winning if Mr. Tauman didn't put the prison system on trial?

"We need to show the jury I was acting in self-defense!" I said again, but Mr. Tauman continued to disagree.

K. W. Lee

One day, I received a letter from a newspaper reporter from the *Sacramento Union* named K. W. (Kyung Won) Lee. He said he wanted to meet me in person, and I wrote back saying I would gladly meet him. However, when I mentioned K. W. Lee's planned visit to Mr. Tauman, he said, "I advise you to stay away from newspaper reporters."

I did not understand this advice. "No, I plan to meet the reporter," I said.

After all, I had nothing to lose, and no reason to keep the outside world ignorant of the gross injustice of my cases. Since I was in the Hole, any visitors I received would see me through bulletproof glass and speak one at a time through a phone link. Late in November, about a month and a half after my death penalty murder charge, two middle-aged men came to visit me. I could tell right away by their facial expressions that both men were Koreans. Mr. K. W. Lee introduced himself and started the conversation by saying he had read my name somewhere.

"I thought it looked like a Korean name," he said. "Are you Korean?"

"Yes, I am Korean," I said. "However, I can't speak Korean anymore for arriving in the United States at an early age."

K. W. Lee asked me about my life, such as when I came to the United States and how I ended up in prison. I explained to him that I came to the United States in November 1964 to join my mother and my younger American sisters. I told him a little bit about my life in the United States and how I was framed for the Chinatown gang murder case. I felt warmth and interest from K. W. Lee and from the other visitor, Mr. Jay Yoo, who told me his name when K. W. Lee gave him the phone. Mr. Yoo smiled warmly and said he was going to law school at UC Davis and would soon take the bar exam. For now, he worked at the Sacramento legal aid center and would try to help with my struggle for justice in any way he could. Once again, K. W. Lee came to the phone and asked me more about myself. Then he asked, "Is there anyone I should contact regarding the Chinatown case?"

"You must contact Ranko Yamada. She can tell you all about it," I said.

I gave him Ranko's full name and address in San Francisco. Even though convicts, especially in my position, naturally do not trust strangers, I felt total trust toward K. W. Lee and Jay Yoo.

By the time our long visit was over, I felt a growing bright light at the end of the long tunnel where I had been in such darkness for four years. It was as if heaven felt my inner tears and sent two angels to guide me. Seeing their interest in my struggle against injustice, I was filled with hope without even knowing whether K. W. Lee and Jay Yoo could do anything to support me. It could have been false hope, but for whatever unknown reason, I had feelings of complete faith in these two good men. I was in the highest state of mind since my imprisonment.

Until then, Ranko alone had shared my struggle, standing by like a great mountain. Now, not only I, but Ranko too, would be encouraged by K. W. Lee and Jay Yoo's involvement in my case, and she would no longer endure my imprisonment alone, so I was very glad, not only for myself but for Ranko's sake. As soon as I returned to my cell, I wrote to Ranko about the visit and told her we now had reason for hope in two trustworthy people we could rely on without second thoughts. K. W. Lee and Jay Yoo might not be able to help, but my first impression of them set up an unshakable faith in their good intentions. I asked Ranko to give whatever information she had about the Chinatown case to K. W. Lee.

Prior to the prison murder case, my situation was hopeless. Ranko must have fully realized this without letting me know. But I continued to cling to false hope for justice. Unwilling for years to let go of false hope, I now had a true reason for hope. Was it the thinking of a madman to have hope because of one visit from two strangers? Perhaps it was the hope of a most desperate man looking for any reason to turn false hope into reality.

I also wrote to my mother about K. W. Lee and Jay Yoo, and informed her that Mr. K. W. Lee might contact her. My mother's reply letter was cold as can be. She was not going to talk to anyone about my case. My mother seemed to fully trust the American justice system. She believed I was guilty in both cases and had no faith in my letters to her about my innocence. Without any care for a suffering son, she viewed me as a disgrace. She and my sister Mary wanted no association with a disgraced man.

In contrast, Ranko neither encouraged nor discouraged my illusions and thoughts about the justice system. She was more silent in her support, showing her noble self only in her actions; that is the kind of person she is. Any time a person speaks of Ranko, it is with deep respect. Her motives are pure, and she is one of those rare people who is modest about past and present accomplishments.

Speaking Truth to Power

I was not aware at the time that K. W. Lee had also contacted my friend Tom Kim, former director of the Korean Community Service Center in San Francisco and activist for Korean and Asian American communities. I had met Tom a few times in Chinatown before my arrest in June 1973. He was aware of my Chinatown murder case and gave his support to me at the time, but like Ranko, he couldn't find any eyewitnesses willing to come forward to refute the false charges against me. The witnesses not only feared the Wah Ching but the SFPD as well. San Francisco police officers on the Chinatown gang task force intimidated people with threats like, "What we did to Chol Soo Lee, we can do to you if you come forward as a witness to anything related to his case."

What disappointed me most was a Chinese American SFPD officer who, at the time of my June 1973 arrest, was aware of my innocence and knew the facts of Yip Yee Tak's murder case but chose to remain silent even when an innocent man might be put to death. Just as a code of silence operates in the criminal underworld, a "blue wall" of silence applies to police officers. Even the public knows this "blue wall" exists. I got a chance to speak with this Chinese American officer ten years later, and I asked him, "Why didn't you bring my innocence to the attention of the SFPD or the D.A.?"

"I had just joined the police force in 1973," he said, "and my higher-ups in the department would not have believed me or would have just ignored me. Back then, only a few Chinese Americans had started to join the SFPD."

I cannot find any excuse for this police officer, who was raised in Chinatown, for keeping his sense of justice to himself. As I see it, he was unconcerned about my case because his main concerns were job security and the "blue wall" of silence. Instead of serving his honorable duty to protect the community, he suppressed his knowledge of my innocence. It seemed he sorely lacked the personal courage required to seek the kind of justice that Dr. Martin Luther King, Jr., championed during African American struggles to gain civil rights. In fact, as the example of Dr. King's life clearly showed, those who do have courage to speak truth and seek justice are not guaranteed success or personal reward. Instead, they might risk their job security, personal safety, and their lives.

When K. W. Lee got involved in my case, he had no way of foreseeing the consequences he might face personally. Other journalists who questioned flaws in the justice system had been known to attract powerful enemies. Before my case was brought to public view by K. W. Lee, another courageous investigative reporter, Mr. Raul Ramirez, wrote in the *San Francisco Examiner* about the case of Richard Lee. Like me, he had been convicted of a Chinatown gangland murder and was serving a life sentence in Tracy, where he was a part of Joe Fong's group of Chinese convicts that I had befriended when I first arrived. Raul Ramirez's articles raised questions about the events leading to Richard Lee's sentence.

Around that time, Richard Lee filed a writ with the San Francisco Superior Court and was granted a hearing to contest his sentence. However, the court did not grant his writ for dismissal or for retrial of his case. Seeing this, the SFPD and the D.A. decided to file a multimillion-dollar libel suit against Raul Ramirez for his reporting on Richard Lee's case. A defense committee on Mr. Ramirez's behalf then hired attorneys who fought a ten-year legal battle until the court finally dismissed the case against Mr. Ramirez. Meanwhile, an untold amount of San Francisco taxpayers' money was spent to prosecute Raul Ramirez at no benefit to anyone, besides making Mr. Ramirez's life very difficult. The injustice of these actions by SFPD and the D.A.—to attack an honest man for doing his job as an investigative reporter—should raise questions about their motives. How do retaliatory lawsuits like this affect citizens' understanding of the legal system, and whom it serves?

Like Mr. Ramirez, K. W. Lee is a great man of the highest order of personal integrity. As long as we have people like K. W. Lee and Raul

Ramirez working as investigative reporters, the public will see the truth about questionable actions. The sorrowful thing is, truth can take such long years to be revealed.

In all fairness to the unselfish and honor-bound among police officers, many in law enforcement also desire great honor. Anyone who does their duty or work out of total unselfishness is someone I can respect.

Harassment

My daily routine in the Hole started with rolling up my mattress after breakfast. If there were letters to write, I wrote on whatever paper or books I could get hold of rather than going to the yard. I didn't start watching TV until late in the afternoon.

One day, I was in the yard and found Aguila on the first floor facing the yard in the K wing PC. I could already guess he had sought PC to escape the NF in East Hall. As the lone Asian, Aguila was under a kind of pressure I understood, so I didn't ask him to explain. Instead, I asked if he knew how the rest of the Asians were doing in the mainline. He informed me that Kim was also in PC in K wing, and Pinoy would soon be joining them in K wing. Steve and Stan, the guys who were half white and half Japanese, had transferred out of Tracy after being in PC. Ray, Andy, Glenn, and Carlo were still in the mainline, but Carlo might soon get transferred to Vacaville.

Most importantly, none of the Asians in the mainline got hurt after the events in the L wing yard a few months back. The whites in L wing yard had targeted me in their war with the Latinos, but they could have used my Asianness as a reason to attack the few Asians I knew in the mainline, simply because prison society was ordered along racial lines. So I felt very relieved to hear news that everyone was all right. I was a bit disappointed with the other guys for resorting to PC, being too weak to stand among the hard-core convicts. However, with only a few months left before his parole date, I could understand that Aguila wanted to go home and feared the gang members.

On my next visit from Mr. Tauman, he brought along a police department investigator, and we went over the case again. Mr. Tauman had found many flaws in the Chinatown case records, and he agreed that reopening the Chinatown case was important to the prison case. I mentioned the visit from K. W. Lee and Jay Yoo, but Tauman still advised me to stay away from newspaper reporters. I kept wishing I had a less passive, more outspoken attorney who would publicly expose the Chinatown case and show how I was set up on the prison case, but Mr. Tauman seemed intent on keeping both cases inside the court system and away from public attention. Believing there should be publicity for the injustice of my case, I went against Tauman's advice and started giving interviews to K. W. Lee.

Prison authorities were wary of news media and knew that K. W. Lee wrote for the *Sacramento Union*. As a result, I started getting mistreated. I was given negative reports for any little bit of prison rule violation, especially for mouthing off at guards. Whenever the guards started problems with me, I usually ended up in solitary confinement. I especially clashed with a new officer named Diaz, who was in charge of the second tier that I was on.

Based on his interviews with me, K. W. Lee wrote a two-part feature news article describing my early life in the United States and raising questions about the Chinatown case. When the story first appeared in the *Sacramento Union,* I was placed in solitary confinement on the first tier in a punishment cell for almost no reason. The cell had a concrete bed and mattress, and a hole in the center of the cell where the toilet used to be. I was allowed to have nothing else. After I was moved there, Diaz and another guard entered the cell with me while I was dressed only in boxers. They handcuffed my hands behind my back, and along with physical intimidation, they trash-talked at me. I talked right back at them since the guards were saying they couldn't be intimidated. Within five minutes, the guards left and closed the cell door.

This treatment left me in a very depressed state of mind. Somehow I found a small pencil and started writing to K. W. Lee on toilet paper about my situation. I got hold of stamps and envelopes from another convict to mail out the toilet paper letter. When K. W. Lee wrote back, he encouraged me to stay strong, but I could see that K. W. Lee was not in a position to investigate the mistreatment of prisoners. In my time in prison, I never wrote to people outside complaining about my troubles inside prison. This letter to K. W. Lee in 1978 was the one and only exception. Anyway, by the time his reply letter reached me, my ten days in total solitary confinement were over.

The harassment continued back on the second tier. Sometimes I returned from court after dinner had already been served to the other prisoners. One time, my food tray was laid out uncovered on the open floor. It took a court order to enforce a prison regulation that my lunch or dinner should be served warmed on a food tray.

Another time, I returned to find one of the better-tasting dinners on my tray, a piece of meat. Before eating, I turned the meat over and saw what looked like a pubic hair. I called to the tier officer, Diaz, for an explanation.

Diaz and the sergeant of the Hole came to my cell, and the sergeant said, "What's the matter?" I showed him the pubic hair on the meat in the dinner tray, whereupon he laughed. "Well, it looks like a hair. I guess the kitchen worker must have lost his hair while he was cooking the meat."

As both he and Diaz continued smiling, I threw my food tray at them, putting whatever food was on the tray all over their uniforms. This resulted in a report of disrespecting the guards and solitary confinement on the first tier once again. This kind of mistreatment continued, and I believe it was motivated by racism. It felt like something more than plain old harassment.

The other nonwhite convicts on the tier knew I had survived a racial setup in L wing, so they decided to give me support in the form of protest actions short of rioting. We knew that convicts trusted by the guards did janitorial jobs like sweeping the mainline tiers, but they were not allowed entry into the Hole. The tier in the Hole was swept by prison guards. Seeing this, convicts in the Hole prepared to protest by saving up their trash items. One day, just after the guards finished sweeping the tier, one of the NF or BGF leaders called out, "Trash out!" And then all the convicts threw trash out of their cells onto the tier. By this action, the convicts gave notice to the guards to check themselves against harassment, or else worse actions could be taken against the guards. After this, the harassment toward me lessened. However, I still would not eat any food left for me by guards when I returned from court.

I saw how the conditions and practices of the prison system could make a grown man act in such pitiful ways, like a boy or a bully would act. Since it was no longer acceptable to hurt convicts physically, it was all about psychological warfare. Convicts were no longer viewed as humans, but as animals in need of taming, like dogs by their masters. This is another reason you found the strongest of human spirits in prison Holes, much stronger than convicts in the mainline who just went along with the program. We said fuck the psychological program—we are human beings and desire to be respected as humans.

By contrast, what the prison guards desired most from convicts was not respect or humanity. They wanted to force us to obey. To this end, most prison guards abused their power over the convicts and tried to demean us. The guards had duties to discharge, but their methods set standards for good versus bad prison guards. Thousands of convicts dealing with guards learned to read the psychological types of guards and gauge which guards were bullies and which were strong or weak. Most prison guards assigned to Holes or adjustment centers, especially the newer guards, were trained to conduct their duties like big bullies who must prove they are better and stronger than the hard-core convicts. Few in number were those guards whose good and firm way of relating to the convicts earned respect from the convicts.

Convicts in the Hole were there to do time, and any convict who got out of line with each other would be killed. However, most followed the code of conduct set by prison gangs, which allowed convicts doing years in the Hole to live side by side without any problems. We were supportive of each other. For example, each race of convicts set up stores to meet the needs of convicts who had no incoming funds from the streets and to provide the disadvantaged of their own race with commissary purchases of soap, tobacco, coffee, and so forth without any obligation whatsoever.

In the daily struggle between convicts and guards in the Hole, it was easier for the guards to pressure a lone Asian than contend with Latinos or African Americans on the tier. The reality is, I received only limited support from the Latinos and African Americans. However, I never asked for their understanding of my position as the lone Asian. To ask for support from others on the tier would be seen as weakness. Determined not to show any weakness, I stood alone.

Movement

Mr. K. W. Lee continued to interview me numerous times, getting the full picture of my life and the Chinatown case. When he was not interviewing me, he read transcripts of my trial and interviewed anyone he could find who might have some facts about the case. I learned later that K. W. Lee put his job and reputation of twenty-five years as an investigative reporter on the line by involving his newspaper's coverage of my case. With the risks involved, K. W. Lee could not afford even the tiniest of mistakes in the articles he wrote. Still, he continued, and in late January of 1978, when the *Sacramento Union* published K. W. Lee's two-part feature article about my life and questionable guilty verdict in the Chinatown case, some concerned Korean Americans decided to organize a defense committee on my behalf.

The Chol Soo Lee Defense Committee (CSLDC) began at the home of Dr. Luke Kim and his wife, Grace Kim, in Davis, California. The Sacramento area had a small Korean population, and a handful of concerned Korean Americans met to form the committee. They were good people. Mr. Jay Yoo, who advocated for Koreans at a legal aid center, was elected to be the CSLDC's coordinator and started raising funds to support justice on my behalf through Korean church communities in Sacramento. As it happened, many Koreans were able to identify with my lonesome journey in the United States and my lonesome struggles for justice. The Sacramento committee grew, and K. W. Lee's articles circulated among more Koreans, gaining more supporters.

Under the leadership of Jay Yoo, support sprang up in other parts of the United States, especially in the San Francisco Bay Area. Koreans started asking how they could help and got in touch with Mr. Yoo to organize more outreach. One of the first Korean churches in America, the Presbyterian Church on Stockton Street, got involved under the direction of Reverend Cha. Mrs. Doris Yamasaki, founding member of a Buddhist temple in San Francisco, also took up the cause. Together, Reverend Cha and Doris Yamasaki started building a Korean CSLDC in the Bay Area. Setting aside their religious differences, they united behind the cause of bringing the light of justice into my dark journey.

Meanwhile, Ranko Yamada visited local colleges, and law students in their early twenties formed an Asian American wing of the CSLDC in the Bay Area. Marking a significant moment in Asian American history, a joint struggle for justice brought together foreign-born first-generation Koreans in the United States with American-born Asians, forming a pan-Asian movement. As news of my plight spread throughout America, the CSLDC expanded from Los Angeles to New York to Hawai'i, and even got attention overseas in Korea. It was a proud time for all Asians to be building a broad-based coalition to work for justice. As the funds for the legal defense of my case started to pour in, Mr. Jay Yoo coordinated the whole effort.

In the beginning, this was all happening without my knowledge. Until just months earlier, my only support had come from Ranko and Reiko. At first, I was unable to comprehend all the support the Koreans and Asian Americans were giving me. But soon, I started writing thank-you letters daily, and hundreds of people had received my personal thank-you letters. It was truly miraculous that one Korean reporter who took interest was able, through his investigative articles, to awaken a great sense of justice in thousands of people on behalf of one Korean doing life in prison and facing the death penalty.

Preliminary Hearing

Two or three months after being charged for the prison murder, a preliminary hearing took place in the Stockton court. At the hearing, the judge ruled that sufficient evidence had been established with Needham's death for me to be held over to San Joaquin County's Superior Court in Stockton for murder charges with the death penalty, and Judge Chris Papas was assigned as my trial judge.

In the trial to come, Mr. K. W. Lee attended almost all of the defense and prosecution motions regarding the prison murder case. Years later, K. W. Lee told me that Judge Papas complained to K. W. Lee about his biased reporting on my case. Yet at the same trial, an elderly female reporter, who was a close friend of the judge, was also writing articles about the case in the *Stockton Record*. In fact, Mr. Tauman said Judge Papas often ate lunch with her. To me, it seemed unusual for a judge to eat lunch with a reporter who was covering a death penalty trial over which he presided as judge. Shouldn't common sense restrict a judge from close relationships with media reporters covering his ongoing cases? After all, even a defense attorney cannot personally approach the judge.

This friendly informality between the judge and the *Stockton Record* reporter perhaps suggests something about a small town in the rural county that provided the setting and the jurors for my trial. San Joaquin County included the small cities of Stockton and Tracy, which were both near DVI prison. Hundreds of prison guards, administrators, free men, and other employees of CDC worked for the Tracy prison and lived in San Joaquin County. If you belonged to this population of just over two hundred thousand people, chances were you knew many of your fellow citizens and belonged to a close-knit community.

When the case started to make headlines in local newspapers, it wouldn't have surprised me if employees of the Tracy prison had discussed my case with people in their families, churches, neighborhoods, clubs, and so forth. Surely, the prison employees would have supported the prison's official version of my case and thus spread the false story to many more people who did not work for the prison system and who knew nothing else about the case.

Meanwhile, more news media started paying attention to both sides of the story. Mr. Raul Ramirez started covering the case in the *Oakland Tribune*. Asian Americans also raised more awareness of the racial injustice in my case. In my cell, I was able to watch some TV networks in Northern California, and I found a half-hour program on Oakland's Channel 2 called *Asians Now,* airing on Saturday mornings.

In early 1978, I received a letter from Professor Elaine Kim, the director and host of *Asians Now,* asking permission to interview me. I consented to her request. It was my first-ever TV interview. Within a few weeks, Professor Elaine Kim, Mr. Han Yun, and Ms. Young Shin arrived at Tracy prison for the interview. I was handcuffed in wrist chains in my front as I was during interviews with K. W. Lee. The TV interview took place in the visiting room on a day when no other prisoners had visitors.

I could sense that Elaine Kim, Han Yun, and Young Shin were a bit nervous. Before the interview, we talked in a friendly tone for about forty-five minutes while the camera and lighting got set up. I learned that Elaine Kim was a professor of ethnic studies at UC Berkeley, Ms. Shin worked for a Korean community center, and Mr. Yun worked as an administrator for an Asian mental health service program. All three were Korean. By the time the interview started, Professor Elaine Kim seemed more at ease with me.

I can understand the feelings they must have had toward me when this may have been their first time inside a prison. They had probably never met a convict, especially a Korean, who was serving a life sentence for a cold-blooded murder involving San Francisco Chinatown gangs as well as facing the death penalty for an inside prison murder. Even though I was handcuffed with wrist chains, two prison guards were ready in case I made any violent movements toward the people who came to interview me. According to state prison rules, convicts' meetings with the news media were supposed to be confidential, so when K. W. Lee interviewed me, no guards were in the room, though they remained stationed just outside of the visiting room door. However, because of the TV crew, it was decided that state prison guards needed to be present during the TV interview for security reasons.

I did not object since I had nothing to hide regarding whatever questions Professor Elaine Kim had for me. In a different sort of way, the questions Professor Elaine Kim asked me during the TV interview were much the same questions as those asked by K. W. Lee. After the interview was over, I asked for the address of Professor Elaine Kim and her associates so I could correspond with them and write thank-you letters to them. Later, I received a nice letter of appreciation for our meeting from Ms. Shin.

Sometime during the months prior to the prison trial, I received another surprise visit from Reiko. This time our visit was through a glass window and phone. During our visit, we didn't speak of the case or the conditions I was living under, but we spoke of our friendship. Even though both of us felt the pain of having to see and talk through the glass booth, I was truly glad to see my beloved friend's face. She came to visit me after she had recently given birth to her first son. I believe it was painful for Reiko to see me in the visiting booth. Perhaps she sensed some of what I was enduring in prison without my speaking about the depths of my struggles for survival. At the end of the visit, Reiko asked, "Do you need anything?"

"All I need is your friendship," I said. But I also mentioned that she could send me a birthday package in August, and that I wanted to read a paperback book titled *Shogun* by James Clavell. I explained that convicts could only receive books mailed directly from a bookstore or publishing company, and hardcover books needed to have the cover torn off. If a family or friend mailed a book, the book would be returned. Reiko said she would send me a food package and also go to the bookstore to order *Shogun* for me before leaving the US.

The visit from Reiko deeply affected me. She was the friend I had known the longest, and her unwavering friendship continued even as we were thousands of miles apart. Living in Kobe, Japan, with her family, Reiko's spirit of friendship continued to reach a convict in prison. Our friendship has the deepest kind of love—spiritual, not physical or personal. Love, I believe, is the highest order of friendship that can be shared between true and unconditional friends. Within a week, I received a copy of *Shogun* as well as the food package after Reiko returned to Japan. After I read the book, I passed it on to other convicts on my tier, who always returned it to me in good condition.

Convicts in the Hole were not allowed to make any phone calls, so during one of my court appearances I requested a court-ordered phone call and was granted ten minutes. That evening, I called Ranko while a prison guard listened to the conversation on another phone. Ranko was upset that I had asked her sister Reiko for food packages. "From now on, send the package slips to me," she said, "and I will mail you the food packages."

Convicts were allowed four food packages per year, and convicts could have up to five cartons of cigarettes in each package. One package could arrive in the month of your birthday, and three Christmas packages were allowed during the month of December, with each package weighing no more than fifty pounds. Ranko stayed true to her word, and in the month of December 1978, I received three food packages for the first time. Each must have weighed the full 50 pounds, a total of 150 pounds' worth of different sorts of foods, along with 15 cartons of cigarettes, which must have been purchased in stores. From 1978 on, I received all four packages each year. After 1980, the food packages were mailed to me by the CSLDC rather than by Ranko or her mother.

Each time I received a package, I was given a third of the food items, along with a few cartons of Camels, from the convict store on the tier. When the gang in charge of the tier store distributed the package items, I still had more items than others. Any convict involved in a prison gang gave his whole package to their gang store, and what little the convicts had in the Hole, the NF and BGF gangs shared equally among their gang members. I would also receive the same amount of food items as other convicts received.

Everything in a prison gang member's possession belonged to the gang, including his life. But as a nongang member, I was free to do as I pleased with my personal property, while respecting and getting along with the gang tier rules like keeping the TV sound low, not throwing out trash on the tier until just before the guards reached the steps of the tier, and not talking loudly. If you wanted to say something to someone far away from your cell, you wrote it on a kite and sent it down the line, which ran from end to end of the tier, by telling your next-door neighbor to pull the line. You never disrespected the rules in your words or actions to other convicts on the tier. The penalty for disrespecting a convict was death. To keep peace and quiet on the tier, all convicts obeyed the tier rules.

You had to keep up your guard at all times. For example, taking a nap during the day or evening was dangerous because that was when convicts were allowed onto the tier two at a time for about twenty minutes to shower and visit other convicts on the tier. I remember one day when the daily time period was just beginning for two-at-a-time showers, the first NF member who came out of the shower stopped by my cell and said, "Hey Lee. Stay alert tonight."

"All right, thanks," I replied.

When the NF member informed me to stay alert, he was warning me that a stabbing was about to take place during the shower period. Sometime after the warning, I noticed when the guard asked one African

American if he wanted to shower, the convict refused. The next African American came out on the tier with his shower gear, but he was also wearing shoes. Then the guard asked two more African Americans if they wanted to shower, and they each refused. Then a second African American came out on the tier for his shower fully clothed, and while the first African American was in the shower, the second guy came over to talk to me. "What's happening, Lee?"

"Not much, just finishing writing a letter, so I can go back to my book. How about you?"

"Nothing much."

I knew the African American who stopped by my cell was friendly, but I noticed he sounded very depressed; his face carried a look of sorrow. I guessed he was the target tonight. I liked the guy, but I couldn't get involved in BGF matters. I could try to warn him, but any other action on my part was not possible under the living conditions on the tier. Then I heard his name being called by another African American in the back part of the tier from the cells occupied by the BGF's tier leaders.

"Well, I see you later on," I said.

"Okay, Lee, see you later." He started walking toward the back of the tier. Then I noticed the other African American just out of the shower. He also started walking toward the back of the tier. I took out my small mirror to watch the stabbing I was sure was about to take place, but then I changed my mind. I didn't want to see a guy I knew and liked get stabbed to death, so I just lay on my bed and listened.

Soon I heard the fast movements of fighting. By the sounds, I knew he was getting stabbed. Then I heard the guard yell, "Stop that shit!" and the sound of a small tear gas gun firing down onto the tier. Immediately, I felt stinging in my eyes and quickly wet a towel to cover my face. All the guards working in the Hole came onto the tier, followed by more guards coming off the mainline. I guessed the guy who did the stabbing dropped his knife or gave it to another BGF member to get rid of it. The stabber was handcuffed behind his back and marched off the tier. Then I saw two guards escorting the victim, whose arms were draped over their shoulders; he was partly walking and partly being carried. I took all this as a good sign that he would survive the stab wounds, but from the look of his clothes, I could see he'd lost lots of blood. After the two African Americans were removed from the tier, each convict was strip-searched and handcuffed to the rail on the tier while all of our cells were searched.

Learning from more experienced prisoners, a convict knew how to hide a weapon well. For example, he could wrap it in toilet paper inside a hollowed out crevice, so the toilet could be used without flushing the weapon down the toilet. Or he could dig small holes in the wall to slide weapons in and cover them with a mixture of concrete dust and toothpaste. Or he could cover the sharp edge of a knife with tape to hide it in his rectum. If he needed to take a knife out to the Hole yard, he put it in his rectum. The convict then didn't use the toilet for two to three days, so the knife would come out easily when he used the yard toilet. Hiding it in the rectum was also the way to transfer a weapon when going from one prison to another.

After the stabbing on the tier, we were placed under lockdown so the prison guards and administration could investigate the stabbing. After about a week, we were let back on the yard. I didn't hear anyone talking about the stabbing. Why he was stabbed was the BGF's business. In the same way, the events in my life—the defense committee, the newspapers and media attention, or just about anything I did—was my own personal business. I did not share it with any other convicts, nor did they ask me about my life. We had no privacy whatsoever, especially in the Hole, so convicts' interactions with the outside world and our inner thoughts were viewed as personal matters that we kept to ourselves.

Any privacy you could get was important, because your life was open to so much surveillance in the Hole. Every movement you made in or out of your cell was watched. Even in your sleep, you were not left alone. After lockdown, the tier guards came down to check on convicts throughout the night, flicking their flashlights into your cell. If you were covered up fully, the guards woke you up in order to see some body part like your head or arm. The guards also read all your incoming and outgoing mail, and the only mail kept confidential was mail exchanged with attorneys, courts, and news media. When you received such confidential mail, the letter was opened in front of you before you could have it.

Lie Detectors

Mr. Jay Yoo and his wife continued to visit me from time to time. Through correspondence, I also stayed in contact with Mr. K. W. Lee about once a month. Since correspondence with news media was considered private, I sealed my letters to K. W. Lee as confidential mail; his letters to me were also sealed confidential. But one day, a letter from K. W. Lee was opened prior to my receiving it. This letter contained flyers about the defense committee's activities. The sergeant and guard who gave me the letter stated that the flyers were contraband, which made no sense. Moreover, this incident showed that the prison administration was going through my mail even though the mail was marked as confidential under the CDC's own rules. Apparently, the prison administration was opening and resealing my confidential mail.

As the defense committee continued building support with more Koreans and Asian Americans joining, I received three Asian American visitors from Los Angeles—Jai Lee, a Korean American activist; Warren Furutani, a Japanese American community activist involved with Asian American programs; and Charlie Park, who had a street background. Jai Lee was about my age and Warren was a few years older. At that time, I was twenty-five. After reading K. W. Lee's articles about my life and the Chinatown case, Warren explained that they were forming a defense committee in Los Angeles and wanted to meet me in person and give me their personal support. Our conversation was natural and enjoyable, like meeting new friends. Toward the end of the visit, Charlie Park asked Jai and Warren to step out of the visiting booth for a minute. After they stepped out, Charlie Park said to me over the phone, "Hey, look at me in my eyes."

"All right," I said, thinking to myself, "what the fuck is this little punk trying to say?"

He said, "Hey, did you kill the guy in San Francisco Chinatown?"

"No," I said without hesitation, looking him straight in his eyes. Our eyes stayed locked together while I thought, "Why in the fuck is this little punk-ass giving me some suspicious fucking question?" I felt like breaking through the glass and kicking his ass. But maybe that was his street mentality, to look me in the eyes and satisfy himself about whether I was telling the truth or not. I guess my answer was good enough for him. I showed no signs of being offended.

Charlie didn't say anything else, but asked Jai and Warren to come back in the visiting booth. I thanked Warren, Jai, and Charlie for their visit and wished them well on their return drive to Los Angeles. They wished me well, too, and promised to continue working with the LADC (Los Angeles Defense Committee) to raise consciousness and awareness of the gross injustice of my case among Korean and Asian American communities in Los Angeles.

In July 1978, to ease any lingering doubts regarding my guilt or innocence in the Chinatown case, Mr. Tauman and the defense committee arranged for a lie detector test to be performed on me by Clive Baxter and Associates, one of the most respected lie detector firms in California and the United States. A two-day lie detector test was set up, in which I was asked different questions about myself and the Chinatown case. Toward the end of the test, the man who was conducting the test asked direct questions like, "Did you kill Yip Yee Tak?"

I responded, "No," which brought the lie detector test to an end.

As the man took off the wire hooks from my chest and fingertips, the lie detector man who conducted the test said I passed all the questions that were asked. Since my answers were clear throughout the test, he decided to take a chance to ask point-blank questions about my killing Yip Yee Tak, even though these sorts of questions were normally not asked. Because of my clear answers of "yes" or "no" to his questions, he felt sure of my innocence of the murder and believed my test answers would unquestionably clear me of the murder. The results of the lie detector test were written up by K. W. Lee in the *Sacramento Union*. His article may have been followed up by stories in other newspapers.

Needless to say, the complete success of the lie detector test was an event much welcomed by the defense committee. Not only had K. W. Lee thoroughly investigated my case in his two-part article, but now my innocence was backed up by a respected lie detector test. This gave people even more reason to feel convinced of the injustice I was suffering.

Habeas Corpus

Only seven months after the CSLDC was formed, it had raised enough money to hire a respected and well-known attorney, Leonard Weinglass, renowned as one of the "Chicago Seven" defense attorneys. In September 1978, Mr. Weinglass worked closely with the CSLDC to file a writ of habeas corpus in Sacramento County Superior Court. Judge Lawrence K. Karlton granted a hearing for the writ of habeas corpus.

Mr. Weinglass then hired a private investigator named Josiah "Tink" Thompson, who thoroughly investigated the case and found new eyewitnesses whom the S.F. police had suppressed before or during the Chinatown murder trial in June 1974. While attending the writ hearing, which lasted about a month, I was transferred to the Sacramento County Jail. I found Judge Lawrence Karlton to be a very dignified judge who paid close attention to details and to the new witnesses. However, he overruled the defense's motion to have the lie detector test admitted into evidence.

While I was in the Sacramento jail's single-cell tier during the writ hearing, numerous defense committee members came to visit me. The courtroom was packed, notably with Korean grandmothers and grandfathers who didn't understand or speak English, but came to the writ hearing every day and saw all the new evidence and the new eyewitnesses testifying in court. I felt a bit overwhelmed by all this support. At last, the light of justice was starting to shine in the writ hearing, brightened by the presence of numerous Korean and Asian Americans in the courtroom. I felt so humbled and grateful in my thoughts and heart to see the humanity and justice in all the people who had taken up my cause.

For five years, I felt trapped in a tunnel of total darkness where not even the thinnest light penetrated, and now the torchlight of justice had finally found me. As the San Francisco police and prosecutor continued to pursue me with no concern for justice, the defense committee pursued the full course of justice in my case. I see tragedy in the way SFPD inspector Frank Falzon and D.A. James Lassart went against the truth, disregarding their own dignity and honor, while a multitude of people united in the struggle for what was right and formed an indomitable will to suppress the evil of injustice. A lone sufferer of injustice may be silenced when he has no support, but when he is no longer alone, the voices calling for justice can be heard loud and clear.

How often do news media tell us about a wrongfully convicted man getting freed after years in prison? How many cases have there been of men on death row who were proven innocent based on DNA evidence? In my opinion, Falzon failed as a law enforcement officer in his duty to protect the public. What he actually accomplished by targeting me was to let the real killer of Yip Yee Tak get away with murder.

During the course of the writ hearing, I met a very special woman named Peggy Saika, who was married to Dr. Art Chen. Peggy visited me at the Sacramento County Jail and invited me to call her at home from jail. In the jail, one phone was shared by twenty-five inmates in single cells and was passed from cell to cell. When it was my turn, I kept my calls to twenty minutes and then passed the phone to the next cell. However, some inmates did not understand the convicts' code of sharing and used the phone for hours before they were almost forced by other inmates to pass it on. Seeing this, I started waiting until two or three in the morning when no one else wanted to use the phone. Then I would have the phone passed down so I could call Peggy, who answered in a very raspy voice.

Years later, Peggy told me that when the phone rang in the middle of the night, her husband, Art, would just pick up the phone and pass it to Peggy, well aware that it was me calling. She tried to answer as if she were wide awake. Her voice was a welcome sound to my ears, and we would talk about whatever was on our minds for about an hour or two. I called her two or three times a week, and Peggy never once hinted at any complaint about my calling at such early morning hours. She understood it was difficult for me to use the phone during normal times, especially when I was in court all day. The way Peggy befriended me in those phone calls meant so much to me. Her and Art's friendship continued, and to this day, we can still share laughter about the late-night calls. After my phone calls to Peggy, I felt as happy as one could feel in jail.

The time I spent in my writ hearing was a happy time for me. Here was my chance to have the Chinatown case opened again for a new trial. I was happy, too, because so many supporters came to the hearing, which had a deep impact on me as a human being. I found Mr. Weinglass to be a highly skilled and experienced defense attorney, who made excellent use of Tink Thompson's findings from his investigation of the Chinatown case. Somehow, he found a new witness who was Chinese, perhaps through contacts in Chinatown. The new witness saw the real killer and could testify that I wasn't the killer, but he feared for his life, as the Wah Ching still controlled the streets of Chinatown. As a result, the witness refused to testify in open court but was code-named Witness X, and was protected with a mask and his voice disguised while he was questioned by Weinglass.

Witness X's interview with Weinglass was covered by Sacramento newspapers and other newspapers. By this time, the defense committee was drawing national attention among Asian Americans. However, Witness X's testimony was not allowed to be admitted as evidence in court since Witness X refused to testify in open court. Still, the defense team found yet another eyewitness, suppressed by the police, who testified that she saw the killer's face just before the killing. She happened to have had a minor fender bender with the killer earlier the same day. She coincidentally ended up standing fewer than fifteen feet from the killing with her friends and recognized the face of the man from the car accident.

The SFPD ballistics expert was also called to the stand, where he admitted to making a "mistake" in his previous assessment of bullets found on the body of Yip Yee Tak and the bullet from the accidental gun firing in my apartment. The bullets did not match, he said. In his original testimony in 1974, the ballistics expert had stated that the bullets that killed Yip Yee Tak and the bullet dug out of the wall of the house next to my apartment were a perfect match—a mistake that my defense attorney Mr. Hintz never even tried to correct, though I repeatedly told him that the bullets from the murder weapon, a .38, could not possibly have matched the bullet from the gun I'd fired because they were different caliber guns.

Having Mr. Hintz as my attorney on the Chinatown case trial was like giving him a shovel to dig my grave, and the grave would have been permanently buried had it not been for K. W. Lee. His reporting of my story exposed the injustice of my case and spurred people of conscience to form the CSL Defense Committee on my behalf. I could have been killed in prison or legally executed, and my death would have gone unnoticed. Thankfully, now I was being resurrected from the grave through the efforts of the defense committee, whose members created a strong family of support.

As the writ of habeas corpus hearing drew to a close, attorney Leonard Weinglass and the defense committee members and supporters who witnessed the hearing seemed very optimistic that my writ would be granted for a retrial of the Chinatown case. When the hearing was over, I was once again returned to Tracy to the same cell in the Hole to await the decision from Judge Karlton. While waiting for the writ decision, I started preparing for the prison case trial, which was still being handled by Mr. Tauman of the San Joaquin public defender's office.

Soon after my return, we heard the sound of gunshots discharging somewhere in the mainline at Tracy. Everyone in the Hole and the whole wing fell silent, listening to round after round of gunfire and wondering what was happening in the mainline. Most of us started getting ready for whatever might come. Knives were dug out of walls and removed from toilet paper and other hiding places. I didn't have a prison-made knife, so I rolled up a magazine as tight as I could and firmly wrapped strips of bedsheet over it to make a club in case rioting spread into the Hole. It was a fearful experience to hear hundreds of rounds of gunfire without knowing what was happening. After half an hour, the guns went silent, but we remained alert until we received news from one of the guards.

We found out a race riot had erupted between white and black inmates in the yard, and the mainline gun tower had started shooting to separate the combatants. Within a week, I was notified by a BGF member that they planned to attack the whites with razors during yard time on another tier. The next day, I heard the K Hole yard gun tower once again shooting off round after round, using shotguns to break up fighting between blacks and whites. Many of the whites got cut with razor blades. No one was killed, but many convicts in the riot got shot with bird pellets. The CDC's rule about guards' use of guns was to use shotguns to break up fights. However, if the guard saw a weapon, the gun tower or rail guards could use the lethal Mini-14 automatic rifle.

At the writ hearing in Sacramento, I had seen many reporters and supporters, and had met Mr. Weinglass and investigator Tink Thompson, who put new evidence before the court and the public that showed my innocence. During that time, I felt like I had gone on vacation from the violent world of prison. Now I was back in the jungle, where survival took over all my thoughts, and I always had to be on guard. I was just another convict on the tier among many others.

Prison guards and administrators knew about my writ hearing, but no one mentioned it or asked me how the case was going. In regards to my case and supporters outside, I kept my thoughts to myself and didn't discuss it with other convicts but continued to follow the routine of life in the Hole. Keeping low-key was important. This attitude was respected by other convicts, who knew I was in a struggle for my life with the courts. If I won an overturn of the Chinatown case, I still could have life in prison if I lost the prison killing case.

Preparing for the Prison Murder Trial

Soon after I returned to Tracy, Mr. Jay Yoo visited me to discuss preparing for the upcoming trial of the prison murder case. Judge Karlton's decision on the writ hearing was expected within sixty days. If he ruled in my favor, then I would no longer face the death penalty. At this point, Jay Yoo asked if I still wanted Mr. Tauman to represent me on the prison case. Would I allow Mr. Weinglass to take over instead? I thought about the question. Mr. Tauman did not do a great job in addressing the Chinatown case, but he was at least willing to look into it. Plus, he knew the Stockton court system well. I informed Mr. Yoo that Mr. Tauman would continue to represent me for the prison case trial.

On January 19, 1979, jury selection started for the prison case. Meanwhile, the public defender's investigator had been unable to find any convict witnesses in the L wing AC. Even the African Americans refused to testify, preferring to remain silent. On the other hand, white convicts had vented their anger at me by telling the investigator, "They [the court] should kill the motherfucker" with the death penalty. The whites had planned to kill me on October 8, 1977, but their plan had failed. So now they wanted the courts to kill me.

I continued to ask Mr. Tauman to put the prison system on trial. I tried once again to explain why this was so important. My case of self-defense would have spoken for itself. Mr. Tauman still decided against bringing up events and issues leading to my self-defense against a group of whites, in which one died by his own weapon. Instead, Tauman decided the case would depend on staking my word against the testimony of two white prison guards. My history of good conduct in Tracy would back up the idea that I was defending myself. With Tauman's defense strategy set up this way, the jury selection began. At this point, Tauman brought in a white woman, who was supposedly an expert at picking the right jury for my trial. She even gave advice on how I should dress to better impress the jury. The color she chose was tan clothing and even tan-colored shoes. It took about two weeks to select twelve jurors and three alternates—a jury of all white men and women.

Shortly after this, Judge Karlton handed down his decision. He granted my writ of habeas corpus on the basis of the suppression of material evidence by both the police and the prosecution. He had decided to overturn my Chinatown case murder conviction! His decision made bold headlines in the *Sacramento Union* newspaper. However, the joy about Judge Karlton's decision was short lived because the San Francisco prosecutors immediately appealed Karlton's decision to the Stockton Superior Court, the same court where Judge Chris Papas was about to preside over my Tracy prison killing case. I felt the trial should have been postponed until the California Appeals Court made a decision regarding Judge Karlton's overturning of the Chinatown conviction, but it wasn't. As a result, Karlton's decision had no effect on the prison killing trial. Even though my prior murder conviction had just been overturned, I still technically had the prior conviction, so the trial proceeded as a death penalty case. This news came as a shock to my supporters, who packed the courtroom for the prison killing trial.

Packed Courtroom

The trial began in February 1979 in the Stockton Superior Court. Judge Chris Papas immediately instructed the jury to disregard Judge Karlton's decision. Mr. Tauman objected, but was overruled. From the start, the trial looked to me like it was going to be one-sided. I noticed Judge

Papas repeatedly overruled objections by the defense counsel and refused to grant the defense's motions, yet he allowed the prosecution to
introduce much hearsay into the evidence. I was unaware of a prior meeting between Mr. Tauman and Mr. Weinglass to discuss the prison case
trial. I assume Tauman did not share his strategy with Weinglass at all
and was intent on handling the case on his own. However, I soon started
to feel uncomfortable about my choice of a lawyer. Still, I had decided
on Tauman and didn't want to change my mind and ask Weinglass to
take over.

Looking around the packed courtroom, I recognized some of the
people I'd seen a few months earlier at the Sacramento writ hearing, such
as Mr. and Mrs. Jay Yoo. Also, I noticed many young Asian American
college students, many more this time than I'd seen before. By the time
of the Stockton trial, college students had formed defense committees in
the San Francisco Bay Area, Los Angeles, and New York. The multiple
defense committees accepted Mr. Jay Yoo as the national coordinator for
the Chol Soo Lee Defense Committee movement. Peggy Saika teamed up
with college students in the Bay Area and New York, while Warren Furutani, Jai Lee, and Charlie Park, along with Kelly Chung, whom I met
through letters and a few calls, inspired many more people to join the
defense committee in Los Angeles. Some of those working on the committee with Warren, Jai, and Charlie included students in their second or
third year of college who visited me in 1978, so I spotted many familiar
friendly faces in the crowd.

I also saw many Korean elders at the trial, too. Most first-generation
immigrant Koreans spoke no English but had heard about my case through
their Korean churches and Korean Buddhist temples. By comparison,
most of the young college students were not Korean but were second-,
third-, or fourth-generation Asian Americans of Japanese and Chinese
descent. This mixed group of supporters attended every day of my prison
case trial. Some came from the San Francisco and Sacramento areas and
others from as far as Los Angeles. The CSLDC members and supporters
all took pride in being part of a historic multiethnic, multigenerational
Asian American coalition, united in a common cause to seek justice on
my behalf. They came together from many different walks of life, all joining forces.

As the national coordinator, Mr. Jay Yoo wore a suit whenever he
met with the Korean community. But sometimes I saw him wearing a
black leather jacket like the kind preferred by the Black Panthers. Koreans were able to relate to me because I was born in Korea and they un-

derstood the isolated life I had in America. Like me, they had also come to America with dreams without speaking English. When they arrived in the US, they felt subjected to great injustice just like I endured as a Korean in America. What happened to me could easily have happened to them and their children growing up in America. The illusions Koreans had about the American dream clashed with the realities of difficult adjustments to American life. On the other hand, young American-born students who grew up in the civil rights era viewed my case as a political cause. With Asian unity behind a shared cause, they believed they could greatly empower Asian communities politically and provide political education for forming stronger Asian alliances.

It was clear the Korean community supported me, as did various Asian American college students. Even though heated differences sometimes arose about reasons for supporting me and the cause of justice, all of the defense committees spoke in unison about the goal to free me from injustice. Their unity achieved a great victory—a winning force for overturning the Chinatown case. Now I, with national support from Koreans and Asian Americans, looked to break the second chain of injustice by facing the challenge of the prison case trial.

Hearsay for the Prosecution

For the prison case trial, we faced a biased judge and jury who seemed to have presumed my guilt before the trial even started. The prosecution's opening statement to the jury summarized the case as follows: The defendant Chol Soo Lee was working for the NF as a hit man to kill the white biker in the L yard. The defendant used two prison-made knives according to prison guard witnesses, and the prosecution's key witness would substantiate this theory.

Mr. Tauman decided not to give an opening statement. This was a great mistake. He should have made an opening statement to frame my actions as self-defense. Apparently, Mr. Weinglass had urged Mr. Tauman to make this argument up front and severely criticized him later for not doing so. I agree that he should have planted in the jurors' minds the concept of self-defense as soon as possible. Instead, he waited until after the prosecutor presented his whole case, which weakened the defense's main argument. The jury was primed to buy the prosecutors' story, so the defense's belated claim of self-defense seemed like a cheap shot. Had Mr. Weinglass handled the case, he might have influenced jurors to keep an open mind. As an experienced criminal trial attorney, he would never have made Mr. Tauman's mistakes. As it was, the case seemed like a lost cause.

Why did I keep Mr. Tauman as my lawyer? My confidence in him predated my meeting K. W. Lee, Jay Yoo, or anyone on the defense committee. He was the first person I knew who reviewed the Chinatown case and said we needed to go after that case before the prison case came to trial. So I was grateful to him and bonded with him, and felt some loyalty to him. And even though Mr. Weinglass and Tink Thompson got all the evidence to create a winning case to overturn the Chinatown murder conviction, I believe it was Tauman's research that first shed light on the unfairness of the Chinatown trial and showed how defense attorney Hintz helped the prosecution, Frank Falzon, and James Lassart suppress eyewitnesses.

But I overestimated Mr. Tauman as a trial lawyer. He seemed weak throughout the trial. It may be unfair to Tauman to second-guess his thoughts, and I'm sure he did the best he could. I clearly had a choice between Tauman and Weinglass, and I chose Mr. Tauman. However, I wish someone could have helped me choose more wisely. Mr. Jay Yoo had experience in legal matters, and I wish he had explained to me the advantages of a highly skilled versus a less skilled attorney. I will never know if the outcome would have been different with Mr. Weinglass in charge through the whole trial.

Also, perhaps we were all reassured by the huge victory of overturning the Chinatown case, which left us overconfident about winning the prison case. Perhaps we all believed my freedom was within short reach. Regardless, I can't now second-guess what people were thinking when the prison case trial started.

As the trial got under way, the prosecution called its first witness to the stand, the San Joaquin County coroner. The coroner testified that Morrison Needham died of one wound to his throat and was stabbed in two other areas. There were tiny drops of blood on one of my shoes and a bit of blood on the left side of my pants. However, the coroner could not determine conclusively that it was Needham's blood on my shoes and pants.

Next, the yard watch prison guard testified. He said he heard the whites say, "Are you guys ready to get down?" and interpreted this as a sign of trouble. He then saw the group of five or six whites start to walk toward the weight-lifting area, with Needham being the last white to cross over between the white and black areas. After hearing the troubling remarks, the yard guard phoned the gun tower guard. While on the phone with the gun tower, the yard guard saw me walking toward the handball area, with Needham directly in line with my path. He testified that in the few seconds after I reached Needham, he saw me make stabbing motions with both my hands and then heard the gun tower guard yell "knock it off" as I backed away from Needham toward the table where I had been sitting earlier playing chess. Before reaching the table, the guard testified that he saw me throw an object on the roof of L wing.

Then Mr. Tauman cross-examined the yard guard. Did he at any time see any weapon in my hands? The guard answered "no." At a distance of twenty feet from where Needham and I met, did he see any weapon in my hands? Again, he answered "no."

I think Mr. Tauman failed to ask a number of questions that might have given a clearer picture of the situation. He did not ask the yard guard to identify where the whites had positioned themselves. They were right under the windows of the L wing building, where they easily could have received weapons passed through the windows of the cells just above them. He also did not pose any questions to clarify that convicts usually prepare to stab their victims by grabbing hold of the victim and then stabbing. Tauman's questions for the yard guard were weak.

The gun tower guard then took the stand. His testimony matched that of the yard guard, but provided some additional details. From his position sixty feet away at the northeast edge of L wing with a clear view of the whole yard, the gun tower guard saw the group of whites after receiving the phone call from the yard guard about trouble brewing in the yard. With a command view of the yard, the gun tower guard witnessed the scuffle, but did not know who started the fight. He had a clear view, especially of my left side, and said he saw my hands and arms make stabbing motions in the areas where Needham was stabbed. He said I used two weapons—one in each hand—but he didn't see me reach for any weapon or see any weapons in my hands prior to the scuffle. After I walked away from Needham, he saw me throw something up onto the east-side roof.

Again, Mr. Tauman's cross-examination questions were weak. He should have tried to clarify from what the gun tower guard saw that the whites must have crossed over to the blacks' area. This would have shown how a whole group of whites were coordinating aggressive action prior to the actual confrontation. Instead, the tower guard never considered the idea that Needham and the group of whites had been planning to attack me first.

Prosecutors then put their key witness on the stand, a former NF member named Ray Contreras. Contreras was a self-admitted perjurer, who was given immunity for nine counts of murder, released from prison, and put in the Federal Witness Protection Program—all in exchange for his testimony against me and cooperation with state and federal investigations of the NF leadership under the RICO (Racketeering Influenced and Corrupt Organizations) Act. By reputation at Tracy, Contreras had been a known ass-kisser to the NF leader in East Hall. He conducted himself as a kind of NF underling, so it surprised me to hear NF gave him the high rank of lieutenant. To me, this suggested a weakening of the NF leadership, compared to the strict standards of NF's top leaders like Babo, "D.R." Joe, and other members who did time in the Hole or adjustment centers and conducted themselves as serious-minded convicts. I think the simple fact that Ray Contreras was on the witness stand against me and was involved in the RICO investigations made him look as if he were an important soldier in the NF ranks when in reality, he wasn't.

Contreras started telling a secondhand story he had heard. Over the defense's objections, Judge Papas allowed his testimony, giving the prosecution the green light to use unreliable information as evidence. This totally contradicted the judge's ruling against the defense when he refused to allow witness evidence found by the public defender's investigator because he deemed it secondhand testimony. As it happened, strangely, the public defender's investigator had died just one day before the trial. I wondered about his unexpected death just before the trial. Could he have discovered leaders of the NF in East Hall who would have testified on my behalf and verified that I had no ties to the NF? Meanwhile, prosecution witness Ray Contreras was allowed to tell a totally fake story in court about an Asian prison gang with ties to NF. Even the CDC knew no such gang existed in Tracy. Yet this lowest of the low was allowed to testify with false information simply to provide the prosecutors with a motive to use against me.

The truth was well known within Tracy prison that I knew many NF members and just as many BGFs. I suffered about two and a half years in the adjustment centers, and for the past year and a half, I was on the same tier with NF and BGF members in the K wing Hole. It was the prison administration's decision, not mine, to house me with the NF and the BGF. My official prison records showed I had no ties to the NF and BGF. I was transferred to L wing by the prison administration, perhaps to see if I would trade information about the NF for my own life. Even according to official information on record with the administration, it was known that the whites were setting me up to be killed.

As for Asians at Tracy, the truth was that I broke ties with Joe Fong's Chinese group in Tracy so I could help out the ethnically mixed group of Asian newcomers to Tracy. Meanwhile, Contreras estimated that there were eight to nine members in the so-called Asian Family gang. Yet not one of these individuals could be identified by the prosecution, and none could be found to testify. This ex-NF rat's testimony about made-up ties to a gang reminded me of the Chinatown trial, where I was pegged as a member of the Ski Mask gang, who presumably hired me out to the Wah Ching as a lone hit man. That story was totally trumped up to supply a motive. Now here was the same shady and low tactic all over again. By using Contreras, the prosecution tried to show that my involvement with NF gave me a motive for first-degree murder.

The guards' eyewitness testimony had only proved that there was a scuffle between me and Needham. Both guards testified to seeing no weapons in my hands just before the scuffle; they didn't know who had the prison-made knife, and never saw a knife in my hands. But now Contreras testified that two knives found on the rooftop were gang-specific knives. He claimed that as an NF leader, he knew the NF had ordered me and other prisoners to make knives and that they supplied me with knives to use because I was second in command for the Asian Family gang, which was allied with NF.

This was a totally manufactured story. How could a group of eight or nine ethnically mixed Asians agree to get involved in prison gang warfare and work side by side with the NF? By association with the NF, the so-called Asian Family would have made enemies of La Eme and AB Bikers, together with members numbering in the thousands. There was no benefit in belonging to a so-called Asian gang with ties to the NF because that would have invited danger and imminent death.

Here is the true story. I knew the top gang leaders and had friendly interactions with all of them. I knew Babo and D.R. Joe Gonzales were the supreme commanders of the NF, Mark was the top officer above all BGF leaders in Tracy, and Spider presided over all white bikers and Aryan Brotherhood members. I think Spider must have also bought the false idea that Asians were involved in prison gang warfare. It was too bad that Spider, knowing me as well as he did, would not reason with me when I tried to talk to him in L wing yard. By attacking me, the whites fell for the prison administration's setup. As for the NF and BGF leaders, I tried to maintain good relations with both, so whenever a problem with

Latinos or blacks arose, I could talk to their leaders and they would have my back. I did this mainly to help the Asians avoid violent conflicts with other racial groups.

For example, after I was transferred to the East Hall, I found out that the NF was investigating how the whites got baseball bats for their attack on the NF. They suspected involvement by Joe Fong and the rest of the Chinese. Even though I was not a spokesperson for the Chinese, the NF leadership of the East Hall questioned me closely about whether the Chinese helped the whites get the baseball bats. They suspected the Chinese because Chico, David, and a couple of others worked in the tool and equipment rooms of the Tracy yard. I answered firmly that no Chinese or Asian had anything to do with the whites getting baseballs bats. I defended the Chinese in the strongest terms possible because I knew if the NF believed that the Chinese helped the whites, the Chinese would end up on NF's hit list. I explained to the NF leadership that Asians working with whites was a ridiculous idea because we stand alone and do not get involved with any gangs. Why would we endanger our lives? I know the NF leadership of East Hall believed me, and as far as I know, Joe Fong and the Chinese were never placed on the NF's hit list.

For Judge Papas to allow Ray Contreras to tell such outrageous lies in the courtroom showed how one-sided the trial was. With Papas overseeing my trial, Contreras was encouraged to commit perjury. It showed how desperately the prosecution wanted to win the trial and have me dead. Judge Papas controlled the jury by allowing the prosecution's motions and refusing to admit evidence gathered by the defense. He also disallowed witness testimony that I was not the killer in the Chinatown case and did not allow the jury to be informed that the Chinatown murder conviction had been overturned on a writ of habeas corpus.

Meanwhile, the jury appeared fearful to see so many of my supporters in the courtroom. Few Asians lived in San Joaquin County, and perhaps the white jury resented the presence of so many Asians observing the trial. Many Korean elders attended the trial not only to support my cause but also to witness for the first time in their lives a fair and just trial. They were disappointed. Judge Papas and the *Stockton Record* news reporter both displayed an us-versus-them mentality—whites against Asians—that revealed the blatant racial biases throughout the trial. Some of the elderly supporters were scared by severe and intimidating security measures, whereby they were searched and photographed before admission to the courtroom. I was disappointed that Mr. Tauman did not object to the threatening security measures imposed on my supporters or more forcefully protest Judge Papas' actions. The prosecution got everything they wanted before the trial started, while the defense always lagged behind.

Witnesses for the Defense

Now the defense had a chance to present its case. One of the most interesting defense witnesses was a man from the Los Angeles County Sheriff's Department, a county jail guard who gave a firsthand account of guarding Needham in the L.A. County Jail. This guard voluntarily testified on behalf of the defense, an event rarely heard of in law enforcement. The county jail guard testified that Needham raped other inmates and assisted two hanging "suicides" in the L.A. County Jail. In many cases, he said inmates can harm another prisoner without leaving evidence of having done the harm. It is much easier for a guard to call a hanging a suicide than a homicide, which would require a full investigation leading nowhere.

The L.A. County Jail guard testified that Needham was a white supremacist and a member of the Aryan Brotherhood, a neo-Nazi prison gang. Within a CDC prison, it should be no surprise and obvious that Needham would attack no white convicts but would instead target nonwhites like me. In fact, Needham was heard bragging to other inmates at the L.A. County Jail about his pledge to kill no white convicts once he entered the California prison system. The guard concluded by saying that he wanted to take the time and trouble to testify on my behalf because in his view, Needham was a bad character.

After that witness, very few other defense witnesses took the stand. Witnesses found by the public defender's investigator were disallowed by the judge. After the investigator died just before the trial, Mr. Tauman sent new investigators to East Hall to interview NF leaders and to interview Ray Contreras. But I wondered why Tauman didn't seek NF members or leaders who could contradict Contreras' testimony. Why didn't he find witnesses to testify that my life was under threat by the whites—a fact that was well known even among numerous prison officials? There were other possible witnesses who might have supported my defense. Why didn't he address issues that could contradict the prosecution's case and strengthen my defense before I took the witness stand? Instead, it seems Tauman believed my own testimony would be enough to counter that of the two prison guard eyewitnesses.

Mr. Tauman spent about half an hour at the court building preparing me, which seemed to be a very short time to prepare a defendant to testify in any trial. I wanted to testify about the prison system and how they set me up with the transfer to L wing. I wanted to describe the whole chain of events leading up to October 8, 1977, starting from my arrival at DVI. But Mr. Tauman said I should limit my description of events to the L wing yard and not bring up the whites' prior threats to my life while I was working in the kitchen. And I was not to refer to any other witnesses involved in the trial.

Finally, I was placed on the witness stand, facing the jury, who looked back at me with expressionless stone faces. I testified that I saw Morrison Needham for the first time when Aguila and I were briefly on the first floor of L wing before transferring to L wing's third floor with the blacks and whites. I spent about two weeks in the L wing AC, aware that my life was under constant threat by the white bikers and Aryan Brotherhood members. Even the prison guards warned me about it. In fact, everyone in the yard, including the guards, expected the whites would attack me sooner or later. It would have been a sign of weakness if one of the newly arrived ABs didn't attack me. In the yard, I noticed that the blacks, mostly BGF members, kept to the east side, and the whites, mostly bikers and ABs, kept to the west side. To stay in a neutral zone between the blacks and whites, I sat at a table near the yard guard fence cage. Even though I knew many of the blacks and whites individually, I was in a weak position, caught between the two racial groups.

Aguila and I sat at that table for four hours every day, along with Johnny Spain. Spain was a Black Panther, but not a member of the BGF. As one of the San Quentin Six, he was viewed as a political prisoner and uninvolved in prison gangs. He wanted to be a lawyer and had done much more time than I had. In L wing yard, Johnny Spain played chess with me every day while fully aware that the whites in L wing were planning to attack and kill me. He was in harm's way if the whites decided to rush me at the table, as was Aguila, who sat with us or stood around toward the black side exchanging short conversations with BGF members. If a group of whites had rushed at me, I believe Johnny Spain would have fought the whites with me because he sat with me every day like a rock, holding the full wisdom of an older convict.

I continued to testify. As I played chess with Spain on October 8, 1977, I noticed a group of whites crossing over to the black side in clusters of twos and threes. It was a hot day, but they all wore sweatshirts or prison blue jackets. Without a word being said, Spain sent me a warning signal with a flick of his eyes and small upward movement of his head toward the whites, but he did not get up from the table. By now, there were six or seven whites on the east side of the yard, mostly putting some weights together in the weight-lifting area. Needham was the last of them to go over there, walking by himself at a slow pace. He wore a light gray sweatshirt. He was about fifteen feet from the whites in the weights area and about twenty feet from the table where I was sitting.

I thought to myself, the whites have crossed over so they can control the west side of the yard and fight any blacks who might give their support to me. Once that last white guy joins up with the rest of the whites, their whole group will be together. Then they will organize themselves to carry out their plan to charge at me. But if I move fast, I still have time to attack that last white guy before he joins the group. I can attack him by myself and start fighting him with my fists. I assumed that Needham and the other whites would never expect that I would attack their group by myself.

At a fast pace, I walked toward Needham, watching him from the side of my eyes. Since his focus was probably on joining the other whites, I surprised him. Within inches of each other now, both of us acted on reflex. He turned and grabbed the left side of my tank top. My left hand and arm went toward Needham's grip on my tank top. I knew what the grabbed tank top meant and saw him reach with his right arm toward his pants. I twisted myself sideways and reached with my right hand toward the same area he reached for. Under my hand, I felt a hard object like a prison-made knife handle. Needham weighed about 170 pounds and was 5'11" in height compared to my 135 pounds and 5'4" height, but I moved faster. By luck, I got hold of the knife and started stabbing. I can't recall how many times I stabbed him because the incident happened fast, in maybe two to three seconds. The sound of the guard yelling "Knock it off!" reached my mind during this life-and-death struggle. I got loose from Needham's grip with no idea of how badly I may have stabbed him. As I started to walk backward, Needham made no further attempt to attack, which gave me a clue he was hurt.

Then I looked to see if the whites in the weights area were getting ready to charge at me. Looking around for a safe place to throw away the knife, I saw a low roof, where I tossed it. By that time, the alarm had sounded, and a group of prison guards were coming through the yard gates. I heard someone say, "That's him!" Then I was pushed against the fence of the yard cage with my arms in the air and slapped with handcuffs to my back. This happened so fast I didn't get any chance to look back at the scene in the yard.

I was taken to the prison hospital and ordered to take all my clothes off for a strip search. After my boxers were returned to me, I was once again handcuffed and escorted to the K wing Hole and held there for six or nine hours before being charged with murder with the death penalty. I was shocked to hear the outcome of my scuffle with Needham. The Stockton court inspector testified earlier that he saw me turn pale when the charge was read. This is all I recall of my testimony.

After I finished, the prosecutor cross-examined me. I stood firmly on the truth of my testimony. The prosecutor then put on a rebuttal witness. Mr. Tauman had no more defense witnesses, and both sides rested their cases. The prosecutor summarized the state's case against me. When Mr. Tauman summarized the defense, I noticed some of the men on the jury were nodding off to sleep. The prosecutor was given a second chance to make a closing argument to the jury and finished with an even stronger summary.

The next day, Judge Papas handed down a long list of jury instructions, saying the jury could only find me guilty of first-degree murder or manslaughter or else find me not guilty. Watching the jury's body language, I saw clear signs that they were predisposed to a verdict of first-degree murder based on Judge Papas' instructions. A person can read unspoken messages by watching body language and facial expressions, and listening to the tone of voice in which words are said. I think unsaid messages informed the jury throughout the case, most significantly during the opening remarks to the jury when Mr. Tauman should have advanced the self-defense theory and failed to do so.

Now the jury went out to deliberate. On the second day, the jury returned to court and asked the judge to clarify the jury instructions. The jury deliberated another day and came back with a verdict of guilty of first-degree murder. This was no surprise to me. It was a one-sided trial from the start.

After the jury verdict, I asked Mr. Weinglass and Mr. Tauman to go ahead and let them push for the death penalty. With the death penalty, I would receive a far better review of the case and a better shot at getting an appeal through to the California Supreme Court, where the chief justice was Judge Rose Bird. In truth, I preferred the death penalty over facing a life sentence without chance of parole. By now, I had already spent three and a half years in adjustment centers, and during the last eighteen months, I'd lived in the K wing Hole among hard-core convicts who sought only self-dignity and kept their sanity by not being broken or defeated by the prison system or by injustice. At the time of the prison case, I was twenty-six years old.

Death Penalty

Judge Papas instructed me to bring over my night needs as the jury was expected to remain for the penalty part of the trial. The next day, Mr. Weinglass took over for the penalty stage and called his first witness, Dr. Elaine Kim. I had been corresponding with her since the *Asian Now* interview, and she understood parts of my life in Korea. The first letter I ever wrote her was a poem that she kept and showed to the jury. The second person to testify on my behalf was Johnny Spain. As soon as his name was mentioned on the witness stand, a few men on the jury rolled their eyes because they knew he was involved in the George Jackson incident in San Quentin. The jury had a terrible attitude toward my case in general. I doubt any of them were ever caught up in the California prison system or gang violence, or had any exposure to a reality-based understanding of the case.

Johnny Spain testified that I was playing chess with him when he saw a group of whites coming over to the African American weight-lifting area. He had a clear view of me as I walked toward Needham and saw that I carried no weapon. He saw Needham grab me to get a good hold, and saw a very short struggle between myself and Needham until the prison tower guard yelled "knock it off." Spain also testified that he could that see a few of the jurors were nodding off to sleep.

Meanwhile, the prosecutor viewed the jury to see their reactions to Elaine Kim and Johnny Spain's testimonies. He looked confident about the jury's demeanor. After the two defense witnesses testified, he rested his case without putting any more witnesses on the stand. During closing remarks, Weinglass addressed the jury as to why I should not be given the death penalty, and the prosecutor explained why I deserved it, as he was allowed the last word before jury deliberation. Judge Papas then instructed the jury about deciding between the death penalty and life without parole, and prepared the jury to deliberate at the hotel the next day.

On the first day, the jury was unable to reach a decision, but on the second day on March 22, 1979, the jury recommended that I receive the death penalty. Judge Papas thanked the jury, dismissed them, and set May 14 for the formal sentencing date. By law, the judge could still sentence me to life without parole, but the jury advised death.

Afterward, Mr. Weinglass told me there were good grounds for appeal because of the judge's unfair jury instructions and his admission of hearsay evidence in allowing the NF snitch's testimony. I was confident that Mr. Weinglass would handle my appeal, but I felt emotionless, knowing that in two months I would be sentenced to death.

When I returned to the K wing Hole, the whole of Tracy prison was aware of the jury's death penalty recommendation in my case. However, I did not discuss the trial or the sentence with anyone but went about my normal routine. I was outwardly calm, but other convicts were aware of my explosive state of mind. As a show of support, some came up to me and conducted short conversations, offering whatever they had, such as books, smokes, and coffee. I declined, but thanked them in a calm way.

I felt no emotion. Instead, I thought about killing the prison guard, Diaz, through the bars. I could surprise him during the clothing exchange when I got my prison jacket. But he seemed aware of my thoughts and stood as far away from the bars as possible while exchanging my clothes. I thought hard about how to kill Diaz. Then I changed my mind. There would be no turning back if I stabbed him. Diaz had been hard on me ever since he started working in the K Hole, but I realized that killing him would be a sign of weakness. To truly be a hard-core convict, you must overcome anything the prison system or the guards put you through. You stand up and face them eye to eye as if to break them. I was at a low point in my time in prison. The reality was I would be sentenced to death. Even if I won my appeal on the Chinatown case, I would go through another trial and still face a life sentence. Already, I had reached the farthest extremes of living up to the convicts' code of conduct.

The prison guards left me alone, aware of what I was going through. They stayed away, knowing I might strike if they provoked me. They were nothing but cowards who only found courage in groups, and they probably assumed I was supported by the NF and BGF, who were fearsome enemies in the guard's eyes.

I should clarify that I took no pleasure in the death of Morrison Needham, who was yet another casualty of the prison system. But my life depended on defending myself against him. Most convicts in my situation would not have survived or would have sought PC rather than stand up to an enemy against overwhelming odds. I believe all the Asians in the California prison system who followed my case took pride that I was an Asian convict who stood up when set up to be the target of twenty-five whites and survived without protective custody. But in the end, my type of self-defense against the whites in L wing resulted in murder charges against me.

All my life I had been struggling to stay alive, starting from my birth in Korea, facing racism in American schools, experiencing difficult teenage years, being sent to state prison, and finally receiving the death sentence from a racist jury and judge. I had survived this far, and now I would face the death penalty as an ultimate test of my survival skills, not only in the courts, but in San Quentin penitentiary, which was ruled by La Eme and the AB. I had already realized an even more serious life-and-death struggle lay ahead of me at San Quentin on Death Row.

I kept all those thoughts to myself and wrote thank-you letters to my supporters, gathering strength from the personal way many people had befriended me. I wrote that the death penalty was another struggle for justice in which I hoped to prevail. My letters to Ranko and Reiko were much more personal as I continued to seek their personal affections and asked them not to lose hope. As I received many letters of encouragement and support, I noticed a lot of them talked about building a movement for justice. The movement to Free Chol Soo Lee was gathering strength across the United States.

"Freedom for Chol Soo Lee!"

On May 14, 1979, I was driven to court by Sergeant O'Neill with other prison guards in a car with me. When I appeared in court, the courtroom was packed with my supporters and many Stockton court guards who watched for any signs of trouble. The prosecutor argued before Judge Papas that I should be given the death penalty and not life without parole. Mr. Weinglass argued that I should be given life without parole and not the death penalty. With a bit of a smile at the attorneys and the supporters in the courtroom, Judge Papas announced the sentence of death and instructed that I be transferred to Death Row in San Quentin. After the judge announced my death sentence, I heard a young college student named Jeff Adachi shout out, "Freedom for Chol Soo Lee!" The other supporters followed his lead in chanting, "Freedom for Chol Soo Lee! Freedom for Chol Soo Lee! Freedom for Chol Soo Lee!"

As Judge Papas ordered everyone be removed from the courtroom, I noticed Sergeant O'Neill giving high fives to the other prison guards. I hadn't thought O'Neill was that racist, but I guess he was putting on a show while transporting me back and forth from Tracy. The death penalty sentence was a victory for the prison guards and the white convicts.

The prison guards failed in their effort to set me up to be killed by white men, but won their victory through a racist court system. Now they were exchanging high fives over a man's death sentence. It made me wonder what kind of man finds joy in another human being's death. Where was the sense of humanity in those prison guards and white court deputies who smiled from ear to ear as if my death were some personal victory?

I said nothing, but held my head up high and showed no emotion. I heard the continuing noise of chanting and clapping outside in the hallway, and as I was escorted out of the courtroom, the supporters saw me and chanted even louder, "Freedom for Chol Soo Lee! Freedom for Chol Soo Lee!" As I crossed the hall between two lines of courtroom deputies, the deputies linked arms to hold back the chanting and clapping crowd. Wearing handcuffs, I saluted my supporters, raising both arms with fists clenched in defiance.

Across the hall in another room, some new guards escorting me put me through a routine strip search. During court appearances, I wore personal clothes and shoes that the defense team had given me to wear. After the strip search, these civilian clothes were returned to me for me to put back on. Then I was handcuffed to the waist and put in leg irons as the new guards prepared to escort me to San Quentin. I was surprised to realize I was being transferred to Death Row so soon after being sentenced to death.

I sat in the back of a car with two prison guards in front and two more guards following in another car. The prison guards drove through back roads, avoiding the freeways, until we reached the San Francisco Bay Area. During the two-hour trip to San Quentin, not a word was exchanged between me and the prison guards as I sat in the car enjoying the view. Across the Richmond Bridge, I saw a sign for the road leading to San Quentin penitentiary. Eventually, the car slowed down in front of two large steel gates. Inside was a parking lot and tan-colored buildings. The car pulled up in front of the guard entrance building, where I was escorted inside with the court order for my death sentence. My leg irons were removed, and now two San Quentin guards took over as escorts. I was inside of San Quentin.

Deuel Vocational Institution (DVI) in Tracy, California, 1977. Courtesy of K. W. Lee and the K. W. Lee Center for Leadership.

K. W. Lee's first meeting and interview with Chol Soo Lee at Deuel Vocational Institution in 1977. Courtesy of K. W. Lee and the K. W. Lee Center for Leadership.

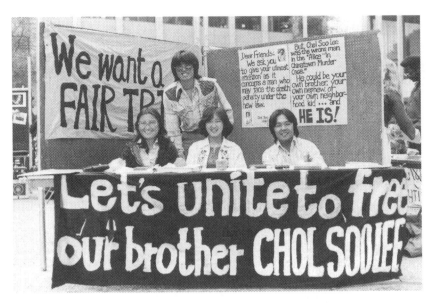

Information booth and petition drive sponsored by the Bay Area Chol Soo Lee Defense Committee and the Korean Students Association from the University of California, Berkeley, at a local San Francisco event in 1978. Courtesy of Gail Whang and the K. W. Lee Center for Leadership.

Jam session in Los Angeles during a joint meeting between the Bay Area Chol Soo Lee Defense Committee and the Los Angeles Chol Soo Lee Defense Committee in 1978. Courtesy of Gail Whang and the K. W. Lee Center for Leadership.

"Free Chol Soo Lee" rally in Sacramento, 1978. Courtesy of the K. W. Lee Center for Leadership.

Pan-Asian, multigenerational rally held in front of the Stockton Court House, 1979. Over 150 people from all of the California Chol Soo Defense Committees were in attendance. Courtesy of Gail Whang.

Rally in front of the Stockton Courthouse, 1979. Courtesy of the K. W. Lee Center for Leadership.

"The Ballad of Chol Soo Lee" was recorded and produced in 1978 to raise funds for and increase awareness about Chol Soo Lee's case. Musicians on the recording included Jeff Adachi, Shiu-Wai Anderson, Peter Horikoshi, Robert Kikuchi-Yngojo, Duke Santos, and Sam Takemoto. Courtesy of Jeff Adachi and the K. W. Lee Center for Leadership.

Monday, March 31, 1980

KOREAtOWN

The English Language Voice of the Korean American Community

Vol 1. No. 24

35 cents

Chol Soo wins battle

Release order upheld in 'Chinatown' murder

By K.W. LEE
Editor

Death-row inmate Chol Soo Lee's seven-year nightmare in the "Alice in Chinatown" murder case is over.

The 27-year-old Korean immigrant — on San Quentin death-row for a crime he says he didn't commit — has taken one giant step toward the freedom that for so long has eluded him.

Supporters of Lee's battle for life and a new trial were elated, as the 3rd District Court of Appeal in Sacramento unanimously upheld on March 21 a Sacramento judge's release order wiping out Lee's 1974 San Francisco Chinatown murder conviction.

THE APPEAL COURT'S ruling killed the death penalty hanging over Lee for the 1977 prison-yard slaying of a neo-Nazi fellow inmate while Lee was serving a life sentence at Deuel state prison for what has come to be known as the "Alice in Chinatown" murder.

The immigrant, then 20, was arrested on June 7, 1973 for the streetcorner slaying of gangland figure Yip Yee Tak in San Francisco four days earlier. Because of the surrealistic circumstances surrounding the Tak murder and Lee's subsequent arrest and 1974 conviction, The Sacramento Union's 1978 investigative series depicted the case as that of an "Alice in Chinatown."

On Jan. 19, 1979, Sacramento Superior Court Judge Lawrence K. Karlton — now a federal judge — ordered Lee's release on a writ of habeas corpus, on the grounds that the prosecution failed to provide material evidence to Lee's attorney in his 1974 trial in Sacramento that could have altered the outcome of that trial.

Subsequently, however, the death-penalty prison murder trial was forced on the defendant in San Joaquin County Superior Court, although his Chinatown conviction — the very basis for his death penalty — had been just overthrown by Karlton. Lee claimed self defense in the prison killing case.

THE SAN JOAQUIN COUNTY prosecution — trying Lee on the prison case — immediately appealed the Karlton ruling.

Continued on Page 10

CHOL SOO LEE

Headlines from *Koreatown Weekly* on March 21, 1980, announcing the Sacramento District Court of Appeals' decision to uphold Chol Soo Lee's writ of habeas corpus petition and order that the conviction for the 1974 Chinatown murder case be set aside. *Koreatown Weekly* was the first national English-language newspaper for the Korean American community. Courtesy of K. W. Lee and the K. W. Lee Center for Leadership.

"Free Chol Soo Lee" rally held at the gates of San Quentin State Prison in 1981.
Courtesy of Gail Whang and the K. W. Lee Center for Leadership.

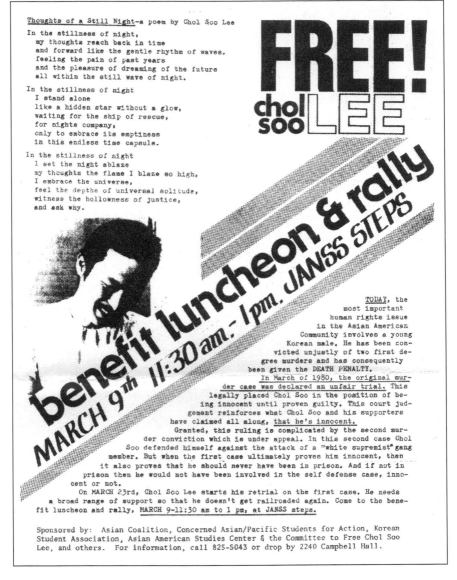

Flyer for fund-raiser and rally at UCLA in support of Chol Soo Lee's retrial of the Chinatown case in 1982. Courtesy of the K. W. Lee Center for Leadership.

A special victory issue

Vol 3, No. 22

KOREAtOUn

The English Language Voice of the Korean American Community

Monday, October 11, 1982

Three years old

Chol Soo Lee is innocent

'MY VICTORY IS YOURS'

Full pardon sought

With the first of the two murder cases cleared, Chol Soo Lee's defense team isn't merely waiting for a ruling from a Sacramento appeals court on Lee's appeal in the second case stemming from the 1977 prison incident.

His team is shooting for full pardon from Gov. Brown in the waning hours of his four-year term.

The appeals court has been sitting on the San Joaquin County case for two years, and this unusual inaction is interpreted as a hopeful sign that the court may see some merit in Lee's assertion that his second conviction was a miscarriage of justice. The appellate court has been waiting to see what would happen in his Chinatown murder retrial. Now that Lee is cleared in the first killing case, the appeals court will decide on Lee's appeal Oct. 8).

If the court rules in his favor and a new trial is granted, defense attorneys J. Tony Serra and Stuart Hanlon will seek his release on bail. If his appeal fails, a full pardon will be sought from the governor.

But Lee wants a new trial, not a pardon, according to his lawyers.

MOMENTS TO SHARE — Members of his defense team savor victory with smiling Chol Soo Lee in a court conference room shortly after the not-guilty verdict was read. From left: Sookie N. Choo, investigator Josiah Tink Thompson, J. Tony Serra, Chol Soo, and Stuart Hanlon

Diary of

Photo of Chol Soo Lee's legal defense team following the San Francisco Superior Court jury's decision to acquit Chol Soo Lee of the murder of Yip Yee Tak in the retrial of the Chinatown murder case in 1982. *Left to right:* Sooknam Choo, Tink Thompson, Tony Serra, Chol Soo Lee, Ranko Yamada, and Stuart Hanlon. Courtesy of K. W. Lee and the K. W. Lee Center for Leadership.

Chol Soo Lee and his supporters celebrate his freedom on March 28, 1983, after California Superior Court judge K. Peter Saiers ordered Lee's release from San Quentin State Prison. Courtesy of K. W. Lee and the K. W. Lee Center for Leadership.

Chapter 5

San Quentin

Gauntlet

I was escorted into a small building used for R&R. The wrist chains were removed, and once again I was strip-searched. They kept my personal clothing but allowed me to keep a pack of cigarettes and the street shoes I'd worn to court. When I was led out of R&R, a guard informed me in a soft tone that I would be held in the AC, the San Quentin Hole, until I was transferred to Death Row. Upon entering the first floor of the Hole, I was taken to a small cell with one wall and bars on three sides, where I was once more strip-searched and handcuffed behind my back. Leading me by the chains between my hands, the guard then took me through the west side of the tier. The tier seemed louder than the Hole in Tracy, and I noticed a mix of races among the convicts, but I didn't see anyone I knew. I was aware that everyone at San Quentin knew from the news media that I was coming. We reached the back of the tier, where there was a gate and five strip cells (empty cells where prisoners are placed without clothes) with double doors. After being locked in the strip cell, I backed up to the cell door and held my hands out through the food chute to have the handcuffs removed. I noticed the mattress cover was torn, and my bedding rested on a solid concrete platform. Then I heard an African American voice call out, "Hey, new guy in back—you all right? You need smokes or anything?"

"No, but thanks," I said.

By this time, dinner was being served, and I got my first taste of San Quentin food, which was a lot worse than Tracy food. When hot food was served on the mainline in Tracy, it wasn't that bad, but the food in San Quentin's Hole was cold and mostly flavorless. I spent that night in the strip cell.

At 9 a.m., a guard came to escort me to Death Row. As always, I was strip-searched and then handcuffed in back before the cell door opened. I was escorted to a cell at the front of the tier for another strip search, then waist-chained with my hands cuffed to the side. No leg irons were used because they are against the law for escorting a high-security convict inside the prison. In leg irons, he has no chance to dodge attacks against him. Sometimes the most dangerous convicts are escorted with waist chains and long chains attached to a neck collar, like a dog.

The guard said he was taking me to the prison hospital for my health checkup. This sounded to me like a humorless joke. The CDC wanted to make sure you were healthy to be executed. As the guard brought me outside, I noticed it was a clear warm day. To my left, a nine-foot-high fence with gun rails and two gun towers surrounded all sides of the Hole lower yard. The fence also separated us from the North Block upper yard for the mainline. Ahead of me in the lower yard, I saw a mass of convicts. As we neared the mass of convicts, the guards shouted, "Escort!" and directed the prisoners to stand aside and let me pass through. As a rule, convicts must move back at least ten feet from an escorted convict. This time, however, the lower yard was so crowded that the convicts were only a few feet away from me when the escorting guard led me right through the middle of the throng.

Suddenly, a white convict rushed at me from the left, lunging with his prison-made knife. I deflected his attack by pivoting to the right. The knife just missed my elbow. He tried again to stab me. By then, the nearest guard used his bully club to shove the white convict back, shouting "Escort! Escort! Need cover!"

Gun rail guards ran to positions overlooking the scene. An additional prison guard stationed himself to my left. By then, my assailant had retreated, making his way toward the back of the crowd. Now I had escort guards on both sides, and guards armed with Mini-14's tracking my movements from the gun rail atop East Block. As I walked with the escort guards through a corridor of cleared space, the gun tower guard walked alongside high above. The Mini-14 was a sign to the convicts that the guards meant business.

At this time, the upper yard was fully packed with four or five hundred convicts. They all faced out toward me in total silence; it was so completely quiet that you could hear a pin drop. I kept my head up and walked at a normal pace, looking straight ahead. The prison gangs had been informed ahead of time that a hit man was coming down, and now hundreds of convicts stared at the lone Asian in waist chains, escorted by three prison guards. Between East Block and the upper yard was a space of twenty-five feet, and I continued to walk at a normal pace, signaling to all who stared at me that my life was mine. I have to admit that inside I felt shaken by the attempted stabbing and by the silence of the whole upper yard. This silence seemed to me to spread throughout the prison, filling up the full seventy-five yards' walk to the prison hospital.

It was my second day in San Quentin, and the attempt on my life was no accident. It was a planned hit by the Aryan Brotherhood. I successfully blocked the knife thrown at me by the AB assassin, but the attack would have been fatal if he had succeeded in hitting me and a team of other ABs jumped in on the hit. Luckily, the prison guards' fast reactions to the first attack kept the others in check. I was right under the gun rail when the hit was attempted, but I managed to keep a clear head, allowing the escorting guards and gun guards to quickly recognize their positions around me. If I had run from the scene of the hit, I would have created confusion, allowing the rest of the AB hit team to stab me during the commotion. This seventy-five-yard escort to the hospital was one of the most difficult walks in my life. I had to keep a level head and remain calm with all the hard-core convicts observing me for the first time.

I can't put into words what this world of the self-enforced convicts' code of conduct is like so that you who live in free society can understand my position. Over the years, I gradually gained training and expertise, starting with my teenage life in the streets, then my experience in CYA, then county jail, and then the violent world of state prison among hard-core convicts. A normal person without this kind of background would not be able to survive in state prison or understand how anyone could live in such a cruel and inhumane place.

If a normal person could experiment with trying to live like a convict, he wouldn't last a day in a state prison like San Quentin, Soledad, or Folsom, where each convict does not view other convicts as human beings but cares only about his personal safety. Normal links to our humanity are lost in the daily focus on survival. As an outside observer, if you saw how we conducted our daily lives, you couldn't even come close to understanding how we think in order to make a life for ourselves in prison. You'd need to see, hear, and smell real blood to fully feel the inner state of a convict who has been stabbed. You'd need to be the stabber. It is almost like the life of a gladiator who may be called upon to kill or be killed at any time. To survive, the gladiator has no choice but to engage a kill-or-be-killed mind-set. But even a gladiator's life is not as bad as a convict's. Gladiators are given weapons, and they fight out in the open arena; they kill or die with a kind of honor. But for convicts, killing or being killed is mostly a surprise event. There is no honor in seeing the blood of a human being on the prison yard ground. If people in free society truly cared about and understood the lives of convicts, it would be impossible to continue treating us as disregarded living things. Instead, they look away and try to dismiss from their awareness the fact that convicts are human beings.

Delivery

Without a word exchanged between myself and the escorting guards, we reached the hospital in a state of high tension. The prison doctor examined me thoroughly. There was no need to say anything. I just listened to what the doctor said. He found my physical health to be in very good condition. Now I had permission to die in the gas chamber.

Next I was escorted by two prison guards with a gun rail guard still tracking me to North Block. Passing through the North Block gates, I stood in front of the elevator. Next to the elevator was a green door, which led to one of the gas chambers. This elevator made only two stops: ground level where we now stood and Death Row. We boarded the elevator, rising to the fifth floor at the top of North Block. Still in waist chains, I was taken to a small conference room to be processed by the prison administrator (PA) in charge of Death Row. A lieutenant sergeant waited for me there. I felt like a human delivery package sent to Death Row. I was ordered to sit down in front of the PA with a guard behind me. With a hard smile, the PA said, "You know there was an attempt on your life by the Aryan Brotherhood while you were being escorted to the hospital."

"Yeah, no kidding," I thought.

The PA continued, "Since there was an attempt on your life, today you will always be escorted by two guards. As for your program on Death Row, you have none. Just recently, a few white prisoners were attacked and now there are two yard groups, one for whites and one for minorities. Since there are La Eme members in the minority yard, you can't go to the same yard with them because we know your previous association with the NF. You might kill a La Eme or they might kill you, so we are not taking any chances by putting you in the same yard. You will be allowed to shower every day. According to your rights, we have to give you one hour of daily exercise, so the shower room will be your exercise room. If the guards have time, they will take you to the yard located on top of the roof for you to exercise there alone. Do you have anything to say?"

Knowing my request to join the minority yard would be denied, even though I had no problems with La Eme, I just shook my head from side to side. It seemed that I was being given special treatment. Did the prison administration aim to break me down mentally by not allowing me to go to the minority or white yard? As I was led toward my cell at the back of the east side tier, I looked at some of the Death Row convicts. There were as many minorities as whites. I saw several African Americans, and in cell number eighteen, I saw a Latino with a prison tattoo, whom I guessed was a La Eme member.

I was escorted into cell number thirty-four, and the chains and handcuffs were removed through the food chute. Right away, I noticed how small the cell was, about four by nine feet, with a solid concrete bed and a mattress and a stainless steel toilet and sink at the back. Standing up, at my height of 5'4", I could reach both walls across the cell's width with my hands.

Alone in my cell, I considered my next moves. The first order of business for any experienced convict transferring to a new prison was to learn who the other convicts on your tier were and who carried weight. This was to anticipate how to establish your territory when you arrived. Back when I was still in Tracy, I had done some research to get ready. In Tracy, the prison gang intelligence system was good enough to track the movements of other gangs and identify enemies or allies at other prisons. I knew some friendlier NFs might offer advice, and I had asked the NF leader in charge of my tier if he knew anyone on Death Row. He had said, "You can rely on a Native American guy named Chief from Fresno. Also, there is a La Eme named Nico on Death Row. You need to watch out for Nico. And there are two Hell's Angels bikers. You should keep your eyes on them, too."

I never underestimated possible enemies in my surroundings. Underestimating enemies amounted to comforting yourself with false beliefs, which could be fatal. This was the case of the white bikers and the AB in Tracy's L wing whose overwhelming numbers against me gave them a false sense of security. Their fatal mistake was to assume I would not fight back. Instead, I maintained the view that I should always be ready for any kind of attack. That is why, when I first saw the hundreds of convicts in San Quentin's upper and lower yards, I stayed alert to incoming attacks. Aware that I was entering many different territories, I was fully prepared to deflect other convicts' moves with lightning-quick reactions.

Now that I had survived crossing the crowded San Quentin yard and had arrived safely on Death Row, I needed to get in touch with the

Native American named Chief as quickly and quietly as possible. Instead of using another convict to get a message to Chief, I decided to use an African American prison guard who went from cell to cell with the dinner cart. When the guard stopped at my cell, he had a friendly look. He looked like a mid-level experienced guard. I asked in a friendly way about the food on the dinner tray, and then I said, "Officer, is there a Native American man named Chief on Death Row?"

The guard knew what I was getting at. "Chief is on the other side of the tier," he said.

I said, "When you go over to the other side, could you please tell Chief that Lee from Tracy just arrived on the tier and ask him to stop by my cell?"

"I will tell Chief your cell number," he said.

"Thank you," I replied.

My second order of business was to make a weapon. I needed some kind of prison weapon as soon as possible for self-protection, just in case anything went down. First, I searched the cell to make sure nothing had been planted there by the guards to set me up. I combed through everything for a hidden weapon and found nothing. Then I searched the cell for metal for a knife but found it impossible to cut out a piece of the stainless steel sink or toilet. I was in a bad position. I needed a weapon. Then I looked at my street court shoes, which were made of leather and rubber. When I took the interior sole of the shoes apart, to my surprise, I found in each shoe a steel shank about three inches long and half an inch wide. I took out one of the shanks.

Later that night, I attached a paper and cloth handle to the steel shank to make it longer, then sharpened the steel on the concrete floor. It took two hours to fashion a one-and-a-half-inch double-edged pointed knife. This was the first prison-made knife I had ever made. With the handle, the knife was five and a half inches long, with a strong metal blade that would not bend if the knife were used. Satisfied the knife would work well, I took the handle apart, removed the second shank from the other shoe, and hid both pieces in the middle of my cotton mattress. Just in case my street shoes were taken away, or if I were moved and put through a metal detector, I knew not to hide the metal back inside the shoes.

Some may ask why I started making prison knives so soon upon my arrival at Death Row, especially if I was trying to avoid any problems. San Quentin was full of potential enemies with the gangs of AB, La Eme, and the Bikers. There was no question I had enemies, even though

I had tried my very best not to make any. In Tracy, I had gotten along well with Spider, the white biker leader, when we played poker together and both ran poker games, but my friendly rapport with him ended because Tracy officials labeled me an NF associate. The prison administration continued to link me to NF even after a San Joaquin Superior Court judge legally cleared me of NF association. In L wing, the five or six whites who followed Spider should not have considered me their enemy or planned to kill me because of their war with NF, but they did.

Then, after Morrison Needham's death in the L wing yard, California prison officials viewed me as an associate of NF because of Needham's death. Yet the NF had never planned Needham's death in L wing, and neither had I. Prior to his death, I had never identified Needham as my enemy. We had seen each other in L wing, but I didn't know he had just arrived at Tracy, and I never formally met him. I knew nothing of his background. I didn't know if he was involved in AB's war with NF. As for the BGF members in L wing, they knew the whites planned to kill me, but said nothing about Needham.

Meanwhile, my case was getting full coverage by newspapers in the Sacramento and the Bay areas. Prison gangs read newspapers or watched television news, which were often good sources of intelligence. However, in my case, the newspapers provided false information because they kept mislabeling me as an NF associate. Because of this, I got on the AB's hit list, and very possibly on La Eme's hit list too. I knew I had enemies. Everyone saw obvious proof of this when an unknown white man tried to kill me on my second day in San Quentin. My life was known to be in danger in San Quentin, where La Eme, AB bikers, and BGF dominated. The prison administration at Death Row officially confirmed this by segregating me from both the white and minority yards.

All this is to explain why I decided to arm myself. On Death Row in San Quentin, I was in the enemy camp, where Nico of La Eme or a white biker might try to make a hit on me. I needed a weapon to defend myself. Now that I had a weapon, I needed to find sincere allies on Death Row if I wanted to survive. I was looking toward Chief, whom I had yet to meet, to be one of them. I needed to find out the background of all the convicts on Death Row: who was who, and which gang members were on this tier? I also needed to know how much influence Nico wielded and where the non–Death Row convicts were held.

I had arrived on Death Row after six and a half years of imprisonment, with most of that time done in the Hole and adjustment centers in the company of NF or BGF gang members. I had learned a lot of survival skills and ways to avoid confrontations. Now I prepared to strengthen myself mentally against the prison administration's policy to restrict my contacts with other convicts on Death Row. They had put me on total lockdown except for a daily shower, and I viewed this as a strategy for breaking me down mentally. I wondered, "What if they don't need to put me to death in the gas chamber? What if the other convicts and the guards finish the job themselves?"

Chief

A Native American man, 6' tall, weighing about 200 pounds, and wearing a long ponytail, soon stopped by my cell and said, "My name is Chief. The guard said you want to meet me."

"My name is Lee," I said. "I just came from Tracy, where I was told to look you up when I arrived here." When I mentioned the homeboy, the NF leader, in the Tracy Hole, Chief seemed to open up and trust me.

"So what's happening on Death Row?" I said.

Chief said, "A while back me and another guy stabbed Charlie, the leader of the whites. He's in cell thirty-two, two cells away from you. After that hit, the administration split the yard into two groups, one white and one minority. I should tell you there are about twelve BGFs on the other side of the tier, and a small group of Latinos in a gang called Texas Syndicate (TS). But most guys on Death Row are weak, doing their first time in prison."

"I was told by the PA that there are La Eme members in your yard, and because of them, I can't go to the minority yard."

Chief said, "There's only one La Eme. His name is Nico. If you want me to hit him, I will."

I said, "No, let's hold off on hitting Nico for now."

I already had enemies in AB and among the white bikers, and the last thing I needed was to make an enemy of La Eme, the most powerful gang in the California prison system. La Eme and AB were allies, so hitting Nico would make all these gangs come after me.

I asked, "Chief, where you at?"

Chief replied, "I am not with NF but with a Native American gang called Bulldog. We are allies with NF since all of us come from Northern California."

"Thanks for the info, Chief. Let's talk some more another time."

"All right, Lee. You need anything?"

"Yeah, I haven't got my prison property yet. I could use some smokes, coffee, books, and some stamped envelopes."

"I don't smoke, but I'll have some tobacco and other things sent over today," said Chief.

"Thanks," I replied.

The prison guard had let us talk for twenty minutes while he leaned back against the rail to overhear our conversation. I could see Chief must have some pull and influence on Death Row for the guard to escort Chief over to my side of the tier and let us talk as long as we wanted. During the conversation, I checked out Chief just as he was checking me out. We had both proved ourselves as convicts in Tracy, and Chief had gotten information about me before I arrived at Death Row. That information must have been solid for him to offer to kill Nico just so I could come onto the minority yard. That surprised me. It showed that Chief already had much regard and respect for me based on what he'd heard from convicts at Tracy. Even though we were meeting for the first time in our lives, I found Chief to be a solid convict to have on my side.

That same day, Chief sent over through a guard the items I requested, including stamped envelopes and a half-sized pen. I'd never known companies made such small pens—only four inches long! I wrapped the pen with some paper to lengthen it for easier writing. Using the prison-issue writing paper, I wrote my first letters to Ranko and Jay Yoo to let them know I was at San Quentin Death Row, and I gave them a PO Box number for receiving their letters. However, I didn't tell them about the troubling conditions I faced in San Quentin.

Welcome Visitors

San Quentin is located in Marin County across the Golden Gate Bridge from San Francisco. This makes it easier to receive visitors from the Bay Area. My first visitors were Jeff Adachi and David Kakishiba. Jeff was planning to go to law school, and David was the executive director of the Berkeley Asian Youth Center while he attended UC Berkeley. Jeff was full of smiles and did most of the talking in a happy voice, whereas David spoke little but was full of laughter. I found their visit very comforting. I didn't tell them about my problems with restricted yard time and twenty-four-hour lockdown. Instead, I told them I was doing well and in good health, and we talked about the defense committee.

Death Row convicts were locked in a visiting booth while talking to visitors one at a time through bulletproof glass and a telephone. Some weeks I had two or three visits, which felt very uplifting. While forced to do hard time on Death Row, I accepted my visitors at a personal level rather than seeing them as political activists. At the time, I wasn't thinking in terms of their higher ideals of Asian American empowerment and unity.

I also started receiving visits from people of high social standing, such as the Buddhist monks who helped build the first Korean Buddhist temple in the San Francisco Bay Area, working with my mother's friend, Doris Yamasaki. To this day, Doris is like a big sister to me and has always shown me kindness since my arrival to the United States. There was also a Korean counselor who visited with gifts of books on Korean history. A modern Korean writer who lived in England even visited me, as did Lee Tai Young, Korea's first female lawyer and first female judge, whose husband was also a highly respected politician. I also saw Ms. Chong, who formed a CSLDC in Hawai'i, and Dr. Duk Choi, whose elder brother was the highest-ranking federal appellate judge of the Western states of the US and thought to be a possible appointment to the US Supreme Court someday.

Another visitor was Robert Aitken, a highly respected American Zen master from Hawai'i, who first learned to practice meditation when he was held as a Japanese prisoner of war during World War II. He came to see me several times with his wife when they were in town visiting the Zen center in San Francisco. During his visits, Aitken, who had very piercing eyes, tried to teach me the simplest form of meditation— breathing. I didn't feel like a celebrity with these high-profile visits but felt them more as personal moral support in my struggle for justice.

Another esteemed visitor was Reverend Cha, the leader of the Korean Protestant church in San Francisco, located on Stockton Street in Chinatown. This church community existed when I first arrived in America in 1964. If only I'd known about it, I could have attended this church to relate with other Koreans and receive some counseling and support. But back in 1964, I was unaware of this church, and there was no Korean community center in San Francisco to help me adjust to life in America. However, the first Korean American community center got established on Fulton Street in 1970 by Tom Kim, whom I'd met a few times in Chinatown. Without my knowledge, Tom Kim had tried to raise funds for me after my arrest in June 1973.

Another visitor I received was Mr. Frank Yoon, who used to work with Tom Kim and knew me when I lived in San Francisco. He loved riding his motorcycle, which he continued riding until he died from cancer in the mid-1990s. Looking back at the history of these pioneer community organizers, I now sincerely hope Korean Americans will carry on the spirit of Frank Yoon, Tom Kim, and many others, whose life work, in small and major ways, improved life for many Korean Americans.

My visitors were mostly supporters from California, but some came from as far away as New York and Korea. I continued to receive many letters of support to uplift my spirit, and each day I woke up feeling renewed as a result. Most days, the first thing I did in the morning was roll up my mattress to the end of my concrete bed and fold my blanket to cushion the floor. Sitting on the blanket, I used my bed as a table to write thank-you letters in reply to the letters I received or to review a list of names and addresses of people I met through visits or correspondence. When not writing, I passed the time reading or even tried meditating as Mr. Aitken had taught me. Around 4 p.m., I turned on the color TV that the defense committee had given me and tuned to Channel 12 to watch local and world news and other TV programs until 11 p.m. Then I unrolled my mattress to read some more before going to sleep around midnight.

Parlay with Nico of the Mexican Mafia

By formal agreement between minorities and whites on Death Row, everyone kept the noise down after 10 p.m. by lowering the volume of their TVs and not talking to convicts in other cells. It was a peaceful agreement to support those who wanted to sleep early. We convicts on Death Row might not get along well enough to coexist in the same yard, but we all agreed to follow these unwritten rules. We also tried to respect other convicts when they passed by our cells by refraining from hurling insults. Since I was on lockdown almost twenty-four hours a day, with only fourteen square yards for exercise inside my cell, I thought it was time to talk to Nico about the yard situation after four months of my situation. Nico knew why I wasn't allowed in the minority yard, so one day when I saw him passing my cell, I called him over and said, "The PA on twenty-seven said if you and me are in the same yard, we will try to kill each other. I got no problem with you. So what's happening?"

Nico said, "The PA told me the same thing."

"That so?"

"Three or four times. I might believe them if they said it once, but after three or four times, I stopped believing them."

"Listen, I got no problem with you," I said. "I give you my word—I will not harm you in any kind of way. So why don't you let the PA know there is no problem between us?"

A self-respecting convict will do his utmost to back his own word, so when I gave Nico my word, he had to accept I was sincere. He said, "I believe you. I think the man was playing games with both of us. I'll let the PA at twenty-seven know there is no problem between us."

"All right. That sounds good. Just like you keep your word, I'll keep my word."

Nico's escorting guard stood nearby and overheard the conversation.

By pulling Nico aside in this way, I let him know he had my word that nothing would happen between us in the yard. As a convict, he had to tell the prison administrator to let me into the yard with him because if he didn't, he would seem weak for fearing to disagree with the administration's idea that there was a problem between us, so I knew Nico would not make any problem for me.

After that, I was finally let out of my cell to go to the minority yard with all the rest. There, I was welcomed by Chief, who was glad to see me, and I met some African Americans in the yard, who also seemed glad I was let out. I told Chief about my conversation with Nico, and Chief agreed we would do nothing to Nico as long as he fell in line and helped us. I told Chief, "Just keep a close eye on Nico as I would."

Since I had been imprisoned for nearly eight years and most of the other guys on Death Row had fewer than three years, they turned the yard over to me to run it. Before I came out to the yard, Chief ran the yard, but with me there, he listened to me closely. I had been on lockdown twenty-four hours a day, yet within a few days in the yard, I was running it. All the prisoners on Death Row had been convicted of at least one murder, but only Chief really knew the convicts' code; the rest were less experienced. Though Nico was an experienced convict and a La Eme hit man, he seemed to me a bit weak in terms of the way convicts should carry themselves. I saw no threat coming from Nico because he saw that Chief and a few others were in line with me, so the yard remained peaceful in terms of the convicts' getting along with each other.

I felt good to be finally let out into the yard after doing such hard time for four months. I came out to the yard in high spirits. Also, I was glad both Nico and I did not fall into a trap devised to set us up against each other in a small game of divide and conquer. The prison guards and administration were masters at pitting convicts against each other, for as long as the convicts stayed busy killing each other, their aggression would not be aimed against the guards and prison officials. However, I knew I had to always stay alert with Nico because he might receive orders from La Eme leadership to make a hit on me.

Hooty

A newly arrived Death Row prisoner, a Native American named Patrick "Hooty" Croy, was placed in cell thirty-three, right next to my cell. He was new to prison. I told him my name and explained that he would be coming out to the minority yard with me and another Native American, Chief. Next time I was allowed out to shower, I placed on my bar a few items from the prison commissary, such as coffee and stamped envelopes, and told the guard to pass those items to the new prisoner. Though Hooty was new, I took care not to go near his (or any other convict's) cell, as there were many cases of stabbings through the bars with prison-made spears.

However, Hooty seemed to be all right and not a baby killer. This was confirmed the next day when Hooty came out to the yard and I introduced him to Chief and a few other convicts. Hooty was about 5'5", but well built. He knew how to carry himself well, and both Chief and I embraced him like a brother.

Hooty told us his story. This is how I recall it: "I am from Northern California and belong to the Karuk/Shasta Nations. One evening, my sister Norma Jean and I had gone out drinking and were on our way home when three white sheriff deputies stopped our car with their guns drawn. Before we even got out of the car, they started shooting at us." Hooty showed us a large scar on his arm where he was shot. He continued, "I had a gun because we were out in the middle of nowhere in a backwoods area where few people live. Everyone around there carries guns. After the deputies started shooting, I shot back and killed one of them before being wounded myself. After I was down, more deputies arrived, which may have saved my life and my sister's life since the two deputies seemed about to kill us both in cold blood. We were both found guilty of first-degree murder: I got the death penalty and my sister got life." *[Editorial note: Patrick "Hooty" Croy served twelve years on San Quentin's Death Row and was acquitted in a 1989 retrial with defense attorney Tony Serra. His sister, Norma Jean Croy, was released in 1997 after serving nineteen years.]*

Hooty didn't say nor did Chief or I ask if his sister's life sentence included the possibility of parole or not. After hearing Hooty's story, both Chief and I were impressed. Within a short time, Hooty carried himself like a convict. Chief and I took a liking to him and took him under our wings, which meant his problem became ours if he had any problem with another convict.

I soon found out that Hooty liked to play chess, which he learned in county jail. His chess games were strong, so every afternoon in our cells we played one or two games. Each game lasted two to four hours, which gave us time to study each move for its effect on the whole game. Unlike many chess players, we didn't make any move without thinking through the outcome, and if we traded captured pieces, the move would be made to full advantage in targeting another piece or gaining the upper hand. We each had our own chess set with the squares numbered one through sixty-four. To play, we called out moves by numbers, such as "sixteen to thirty-four." Using numbers was a clearer method than using traditional labels, like "pawn to king four." When we played in our cells, I never lost a single game to Hooty, but now and then, we played chess on the yard where Hooty won about three in five games. In the yard, I was always on sharp lookout for other convicts' movements and couldn't concentrate on playing chess.

Another distraction came from hearing shotguns firing regularly in the North Block upper yard, east of Death Row. At the time, I guessed this had something to do with black-on-black conflicts, because interracial warfare would have prompted the administration to separate yard times by race as they had done with Death Row. I believe the guards used shooting to break up attacks between convicts as a way to keep them oppressed and angry at each other. It was the same old divide-and-conquer method to divert anger away from the guards and administrators.

The administration went to any lengths to deter unity among the convicts. They tried to prevent the nonwhite races from uniting in common cause against whites, and even used white convicts as tools to deter race-based unity among white convicts. This manipulation of racial tension by the prison guards and administration is one reason they were so hated by the convicts. For our own personal survival, convicts continued to fight against each other, yet all the while we were fully aware that the prison administration and the guards were the real enemy.

Jackson and Black

As we continued to school Hooty, he accepted our friendship and fell in line with Chief and me. Five days after Hooty's arrival, a new Latino named Pento arrived on Death Row. Pento may have been a La Eme member or associate, as he fell in line with Nico and kept at a distance from me and Chief. Pento belonged to one of the many Latino gangs in Los Angeles, and he tried to carry himself as if he were an experienced convict but without understanding that he and Nico stood no chance against me and Chief with our experience. Now and then, I saw Nico and Pento talking, and sometimes I saw the dirty look Pento tried to give me.

I wanted to tell him, "Dirty looks don't kill anyone. When you want to kill someone, you smile and get as close to him as you possibly can." But he was new, and maybe he thought that looks scared people. In the penitentiary, looks only got you killed if you looked the wrong way at some convicts who viewed it as a threat. I thought about hitting Nico as well as Pento, but I had to keep from drawing heat from La Eme members who controlled San Quentin. So as long as Nico and Pento looked like they were making no moves toward me, I held back.

One day, when I was returning after yard hours from seeing a visitor, I reached my cell and Hooty asked me to pull the line from his cell to mine. A note was on the line from Chief saying that two African Americans were bragging to others in my yard about how they planned to make a hit on me. Even before reading the note, I could guess this concerned the two young African Americans named Jackson and Black, who tried to pass themselves off as members of the Crips. I knew they were not serious in their bragging but just trying to make a name for themselves. If you plan to make a hit, you don't talk to anyone about it; you just make the hit. Chief's note asked me if we should go to the yard packing knives, so I sent Chief a note saying, "No, first let's discuss the matter of Jackson and Black."

The prisoner known as Black was called so for his very dark skin. Black was sentenced to death for the rape and murder of two elderly women. Jackson had committed a similar crime. Both Jackson and Black didn't deserve to be called convicts from what I had seen of them. They carried themselves like street teenagers who had no clue about the convict mentality and code of conduct. As for bragging about making a hit on me, they were just trying to impress other convicts with how tough they were. They had nowhere near my level of experience, and their empty boasting was pathetic. I didn't lower myself to their level or take their threat seriously. When a convict says, "You got my word on it," it means he is ready to back his word with total aggression and enforce his words with death. Jackson and Black's hollow words, which I knew they would not back, set them up to be killed or made into punks or PCs forced off the yard that I controlled.

But just in case Jackson and Black needed to be hit, I sent a note to Hisi, the BGF's leader on the west side of the tier. In the note I said, "Jackson and Black have given other convicts reason to hit them both. Since they are African Americans, I want your consent for the hit, and I need your response as soon as possible."

I sent Hisi this note even though there were no BGFs in my yard and the African Americans in my yard had no high status in African American circles. Hisi's reply note that afternoon said, "I am aware that both Jackson and Black are creating problems but give them another chance. They are young men who don't understand what they are doing. Try to deal with them best as you can, but if they make any threats to you in the future, then do what you got to do."

Hisi asked me to give them a chance, but if I took the threat seriously, I could have taken action right away. Jackson and Black were in their early twenties and didn't understand the convicts' code, so it was best to just ignore them. However, if they made any further threats, now I had the full sanction from the BGF to kill them. Whatever I did was a life-or-death decision for them, but I had to follow the convicts' code to survive within the convict's world and do my utmost to stay out of a conflict that could lead to my death.

The next day in the yard, I called a meeting of everyone except Jackson and Black, who knew they were in serious trouble and kept as far from me as possible by staying near the gun tower guard hut in the front of the yard. Speaking to the rest of the prisoners, I said, "I appreciate those of you who gave me a message of concern regarding Jackson and Black. They are like teenagers in the grown-up world of convicts and they pose no threat to me, only to themselves. So here is what we are going to do to put them in check and prevent any more problems. None of us will speak to or have any interaction with either of them. Do all of you agree with me on this plan to straighten them up and keep them in line?"

All the guys in my yard knew took my words seriously and completely ignored both Jackson and Black. They knew that contact with Jackson and Black would pit them against me, which no one was prepared to do. Meanwhile, I called Chief and Hooty aside to give Hooty morc schooling in how to act like a convict. I said that Hooty should write a note to Hisi saying that two African Americans in my yard were creating unnecessary tension by showing off and that we might need to hit them both if they didn't change their ways. "The note should say I'm holding back on hitting them for now, but I understand we have Hisi's consent to hit them if they step out of line," I said. "Are you both with me on this?"

Chief agreed right away, and Hooty said, "I will back your play any time."

In this way, the problem with Jackson and Black was resolved without any use of violence. The next time Jackson and Black were supposed to come to the yard, Jackson didn't show up. I found out from the prison guard that Jackson had asked to be placed in protective custody. Black continued to be ignored by everyone in the yard. During the next yard call, Black didn't come out to the yard but did not ask to be in PC either. Both Jackson and Black had gotten the message and viewed their lives as threatened. As I had predicted, both were cowards. I had guessed ahead of time what they were likely to do. I didn't take their threats to me seriously, but they took my threats seriously.

Taking Care of Carlo: Part I

One day after my ordeal with Jackson and Black, a prison guard escorted a white prisoner in his midtwenties to my cell. Standing in front of my cell bars, he said, "My name is Carlo. The PA put me in PC because I was convicted of raping and murdering a twelve-year-old girl. I tried to go onto the white tier, but the guys refused to have me on their yard. But I swear to you, I didn't rape or kill the girl. I was framed on the case, I swear! So I want to ask you, will you let me come onto your yard?"

Just by looking at him, I could tell Carlo was new to prison. There were three ways I could answer his request: (1) say no, (2) have him pay a sum of money, or (3) consent to his request. Carlo seemed sincere, and considering my own case of being framed, I told Carlo, "You can come onto my yard. And I'll talk to everyone so no one gives you problems."

Almost with tears in his eyes, Carlo said, "Thank you, Lee, thank you."

I think his eyes got moist not only because I allowed him on my yard, but because someone believed in his innocence of the crime that put him on Death Row. Seeing his reaction, I believed in him and was glad to help. But I didn't show any emotion in my eyes or face.

On the next yard day, Carlo was allowed to come to the minority yard. I told everyone that I believed him to be innocent, and that no one should give him any trouble. Everyone in the yard listened to me, and Carlo had no problems with anyone. On Carlo's first day in the yard, he hung around with me a lot, but within a week he was getting along well with the rest of the guys.

The reason I say the minority yard was "my yard" was because the other condemned men viewed and respected me as the leader of the yard. Whatever I said, they listened to without any questioning. This was one reason why Jackson and Black bragged about planning to kill me. If that had scared me, then they would have controlled the yard. They were lucky that I was not a hot-headed man, for if I had been, then I would have hit them on the next yard outing.

I kept my yard running smoothly and free of problems.

Robert Harris

One night at around 8 p.m., the whites got some prison-made wine and made a lot of noise by talking to each other in their cells as they continued talking loudly into the night. Since the prisoners were on lockdown for the night, the guards viewed wine and the noise as harmless. However, the minority yard and the white yard had a mutual understanding that each side should respect the other by keeping the noise level low after 10 p.m. for the sake of those who wanted to sleep. On this occasion, the whites could have enjoyed their good time talking loudly all night, if they had given the minority yard prior notice of their plan to party all night, but no notice had been given. The time was nearing 3 a.m. when I said in a low voice, "What's happening, Charlie?"

Charlie, who was the leader of the whites, was two cells away from me and understood my question. "All right, Lee."

Then out of nowhere, a white guy shouted down the tier, "Who the fuck are you, you fucking chink telling us to shut up!"

I was shocked to hear this, but remained calm and asked, "What is your name?"

"My name is Robert Harris, you fucker Jap."

"What cell are you in?"

"Cell nineteen."

Robert Harris continued spewing racial names at me for another five minutes. This was just as well because it made everyone aware that his racial name calling was an act of full disrespect to another convict.

Since Harris was in the white yard group, however, he and I might never encounter each other in person, so for him to act like a brave cell warrior was ridiculous and cowardly. When he finally stopped calling me names, the rest of the tier had already gone quiet. All the convicts were fully aware that Harris was now a marked man who had to be hit for disrespecting me and for insulting Asians as a category.

Next day in the yard, I called Chief aside and asked him, "What's happening with Robert Harris?"

Chief already knew I planned to make a hit on Harris. "You want me to try to hit him?"

"No. It's not only me Harris has disrespected but Asians as whole group so I have to hit him myself, first chance I get. What is Harris in for?"

It turns out Harris had planned an armed bank robbery and car-jacked a car driven by two teenagers who were cousins. One was the son of a police officer. Both were eating hamburgers in the car when Harris and his friend ambushed the car and killed them. After both were dead, Harris supposedly finished the rest of their hamburgers. After getting this rundown on Harris, I viewed him as more of coward than a cold-blooded killer. From my point of view, getting a car to rob a bank didn't call for killing anyone. Harris carried out a senseless killing of two innocent teenagers and eating their leftover hamburgers was just a stunt. Both actions—the killing and eating the hamburgers—suggested that Harris was showing off how tough he was to impress his friend. These were the actions of a coward, not a real criminal. A real criminal who needs a car for a bank robbery would achieve his purpose without hurting anyone unnecessarily.

Now Harris had tried to show off how tough he was to everyone on Death Row by calling me racial names from the safety of his cell and segregated yard groups. I would bet my life that Harris would never have tried to show off if he and I were in the same yard group.

Convicts' Code

The convicts' code of respect is so clear-cut that if a convict was (or thought he was) disrespected by another convict, the convict, to retain his honor, would be forced to take direct action to kill whoever disrespected him. If he didn't take action, this would be viewed by other convicts as a sign of weakness. Once convicts see weakness in another convict, they will take advantage of the weakness and start exploiting him into giving up his personal items, which can lead to his becoming a punk. In the world of prison, what matters most for every convict is keeping his honor. To free society, this code of honor may seem like madness, but if you're in prison, upholding the code makes getting along much more easily, for each convict will keep himself in check around other convicts to prevent his words and actions from being viewed as disrespectful to other convicts.

Here is another example of how the code of honor works. Basketball games among prisoners could get fairly rough, like football. One day during a game, Hooty and I were playing on opposite teams, and he was playing too rough and ended up hitting me hard on my front tooth in view of everyone. Seeing this, Hooty took a defensive stance as if ready to fight me, and everyone else stopped and stood still on the basketball court to see what I would do. Hooty got ready to fight because he didn't realize that a convict doesn't fight when disrespected, but will try to kill the guy who disrespected him. In all my years in state prison, I never witnessed a fistfight, only stabbings.

I knew Hooty had been playing a heated game of basketball, same as me, and he hit my teeth by accident. So I said to the rest of the prisoners, "Come on, let's keep playing," much to everyone's relief. We finished the basketball game even though everyone still felt the tension of what could come between me and Hooty. Afterward, Chief came over and asked me, "Are you all right?"

"I am all right. Don't worry about it," I said. But in fact, I was angry. Hooty's action was an accident but still bordered on disrespect.

The real reason Chief came over was to see if I wanted to take action against Hooty. Even though both Hooty and Chief were Native Americans, Chief's loyalty toward me was set in stone, and he would stay out of my way if I wanted to stab Hooty since Chief and I held the same enemies in common, and Hooty was an outsider. But I knew that in his heart, Chief viewed Hooty as a little brother and wanted badly to talk me out of taking action against Hooty. I also liked Hooty, so I had already made up my mind. To relieve the tension among all of us, I told Chief, "Tell Hooty to be more careful next time we play basketball."

Chief gave a big smile, knowing I was giving Hooty a pass. "Thanks, Lee. I'll let Hooty know not to get too careless during any basketball game in the future."

After we returned to our cells, each member of the prison minority yard was allowed to shower, one at a time. After dinner, Hooty called me on the pull line with a page-long letter of apology for hitting my teeth, saying he would be more careful next time we played basketball and to please accept his apologies. I knew Hooty wrote the letter out of strength and not weakness because his apology aimed to resolve the problem. Chief must have told Hooty that if I took the basketball incident in the wrong way, it could have cost him his life. Though Chief had talked to him, Hooty also needed reassurance from me personally that I held no ill thoughts toward him. I too saw Hooty like a little brother and wrote a short note to accept his apology. We were still friends, which felt like a great relief. Like Chief, Hooty was a convict I could rely on to back me up. This incident shows how a very small problem could have gotten out of control and caused blood to be spilled if we hadn't thought clearly about how to resolve it promptly. This minor matter could have resulted in Hooty getting killed.

The convicts' code also aims to enforce rules which people in free society can't enforce. For example, convicts deal most harshly with anyone convicted of molesting, raping, or killing children. Some of us saw a newspaper article about a man sentenced to death for the unthinkable crime of raping and torturing with pliers a two-year-old baby. It sickened us to be aware of such inhumanity. Free society should know that many convicts have babies and wives outside of prison and feel protective toward our own families, which is one reason why convicts enforce a code that child molesters and baby killers must be killed.

When this baby torturer arrived on Death Row, he was placed in protective custody in a cell near the shower room. Everyone knew he wouldn't last a day in any yard group. Whenever I came out to shower, I looked him over. He looked like a very successful businessman, but I could see cold rage reflected in his eyes. Passing by his cell, I saw him standing two feet back from the bars. He stood with assertiveness and looked back at me with cold expressionless eyes. I tried to talk to him in a friendly way to gain his trust or confidence, and even went up to his cell to open up a conversation, but he stayed where he was and made no responses to my friendly gestures. He must have known I was trying to persuade him to come out to the yard so we could kill him. The prison administration had probably warned him that people would act friendly to lure him into the yard. After a few attempts, I gave up but continued looking for other opportunities to kill him. However, he never went to the yard by himself, which prevented my having any chance to spear him.

This scenario is an example of the unwritten rules that all convicts hold in common and try to enforce, compared to people of free society, who do not have the will to enforce such rules and trust the courts to enforce the law. In describing this, I am trying to explain why I would be seeking to set someone up to be killed, while at the same time hundreds or even thousands of people were trying to free me from prison and achieve justice in my case. I can only justify myself by saying that I found it necessary to live by the convict code as long as I was in prison.

As life on Death Row continued in this way, I waited to hear from the court of appeals on both of my cases. Then it happened. On March 21, 1980, the Sacramento District Court of Appeal upheld Judge Lawrence Karlton's decision to overturn the Chinatown case conviction, and I was transferred to the San Francisco city prison for arraignment court.

Margie

Upon my arrival to the San Francisco city prison, I called my sister Margie, whom I had not seen or spoken to for many years. Two years earlier in 1978, Margie had written me a letter asking me to adopt her. At the time, Margie was fourteen years old and needed guidance since she was no longer able to bear living with our mother. I had written back to say yes, but I was unsure if I could adopt her from prison. Since then, I had not heard from Margie, and I was very concerned about her well-being. Now, in 1980, while I waited to enter a not-guilty plea in arraignment court, a city prison guard informed me I had a visitor. The guards knew I was in San Francisco for a short court appearance, so they allowed me to have a special visit during nonvisiting hours.

I entered the visiting area, and through the glass, I saw my sister sitting with a baby in her arms. She watched me approach, smiling brightly, with the phone receiver already in her hand. I felt so good to see her. Among all my family members—my mother; my white sister, Mary; and all the cousins from Korea now living in America—I cared for Margie above all others, for her life was the most similar to mine. Both of us grew up fending for ourselves, and perhaps this created a special bond between us. As I picked up my end of the phone, I said, "Margie, how are you doing? I am very glad to see you, and who is the baby?"

Wrapped in a blanket, the baby looked like a newborn, maybe a month old. With a shy smile, Margie replied, "I am fine. This is my baby. Her name is Mary."

I looked at my sister. At sixteen and a half years old, she looked so young and innocent in her obvious joy to see me and to be a proud mother. Margie never let go of the baby, holding the baby in her left arm and the phone with her right hand. She said, "And this is my husband, Tom. He don't speak too much English but say hello to him."

Margie gave Tom the phone. He appeared four or five years older than Margie and had a serious face. I learned later that his parents, brothers, and sisters came from Vietnam and were Chinese-Vietnamese. I said, "Hi, Tom. I am glad to meet you."

"Hello." He returned a bit of a smile. I think "hello" is about all he could say in English as he seemed shy to say anything more.

"Tom, I hope you're happy with my sister and your new daughter."

Tom just nodded his head and returned the phone to Margie. Margie said, "I live with Tom and his parents on upper Grant Avenue in Chinatown. I am happy with Tom, and his family treats me as a member of their family. Tom has six brothers and two younger sisters, and most of us live in the same apartment. How have you been, brother?"

"I am okay, Margie. I have a retrial on the Chinatown case soon and am waiting for my appeal on the prison case. A lot of people are helping me and I am hopeful I could be free soon."

I felt great about seeing Margie, my new baby niece, and new brother-in-law, Tom, who seemed like a solid guy Margie could trust and rely upon. I felt secure to know that Margie was well taken care of and had been fully accepted into Tom's family. As it turned out in years to come, Margie and Tom went on to have two sons. Alex was born soon after Mary (I sometimes wonder if Margie named her first child after our sister Mary, but I never asked). The second son, Jonathan, was born in the late 1980s. After that, Margie was three months' pregnant with a fourth baby when she got shot as an innocent bystander during a Chinatown gang war and lost the baby she was carrying. During that painful time, I knew about her financial situation and tried to give her whatever support I could. But Margie was tough and had a strong husband in Tom and a mother-in-law who treated Margie like a daughter and her children as favorite grandchildren.

Reflecting on my family, I always felt distant from my mother and white sister, but felt no wall between me and Margie. I didn't see Margie during the first nine years of her life until I moved to Chinatown, and even then I only saw her once in a while when Margie's father, Frank, encouraged me to spend time with her, pick her up after school, or take her shopping downtown. Margie and I actually spent very little time together, yet she continued to reach out to me after her father's death and came by to see me at Jim's hamburger restaurant when I worked the graveyard shift in 1972.

After my arrest in June 1973, two or three years later, Margie's grandmother was killed in an accident in Chinatown, and my mother took Margie into her custody. Like me, Margie ran away from our mother, back to Chinatown. Margie realized that our mother and white sister didn't care much about her, just as I had experienced. Even before our teenage years, both Margie and I found ways to survive on our own. For me, survival led to Juvenile Hall and three stretches of time in the CYA system—eighteen months, then six months, then nineteen months—all before I turned eighteen. I don't know all that Margie had to go through, but by age fifteen, she found life with Tom, which may have saved her life. So I will always be grateful to Tom and his family for taking her in as family. At the time I am writing this book, Margie and Tom are still together and I believe they are meant to be soul mates for life.

Even though Margie was so young when I was arrested in 1973, she never forgot her brother. As I write this, Margie is going into her forties and I am in my early fifties. It is my great hope that someday soon Margie and I will be reunited and can reflect together on the past and on the strong bond between us. I say this because we have not spoken for over ten years; a rift was caused when I lashed out at her in anger and pain. But to me, Margie will always be my beloved sister, no matter what turns life may take for either of us. Both Margie and I are survivors.

As for Margie's 1980 visit to me in the San Francisco jail, I was so overjoyed to see her and to hear that she was happy with her life. But even though I was given all the time I wanted for the visit, we ran out of things to say after about an hour. So I said, "Margie, I got to go now, but I'll stay in touch and call you often as I can. Don't worry about me. I be okay. You take good care of yourself and your baby, OK? I miss you very much, but I will be out soon and I'll do anything for you."

Margie looked sad. "Brother, I'll see you soon, and I hope you get out soon."

I sat there with mixed feelings, watching them leave. I think we were separated from some of our emotions, but her visit was still one of the brightest days of all my years of imprisonment.

I went to arraignment court the next morning and entered a plea of not guilty to be held over to San Francisco Superior Court for the retrial of the Chinatown case and was transferred back to San Quentin's Death Row later that afternoon.

Soon afterward, the defense committee realized there would soon be a retrial of the Chinatown case, and the committee's efforts picked up momentum. Mr. Jay Yoo reached out to Korean church ministers and other American social justice organizations, while younger CSLDC members reached out to college students and Asian American communities all across America, and even in Korea. All the outreach was positive. I received more letters and visits from leaders of various organizations as well as visits from people on the defense committee who stopped by to see how I was doing.

Even my old friend Cecil, who was half Korean and half Japanese, started to visit me. I had known Cecil and her brother since 1971, but Cecil had decided after the birth of her son, Tomo, to stay away from political movements or organizations. Despite this, even she felt the need to support the cause of justice by joining the defense committee. She started visiting me as a friend to give me her personal moral support. The support movement on the outside was gaining strength.

Rumors about Nico

One day just before yard time, I was called out for a visitor. After my visit was over, the one African American guard who worked on Death Row escorted me back to my cell. He was an experienced guard in his late thirties, and I got along well with him. Most of the time, I had two escorts, but due to a shortage of guards, he took me by himself. On the way, he said, "Hey, Lee. Nico just got busted for bringing two pieces in his coffee tumbler to the yard."

"Thanks for the info," I said.

This guard knew I would not mention what he said to anyone. He was trying to tell me that Nico and La Eme brought prison-made knives to the yard to make a hit on me. When I got back to the Death Row tier, Chief called me over to his cell and passed me a note. I already knew what it would say. Back in my cell, I read, "Nico got busted for taking two pieces to the yard today. I think you was the target. What you want to do about it?"

I wrote a reply note, "Wait until we get to yard, and we will talk about it."

When I came out to shower, I passed my note to Chief. Death Row is a small group within San Quentin, so I was sure news had gotten around to everyone about Nico trying to take two knives out to the yard. Using his coffee tumbler was such a dumb way to sneak a knife onto the yard; I almost think Nico wanted to get busted because it was such a dumb move. During the next yard call, Chief and I got together, but much to my surprise, Nico also came out to the yard. I thought to myself,

"How could this happen? Nico is out in the yard after getting busted with two pieces? He didn't even get locked down for ten days, which was the routine treatment for any convict caught with a prison-made knife. Yet here he is, hanging out with his homeboy from Los Angeles, looking guilty. I could see the fear in him, worried about how I would respond. This has got to be an administration setup, to set me and Nico against each other."

I called Chief aside and asked, "What happened?"

Chief said, "Nico came up the stairs and almost passed through the yard gate when his escorting guard checked his coffee tumbler and found two pieces. Maybe the pieces made a clinking noise inside the coffee. Then Nico was taken back down to his cell."

I looked around the yard. About fourteen condemned prisoners were out in the yard with no movement. A few groups stood around just talking. Hooty leaned against the fence near me and Chief. Nico with his L.A. homeboy, Pento, stood near one corner where the gun shack was located. Nico seemed lost, like he didn't know what to do. He watched me, Chief, Hooty, and the other prisoners in the yard. After his attempt to bring in knives the day before, everyone was alert. I could feel the tension level was high because nobody knew who Nico was targeting.

I told Chief, "The way it look to me, Nico wanted to get busted. Chief, do you know if Nico and his homeboy from L.A. was having problems with anyone in the yard?"

"No, not that I know of."

I said, "Well, that only leaves me as his target for the hit. Or possibly you. But why did Nico wait so long before making his move, since we have shared the same yard for six months?"

After a few moments thinking about it, I said, "Listen, Chief. I really don't want to make a move on Nico unless we know for sure Nico's target was me or you. There are just too many La Eme members in San Quentin. That's an enemy we don't need." I explained to Chief that once we made a move on Nico, we'd have to hit his homeboy, too, and any future convicts we saw on Death Row with any connection to La Eme. The current situation looked more and more like a setup by the prison administration. I said, "So for right now, let's postpone hitting Nico until we have all the facts."

"Whatever you say, Lee." Chief was far from hotheaded about making a move that could embroil us in prison gang warfare and force us to continue making hits on any La Eme members or their associates.

Unlike in Tracy or the San Quentin mainline, we didn't need gang warfare on Death Row.

Although I knew Nico's target must have been me or Chief, or both of us, I said, "Chief, let's see if Nico tries another move or not. If he gets reinforced by another La Eme coming to our yard, then we might need to make the first hit before La Eme gets organized. But for now, let the matter rest."

Chief agreed with me fully, seeing the way my mind worked. We had been in the same yard for the past year, and Chief realized I could think clearly. He respected the complex balancing act I maintained, avoiding any unnecessary hits, as I did when handling the problem with Jackson and Black. Within a few days, the Death Row yard calmed down and went back to the usual routine. Nico and his homeboy kept their distance from me and Chief. I think Nico was a bit scared and keeping a low profile to try not to draw more attention to himself and to let the tension in the yard ease back to the level it was before he tried to bring in pieces.

I knew there had been a bad argument between Nico and an African American in the yard, which progressed to a fistfight, the one and only fistfight I'd ever seen during all the years of my imprisonment. Differences between convicts were normally settled with stabbings. This other dispute could have been the reason Nico tried to bring pieces up to the yard. Either way, I needed to show everyone that no problem existed between me and Nico, to calm the tension in the yard. Whenever the tension level flared up, each convict got ready for anything to come down, which made for an explosive atmosphere ready to go off at any moment.

But I continued to keep my eyes on Nico, as did Chief and Hooty. After a few weeks, Nico must have seen the tension level drop with me paying him no attention, so he started to mix with others again, but his homeboy, Pento, kept his distance and took no part in yard activities other than talking to Nico. I did have a few short conversations with Pento just to check him out and learned he had no prior prison experience, just some county jail time and involvement with a Los Angeles Latino street gang. Still, he knew how to do his time and carry himself like a convict who is confident of taking care of himself. Without Nico's presence, however, I believe Pento would have felt a lot less confident, the way most street gang members feel insecure alone but are full of bravery among fellow gang members. I didn't see him as my enemy, but still kept close watch on him due to his relationship with Nico. As for Nico, he still seemed wary around me in the yard. He must have received information connecting me to the NF from other prisoners or newspaper articles, and he didn't know how strong that connection might be. He also didn't know how close he had come to being hit by Chief soon after my arrival on Death Row.

Still, I knew that sooner or later, I would have to make a move on Nico, for Nico and his homeboy from Los Angeles presented a danger to my life. Nico must have been aware of the situation, but both of us were postponing the confrontation for as long as possible. And while Nico didn't know how to bring knives up to the yard, Chief and I could do so if we needed to.

Court Appearances

On July 21, 1980, I appeared in San Francisco County Superior Court before Judge Robert L. Dossee. The judge set a date for the retrial of the Chinatown case, but the trial kept getting postponed for legal reasons. Each time when I was transported to San Francisco for a court appearance, the courtroom was usually packed with people supporting justice for my case. The courtroom assigned for my trial had bulletproof glass almost to the ceiling, dividing me from my supporters. For each court appearance, I was in San Francisco for only two or three days, and apart from legal documents, wasn't allowed to bring personal items from San Quentin. In the maximum-security section of the county jail where I was held, there were five single cells with a shower on the tier and a mesh fence keeping maximum-security prisoners from having any contact with mainline county jail prisoners.

During these times in the San Francisco jail, I received visitors from the Korean Buddhist temple or Korean church each day. Different groups supported me in different ways. For example, one day my mother's friend, Doris Yamasaki, gave me rolls of quarters and a list of Korean people to call to thank for their support. The maximum-security section had a pay phone on a wall, and I used all the quarters to call and thank many people. During another stopover in San Francisco, one day I received about fifteen visitors, all of them Christian reverends led by Reverend Cha, who was working closely with Mr. Jay Yoo.

Unlike the Asian Americans on the defense committee, who were mostly young college students, Koreans in the San Francisco Bay Area included people like Mr. Steve Hong, a respectable and conservative businessman, whom I held in high regard. Each subgroup within the movement wanted to support the cause for their own reasons and in their own ways. Consequently, the first-generation, immigrant Koreans could not relate to the ongoing disputes among some younger American-born Asians on the CSLDC, who sometimes clashed over differences of political philosophy. For example, some wanted to emphasize my innocence as a symbol of how the entire justice system was corrupt, such that justice was nearly impossible to achieve through any legal procedure. Others who chanted "Freedom for Chol Soo Lee!" believed that the legal system could be used to overturn the wrongful conviction and wanted to stay focused on the courtroom battles to secure my freedom. Between these two ideological camps, one question remained unanswered: If Chol Soo Lee wins freedom from incarceration through legal procedure, what will it mean to gain freedom without justice?

First-generation Koreans like Steve Hong wanted no part of this infighting with the younger Asian Americans involved in the CSLDC. As for me, I was mostly unaware of it. When it came down to support given to the cause of justice on my behalf, I mainly saw how everyone united together, for which I am grateful to this day and will be for the rest of my life. Meanwhile, most of my attention stayed focused on fighting my own battles that none of the Asian Americans, Korean immigrants, or anyone on the CSLDC had any idea were taking place.

Nonviolent Protest

After living on Death Row for a year, I was tired. Death Row prisoners were treated in a way that was similar to convicts in the Hole and lockup units. The prison administration didn't give us any kind of program, just yard time and showering. I had been almost trouble-free on Death Row, but conditions looked to remain inhumane. One day, I asked all the guys in the yard for a meeting. At the meeting, I explained how we were denied programs such as access to the law library, prison library books, more time on the yard, contact visits, church services for those who wanted to attend church, and so forth. Even though we were on Death Row, we still had some rights. Requests to improve living conditions for prisoners on Death Row had been turned down without any concern by the administrators. Now I proposed that we should organize a protest, using methods such as news media publicity or throwing water on the prison guards—the kinds of protest that stopped short of violence against the guards.

All the prisoners in my yard seemed excited about protesting Death Row conditions. I informed them we would start the next day. This would give me time to contact the whites and invite them to join in. Also, I was aware that among the few prisoners serving their first sentence on Death Row, one or two were giving the guards information about any movements in our yard. Therefore, I expected the prison administration and guards would be ready, since there was a good chance that information about my plans to protest would be passed on to them.

After returning to my cell, I wrote a note to biker Charlie who ran the white yard group, telling him of our plan. Later that day, a short note from Charlie was passed on to me, which stated, "We discussed your yard's plan to protest conditions on Death Row and have decided not to join in. Instead, we will continue to file for our rights in court to improve the conditions on Death Row. We will support your protest by refusing all activities. We won't go to the yard or come out to shower. That is all the support our yard is willing to give."

Charlie's note was clear—the whites did not want anything to do with the minority yard protest; they accepted the conditions of the Death Row administration to keep the prisoners divided. Their ongoing efforts to file writs in court were BS, for courts will always side with the prison administrations on how to run the prison. As to their offer of support by not showering or going to the yard, they knew that once the protest started, Death Row would be on lockdown anyway with no yard or shower calls.

The reason for not having yard every day was that the east side tier of Death Row held only a few prisoners—about a dozen BGF members and a few TS members—and none of the east side prisoners had death sentences. By comparison, the west side of Death Row was full of condemned prisoners, with a small yard shared by different groups that took turns going out every other day. That was the only program we had— just a few hours of yard every other day, with basketball and chess the only activities allowed. In this way, Death Row prisoners were treated the same as convicts under disciplinary lockdown, though most Death Row prisoners had clean disciplinary records.

The only problem among Death Row prisoners arose when two white leaders were attacked by minorities after the whites tried to gain leadership of running the yard. This white dominance of the yard was favored and encouraged by the Death Row administration, perhaps to find an excuse to divide the Death Row prisoners. The attack on the two white prisoners gave the administration an excuse to divide the yard, giving whites their own yard. Since there was no prison gang violence on Death Row, establishing an all-white yard was an outright racist practice by the administration. This social segregation maintained racial tensions between whites and nonwhites, and gave Death Row white prisoners their own yard like they wanted.

After the note passing between Charlie and me, the next day members of the minority yard started throwing chips out of their cells onto the tier and burning whatever could be burned, mostly newspapers and magazines. No prison property was destroyed, such as our mattresses, blankets, sheets, towels, pillows, and so forth. It was a mild protest, and no prison guards came onto the tier to shut the protest down. Instead, they allowed the frustration of prison inmates to vent itself out during the protest.

Near Asphyxiation

On the third day of the protest, I had a small pile of newspapers out on the tier ready to be burned, along with some newspapers Hooty put out. Just as I was about to set fire to this pile, a gun rail guard standing in front of my cell called out, "Lee, burn whatever papers you've got there, but after that, no more burning."

I had a tumbler of water in my hand, and in an act of defiance, I said, "Fuck you!" and threw the water on the guard. Then I lit the pile of newspapers. The guard got pissed off at me for throwing water on him and soon returned with a fire extinguisher, which he aimed directly into my cell. My whole cell filled with a harsh fog of fine white dust. I couldn't see anything. The white dust cut off all the oxygen in my cell. I couldn't even call out for help, as I couldn't breathe in. In truth, what came out of the fire extinguisher was death. I thought to myself, I am finished. I'll die soon if I can't breathe. I was choking on the fine dust as I stood in my cell. After standing there for a minute, I remembered the central heating system was on and warm air was entering my cell from it. As soon as I realized this, I wet my towel as much as I could, and with the wet towel covering my head, I went to the air vent to breathe the life-saving incoming air. To my good fortune, the air vent was on because during different times of the day, the air was off. I breathed through the air vent for about twenty minutes until the fine mist of dust started to settle down, and I could breathe again and talk. The first thing I said was, "Hey Hooty, are you all right?" I knew some of the dust from the fire extinguisher had gone into his cell, too.

Hooty said, "I am all right, but the dust is everywhere in my cell."

"Good. Let's clean this dust out of our cells."

Hooty had no idea how close I came to dying and I didn't know how much the fire extinguisher spray entered his cell, but I was glad we both came out alive because I didn't hear any sound from Hooty during those twenty minutes of breathing at the air vent. He may have done the same as I did by breathing through his air vent, too. I didn't know if the gun rail guard knew how close he came to killing us, but when I saw him walk past inside his gun rail, I threw my water at him again. Had I died because the guard aimed the fire extinguisher into my cell, my death would have been ruled accidental, and no action would have been taken against the guard.

We protested for the rest of the day, but by the fifth day, no one had any more heart to continue, and the protest stopped as it had run its course. Some months later, Death Row prisoners were offered more programs, so I think our protest helped bring about the change.

Taking Care of Carlo: Part II

When the protest was still going, I was standing in my cell one day when I saw Carlo out on the tier sweeping up the mess we made. No prison trustee worked on Death Row, so seeing Carlo on the tier surprised me, as we were still on lockdown. I truly didn't know what was going on with Carlo, but I could see he was cooperating with prison guards while we were still on protest against the conditions on Death Row.

When Carlo came by, I said, "Carlo, put the broom down and don't do the guards' work."

"No, I got to do this," he said. "The guard asked me to clean up the tier."

By now, Carlo had been on the minority yard for about six months and was aware that cooperating with guards was a no-no. Once again, in a gentle voice I said, "Carlo, go back to your cell. We are still on protest."

"No, I got to do this."

Carlo refused to return to his cell after two warnings. I guess he thought that by kissing the guards' asses, they would be his friends and help him while he was on Death Row or maybe help his case in return for his cooperation during our protest. But Carlo's cooperation with the prison guards was unacceptable to the convicts in the minority yard. Next day, we were still on lockdown but were allowed to shower, so I took one of my prison-made knives made of the shanks of my personal shoes and passed it to Chief with a note that read: "Take care of Carlo."

As I was returning from the shower, Chief gave me a slight nod. I would have hit Carlo with Chief, but the gun rail guard had just given me a disciplinary report for assaulting a prison guard by throwing water at him, which meant I was placed on ten-day lockdown. After five days, the minorities were allowed back on the yard, and I saw Chief go by with his eyes looking straight ahead. After about forty-five minutes, I heard a single shotgun blast, and about a minute later, I saw Carlo being escorted by a prison guard. He appeared to have three stab wounds. As he passed by my cell, he gave me a sad look. I returned his look with expressionless eyes.

All Carlo had to do was listen to me and stop cooperating with the guards. Since Carlo decided it was more important to cooperate with guards than with his fellow prisoners, the hit he received was all due to his ass kissing of the guards, especially during a time when his fellow prisoners were protesting. All the months that Carlo was in my yard, no one bothered him or tried to take advantage of him. No one made him pay to be in the yard or said anything to him about his case. Instead, the prisoners on my yard accepted Carlo as I did. But when Carlo cooperated with the guards, he was viewed as likely to cooperate in other ways, by telling guards information he might pick up in the yard. Among the convicts, no one thought anything about Carlo getting hit. Everyone knew he had it coming. The hit on Carlo was just a small example of how seriously convicts took these issues while doing their time. The prison administration blamed me for giving orders to Chief to stab Carlo, and I was moved to a solitary cell in back of the AC Hole for ten days. Then I was returned back to Death Row's west side, near the front of the tier where sunlight filtered through dirty windows and gave a little better lighting.

More Visitors

One day, I was informed that I had an attorney visit. I was surprised to be led out to the main visiting room in wrist chains into a barred cage where a young Asian American lawyer named Don Tamaki was waiting. Mr. Tamaki had confronted the prison officials about prisoners' rights to have full contact visits. Mr. Tamaki seemed upset we still had to visit inside a cage. Sitting across from me in the barred cage, he asked, "How are you doing? How is everything going?"

"I am fine and in good health." I didn't discuss any details about life on Death Row.

Don Tamaki was not my lawyer but part of the legal team, which included Sooknam Choo, John Young, Gary Eto, Mike Suzuki, and Jeff Adachi, along with other Asian Americans who were all enrolled in law schools. Gary Eto had made several trips from Los Angeles to the Bay Area to visit me with Jeff Adachi, who was at Hasting Law School in San Francisco. All of these young law students eventually became very successful lawyers and remained committed to helping Asian American communities in California. While students, they got involved with my case by doing research, supervised by my attorney, Mr. Leonard Weinglass.

At the time, I believe Don Tamaki was heading up several causes related to Asian American communities. The hour-long visit went well, but I could see he was upset the whole time with the way prison officials had arranged our meeting inside a barred cage. He visited me again six months later under the same conditions to give me his in-person moral support, and again he still seemed frustrated with the visiting conditions in the cage, with me wearing chains. Mr. Tamaki may not have realized that he was the first and only attorney I was ever allowed to visit person-to-person like that, even inside a cage in San Quentin's main visiting room. Don Tamaki was slender with an average Asian male's height, but he knew how to carry his weight with more command and clout than the other attorneys who visited me through the glass booth. Mr. Tamaki demanded to be allowed to see me in person, while the others might have followed the prison guards' rules without thinking to challenge authority.

Among the law students was one female named Trina, who was from Los Angeles and was attending Hastings Law School in San Francisco. Trina visited me once or twice a week and was very sweet in every sense of the way a woman can express herself to a man. Naturally, I started to develop personal feelings toward Trina, even though I still held my deepest affection for Ranko. Over the years, even before the defense committee started, I had written numerous times to Ranko to express my deepest affection for her, but she replied with nonpersonal letters—about one for every three I wrote her. Meanwhile, as Trina continued visiting me, my personal feelings grew toward her, to which she responded well in both letters and visits that went on for about eight months.

Then one day, Trina visited me with a sad expression in her eyes. She said, "I'm quitting law school and moving back to Los Angeles to be with my family."

"I wish you the best," I said. I sensed I would never see her again.

By then, I had grown very fond of her and looked forward to her visits and letters with much affection. But when she told me the sad news, I was not free to discuss her decision. Much as it pained me, I did not try to talk her out of it. As she usually did, Trina held her palms up and pressed them against the window as if to hold my hands and my feelings through the bulletproof glass. With tears in her eyes, she promised to continue corresponding through letters as we said our goodbyes. She did write to me every so often until I was free, but we never saw each other again. Even to this day, I feel thankful to Trina for her friendship and affection.

There were other females who visited me, but only two—Trina and my old friend Cecil—aroused feelings in me anything near to my affection for Ranko. Because of my feelings for Ranko, however, I often asked about Ranko, even when my visitors were females seeking a personal exchange of feelings with me. As for Ranko, I never mentioned my feelings for Trina or Cecil to her. Ranko might have felt glad for me that I had female companions on the outside, but my feelings toward Ranko were too strong. I was unwilling to let go of Ranko.

Jose of Texas Syndicate Makes Peace

While returning from the yard one day, handcuffed behind my back with an escorting prison guard, I passed through the dimly lit back of the tier, where TS members were laughing, joking, and drinking prison-brewed wine. Midway down the tier, I heard a noise, then a lightbulb and socket burst through the bars of a TS member's cell. A piece of the socket struck and cut the side of my nose. The whole tier got quiet. I looked at the TS member, whom I knew slightly and then continued on down to the tier to my cell. On the inside, I was exploding with anger, but outwardly I looked calm except for the look in my eyes.

A guard asked, "Do you want to be taken to the prison hospital to get the cut on your nose treated?"

"No," I said, even though it was more than a slight cut and would take some time for the bleeding to stop. I thought, "Why did this TS declare war on me for no reason whatsoever? As long as I've been on Death Row, there have been no negative words exchanged between me and any TS members. Now how should I retaliate?" Later that day I received a long letter of apology from Jose, who threw the light socket at me.

I wrote a short note in reply: "Stop by my cell next time you're on the tier for a shower." After his shower, Jose stopped by. He stood so near my cell I could have grabbed him or speared him through the heart. The escorting guard was aware of what Jose had done the day before, so he stood back to allow me and Jose to talk over the matter between ourselves. The first thing Jose said was, "Lee, I didn't know it was you who was going by my cell. I am very sorry I cut you on the nose. I was drunk. I'm here to apologize for what I did yesterday,"

Jose and I were in different yards with almost no chance of being put in the same yard, but he knew there were other ways he could get hit, such as during transfer to another prison, or through someone else in his yard, or by getting speared through the bars or shot with a zip gun, and so on. Listening to him, I could tell he was sincere as well as afraid.

I said in a serious tone, "Jose, I accept your apology, but there's a problem. Everyone on the tier is aware you cut the side of my nose with the light socket. People were laughing about it afterward, and it made me look bad to the whole of Death Row. So here is what I want you to do. After you return to your cell, I want you to holler down to my cell and apologize so everyone can hear you."

I knew I was pressing Jose hard, for he was nineteen cells away, but I felt forced to find a way to settle the problem between us and restore respect for me from all convicts. Understanding the situation as I did, Jose said, "I will do what you said." He left to return to his cell. In a few minutes, I heard Jose shout, "Hey, Lee! I am sorry for what I done yesterday and I apologize to you for my actions."

"All right, Jose, your apology is accepted," I said.

I was glad the matter could be settled by hollering an apology down the tier. With Jose's apology, the matter was resolved without loss of respect, and we avoided unnecessary bloodshed.

Stanley "Tookie" Williams

For a while in early 1980, the prison administration could not determine if my death sentence still stood after the Chinatown case was overturned, so they sought clarification from Judge Chris Papas. During this time, I was looking out of my cell one day and saw a new prisoner arriving on Death Row. I was surprised to see an African American, about 5′8″, who was very well built—one of those guys who looked like he worked out with weights all his life. I saw no softness in him, as he was escorted down the tier, handcuffed behind his back, facing straight ahead, and keeping his expression solid. He looked like the kind of convict you stay away from if you don't know him. I soon received a kite note from Chief informing me that the new convict's name was Stanley "Tookie" Williams, who was one of only three still living founding members of the Crips, a street gang in Los Angeles. Another known member of the Crips was already on Death Row, "Big Buff," who was over 6′ tall and also solidly built.

The day Tookie arrived I was on twenty-four hour lockdown (except for showering) because the prison administration had come down on me again, and so I hadn't gone out to the yard for a few months. Soon after Tookie arrived, I was transferred to the back of Death Row's west side where the BGF members were housed and put in a cell next to the BGF's leader, Hisi. At that time, Hisi's group was engaged in a power struggle within the BGF. A few cells away was Big Red, whom I had known in Tracy and who had been stabbed by Jo-Mo. When I talked with Big Buff or Big Red, we didn't have much in common and little was said, but I got along well with Hisi for some reason. We talked about anything to pass the time, with mostly Hisi talking, as I was not much of a talker. It was more of an open conversation, and other BGF members would join in the conversation without cutting in disrespectfully. If they cut in on a private conversation, that would be taken as a sign of disrespect.

Now and then, I would call out to Tookie, but I had trouble pronouncing his nickname. When I said "Tookie" it sounded funny, like "Taki," and Big Buff would try to correct me, "His name is *Tookie.*" Tookie would respond calmly, aware that I was not making fun of his name. He knew from Big Buff and others that I was a solid convict on Death Row, and no one laughed at the funny way I pronounced his name.

At this time, Big Buff and Tookie were also on lockdown, and like me, they were not allowed to go to the minority yard. However, after a few months, the guards saw that I got along well with Hisi and the BGFs, so the Death Row administrator asked if I wanted to go to the yard with the BGFs. I agreed. During next yard call, I was allowed to go out with about a dozen BGFs. As soon as they were on the yard, the BGFs started their routine, running around military style, with someone sounding off to encourage those exercising. I tried to join in but was out of shape from being on twenty-four hour lockdown, so I spent most of the time watching the BGFs and keeping to myself. Meanwhile, Hisi and BGF members, who had been talking to me for the past few months, seemed to keep their distance from me. I took this as a bad sign and didn't feel comfortable at all, like I didn't belong in the yard with them.

After we were returned to our cells, I thought it all over. First, why did the BGF keep their distance from me without introducing me to

everyone on the yard, as if I were an intruder? Second, would my association with the BGF in the yard continue in future lockup units? I knew
it would be another five or six years before I'd be allowed back on the
mainline. Would going to the BGF yard draw attention to me as an associate of the BGF, the way I was viewed as being linked to the NF in
Tracy? I decided there was no place for me in the BGF yard.

That night, I called to Hisi and said, "I don't feel right about going
out to your yard. If I keep going to your yard, it's going to draw more
attention to me in future."

"I understand your position. It's cool. No offense will be taken. You
still good with us."

By letting Hisi know ahead of time of my decision to discontinue
going to his yard, I maintained mutual respect between Hisi and me, and
avoided being viewed as weak.

Hitting Harris

A few weeks later, I received word that Robert Harris had messed up in
his white yard group and was placed in the minority yard. Placing a
white convict in an all-minority yard was a very unusual move by the
administration. When Jackson and Black had messed up in my yard and
stopped coming out for fear of what might happen to them, they were
not given a choice to go to the white yard. On the other hand, for Robert Harris to come into the Death Row minority yard looked to me to be
some kind of setup by the administration.

Within a week, I was informed by the Death Row prison administration that Judge Chris Papas' death-sentence order would stand as
ordered in May 1979 until the outcome of my appeal of the prison case.
Also, I would be released back into the minority yard. Since Robert Harris was now in the minority yard, I saw this as another setup. The prison
administration was fully aware there was a serious problem between
me and Robert Harris, because six months back Harris had challenged
me with racial slurs at night when the whites were drunk. In fact, everyone on Death Row knew a confrontation would arise if we both came
out to my yard.

I think the prison administration first removed me from the yard
for about three months and then placed Harris in the minority yard in
order to increase the level of intensity between Harris and me. Harris
would never have gone into the minority yard if I had already been out
there. The prison administration knew Harris was a cell soldier with a

big mouth—maybe that's what got Harris into trouble in the white yard, where he had been for two years. With informants in both yards, the prison administration must have known a violent confrontation between Harris and me in the same yard was inevitable.

At the time, I didn't own a piece, so the night before I was due to be released back into the minority yard, I asked Hisi if BGF could get me a piece. Hisi had a prison-made double-edged flat piece about eight inches long, which he arranged to be passed on to me. The next day at yard call, I checked to see who the escorting guards were and noticed the African American guard who was friendly and sometimes passed on information to me. He was the same guard who had told me that Nico got busted for trying to take pieces up to the minority yard.

I guessed this guard might not give me the full strip search, so I taped the piece to my back. When he came to my cell, I went through the routine of standing in front of him, just lifting my feet without turning around or bending over. Other Death Row guards would have made me turn around for a full strip search and bend over for an asshole reach, but I guessed correctly—the guard didn't make me turn around before handing back my clothes and shoes. This African American guard, who looked to be in his forties and had worked in the California prison system for many years, might even have known I was packing a piece and decided to let me take care of business, knowing Harris was my target. Harris had been bragging about all the interviews he was getting from the news media because he was among those first in line for execution once the death penalty law in California was reenacted in 1977 after being ruled unconstitutional in 1976. As I said, he was all mouth.

I was the last one to come onto the yard, which was already active with almost everyone playing basketball at the far end. The only two not playing basketball were Pento, Nico's Mexican friend from Los Angeles, and Robert Harris. Pento and Harris stood near the court by the chin-up area on the east side of the yard. I noticed the gun rail guard was not following his usual routine of walking all around the fence enclosing the yard; instead, he stood or walked near Harris on the east side. As soon as I got into the yard, Harris came over and said, "I am sorry about calling you names a while back. I hope you accept my apology?"

I looked him in the eyes and said, "What took you so long to apologize?"

I walked away from him, thinking if Harris had apologized to me prior to my coming into the yard, I could have accepted his apology and the violent tension between us would have been dropped. Now that I was in the same yard, Harris was so scared that the first thing he wanted to do was apologize, but now it was too late to accept because I had brought a piece out with me. There was no way I could take the piece back off the yard, as we were strip-searched before being escorted to our cells.

When the issue with Harris first came up, I had told Chief that it was a personal matter between me and Harris because his racial name-calling disrespected all Asians, and I had to stand up for my race against any disrespect toward Asian convicts. I truly wished Harris had apologized to me right after sobering up or anytime in between the incident and coming face-to-face with me now. As it was, all the convicts in the yard, as well as the gun rail guard, could feel my tension toward Harris. All the convicts stayed in the rear of the yard, and I walked back and forth in the yard. Meanwhile, Harris started showing self-defensive martial arts moves to Pento and must have asked Pento to watch his back, in case I tried to hit him from behind.

I paced the yard for a half hour, looking for an opening to hit Harris. Then it came by chance. Just when I happened to be ten yards from Harris, I heard shotguns start going off, round after round, down on the North Block yard. The gun rail guard turned and leaned over the roof of the Death Row yard to see what the gunfire was about. This was the best opening I could get. I took the piece from my back and made a fast rush at Harris. As I was stabbing Harris, next thing I felt was my body flying up in the air.

I landed about eight feet away from Harris, bleeding from many parts of my body and realized I'd been hit with shotgun pellets mainly in my knee, which is why I went flying. One of the pellets hit a vein on my right upper arm and blood spurted out of my arm like a fire hose. I sat up with blood pouring out of my arms and legs, and other places. The other convicts started coming over to help me up but were ordered to stop by the gun rail guard. Still, Chief came over with a handkerchief, which I tied around my arm. I knew Harris was bleeding, too, but I saw him standing up checking his body, a sign that I didn't seriously stab him. Later I found out that I stabbed him twice—once in the side of his neck and once near his kidney area, but with no serious wounds. I was bleeding badly because the guard had shot me from within ten feet away. At San Quentin, gun rail guards usually used shotguns packed with bird-shot pellets to shoot at convicts when breaking up a stabbing incident. The shotgun pellets were nonlethal, but if the guard had shot me in the chest at that close range, I might not have survived.

The first guard to come out to the yard was the African American guard, but before he arrived, I was able to hide the piece under my shirt. Since I was bleeding a lot, he didn't put any handcuffs on me. As he escorted me, I limped slowly off the yard and down the stairs on the West side of the tier. Just as I reached Hisi's cell, I told him where the piece was, and as I turned around, Hisi took the piece out of the place where I had hidden it under my shirt in back.

I was taken to the prison hospital, where I saw a dozen African Americans all standing around the doctor's office with handcuffs on, so there must have been black-on-black fighting on the North Block yard. I waited for my turn to see the doctor, and while waiting, I saw Harris getting escorted into the hospital in handcuffs. As he passed by where I was seated on a hospital gurney, Harris put on an angry look, acting as if he wanted to start a fight with me. I thought to myself, "Harris, you're so brave now that an escort guard is with you, when less than an hour ago you were apologizing to me face-to-face. All this brave acting shows how big a coward you are." I regretted not stabbing him hard enough. My aim was not to kill him but to teach him a lesson. If I had killed Harris, I would have had no chance of getting out, but by just stabbing him, I knew the D.A. wouldn't accept an assault case because there were too many stabbings in San Quentin, and the Marin County D.A. only accepted murder cases.

Shortly after Harris passed by, I was seen by a good-looking young woman doctor, who asked me to remove all my clothes to check over my body, including my private area. I had a bit of a laugh within myself because a woman was touching my private area for the first time in eight years, and it took a shotgun to get me there. To be sure that I was not shot in my private area, I was given an anti-infection shot, and the doctor prescribed pain tablets two times a day. I was escorted back to Death Row in handcuffs and placed in a total isolation cell in back of the west side tier. There were five isolation cells on Death Row, and my cell gate was closed, but the guard left the door open. I was surprised to hear Chief's voice in the next cell. He sounded like he had gone mad, as he was cursing and shouting at all the guards who passed by and throwing water at them. I'd never told Chief I planned to stab Harris that day, but the prison administrator had him thrown into an isolation cell anyway just because Chief was close friends with me, perhaps in an attempt to set up Chief to turn against me by unfairly punishing him for a deed I did alone.

When I was examined by the prison doctor at the hospital, the vein in my arm had stopped bleeding. Most of the shotgun pellets had hit me in the knee area. The pain medication the doctor provided did not give me much relief but kept me awake, so I stopped taking the medication at night. But then, I would be awakened by cramps in my calves two or three times at night, yet I knew it was useless to request seeing a nurse or doctor about the pain in my knee and nightly leg cramps.

I received a disciplinary report for assault and possession of a prison-made knife, and the case was referred to the Marin County D.A., who refused to prosecute both charges. After I was thrown into the isolation cell, the prison guards searched Hisi and another BGF member in the cell next to Hisi's and found the weapon. The African American guard who escorted me to the yard and then to the hospital also came under suspicion that he had allowed me to carry the piece to the yard and get rid of it afterward, but nothing came of it. I believe the guard was fully aware of how to handle his job due to his long service as a guard and understood how white prison administration set up enemies to fight each other. While I was in isolation, he once came by and asked, "You doing all right, Lee? How is your knee?"

"I am all right."

"If you need anything, let me know, and I will bring it for you."

"Thanks."

By asking if I needed anything, the guard meant he would deliver items such as books, smokes, and coffee from other convicts on Death Row. Convicts in isolation for disciplinary reasons are not allowed to have anything, but through guards, I had already received tobacco, books, coffee, and edible items from the commissary. I sent some of these over to Chief, who was back to his normal self after acting out on the first day in the isolation cell. After ten days, Chief returned to his cell, and I was once again moved to a cell near the front of Death Row.

A few days after coming out of the isolation cell, I was taken to court in San Francisco for a trial motion hearing. I told Mr. Weinglass why I got shot, but he was highly upset that I had gotten involved in stabbing another prisoner while he and so many supporters were trying to get me out of prison. Here is what Mr. Weinglass failed to understand: Yes, I was fully aware of his legal efforts and the mass support of people trying to free me from prison, but before I could be free, I needed to stay alive. I was forced to stand up for myself in prison using any way I could to survive, and I could have been involved in a lot more stabbings, such as with Jackson, Black, Nico, and Pento. What Weinglass didn't see were the stabbings I had successfully avoided.

Since I didn't receive any apology from Harris before I went to the yard packing a piece and unable to get rid of the piece in the yard, the stabbing of Harris was not meant to undermine the defense legal team and my supporters, but was carried out with the aim of my personal survival within the prison system. While the outcome of the new trial on the Chinatown case and the appeal of the prison case remained uncertain, my present situation challenged me to survive countless future years in prison should I lose my court cases. I had to have control of my life in prison, waiting out the big "if's" of uncertain legal outcomes. I had to live as a convict until the full chain of injustice was broken to set me free. The bottom line was that I had to survive prison life first if I was ever to be free.

I was also in one of the main prisons, San Quentin, controlled by an enemy that I was forced to make in Tracy in 1977. Moreover, I was up against a racist prison administration that continued to try setting me up to be killed by a white attacker that I had stabbed in self-defense. After being in lockup centers for most of my imprisoned years, there was nothing I desired more than to do my time in peace, but with the racist prison administration's foot on my neck, holding me down to be killed and playing their games to break me down, I saw no other choice than to fight back against the prison administration. To them, it was just a game, but to us convicts it was a matter of life or death. Just as prison guards high-fived each other when I was sentenced to death by Judge Papas, the prison administration was set against me the same way gang members might carry out their duty to kill their enemies.

After I was released from isolation once again, I was placed on lockdown twenty-four hours a day. This lasted for two months before I was allowed back on the Death Row minority yard, and Harris was returned back to the white yard. One day in my cell in the front of Death Row, I saw the prison guard who shot me, and I said to him, "Come over here. I want to speak to you."

I could see the guard's face fill with fear that I might try to hurt him. He came within six or seven feet of my cell and stopped with no intention of coming anywhere near my cell bars for fear of getting hit.

He said, "What is it, Lee?"

"Why did you have to shoot me for?"

"Lee, I ordered you to stop and then gave you a warning shot, but you didn't stop, so I had no choice but to shoot you."

"Is that right? All right."

Relieved, the guard left my cell area. I was surprised by his answer because during the course of making the hit on Harris, I didn't hear anything the guard said, nor did I hear any shots from the shotgun. It seems my mind went blank from the moment I started making the hit until I found myself bleeding on the ground several feet away. Had this happened to any other person? How could I not hear two shots from a shotgun? To this day, I still wonder about this.

Changes

Over time, I noticed changes in the condemned prisoners. I saw other prisoners off and on, depending on whether I was locked down or allowed back on the yard. When I first met them, most were new to the California prison system. But after two years, I could see they had changed the way they carried themselves, with a more serious look in their eyes and their faces set like experienced convicts. They were doing their time far more seriously than when I had first met them, as they had been through prison protests on Death Row, seen others get stabbed, and almost daily heard shotguns fire.

One day in 1981 while we were in the yard, we started to hear shotguns being fired continuously for about ten minutes. Even the Death Row yard guard was firing his shotgun down into the AC yard, even though he was out of range to have any effect on the convicts fighting and stabbing on the yard. Later that day, I learned from one of the guards that the AB and La Eme had been allowed onto the AC yard at the same time. Though the two gangs were allies, some problems soon came up between them on the yard, as both gangs were very hard-core. When both gangs started fighting, it took over one hundred shotgun shots to finally break up the fight. Some days later, a La Eme leader named Moe was brought up to Death Row for being the most violent during the fight between the two gangs. The BGF sensed an opportunity to exploit the situation and started to try to make an alliance with La Eme through Moe in order to isolate the AB gang by breaking up their alliance with La Eme.

Within a month of Moe's move to Death Row from the AC, the prison administration transferred all the La Eme gang members in San Quentin's AC over to Folsom. They then transferred a whole new group of La Eme members to San Quentin's mainline and some La Eme leaders to the AC. Less than a week later, a one-sided race riot erupted in San

Quentin. The new La Eme members and their supporters attacked the BGFs and their associates; fourteen African Americans were stabbed on the mainline. It was a clear sign to all convicts that the La Eme was not allied with BGF and would stand by their alliance with AB. The prison authorities had moved La Eme members between Folsom and San Quentin as a way of continuing prison gang wars and crushing any chance that La Eme and BGF might build an alliance.

Moe was one tough leader of La Eme, but after Moe moved to Folsom, his own La Eme gang killed him, blaming him for the fight between the AB and La Eme in San Quentin. During all my years in prison, I saw the prison administration—from the head of CDC down to prison guards—use the same divide-and-conquer tactics over and over again to set up conflicts designed to prevent convicts from creating unity with each other.

Meanwhile, Death Row was getting crowded, filling up fast with new arrivals of condemned men. As a result, the Death Row prison administration classified us into two groups—"A" group for good inmates and "B" group for bad convicts. Those of us in the "B" group, who were all racial minorities, were transferred to the east side second floor of the AC. The AC was the Hole for San Quentin, and was, in fact, the same AC building where George Jackson tried to escape with a gun and was killed by gun rail guards in 1971.

After our transfer to the AC, the poor conditions that the minorities in my yard had protested on Death Row improved a bit. The prison administration opened up the tier so that condemned prisoners had more free time outside our cells and were given some programs to do easier time on Death Row. The AC yard was located between the AC building and North Block, where Death Row occupied the top floor. The yard was divided by big wire fences into three yards with a gun rail and two gun towers. The only exercise equipment provided in the AC yard was weights. Convicts could also play handball against the North Block walls, but I never saw anyone playing handball. Each yard was about one-fifth the size of a football field.

Weights

On our first day of yard, I was placed in the middle yard. The escort locked the gate and moved to the second gate, closing it after I entered the yard. There were some weights in the yard, and under the gun tower, a shower and toilet. After the rest of our group came out, we looked for something to do. The heaviest weight was a bench press weight of 165 pounds, which Tookie and Big Buff took and started working out. Hooty lifted some of the lighter weights, but soon got tired of it. I saw an all-white part on one side of our yard, which I took to be the AB yard. On the other side were African Americans, mostly BGF members, and a few came up to the fence to meet me. While I was talking to one of the BGFs, Big Buff walked by slowly and flashed the Crip gang sign forming his thumb and first finger into a "C." At this, the BGF member said, "Why don't you knock that shit off."

Big Buff continued on walking. Me and Big Buff never had much to say to each other, nor did Tookie and I, so I could see we would have some problems in the near future. I saw signs that Tookie was trying to dominate the yard. Also, with Big Buff showing off the Crip sign, change was coming to the African American prison gangs' power struggles, if it hadn't already started. In all my time in prison, I had yet to see the BGF make hits on the AB or La Eme; instead, they made black-on-black hits. I noticed this, but once again, it was none of my business to ask about prison gangs' activities or involvements. I also noticed that none of the BGF in the AC yard talked about Hisi. Were the BGF in the AC yard at war with Hisi? But again, this was not my business. My concern was with only the convicts in my yard.

After about a week in the AC yard, we found a 500-pound bench weight sitting on the weight bench one day. Tookie and Big Buff went right to it and took turns bench-pressing it. There was also a 285-pound compact weight which Tookie and Big Buff used for curls and back arms, and which Hooty and I could bench-press with a little help from each other. There was also a 65-pound bar.

One day, we were all in the yard, with Tookie, Big Buff, and Chief using the weights; Hooty and I had nothing to do. After waiting for an hour, I said to Hooty, "Let's go over to those guys to find out when they're going to be finished with the weights."

Hooty was just as tired of waiting as I was and replied, "Okay, let's go."

I knew, as did Hooty, that we might face some problems. Tookie and Big Buff were a bit scary, like bullies hogging all the weights on the yard. I didn't know them too well since there was no communication between us. At times, Tookie wore a towel around the yard. When we reached the area where they were using the 65-pound weight, I asked, "When you guys going to be done with the weight?"

Tookie responded to me like I was some inmate in prison, "Just wait your turn."

I took Hooty aside, who seemed as mad as me. I told him, "We are going over there, and after each guy has taken a turn, I am going to take the weight when the third guy finishes, saying, 'It's my turn,' then pass the weight to you. There may be a problem, so get ready to get down."

"Let's go," said Hooty.

Hooty was solid, as I had been schooling him since his arrival at Death Row. Here Hooty and I each weighed under 135 pounds but were going over to face two monster guys—one over 6' tall and another 5'9", bench-pressing over 500 pounds—to show we would not be bullied. If they wanted a problem, both of us were ready to get down, if not today, then at a later date when I could bring a piece out to the yard.

Hooty and I then walked over to the area where Chief, Tookie, and Big Buff were using the 65-pound weight. When we got there, they didn't even look at us, as if we didn't exist. Big Buff was curling the weight, then Tookie, and Chief went last. Just as Chief finished and before he could pass the weight back over to Big Buff, I took the weight from Chief, who look surprised and said, "What you doing?" He sounded upset.

I said, "We waited our turn. After me and Hooty is done, you guys can take your turn."

The expression on my face said that I was ready to get down. As I started doing the curls with the weight, Tookie went off by himself hollering, "I want to break these motherfuckers . . . break their fuckin' neck."

Tookie paced around the yard speaking to himself as both Big Buff and Chief left the area, while me and Hooty continued to lift the weights. I knew Tookie was big time on the streets and was used to getting his way, but this was the penitentiary where there was no room to show weakness. No matter how much weight they could lift, even the biggest and baddest convict could be killed by the smallest. As I expected, the showdown between Tookie and me had finally come. Now I could make my move first on Tookie or wait to see which way he would go—he could either share everything in the yard or else he and Big Buff would have to make a move on me.

After me and Hooty were finished with the weights, I told Hooty, "Keep your eyes open and stay alert in case Tookie and Big Buff try to make a move."

I knew Tookie was new to the penitentiary, but by now Tookie surely knew that every convict must stand up for himself when disrespected. Hooty and me were disrespected first by being told to wait as if we were weak prisoners, but I didn't show disrespect to Tookie when he said, "Wait your turn." They could have continued to lift weights with us by waiting their turns, but Tookie walked away with Big Buff and Chief following him.

After me and Hooty were done lifting the weights, Chief came over to us and said, "What the fuck you guys start?"

In an angry voice, I told Chief, "Check yourself. First of all, you supposed to be with us. Me and Hooty waited our turn. Don't come over to me starting shit over the weights because the issue is settled." I told him we should all get along and share everything in the yard, otherwise there would be problems. "You decide which way you want to go," I said. Before he could respond, I walked away. Talking any more would lead to infighting between Chief and me. Hooty soon joined me in walking around the yard. I noticed Tookie had calmed down and was talking to Big Buff. I am sure their conversation concerned me and Hooty, and whether the street or convict thing was the right thing to do.

Hooty said, "You're right, Lee, to tell Chief off about where we stand. Even though Chief is my Native American brother, I will stand with you if anything comes down."

To lessen Hooty's concern, I explained that Tookie was new to prison. "He possibly don't even know how to make a piece yet, and I already have a piece. But I don't think Tookie is looking for problems. He's still thinking the way he thought in the streets, but he is aware we don't fight in prison but only go for the kill."

I told Hooty that in the future we should ask Tookie to teach us how to lift weights. That way, we would give him his due respect while keeping our own self-respect. Tookie would see we were trying to get along with him in the yard. By taking our turn to lift weights, Tookie should understand we were standing up for ourselves but meant no disrespect toward him. We might have to watch out for Big Buff, who was a bit of a show-off and bully. But whatever Tookie decided, Big Buff would go along with, so we should just watch Tookie's moves.

"When we lift weights with him, he might use the 65-pound dumbbell to make a move against me, or when I'm on the bench, he might drop the weight down on my throat, but for now," I said to Hooty, "just stay cool."

As me and Hooty continued walking around the yard, Chief joined us. This action showed to Tookie and Big Buff that Chief was still with me and Hooty. When Chief joined us, he had calmed down and walked quietly. I sensed he realized he was in the wrong and was trying to correct himself by joining us. None of us felt the tension we had felt about an hour before. I also noticed that Tookie kept a hard face as always but had relaxed. I took it as a good sign to see no angry tension on his face. Tookie probably realized no disrespect was intended over the weights, and he may have respected the way me and Hooty stood up for ourselves as equals in the prison system against the superior size and strength of him and Big Buff. As we walked around the yard a few times, I felt the tension in the yard lifting, and there was no exchange of hard looks.

During our next yard day, which was every other day, me and Hooty went over to Tookie, who was getting the weights together. I asked Tookie in a normal tone of voice, "Tookie, if you don't mind, how about letting me and Hooty lift weights with you, so you can teach us how to lift weights?"

I saw no tension or anger in Tookie's eyes or face. He looked at me for a few seconds as if thinking it over, wondering if my words were sincere or if I might try to make a move against him using weights as my weapon. After a long moment, he replied, "That sounds good to me."

We started working our bench press with the 165-pound weight to build chest muscles and did curls with the 65-pound dumbbell to build our arms. When I was underneath the weight, Hooty or Chief helped me, as I needed assistance to lift the 165-pound weight off the bars. As I bench-pressed, Hooty or Chief positioned himself near the top of my head to give support while I finished a set of ten. When my strength started weakening, they assisted by lightly lifting the weight. In turn, I also supported Chief or Hooty. During Tookie's turn, Big Buff watched over him, as Tookie did the same for Big Buff's turn. All five of us lifted the weight, taking turns. I saw no tension in Tookie or Big Buff, only a bit of caution, which Hooty and I also felt.

When it came to back arms, Tookie taught me, Hooty, and Chief how to work out. Since we didn't have the massive weight-lifting power of Tookie and Big Buff, we used the 65-pound dumbbell for back arms and did three sets of ten on the bench lying down and five sets of ten standing up, along with another back arm form called "kick outs." By the end of our yard time, a few smiles were exchanged between all of us. I believe Tookie thought I was sincere about wanting to learn weight lifting without any ego trip over who was running the yard. With only five of us in the yard, Tookie showed no signs of "I am better than you," but accepted both me and Hooty without any power tripping. Big Buff might not have acted that way on his own, but he fell in line with Tookie, so that the day ended with all of us on equal terms with mutual respect for each other. All of us were in a good mood when we returned to our cells.

Within a very short time, Tookie saw that I was sincere about wanting to learn how to lift weights and wanting all of us to get along well in our yard. At times, Tookie would seek my advice about small matters regarding prison life and how to best survive within the racist California prison system and be aware of different gangs. It was clear that Tookie would always remain a Crip while in prison, and the Crips within prison would follow his lead. This made him a very dangerous target, especially among the BGF, who sought to be the sole African American gang within the prison system and were committed to breaking down the Crips and Bloods from Los Angeles and recruiting them for the BGF. Killing Tookie might help break down the Crips in the California prison system, so it was natural in the prison world for a gang like the BGF to go after someone like Tookie. Convicts of Tookie's stature posed danger not only to BGF, but to other prison gangs as well, depending on who might draw Tookie to their side as an ally.

At this time, both Crips and Bloods were coming into their own as prison gangs. In the late 1970s, so many Crips and Bloods were sentenced to California prisons that the BGF could not control them, especially when the BGF was involved in its own internal gang warfare. Still, the BGF remained the most powerful African American gang within all California prisons. If the BGF had stood in total unity, they might have prevented the Crips and Bloods from establishing their own prison gangs, but it would have taken many stabbings and killings to bring the Crips and Bloods into line with the BGF as the sole African American prison gang. This unity could have posed a great threat to the prison administration, and especially to the guards, who continued to encourage the BGF's internal conflicts and disunity, and worked to incite attacks against the BGF by the AB and La Eme.

It didn't happen while I was still in San Quentin, but an attempt on Tookie's life did take place after he was transferred to the "A" group of Death Row. He was stabbed a number of times in the "A" group yard by another Crip gang member because rival Crips on the outside were fighting against each other, and one of Tookie's enemies brought that war to

Death Row. I was sorry to hear the news that Tookie got hit, but glad he survived his wounds.

As it turned out, Tookie and I became good friends—as good as the prison system can allow—during the time we did together on San Quentin's AC Death Row tier. While Tookie was in the cell next to mine, we got along well and gave each other items from the packages we received from outside. Something Tookie enjoyed the most was chocolate chip cookies. As much as he liked them, he would unselfishly send me over two or three packages of cookies, which he did not share with any other convicts on the tier. In turn, I would also send over to him some Asian snacks, which Tookie tasted for first time in his life. Tookie would ask me, "What's this, Lee?" or "What that you send over?"

"Just eat it. It's good stuff."

Sometimes I sent him some dried squid, which I am sure Tookie never would eat on the streets. Tookie would say with a loud laugh, "I don't know what's this stuff you send over, but it's good!"

I also shared my food packages with others in the Death Row AC yard, who shared whatever they had with me and any convicts they felt a close bond with. In my yard, there was no tension but only good feelings of camaraderie exchanged between us. On nonyard days, even though we were in the Hole, we kept our minds busy to pass the time in our cells. Since Hooty's cell was too far away, we could no longer play chess like we used to. So Tookie and I started playing chess. I am not sure where he learned to play, but most likely in the L.A. County Jail. I taught him to put numbers on his chess board to match my chess board numbers. Tookie was a good player. I had a difficult time winning a chess-by-numbers game against him; he won more often than I did. Tookie also kept busy by reading and making paintings and drawings. As for me, I passed the time reading letters from supporters, and I wrote many thank-you letters in return.

CSLDC Actions

One day, I received a letter from Mr. Steve Hong, a member of the San Francisco Bay Area Chol Soo Lee Defense Committee. Enclosed with Mr. Hong's letter was a list of the names and addresses of about fifty Koreans. The letter explained that these Koreans had donated funds to support my cause for justice. He asked me to write a thank-you letter to each person on the list, which I gladly did. Mr. Hong must have put a lot of time and effort in gathering support on my behalf, as well as in collecting the name and address of each person on the list. I drew much strength from the letters and visits I received. Letters arrived from all over the country, and I wrote a thank-you letter for each one I received. Writing so many thank-you letters kept my mind active as well as hopeful for justice and freedom as the time neared for the retrial of the San Francisco Chinatown case.

I continued to receive visitors—Jeff Adachi, David Kakishiba, Mike Suzuki, Gary Eto, and other members of the Bay Area CSLDC. During these visits, I accepted their personal friendship, and we carried on with general conversation. We mostly didn't discuss any serious matters regarding the activities of the defense committee so I was not told about the strong disagreements within the movement between immigrant Koreans and younger US-born Asian American members over the committee's direction and goals. The Asian American activists who supported my cause were struggling against racist injustice and saw me as a racial political prisoner. And even among young Asian Americans, ideological differences led to competing factions. One side believed total commitment to my freedom should be the committee's single-minded goal, but the other side wanted the national movement to pursue a broader political agenda. Some had joined the CSLDC solely because they wanted to free me from unjust imprisonment and objected to others using my case as a tool to advance larger political aims.

At some point, the divergence in goals became so great that some defense committee members split from the "Free CSLDC" to form a spin-off committee, named "Friends of CSLDC." Most committee members did not want to stop trying to free me of unjust imprisonment, so the "Friends of CSLDC" ended up winning over the most supporters. As for the politically minded committee members, I had only met two members. One was Jai Lee from Los Angeles, who was one of the first people ever to visit me at Tracy in 1978, along with Warren Furutani and Charlie Park. The second person was Gail Whang, an Oakland high school teacher, who had visited me a few times since my transfer to San Quentin.

One day in 1981, Gail visited me to ask if a "Free Chol Soo Lee" rally at the gates of San Quentin would be all right with me.

"Was this approved by Mr. Jay Yoo?" I asked.

"Yes," Gail said, "and Reverend Cha and other church members want to come, along with many other Asian American supporters."

"When will this happen?"

"We plan to rally on Saturday at 11 a.m."

"Okay," I said, "that's okay with me."

This was the only time a Free CSLDC member ever involved me in decision making, though at the time I didn't know Gail was from Free CSLDC or that the rally was a political protest action. Saturday morning arrived, and Gail visited me again. She said, "Over one hundred people have shown up for the rally and more are still coming!"

That day was a nonyard day for my yard group, but on the next yard day, some convicts on the BGF yard spoke to me through the fence. They said that the Saturday yard group overheard the rally protestors chanting, "Free Chol Soo Lee! Free Chol Soo Lee!" I think the people in my yard and the BGF yard all felt that justice for my cause served justice for many convicts. If I received justice and got freed, they could feel that at least one convict had won his struggle against unjust court and prison systems. All convicts could share in this victory.

In late fall of 1981, Mr. Jay Yoo visited me and said, "Mr. Weinglass will be withdrawing as your attorney."

"Why?"

"The defense committee ran out of money to pay Mr. Weinglass's fees," he said. Jay Yoo explained that Weinglass planned to move his law office from Los Angeles to New York, and the CSLDC was seeking a new lawyer for me. "This time, we want someone who is based in San Francisco," he said.

I asked Mr. Jay Yoo how everything was going. He didn't mention the tension between Koreans and Asian Americans on the committee. Instead he said, "More and more Koreans are supporting you across the US and in Korea." He told me that my case was the inspiration for a dramatic radio program series and a three-volume comic book in Korea, and someone in Korea was even writing a book about my case. However, the organizers of these projects had never contacted the defense committee or signed any contract to contribute money to my cause, but the radio program and comic book series were popular hits in Korea, and as a result, many people in Korea were donating money to a branch of the defense committee set up in Korea. Mr. K. W. Lee planned to visit Korea and smuggle out some of these funds since Korean law did not allow anyone to take more than $10,000 out of the country. "The defense committee is doing all it can to build your legal defense fund," Jay Yoo said.

I didn't ask Jay Yoo how much money had been raised so far, but he said that the fund would be used up by the time the Chinatown case was ready for retrial. "Meanwhile," Jay Yoo informed me, "Mr. Tink Thompson, the private investigator, has been finding more evidence against the real killer." He explained that Tink Thompson's newfound evidence would be presented to the San Francisco District Attorney in hopes that the D.A. might be convinced of my innocence in the China-town case so I wouldn't be forced to go through a retrial. We both agreed the Court of Appeals judges must be waiting for the results of the Chinatown retrial before making a decision on my prison case. It was an informative and good visit from Mr. Jay Yoo, and as the visit was ending, I thanked him deeply for his continuing support. As for the loyal support from Koreans in America, I asked him, "Please try to express my thankfulness to my Korean supporters."

Maybe it was a good thing that I was kept mostly in the dark about defense committee activities in Korea and throughout US cities, while Mr. Jay Yoo coordinated the defense committee movement, allowing each regional committee to function on its own. I needed all my energy and intelligence to focus on survival in prison.

While my case had made me an international cause célèbre, my role as a celebrity was almost completely symbolic. The immigrant Korean small business owners and elderly grandparents who joined Korean temples and churches related to me simply because I was a Korean immigrant. Perhaps my case made some Koreans feel protective about their own children's struggles. Or maybe they felt for me in terms of the racial issues and hardships they had endured personally, as Korean Americans mislabeled as Chinese or Japanese, when they saw how my Asian face was enough to convict me of Chinese gang activity. They must have identified with my experience in America and felt it as their own. I received such strong support from Korean communities as a Korean struggling for justice and for recognition of my Korean identity, distinct from the Chinese or Japanese. I should have been recognized as a Korean from the start of the case; that fact alone should have ruled me out as a suspect for a Chinese gang murder.

Vincent Chin

While my case was undergoing trials and appeals, a racially motivated murder grabbed the attention of Asian communities around the world when a Chinese American became the victim of a brutal anti-Japanese hate crime at a time when racist propaganda blamed Japanese imports for hard times in the American auto industry. Vincent Chin, a young man in his twenties, was celebrating his bachelor party with friends at a bar in a Detroit suburb when two white men targeted him for a fight.

They picked Vincent Chin, a Chinese American, to blame for the layoffs of American auto workers. After refusing to fight on a night of celebration before his wedding, Vincent Chin later left the bar alone. The two white racists, imagining they were standing up for white American auto workers, chased Vincent Chin in their car and then beat him to death with baseball bats.

The news of how Vincent Chin met his death outraged Asian American communities, and committees formed all across America to demand "Justice for Vincent Chin." Eventually, the two white men were allowed to plead guilty to manslaughter, even though two men chasing down one man and beating him to death was obviously premeditated murder. To the disgrace of the US judicial system, the white judge sentenced the killers to three years' probation and payment of a fine so low it could have been monthly car payments. This sentence amounted to consent for racist white Americans to kill Asians or any minority members. In other words, the brutal murder of Vincent Chin was acceptable to the white court system.

Aryan Brother Billy Ray in the Yard

Within a few months, the five of us in the AC Death Row yard—Tookie, Big Buff, Chief, Hooty, and me—were getting along well, and there was no tension in the yard. One day, Big Buff was reclassified to the "A" group and given notice to be transferred back to Death Row North Block. Both Big Buff and Tookie had been placed on twenty-four-hour lockdown since their arrival at Death Row because they were members of the Crip gang—yet whites who belonged to the AB, the Bikers, or other white racist gangs were never placed on lockdown upon arrival. Tookie, Big Buff, and I were all locked down without any disciplinary reports against us, but white prisoners who were involved in prison or street gangs received far better treatment and were allowed to mix with the others on the white yard (unless placed on PC status for molesting or raping a minor).

We received almost no news about program changes on Death Row, but I heard the Death Row prisoners in North Block were now allowed out onto the tier and had more yard privileges. They also had access to church services and educational programs. People from outside brought in more programs. Meanwhile, incoming condemned prisoners now outnumbered the sixty cells in Death Row, so the TS members and Hisi's BGF members, who were not condemned men but had been housed there, got transferred out. I also learned that the Death Row prison administrator had devised a new classification plan for Death Row prisoners, dividing us into A, B, and C groups. He opened up another Death Row in "A" Block with more privileges for "A" group prisoners, including contact visits. Prisoners belonging to "A" group were basically treated like the convicts on San Quentin's mainline.

As for those of us still housed in the AC, our only program was yard privileges every other day, same as for others locked down in the AC Hole. We had only about eight condemned prisoners on the whole tier, which could hold twenty-five prisoners. I started feeling angry about the racist treatment of putting only the minorities from Death Row in the lockdown of the Hole. For example, a convict who was sentenced to death for killing another convict in prison—just as I was—was allowed into the white yard upon his arrival to Death Row because he was white. Once prison classification found you guilty of assaulting another convict, you were sentenced to eighteen months in the Hole for possession of a knife, and up to five years for stabbing or killing. Yet I was sentenced to the Hole time indefinitely. This showed the difference in treatment between white and nonwhite convicts who are sentenced to death for crimes committed inside a California prison.

Chief was the next to return to Death Row, which left only me, Tookie, and Hooty in the AC yard for condemned convicts. However, within a short time, a convict named Billy Ray, who was a member of the Aryan Brotherhood prison gang, was sent to the AC Hole for stabbing another prisoner on Death Row. Billy Ray, who was in his midthirties, stood about 6′ tall and was a very experienced convict. Tookie and I both viewed Billy Ray as an enemy and a threat to our lives because of his years of experience as an AB member in the California prison system. We viewed Billy Ray's transfer to the AC yard as a setup, and very likely I was the prison administrator's intentional target for it. There was little chance Tookie was the target, and Hooty had no conflict with any prison gangs. At first, I tried to keep Hooty out of any plans for making a hit on Billy Ray, but if I was being set up, both Tookie and Hooty made it clear I had their support.

I think this was the first time Tookie was in a position to make a hit inside prison. He and I talked about how we might bring a piece onto the yard to hit Billy Ray. It would be difficult, but I knew some guards who might allow me to smuggle a piece out. At the time, I had a piece in my cell that was about four inches long and half an inch wide. Both me and Tookie understood the politics of prison gangs, and Tookie agreed we needed to make a hit on Billy Ray as soon as possible so he didn't have time to make plans to hit us. If Billy Ray didn't have his own piece, he might contact other ABs and ask them to hide a piece in the yard for him.

I told both Tookie and Hooty, "The longer Billy Ray is in our yard, the more he is a threat. Don't allow Billy Ray get friendly. We all need to keep our distance." As an experienced convict, Billy Ray would size up where we all stood and try to get friendly with any one of us. I explained that acting friendly with your enemy was an old tactic for getting closer to make a hit.

"Hooty," I said, "I don't want to involve you with the hit itself because you don't have problems with any prison gangs. So I'll do the hit with Tookie. But you may be the only person who can bring the piece to the yard." I figured Hooty's hair might be our way to smuggle in the piece. I remembered Chief had tied a piece into his long hair when he carried out the hit on Carlo. In fact, Chief probably used this tactic when he made earlier hits on the Hell's Angel, Charlie, and another biker in the Death Row yard. But here in the AC, the guards used metal detectors.

"Hooty, let's do some trial runs to see how well your long hair is searched before you're allowed on the yard," I said. "Check out how well the guards use the metal detector."

Hooty responded, "OK, I'll see which guards use the metal detector in my hair."

"Once you get the piece in the yard, I'll put a handle on it using a handkerchief," I said. "From there, me and Tookie will take care of the AB. How that sound to you Tookie?"

Tookie replied, "It's a good plan. I'd like to bust that dumbass' head open."

The day Billy Ray came out to the yard, we didn't work out with weights but walked around the yard and let the tension build. I sensed that Billy Ray guessed what might come down against him and was making plans of his own about how to protect himself, as well as how to make hits on me or one of the others. As all three of us walked around, we kept our distance from Billy Ray. This was a sign to Billy Ray that he was dealing with experienced convicts and not some fish just off the bus. Our yard was near the North gun tower, the BGF was using the center yard, and the AB used the farthest yard. This way, Billy Ray couldn't make contact with the ABs two yards away. I was sure he had no allies in our yard. As I walked near the fence dividing our yard from the BGF yard, a BGF who'd known me since I'd been in the Hole called me over and said, "You know you got AB in your yard?"

"I know."

"Lee, if you need help from us," he said, "we can toss a piece over the fence to your yard when the gun rail guard isn't watching. But it be taking a big chance, you know that, right?" The BGFs could succeed if both our yards caused a distraction, some noise to draw attention away from where the pieces were being thrown. But BGF's offer to smuggle a piece to our yard was an attempt to be friendly with Tookie, who was not in communication with BGF.

"I appreciate you guys' support," I told him. "But we have our own plans to bring a piece out. If our plans fall through, I'll keep in mind what you said. Thanks. Let's see how everything works out in the next few days."

While these movements and conversations occurred, the gun rail guards couldn't overhear us, but I am sure they guessed what was happening below them in the yard based on the serious looks exchanged. Billy Ray's life was in danger, even though the prison administrator's plan may have been for Billy Ray to target us. Perhaps they had counted on me and Billy Ray fighting each other one-on-one in an area where I'd be in line to be shot with a Mini-14. If so, the tables had turned, and things were not going as they planned. After the yard recall, Billy Ray was taken back up to Death Row on North Block. It was unheard of that a convict who stabbed another convict in the victim's cell was not given any Hole time, but that's the way it was when the white racist prison administration protected one of their own. Even though Billy Ray had just stabbed another convict on Death Row, perhaps in a gang-related incident, he was allowed to rejoin the rest of the whites on Death Row.

Appeal

Personally, I was very relieved when Billy Ray got transferred back to Death Row, as I wasn't looking forward to a confrontation with anyone— convict or guard. My life was in the balance. With the upcoming retrial of the Chinatown case and my Tracy murder conviction pending in appellate court, California chief justice Rose Bird wrote a short opinion about the case. She said the California appellate court should make a decision on the prison case only after legal findings on the Chinatown case and appeals of Judge Karlton's decision to overturn the conviction were fully settled by the courts. Until these outcomes were determined, I was still sentenced to death according to Judge Papas' order to the CDC, which the Death Row prison administration decided to follow.

Even though Mr. Weinglass had withdrawn from the Chinatown case, he, with his co-attorney, Mr. H. Peter Young, continued to represent me on my appeal. At the same time, private investigator Tink Thompson, who joined the legal team in 1978, continued investigations that yielded new evidence and new eyewitnesses to prove my innocence. The real killer had confessed to a close friend the night after murdering Yip Yee Tak, and Tink Thompson found out the real killer's name and whereabouts. But these witnesses wouldn't testify on my behalf in open court because they still feared retaliation from Wah Ching gangsters who still controlled Chinatown.

Meanwhile, San Francisco police inspector Frank Falzon and the San Francisco District Attorney were committed to prosecuting me as the sole contract killer responsible for Yip Yee Tak's murder. Since the new witnesses could clear me of the crime, the police and D.A. refused to examine any new facts unearthed by Tink Thompson in his three years of investigations. Fully aware of the threat to the lives of new witnesses on my behalf, the police allowed the Wah Ching to intimidate the witnesses without giving them protection against possible retaliation. The police and D.A.'s interests lay with preventing the full truth of the case from ever coming to light. It's a sickening thought that those men who swore to uphold the law and protect the public would compromise the duty, honor, and integrity of their roles in this way. These public officials allowed the Wah Ching to do the dirty work for their efforts to continue prosecuting me for murder. The police and the D.A. betrayed the public trust by covering up information that could clear an innocent man of false charges.

However, in a case such as mine, they couldn't forever hide the truth. Once the flames of justice were lit in people's consciousness, they couldn't ever be extinguished. The torch of justice was passed from one person to another across the US, followed by an army of Asian and American communities. Even as some rested, others picked up the torch, because justice in my case was not only for me but for all Asian communities— past, present, and future.

Until then, Asian and American communities viewed Inspector Falzon as an honorable police officer. But during a TV interview, Falzon gave a clue to his true attitude when he told the interviewer, "We played a fair game regarding Mr. Lee's case." For Falzon, giving an innocent man a prison sentence leading to death row was apparently only "a game," regardless of innocence or guilt, but this game was a life-and-death matter for me. During the trial, the prosecutor's goal was to do whatever it took to convict the defendant. To Falzon, it was all just a game of who held the best hand to win the game; the truth of a person's innocence or guilt was irrelevant to how he played the game.

In the same TV interview, Falzon said, "Mr. Lee had a very competent attorney," when he tried to explain how the Chinatown conviction got overturned. Where the truth is concerned, what did it matter if I had a good or bad lawyer? Was it playing a "fair game" when police officers sent a rat into the tank while I was in the San Francisco County Jail, as if they could get my jailhouse confession from the rat? How was Falzon playing a "fair game" when he suppressed evidence and oversaw falsified testimony by the police ballistics expert to match the bullet from the gun I discharged with the one that killed Yip Yee Tak? When my "competent attorney" got the very same ballistics expert to admit his earlier testimony was erroneous, was that also "fair game"? Or was it only fair when the prosecutor won the game through false ballistics testimony and suppression of evidence favorable to the defendant? Was it "fair game" for Falzon to ignore new facts that could reveal the truth? What else might Falzon have done that is still hidden to me and the public as he went about playing his "fair game"?

When someone was guilty of breaking a law, Falzon's job was to uphold the law, but it troubles me to wonder what laws he was really upholding. What manner of upholding the law did he use in all the other cases he handled? I personally view law enforcement as a noble public service, and I think most police officers do not have any personal thoughts of power tripping from being in law enforcement. But everyone sworn to uphold the law in black and white must be involved at some level in doing their duty in the reality of shades of gray. This is one of the main reasons convicts across the board proclaim their innocence. While convicts may be aware they are guilty of something, we know from the onset of arrest to the moment of sentencing that our convictions were to a smaller or greater degree tinted in gray. A black-and-white law had to be broken for a conviction to be obtained, but rarely does the method for obtaining convictions follow black-and-white adherence to the law, nor does the outcome square precisely with actual guilt or innocence. The convict therefore proclaims his innocence.

The vast majority of law-abiding citizens assume they have never broken a law in their life. Yet when a sign states the maximum speed limit is 35 or 65, any driver who exceeds the speed limit by one mile per hour has broken the law in black and white. But this seems like an acceptable gray area for breaking the law in our normal daily lives. On the other hand, a convicted person who states that his Miranda rights were never read to him is less likely to be believed than a law enforcement officer on the witness stand who claims the Miranda rights were read. Given the existence of so many gray areas of the law, a convicted person claims innocence because he or she knows how much the law is broken to enforce the law. If law enforcement did their duty honorably, going strictly by the law, we might find far fewer convicts claiming innocence.

New Faces in the Adjustment Center Yard

For a while it was just me, Tookie, and Hooty in the AC yard. But one day, I noticed Black being escorted back to our yard. Nothing was said about the past, but I told Black, "It good to see you in the yard."

I knew Black was not a threat to me, and I was glad to see him out of the lockdown he had placed himself on a year ago. Black seemed a little nervous, but said, "Yeah, it's good to be back out on the yard."

We went about our yard routine. About an hour later, we saw a guy named Fields being escorted toward our yard. At this, Black yelled, "Fuck no! I am going to bust him up."

During their time together in the AC, Black and Fields must have fallen out, or perhaps Black blamed Fields for being locked down in the past year. Since both Black and Fields came out to the yard late, I figured they had each been asked if they wanted to be released back into the yard, and both had said yes. But Black's hostility toward Fields was too great for him to be in the same yard with Fields. We just stood and watched for what move Black would make. As Fields entered the yard smiling a bit, Black rushed over and hit Fields in the face. At this point, the AC yard gun rail guard fired a warning shot from his shotgun. Black immediately stopped. AC guards rushed into our yard, and both Black and Fields were handcuffed and escorted off the yard. It was the last time I saw Black during the rest of my time on AC Death Row.

I guess the numbers of Death Row prisoners on the AC yard were so few that the administration was trying to fill out our yard. Within days, our yard gained another new Death Row prisoner named Rudy, a Mexican from a Northern California city. Newcomers to Death Row were almost always housed with the "A" group on the top floor of North Block, so I wasn't sure if Rudy had first joined the "A" group, but had problems causing his transfer to the "B" group. However, Rudy said he preferred the "B" group yard over the "A" group yard. It was none of my business to ask him why, since my interest in those kinds of details only applied to convicts who were a threat to my security. Rudy was about 5'8", 140 pounds, lightly built, but solid and ready to get down if any problem came up. He fit right in with us.

After Tookie started teaching us how to lift weights and build up all parts of our muscles, he talked to us lightly and didn't try to bully anyone. My relationship to Tookie stayed as solid as it could be between convicts. While we were in adjacent cells, now and then, just to play with him, I said, "Send me over some of those chocolate chips cookies!"

"Man, you know I love my chocolate chip cookies," he responded lightheartedly. "This going to be the last bag I send you until my next package." He passed the cookies through the bars.

Tookie was one of the meanest and toughest of men on the streets, but he showed a much softer and quieter side as we started getting along well. Tookie knew I would back him if any enemy of his came onto our yard, and we were both willing to back each other when the prison administrator placed the AB, Billy Ray, in our yard, even though I was probably the AB's target and not Tookie. But we both viewed the AB as our common enemy and were solid in backing each other's play.

I was aware Tookie had many enemies for being who he was, and he relied on me to fill him in on the politics of the convict world and the games the prison administration played to set up a convict or groups of convicts, or to incite a race riot in the California prison system. As Tookie did his time in San Quentin's Death Row adjustment center, he picked up on the convicts' code of conduct and seemed to feel most at ease in the AC yard, where he experienced some degree of safety with just a few of us there. In another yard, there might have been more convicts who would go against him. During yard time, Tookie fully concentrated on lifting weights and refused to converse with anyone in the BGF yard when a few BGFs tried to reach out to get him on their side. He stood on his own as a Crip.

Big Buff and other Crips told me that Tookie's crime was totally unnecessary because he could get whatever he wanted on the streets without personal involvement in any crime. But he smoked a lot of PCP and committed a crime that put him on Death Row. I first met Tookie in 1980, and years later I started reading about him in the newspaper, especially after the April 29, 1992, riots in Los Angeles that erupted when the police officers who assaulted Rodney King were acquitted. By this time, Tookie had written children's books and was widely known for renouncing violence. His message had a great impact on African Americans and non–African Americans alike, and I was glad to see news that Tookie had been nominated three times for the Nobel Peace Prize. I truly hoped Tookie might receive the Nobel Prize for his work promoting nonviolence, for I knew his words and actions were sincere. During the two short years I knew Tookie personally in San Quentin, I had witnessed the change in him. Unlike other convicts whose violence might have spun out of control, Tookie matured into embracing nonviolence. *[Editorial note: Stanley "Tookie" Williams was executed by lethal injection on December 13, 2005, in San Quentin State Prison.]*

Within a year of weight training with Tookie, I was doing close to ten sets of ten bench presses with the 165-pound weight. One day, I decided to try a curl with 165 pounds and literally bent over backward to succeed. With the 65-pound dumbbells, we did back arms and worked out our chests, and I finally bench-pressed the 285-pound compact weight without any help, because the 285-pound bar was too short to bounce off your chest as you could the long bars. I weighed about 135 pounds, yet I could curl more than my own weight and bench more than twice my weight. Since there were no mirrors, we couldn't see how our bodies were building up from the weights, but during a strip search, an AC guard now and then commented, "You're getting built up." However, I never responded to this praise because we all spoke to guards as little as possible.

As weight lifting with Tookie continued, Hooty was soon able to curl the 165 pounds and bench the 285-pound weight. Hooty was about the same size as me but about ten pounds heavier. We didn't praise each other for all the lifting we did, but gave each other nods of encouragement. Rudy was less interested in weights, but sometimes joined us to pass the time in the yard. As for Tookie, he was very serious about weight lifting. Compared to him, we were lightweights, for he was back arming the 285-pound compact weight from the bench. With Tookie leading us in weight lifting, all four of us in the yard were solid and united in mind as well. I trusted Tookie, Hooty, and Rudy to the fullest extent that is possible between convicts.

Hitting Fields

Rudy's cell was in the back of the tier, next to Fields. One day, Rudy came to me saying Fields did a lot of cell soldiering and talking trash from his cell. I told Rudy if Fields kept it up, we would make a hit on him using spears of tightly rolled newspaper. Before planning anything, I talked to a guy I knew in the BGF yard about Fields causing problems. The BGF said, "Lee, we know what's happening with Fields. Whatever business you take care of with Fields doesn't concern us. Do what you got to do." This was a green light to make a hit on Fields.

Next I talked to Tookie. "Fields is the guy Black fired on in the yard few months back."

"Lee, I remember him," said Tookie.

"He is doing lot of cell soldiering and trash talking to Rudy. If he keeps it up, we're going to hit him. After he gets close to Rudy's cell, Rudy is going to spear him through the bars, and if he runs past my cell, I am going to spear him, too."

I told Tookie I'd warn him before the time came, so he could prepare just in case his cell got searched. I knew Tookie wouldn't have a piece or any contraband in his cell, but I wanted him to know the planned hit was aimed at Fields for running his mouth and at no one else. I knew from experience that whenever a hit went down, any convict might get nervous wondering about follow-up hits—maybe he was next? So it was best to forewarn the guys closest to you of what was going down, to keep them calm. About two weeks passed before Rudy approached me again about Fields, who was still trash talking at Rudy from his cell.

"I want to take action against Fields," said Rudy.

"OK," I said. "First, start getting friendly with Fields. For one reason or another, ask him to stop by your cell for short conversations when he's out for showering." I explained that Fields would probably fall for the setup because he hadn't done real time yet.

"Once I gain his trust, then what?"

"You let me know," I said. "Then I'll make a short spear for you. Next shower time when Fields comes close by, hit him. When he runs down the tier, I'll try to hit him again with a long spear. After he gets hit, he won't be doing no more cell soldiering. Plan sound good to you?"

Rudy replied, "Sounds good. I'll get him to come as close to my cell as possible."

I said, "You get the first hit on him, so make it good."

Within a week, Rudy told me in the yard that Fields was ready for the setup. That day, I made Rudy a six-inch spear made out of a sharpened toothbrush and tightly rolled newspaper, and passed it down the line to Rudy with a note: "After Fields gets hit and starts running, take the spear apart and flush the sharp piece down the toilet and then as much of the newspaper handle as you can."

The next day, I passed a note to Tookie about the hit coming down. Then I made a four-foot spear of tightly rolled newspaper wrapped in strips of bedsheet with a small metal piece on one end. When I saw the AC guard go back to let Fields out for showering, I stood on my bed, back to the wall, ready with the spear. Fields was led out, handcuffed behind his back—the normal process for all AC convicts. Soon, I heard him running down the tier. He must have seen me. He stopped against the wall as far as he could from my cell. I just needed him to take another two or three steps to make the hit on him. Then the guard said, "Lee, come on, put the spear down. Come on, Lee."

As the guard pleaded, he too didn't come anywhere near my cell. The alarm went off in the AC second tier, at which point it was useless to hit Fields with the spear I was holding, so I started taking it apart to flush the pieces down the toilet. As I stood taking the spear apart, the escorting officer took Fields and hurried past my cell.

Rudy was able to make the hit on Fields, but he could only inflict a light wound with a toothbrush piece. Both Rudy and I got charged with possession of weapons, and Rudy with assault as well. We both did ten days of lockdown time before getting released back to the yard. Making the hit on Fields was the only way to make him come to his senses and stop making life hard for those around him. When Rudy and I returned to the yard, Tookie, Hooty, and I all got to hear the story from Rudy, who was laughing about the hit. Rudy said, "Lee, it went down just like you said. I got Fields close to my cell by my bed, and I pulled the spear out and made one hit before he took off running down the tier. But the guard watched me for a few seconds before following Fields."

"Yeah," I said. "Fields saw me leaning against the wall, and I couldn't get a shot at him because he was ten or twelve feet away. But Rudy, what you did should shut him up for a while."

I then went over to the fence to talk to one of the BGFs in the adjacent yard.

"Hey Lee, what happening? That should put him back in line."

"We couldn't get good hit on him, but I think Fields will stop cell soldiering," I responded.

Then Mark of the BGF said, "Did you hear what happened on our tier?" Mark explained that the AB and BGF were housed on the same tier, and one of the ABs had sawed off a piece of his cell bar—most likely to hit the BGF tier leader or a BGF who killed an AB in the past. The BGFs heard the AB sawing the bar during the night, so before the AB could make a move, the first BGF who came out to shower went to the AB's cell and kicked out the bar.

"The AB came close to making a hit on one of us," said Mark.

"Well, I am glad to hear all you guys survived." I said. "Anyway, I am going to work out now. Talk to you later."

Even in the Hole where security was tightest, a hacksaw blade could be smuggled in. Maybe a prison guard helped smuggle a hacksaw to the AB in the Hole because the guard knew the prison gangs were divided by gang warfare. A convict with a hacksaw could saw two or three bars off his cell and use soap or whatever to replace the bars to look natural until the targeted enemy gang member came by, escorted by a guard and handcuffed in back. Then the convict would crawl out of his cell for a sure kill on his target. Guards knew how prison gangs tried to kill each other, so if a guard ever saw a convict come out of his cell with a piece, the guard wouldn't worry about getting hit but would leave the convict in handcuffs on the tier and run to the front to sound the general alarm. Here we had the kind of convict in the Hole who, if given a hacksaw blade, would cut through his cell bars—not to escape but to kill an enemy. That shows how divided convicts were within the prison system.

Ranko's Illness

I started receiving letters from an Asian American female supporter named Carol from San Francisco. The writing in her second letter impressed me, especially a sentence that read, "The walls are only so high as you want them to be." After a few exchanges of friendly letters, she started visiting me. I viewed Carol as a woman who had inner strength, and was attractive and about my age. After a few visits, I sensed from Carol her desire to be a more personal friend.

The guards sometimes allowed death-sentence prisoners to make phone calls, and after knowing Carol for a couple of months, I phoned her. During the conversation, Carol informed me that Ranko was very sick, so I asked Carol to visit me as soon as possible so I could hear about Ranko's illness in person. She came to visit within a few days, and soon we were seated in the small visiting booth. All convicts in the lockup unit saw visitors through thick glass and talked to them on a phone. After exchanging greetings, I came straight to what was on my mind. "How did Ranko get sick?" I asked.

Carol said, "Ranko went to a meeting in Los Angeles with some friends, and one night she got really sick, but I don't know how or why. But she returned from her trip very ill."

I believe Carol knew why Ranko got ill, but she didn't want to tell me. The visit lasted about half an hour. I was caught up in my concern for Ranko's health and my personal feelings for Ranko, which Carol didn't want to discuss. It was the last time Carol visited me, and she never wrote to me again.

Still concerned about Ranko, I asked my friend Cecil to visit me, and once again I focused the whole visit on asking for details about Ranko. I had known Cecil for ten years, going back to when I lived for a few months in San Francisco's Japantown. There were feelings between me and Cecil back then, but she was going out with another guy, so I put my feelings for her aside. During this visit, Cecil learned how strong my affections were toward Ranko. This must have affected her feelings toward me, for like Carol, Cecil stopped visiting or writing. I had known Cecil for much longer than I'd known Carol, and to this day, Cecil still comes into my thoughts. I think I caused her pain that last time she visited me in San Quentin.

As soon as I could make another phone call, I called Ranko, who sounded very weak and sick. I tried to comfort her as best I could over the phone, and for the first time since I'd met her, she responded well to my personal comforting of her. Yet after my phone call to Ranko, I fell into very deep depression for being unable to comfort Ranko in person. It was one of the most painful personal experiences of my life. For about three days, I was unable to eat or sleep in my concern for Ranko's well-being. I felt very depressed, and in that state of mind, for reasons I can't explain even to myself, I stayed up all night; at about four or five in the morning, I found myself burning all my legal papers, such as my hearing transcripts. I was sitting on the floor as I kept burning the papers. The Death Row prison guard saw me and came over. He said, "Be careful not to burn yourself, Lee. If you want, later on this morning, I will try to have the doctor see you. Do you want to be seen by the psychologist?"

"I just want to be left alone."

"I understand. Just be careful."

The guards on Death Row were more flexible than guards in the Hole or mainline because they saw a lot of convicts go through difficult times. As long as you were not a danger to other convicts or yourself, the guards were trained or instructed to leave a condemned man alone and let him go through his depression and pain. Other Death Row convicts who knew you were going through a very difficult time also left you alone, but guards would pass by your cell more often than normal. One of the main reasons everyone left you alone was out of fear that your depression was so deep that if they said the wrong words, you might lash out violently at them. So it was in everyone's best interests to leave you alone to deal with your depression, and when you did, no one would say anything about what you went through, as if nothing had happened.

During my years on Death Row, the State of California did not execute anyone, but two condemned men committed suicide. In the past, when a condemned man was escorted by a prison guard, the guard would holler out, "Dead man walking!" as if the living man were already dead. But after a new death penalty law went into effect in 1979, a new rule forbade escorts from hollering "Dead man walking." Instead, I think they tried to kill you within yourself before your execution—by allowing a condemned man in his cell to go through his depression alone, for example. In a state of very deep depression, the convict's spirit was already half dead, and he might take the next step by committing suicide. Every convict on Death Row thought about taking his own life. My own depression came on because I was so helpless and unable to comfort someone I was greatly attached to on a personal level.

Death may hold more value to you if you know you're about to lose your life. As a convict, you survive as you can, but when the pain inside you becomes too great regarding your loved ones, you stop thinking of your own life and only think of those you care for. This pain seems far greater than concern for your personal situation in prison. I was used to the barriers in carrying on a love life while locked down in prison, but how could I show my caring for those on the outside? My depression deepened. I tried to write, or even ask prison guards for another phone call, but it all felt like an empty gesture. In due time, Ranko got well, but the guilty feeling of being unable to comfort her from prison remained with me for some time.

Stuart Hanlon and Tony Serra

Leonard Weinglass was still my appeal lawyer on the Tracy prison case. With attorney H. Peter Young, he defeated the state's appeals to reverse the decision of the Sacramento Superior Court by Judge Karlton, who granted my writ on the Chinatown case in 1979 and ordered a retrial.

Now, the Chinatown case retrial was a reality about to unfold. In 1982, the defense committee found two San Francisco attorneys for the retrial. Their names were Stuart Hanlon and Tony Serra. I had no idea what kind of attorneys they were, but I trusted the defense committee to act in my best legal interests.

I will never forget my first meeting with my new attorneys, Mr. Hanlon and Mr. Serra. One day, without any notice, they showed up for a first visit with me. As I entered the attorney visiting booth, I saw two white men with their noses pressed close to the glass panel, looking totally out of place. Mr. Hanlon was about 5'10", and Mr. Serra was close to 7' tall, with long hair. I felt caught off guard by their appearances. What impression was I supposed to have of my future trial attorneys when I knew nothing about them? I looked at their silly faces filling the small window and thought, "This must be a mistake. Are these the best attorneys the defense committee can find? I am in trouble!" We went through introductions, which lasted half an hour. I was not impressed by either one of them. I thought, "I hope to God the defense committee knows what they're doing."

No one told me that Mr. Hanlon was just starting his legal career, but would turn out to be the most committed criminal attorney a defendant could ever hope to have. As for Mr. Serra, he was already one of the best criminal attorneys in the nation. The defense committee couldn't have found better representation for my upcoming retrial. Also, by this time, many Bay Area "Friends of CSLDC" were enrolled in law school at Hastings in San Francisco (or in Southern California, as in Gary Eto's case), and some, like Sooknam Choo and John Young, were almost ready to take their bar exams. These law students provided valuable legal research for Mr. Hanlon, who laid out the groundwork for the case before the strange Mr. Serra joined the team closer to the trial date.

Meanwhile, private investigator Tink Thompson continued to work with the new attorneys and was discovering piles of new evidence supporting my innocence of the Chinatown murder. He had tried to present the new evidence to the trial judge, Inspector Falzon, and the prosecutor, but the young prosecutor, Arlo Smith, refused to accept it. In the weeks leading up to the trial, I felt very at ease with Mr. Thompson's investigations, the law students' work, and Mr. Hanlon and Mr. Serra's preparations. For the retrial, I was transferred to San Francisco County Jail and held in a maximum-security single cell. After the transfer, I started receiving daily visits from supporters as well as attorney visits.

Doris Yamasaki visited with others from the Buddhist temple, and Reverend Cha brought in a delegation of about fifteen reverends from Korean churches in San Francisco. I could only communicate in English with Doris and Reverend Cha, but Koreans visited me daily to show their support.

The San Francisco County Jail deputy even allowed me to have a visiting area where jail trustees received visitors at about three or six different booths, so I could speak to two visitors at the same time. A normal county jail inmate was allowed twenty minutes per visitor, but no time limit was set on the visits I received. The county jail deputies were well aware I had spent the past nine years in state prison and recognized the sincerity of my support from the local Asian American community. For the first time in my life, I received some kindness from the county jail guards in the form of unlimited visits from people wishing to see me. Also, I was fully buffed out from weight lifting in San Quentin by then, and the last thing the county jail officials wanted was any problems from me. I appreciated the good treatment and remained a model prisoner. In the county jail, the CSLDC movement was shown no resentment of any kind. The deputy just came into the maximum-security section, opened my cell and said, "Lee, you've got a visitor," or "Lee, you have a legal visit," and I would walk out to see the visitor or legal team member. For the previous five years, I had never left my cell without first undergoing a strip search and handcuffing, so this was the nearest to freedom I'd experienced for a long time. Even though my security status separated me from the mainline twelve-man tank, San Francisco County Jail time was easy for me.

However, it seemed there was always someone who wanted to start a problem. One day, I was returning to my cell from a visit and just as I passed by a big white deputy, he ordered me to stop and put my head against the wall for no reason whatsoever. For a moment, I just stood looking at him—he was over 6' tall and buffed like he worked out with weights. Next thing I knew, he shoved me against the wall and shouted, "Put your hands on the wall!"

At this point, I started to fistfight with the deputy as I would have done under the same conditions in state prisons when confronted by a racist or power-tripping guard. But then I stopped myself. I could easily have lost my temper, and this deputy looked like I could have brought him down with a few blows and kicks, but I saw he was power tripping to agitate me into fighting with him. I knew the county jail was not the place to fight with guards. Both of us knew if we came to blows, other deputies would pull us apart and assault me. A few deputies stood nearby, seven or eight feet away, in front of their office and had seen the problem from the start. I saw a look in their eyes as if asking me to back down from this "show-off" deputy. So I put my arms and hands up on the wall and allowed the deputy to pat search me. Had I resisted, as I would have done in state prison, I'd have been charged with assault on a deputy, so I stood down. Afterward, the deputy said I could go back to my cell, which I did, much to the relief of those who would have had to back up the bully of a deputy with no common sense. Fortunately, this incident was the only problem I had with any county jail deputies or prisoners.

During the days leading up to the retrial, the defense committee carried out many activities, alongside investigative news media coverage. Both K. W. Lee and Steve Magagnini from the *Sacramento Union* came to San Francisco, as did Raul Ramirez from the *Oakland Tribune*. Articles about my case appeared in those newspapers almost daily; they also appeared in other local media and in nonlocal news as far away as Korea. Television newscasters got ready to cover the trial while the defense committee gathered supporters to pack the courtroom. Even the prosecutor recruited police officers to attend the trial and support his side of the case. I'd never heard of any prosecutors seeking the support of law enforcement officers in a case that did not involve law enforcement officers, but they were going all out to make a show of support to counter the support I was receiving. As it happened, throughout the trial, a small group of law enforcement officers sat in the spectator section behind the prosecutor's table.

On August 1, 1982, just before the trial began, Freedom for CSLDC took out a quarter-page advertisement in the *San Francisco Examiner* and *Chronicle*. The ad listed hundreds and hundreds of names of individuals and organizations across the United States, as well as international supporters in Korea and Japan, all of whom questioned the injustice of my conviction and demanded a fair retrial on my behalf. The defense committee also sought approval from the presiding judge, the Honorable Robert L. Dossee, to allow my supporters to rally before the trial in front of the courthouse and the police department at the Hall of Justice. The prosecutor, Arlo Smith, opposed the rally, but my attorneys promised Judge Dossee that all rally participants would conduct themselves in a lawful and orderly manner. The judge granted the defense's motion, and the rally was allowed to be held on a weekday. Visitors told me that hundreds of people converged on the rally from all over the Bay Area and Sacramento, and even from as far as Los Angeles, New York, and Hawai'i, as numerous CSLDC members had already traveled to San Francisco to attend the trial. Meanwhile, news media from Korea and Japan, as well as from throughout the United States, all got ready to cover the trial.

On the day of the rally, I heard the sound of chanting rise up from street level to the San Francisco County Jail on the seventh floor of the Hall of Justice. A crowd of voices cried out in unison: "Justice for Chol Soo Lee! Freedom for Chol Soo Lee! Justice for Chol Soo Lee! Freedom for Chol Soo Lee!"

Bulletproof Courtroom

In early August, jury selection began. The courtroom was divided by a bulletproof glass panel, which separated the spectators from the judge, jury, defense, and prosecution tables. Jury selection took almost a week and included about four alternate jurors. Judge Dossee presided over initial trial motions, and then the prosecution made their opening argument, outlining the people's case.

The prosecutor stated that two eyewitnesses would testify that I was the killer of Yip Yee Tak. Testimony would be read to the jury from a third eyewitness who was unable to attend the retrial. Then came the big surprise. The prosecutor explained a motive behind the gangland killing—that I was a hired killer for Joe Fong's gang, a group known to have accepted me in Tracy prison. A prison rat had provided this information to James Lassart, the prosecutor of the original Chinatown case in 1974, who was now a federal prosecutor for the RICO case against the NF prison gang. This trumped-up theory was a total repeat of the past. In the 1974 trial, my attorney, Hamilton Hintz, allowed Lassart to bring into evidence Inspector Falzon's story that I was a member of the Ski Mask gang, hired by the Wah Ching to kill their own advisor, Yip Yee Tak. Now they said I was hired by Joe Fong. After the prosecutor's opening statement, both of my attorneys gave opening statements, outlining the defense's case of mistaken identification by the prosecution's witnesses and argued that the witnesses for the defense, including a Chinese witness, were much closer to the scene of Yip Yee Tak's shooting than were the prosecution's witnesses.

As the Chinatown case retrial began, most of the spectator seating in the courtroom was full of people supporting justice in my case. Many were elderly people from the Korean Buddhist temple and Korean churches, including monks and reverends. There were also law students in their midtwenties, and Asian American community activists like Ranko Yamada, Tom Kim, and Jeff Mori, as well as attorneys like Don Tamaki, Sooknam Choo, and John Young. The latter two had just passed their bar exams and were staying in San Francisco for the trial while their first jobs awaited them in New York City. They were only a month away from starting their careers as new attorneys-at-law. Peggy Saika and her husband, Art Chen, also came from New York to attend the trial. The majority of supporters were defense committee members, including the people who first formed the defense committee in Sacramento in early 1978, such as Dr. Luke Kim and his wife, Grace Kim. I felt that all my supporters gave fully from the heart and took nothing in return.

After the opening statements, the first day in court ended with the hearing of witness testimony slated to begin on day two. After listening to both opening statements by the prosecution and my attorneys, and seeing the supporters behind the bulletproof glass having an impact on the jury, I felt sure I would be found not guilty. My attorneys had given a very strong outline of the case and had witnesses who would back our case fully. From that first day forward, I had no doubt in my mind that justice would be served in this trial. That night, both Stuart Hanlon and Tony Serra visited me and asked, "What do you think about the jury and the trial?"

At the time, I still had a lot of mixed feelings toward both Stuart and Tony, but I replied, "I feel confident about the trial's outcome and feel we have a good jury of open-minded people."

The jury was made up of both men and women, and a majority of white people. All Asians were excused. But it was a very different kind of jury than the one I faced at my first trial in Sacramento. I felt sure the San Francisco jury would handle my case fairly. My overall feelings were very positive, but I felt mixed emotions about getting a second chance to prove my innocence while having had to wait over nine years for this day to arrive.

Both Stuart and Tony were very understanding as they kept me up to date on the defense team's activities. A scale model had been built of the Grant and Pacific intersection as an exhibit to show the jury. Meanwhile, Tink Thompson continued to seek new witnesses who might be willing to testify in open court on my behalf. Stuart and Tony received help from Sooknam Choo, John Young, and other Asian law students. The team worked hard every night going over all the issues of the retrial, seeing if any new motions needed to be filed and strategizing how to handle the prosecution witnesses that included two prison rats from Tracy whom the federal prosecutor, James Lassart, had found to supply my alleged motive and supposed confession to the murder of Yip Yee Tak. One of the rats, Ray Contreras, had already testified against me in the prison case.

Both Stuart and Tony looked tired, but I felt their full commitment to proving my innocence, as they were aware of how much this trial meant to me as well as to the Asian American community. They bore the heavy burden of our hopes and expectations with confidence and great humanity. As a defendant, I could not have asked for better attorneys than Stuart and Tony. But as the defendant, I also watched the courtroom drama unfold knowing the outcome would affect my whole life. At age thirty, I faced a future of great uncertainty. Separate from the outcome of this trial, I had been convicted of a second murder in the prison case still in the California courts. After this retrial, would I still remain on death row or be resentenced to life imprisonment? Or would I have the great fortune to be granted a retrial for the prison case, too?

These were a great many "ifs" affecting my life, which created mixed emotions. I didn't feel beaten down by the legal system, for I felt confident about the outcome of the Chinatown case's retrial. Yet I was fully aware—while my supporters were probably unaware—that there was no way I could survive in prison alone against the powerful gangs of the AB, the Bikers, and La Eme. Ever since the classification committee in Tracy tied me to the NF in my record, I had been living under a death sentence—death by prison gangs—as long as I remained in any California prison. It could truly be called a miracle that I was still alive to receive the support of good will from people on the outside. But did that miracle have a time limit—an expiration date?

I never discussed these issues with people on the outside. Seeing the movement's good will and desire for justice, I didn't want to bring dark clouds over them. Instead, I kept encouraging them to break the chains of injustice binding me to prison. It's as if I never allowed the darker side of reality that I experienced daily in prison to be their concern. I received so much good will from people all across America, as well as overseas from Korea and Japan. The movement to free me was really a struggle for justice for all of us, so that even if I died within the California prison system, hope would still remain because we could truly say we struggled for justice with all our hearts, souls, and minds.

With these thoughts and emotions, I looked forward to the next day. The courtroom was packed as the second day of trial began.

Questioning Physical Evidence

The first witnesses to testify were the San Francisco County coroner and the ballistics expert. The coroner testified about the cause of Yip Yee Tak's death, how many times he was shot, and the execution-style shot to the back of his head. The gun was found in an alley near Pacific and Grant Avenues, and the shell casings for the bullets were not .38 caliber. After the prosecutor finished questioning the witness, the defense cross-examined. Then the ballistics expert testified that the gun used to kill Yip Yee Tak left different shell casings than the .38 caliber bullet retrieved from the building next door to my boardinghouse room. I had admitted in the prior trial that .38 caliber bullets were loaded in the .357 gun I had borrowed from a friend and accidentally discharged in my room. Under cross-examination, the ballistics expert admitted he was mistaken in the prior trial when he matched the bullet I discharged with the .38 gun used to kill Yip Yee Tak. This mistaken match was one of the chief pieces of evidence used against me in the first trial.

I wanted my attorneys to further question the ballistics expert as to how he mismatched bullets from two different guns, which was a scientific impossibility. I told them, "At my first trial, he got away with perjury, and now he wants to get away with saying he made a *mistake?*" But my attorneys replied, "The expert admitted his mistake. The jury knows the truth, so there is no need to question him further."

Testimony from the coroner and ballistics expert took up most of the day, so the trial was adjourned until the next day. Until now, Tony Serra had kept his almost waist-length hair tucked under his jacket, but now he let his hair out. He looked a bit odd and wore an old suit with pants too short for him. But from the moment he made his opening statement to the jury, everyone immediately sensed how good of an attorney he was. Stuart Hanlon dressed in a neat suit, like most trial lawyers, but his opening remarks were just as fiery as Tony Serra's. By appearance, Stuart and Tony looked mismatched, but in fact, one couldn't have asked for a better match. Watching them, I thought about my first impressions of them, looking so silly with their big smiles and faces almost pressed on the visiting booth glass. They were serious lawyers. As I watched them, I was very impressed, and my confidence in them continued to build.

Questioning Eyewitnesses

The next day, the prosecution brought out Andy Mill, their first eyewitness. To us, Mill's testimony sounded like a memorized script. He testified that he was in San Francisco Chinatown eating and sight-seeing. At about 7 p.m., he walked toward the Broadway Street nightclub district. Just as he reached the Northeast corner of Pacific and Grant Avenues, he heard loud gunshots coming from the diagonally opposite corner of the intersection. He looked in the direction of the sound and saw a man lean down over and fire a gun into the back of the head of someone who lay face down on the pavement. He testified that the gunman was an Asian male, about 5′6″ to 5′8″ in height, weighing 140 to 150 pounds. After shooting the victim on the ground, the man ran south on Pacific. When the police arrived, it was still daylight and crowds of people still lingered at the scene. Police officers went around asking for witnesses, and Mill and his friend both told the police they had seen the shooting. Both were taken to the Hall of Justice, where they gave statements about the shooter's height and weight. The police officers then asked them to look at some mug shots of Asian males. Mill picked out two or three he thought resembled the shooter. Several days later, he picked out the shooter from a lineup. At this point, the prosecutor said, "Is the shooter present today in this courtroom?" Andy Mill pointed his finger at me. I was the only Asian, sitting between two white attorneys.

Next, Tony Serra cross-examined Mill. Almost 7′ tall, Tony was a giant of a man, big boned, with long black hair combed straight back. As I recall, Tony said, "Didn't you pick out two or three Asian males from the police mug shot book, in addition to picking out the defendant in the lineup?"

"No," Mill replied.

"Did you notice in the lineup that the defendant was only 5′3″ and weighed far less than the suspect you described on the day of the shooting?

"I think the shooter was less tall and weighed less," Mill responded.

"Did you notice any special features of the shooter?"

"No."

"Did you notice a mustache on the shooter?"

"No, he was clean shaven."

"At that time, did you closely associate with many or any Asians?"

"No."

"You testified to seeing an Asian male, 5'6" to 5'8", about 150 pounds, and clean shaven, and you witnessed the shooting in three or four seconds—is that correct?

"Yes."

"Given that you had no Asian associates, do you think you could identify an Asian male you'd never met in three or four seconds?"

"Yes."

"Were you aware you were in the direct line of fire?"

"Yes."

"Didn't you fear for your life?"

"Yes."

Tony Serra went on questioning Andy Mill very aggressively, and Mill's identification of me as the shooter started looking more and more questionable. The prosecution tried asking a redirect question, but Mill's credibility as an eyewitness had clearly fallen.

The next eyewitness was a white man with a handlebar mustache, who was an older friend of Andy Mill. This witness was about 6' tall, 180 to 200 pounds, and well built. He acted very sure of himself in the way he testified, as he had done during the June 1974 trial and the prison trial's death penalty phase in March 1979. As it happened, this witness used to work for San Francisco Juvenile Hall and was working there on August 16, 1969, on the day I and a few other inmates attacked him and another guard, and escaped from Juvenile Hall.

First, the prosecutor questioned the witness. The witness testified that he was a friend of Andy Mill when both were visiting San Francisco just before Mill was to begin training with the American Olympic ski team. He was standing next to Mill on the northeast corner of Grant and Pacific when he heard loud gunshots from the southwest. He saw the gunman lean over and shoot a man lying on the pavement, then turn and run south. The gunman was an Asian male, about 5'6" to 5'8", 140 pounds, and wearing a leather jacket. The witness's view of the shooter was clear enough to later identify him in the mug shot and the lineup. The prosecutor then asked if the man whom he saw firing the gun was in the courtroom and to point him out. The witness said, "Yes," and pointed at me, and the prosecutor had no further questions.

Since Tony and Stuart were taking turns questioning witnesses, it was Stuart's turn to cross-examine the eyewitness. I had some strong feelings about this witness, whose testimony had landed me in prison for over nine nightmarish years. Two other witnesses had testified that I was the gunman they saw, but this man had taken a strong lead in insisting it was me and may have influenced the others. Clearly he was personally willing to go to any lengths to see me convicted of false murder charges. I had not discussed any of my personal feelings about any eyewitnesses to Stuart or Tony, except for my sense of injustice about the ballistics expert. Yet when Stuart started questioning this witness, it seemed to me that Stuart's gestures and his direct, clear, and loud voice gave expression to my feelings. Stuart used no soft touch to build up his cross-examination; he started in like a charging bull.

As I recall, he asked, "Did you give a statement to the police that the suspect was around 140 to 160 pounds?"

"Yes."

"Did you describe the suspect as 5′6″ to 5′8″ in height?"

"Yes."

"Did you describe the suspect as clean shaven?"

"Yes."

"Did you pick out two other suspects from the mug shot book?"

"Yes."

"Did you pick out Chol Soo Lee from mug shots of Asian males?"

"Yes."

"Were the suspects you picked from the mug shot besides Chol Soo Lee in the lineup?"

"I don't remember."

"Did you pick out the defendant from the lineup?"

"Yes."

"Did you recall seeing a mustache on the gunman?"

"No."

"Did you tell the police the suspect you picked out had a mustache?"

"No."

"Did you work in San Francisco Juvenile Hall in August of 1969?"

"Yes."

"Do you remember seeing the defendant at Juvenile Hall Security Unit, cell B-5?"

"I can't recall."

"At the time you heard the gunshots, were you right in the line of fire?"

"Yes."

"Did you have any fear of getting shot accidentally?

"Yes."

"Did you have only two or three seconds to witness the suspect?"

"Yes."

"Was the street very crowded with people?"

"Yes."

"Yet you were able to pick out the defendant as the shooter in two or three seconds?"

"Yes."

"Is it possible you picked out the defendant from the mug shot book and the lineup because you had prior contact with him in San Francisco Juvenile Hall in 1969?"

"I don't remember the prior contact in 1969 at San Francisco Juvenile Hall."

"Is it true you worked at Security B-5 Unit when the defendant was in custody there?"

"I don't remember."

"Do you recall seeing any Asian while working at San Francisco Juvenile Hall?"

"I may have, but I can't recall."

After Stuart finished, and after the prosecutor's redirect question, the witness left the courtroom looking visibly shaken. The cross-examination of both eyewitnesses by Tony and Stuart made their claims to have identified the gunman seem questionable at best.

The next day before the trial resumed, a Chinese American, who worked at the Hall of Justice, had overheard some police officers discussing how the trial had been fixed because one of the female jurors was close to the prosecutor but lied during jury selection. In mid-discussion of the biased juror, the police officers noticed the Chinese American. Glaring at him, one of them said, "You're going to rat on us, aren't you?"

As it happened, the Chinese American did report what he'd overheard to my attorneys, who relayed the information to the judge. The judge then asked the female juror to come into the judge's chamber along with the defense and prosecution attorneys. There she revealed that she had lied about having no prior personal contacts or knowledge of law enforcement; she was once married to a prosecutor in the San Francisco D.A.'s office. She was dismissed as a juror and an alternate juror took her place. Why she was dismissed was not revealed to the public. To my mind, it seemed unthinkable that the police might try to rig the jury to influence the outcome of the trial. But years ago, it had been unthinkable that I could be arrested and convicted of a murder I did not commit. It seemed Falzon's image as having accurately solved Yip Yee Tak's murder was far more important to the SFPD than justice or truth.

Emotional Support

Every day of the trial, Korean elderly people and business owners, Asian American students, and other CSLDC supporters packed the courtroom to show me their moral support. The elderly Koreans brought packed Korean lunches of *kim-bap* for themselves and other supporters. Most of them didn't speak English. Yet every day they showed up to a courtroom where they were required to pass through a metal detector, and deputies lined the walls to provide security.

During the trial, Sooknam Choo often visited me in the holding cell during breaks to offer encouragement. In the small holding cell with its small window into the courtroom, she shared her anguished feelings for me of being kept in a holding cell during the trial. Even though her visits lasted about ten minutes, her pain of seeing me in the concrete-walled holding cell was far greater than mine, for I had grown immune to feeling pain about being locked in a cell. A few times I'd been kept on twenty-four-hour lockdown for two or four months at time, so this was nothing. Sooknam's pain for me must have been very great when she said, "I would throw away everything, even my attorney's license, just to see you be free for one day." She had tears in her eyes.

"I am okay. I am used to it," I said, wanting to take her pain away.

But Sooknam knew no sane person should ever get used to being locked up in a four-by-nine-foot cell. Sometimes she visited me more than once a day, and at times she smiled and joked, but her eyes reflected inner pain to see me imprisoned even in the holding cell. The only thing that cheered her up was the hope we all felt about winning the retrial.

Meanwhile, Jay Yoo and Doris Yamasaki tried to explain the trial to the Korean elders from the Buddhist temple and Korean churches from the Bay Area and Sacramento. As for me, despite the thick bulletproof glass and tight security in the courtroom, I tried to express my thankfulness to all these supporters, and especially to the elders who must have felt discomfort sitting on the courtroom's hard wooden benches. Throughout the day, I tried to let them know with waves, nods, or smiles that I felt their heartwarming support. Many supporters attended the trial daily. The presence of all this support for justice on my behalf was surely felt by everyone else in court—by the judge, jurors, and attorneys. Even the court deputies lining the courtroom walls treated the supporters kindly.

This was one of the most important times in US history when Asian Americans were united in a common cause. Credit for this historic unity goes to the Asian American students who worked to create an Asian American movement in solidarity around one single issue. A united front of Asian Americans from different ethnic and national backgrounds, and all different ages, sat together in one courtroom, supported by hundreds more who sent their support across the country, and even from overseas in Korea and Japan. Without a word being said, everyone (except perhaps Inspector Falzon and Prosecutor Arlo Smith) felt uplifted and deeply affected by this bright moment of Asian American unity.

It seemed to be an impossible struggle for justice on behalf of a lone Korean in a California state prison, but the Free CSLDC movement continued to draw more support over time against all odds. Rather than quitting after I was sentenced to death in 1979, the CSLDC grew stronger. The number of supporters expanded, and their numerous donations of ten and twenty dollars made it possible to set up a legal defense fund, while Free CSLDC volunteers worked countless hours for the cause and came to witness the Chinatown case retrial with the country's best attorneys, Stuart Hanlon and Tony Serra, representing me (while Leonard Weinglass and Mr. H. Peter Young continued to handle the appeal on my prison case). Moreover, the CSLDC showed no hatred or anger toward the police officer or prosecutor, but stood unconditionally for justice and for exposing how I had become the victim of unthinkable injustice.

As I witnessed my own trial, my strongest feelings were focused on one fact: I was finally receiving a fair trial for a nine-year-old case in which I had claimed my innocence from the day I was first arrested. Now support for that fair trial packed the courtroom, with hundreds or thousands more supporters out there somewhere, caring about the outcome. To me, the trial was not to achieve victory over the court system, police, or prosecutor, but only to prove my innocence of a murder I never committed. Again and again, I thought, "I am finally receiving a fair trial." This single thought remained utmost in my mind as I watched the trial unfold.

Questioning Snitches

The next witness called up by the prosecution was Arturo "Fly" Serrato, a convict I once befriended in Tracy by getting him a job as a welder in the prison industry. This witness had been recommended by James Lassart. As the original prosecutor of the 1974 Chinatown case, Lassart wanted to help Arlo Smith by providing NF members who had already testified against their own gang to be witnesses who could supply my motive. Arturo Serrato had supposedly heard my confession, which was a total lie. I asked myself, "What have I ever done to these people? Their job is to uphold the law. Yet they plan to put NF rats on the stand to testify falsely against me?"

I can't find any excuse for these kinds of actions against me. The police and prosecution were given every opportunity to examine and accept private investigator Tink Thompson's abundant evidence that they had caught the wrong man, but they insisted on continuing their prosecution against me. Not only that, but they seemed eager to prove that *they* were being wronged by the CSLDC and all the support for my retrial. Yet under close questioning by Stuart and Tony, the prosecution's eyewitnesses had given doubtful testimony. Even more embarrassing, now the prosecutors brought jailhouse rats to the witness stand, who swore to tell the truth and then lied. It seemed the sanity of the law had been turned upside down and the police and prosecutor had closed the last door through which they could have exited honorably. They only made things worse for themselves by bringing in the rats.

Arturo Serrato testified that I had confessed to him in the Tracy welding shop. He said I was a member of Joe Fong's gang, which explained my motive for the execution-style killing of Yip Yee Tak during the Wah Ching versus Joe Boys war in Chinatown. Let me point out that this explanation totally contradicted the one invented for the original trial, when my alleged motive depended on supposed membership in the Ski Mask gang, hired by the Wah Ching to kill Yip Yee Tak. The trial and retrial "motives" were completely different! It was as if the prosecutors were willing to invent any motive or story they figured the jury would accept. Here is the truth: Joe Fong and some of his friends did time in Tracy at the same time as I did, and that is how I met them.

Tony Serra cross-examined Arturo Serrato, and not just about my so-called confession. He went after Serrato's character. As I recall, Tony's questioning went like this:

"Are you a rat?"

"No."

"Are you a snitch?"

"No."

"Are you an informant?"

"No."

"What are you?"

"Huh. I guess I am a government witness." Serrato seemed thrown off balance by these simple and direct questions. He appeared to lack confidence. Tony said, "You were a member of Nuestra Familia, right?"

"Yes."

"Now you're testifying against the NF?"

"Yes."

Tony Serra explained that government witnesses received thousands of dollars and immunity for crimes as brutal as nearly shooting the head off a prostitute with a shotgun.

"You say Mr. Lee confessed to you?"

Serrato responded, "We were working in the welding shop in Tracy when Lee said he was a member of Joc Fong's gang and executed the guy for the Joe Boys." Serrato's answer was weak and short. I don't think anyone believed a thing he said about my so-called confession. Tony had discredited Serrato's testimony from start to finish. Seeing this, the prosecutor decided against using the other government rat, Ray Contreras, who had testified against me in the Tracy case. Both Tony and Stuart later said the prosecutor should have put Contreras on the stand because he was a much more confident liar than Serrato. But after Serrato's preposterous testimony, which left the jury shaking their heads in total disbelief, the prosecution rested their case.

Not the Gunman

Now it was the defense's turn to put our witnesses on the stand and build support for Tony and Stuart's opening statements. Our first defense witness had previously served in the US Navy with honor. This witness was an eyewitness to the execution-style death of Yip Yee Tak on June 3, 1973, and had already testified in the first trial. His friend, also in the Navy, had testified in the first trial, but refused to testify for the retrial. But this witness sitting before the court had traveled across the country to take the stand to testify again on my behalf. He said he and his friend were walking through Chinatown, heading toward Broadway, and at the northeast corner of Pacific and Grant, he heard shots coming from the northwest from about sixty feet across the street. He saw the victim lying facedown on the ground, and the gunman, wearing a leather jacket, lean over the victim and shoot him. Then he testified that the shooter tossed a revolver into Beckett Alley and ran south on Pacific.

After the police arrived, the witness said he gave them a description of the gunman as a young Asian American male, about 5′7″ to 5′8″, about 160 pounds, with a clean-shaven face. Later at the Hall of Justice, the witness picked out a few pictures from an Asian mug shot book. He did not pick me out of the lineup, and during the first trial in June 1974, he had testified that I was not the gunman he saw on June 3, 1973. Now, once again, he testified that I was not the gunman he saw nine years ago. Under cross-examination by the prosecutor, the witness stood firmly by his eyewitness account and asserted that I was not the gunman he saw that day. The prosecution was unable to shake him.

The next witness for the defense was a white woman, a new witness whom the San Francisco police had excluded, and whom Tink Thompson had discovered at the time of the Chinatown case's writ of habeas corpus petition in October 1978. This witness was an eyewitness to the crime while touring Chinatown with her friends. She had been looking into a Chinese bakery shop window on the northwest corner of Grant and Pacific when she heard gunshots just ten to twelve feet away. She saw the gunman lean over a body lying on the ground and fire a final shot to the back of the head. Then she saw the gunman run, toss the gun into Becket Alley, and continue running down Pacific toward Kearny Street.

The witness also recalled that the gunman was the same man she'd seen in an earlier encounter that day on Kearny Street. Driving a Cadillac, the man had very lightly hit her car—just a slight bump—while parking on Kearny Street. At the time of the accident, the witness had seen the man clearly. She could see that the man from the minor car accident was the same man who fired the gun into the body lying near the corner of Pacific and Grant. As the witness closest to the shooting, she described the gunman as an Asian male, 5′7″ to 5′8″ and about 160 pounds. The prosecutor tried to redirect her testimony, but the witness was unshakable. She was sure of what she had seen during the shooting and the earlier car accident. She stood solidly on her eyewitness testimony that I was not the man involved in the car accident or the shooting.

Another new witness, a Chinese man in his early twenties, took the stand. Tink Thompson had discovered this young man while working on the writ of habeas corpus petition in 1978. Fearing for his life, the man, who was code-named Witness X, had refused to testify openly in Sacramento Superior Court at the time of the writ of habeas corpus hearing. However, for this 1982 retrial of the Chinatown case, my defense attorneys and Tink Thompson convinced him to take the stand. He looked very anxious as he was sworn in. He testified that he lived in the Ping Yuen housing project, located on Pacific Street between Beckett Alley and Kearny Street, one block from the main hangouts of the Wah Ching gang on Jackson Street. The witness stated he saw the killing of Yip Yee Tak, but feared for his life if he testified as a witness at the original trial. "The Wah Ching could do the same thing to me," he said. He continued to explain that he'd seen me and Yip Yee Tak's killer around Chinatown and knew both of us by sight. As a result, he was certain, "The man I saw run away after shooting Yip Yee Tak was not Chol Soo Lee."

He was the only Asian witness to come forward and testify in open court. There were a few other local Chinatown witnesses the defense team had uncovered, but they were all too fearful of the Wah Ching. One witness was a friend of the real killer who had agreed to testify that the real killer had confessed to the killing right after Yip Yee Tak's death. But this witness was only willing to testify in a closed courtroom without any news media or public spectators, so the witness ended up testifying before Judge Dossee in his chambers. Stuart and Tony requested closing the courtroom for this testimony, but Judge Dossee denied their request.

My defense attorneys never asked the lone Chinese witness to name the real killer. After the witness made it clear that he knew both the real killer and me, and I was not the killer, the defense attorney did not question him further. The prosecutor then asked the Chinese witness how he saw the man running from the shooting was not me, and then said, "No further questions." I was most surprised that the prosecutor didn't ask the witness to name the real killer. It was as if the prosecutor had no interest whatsoever in asking the Chinese witness about the real killer of Yip Yee Tak—no desire in seeking the truth to solve the crime.

After the Chinese witness testified, the defense team met with me. Stuart and Tony felt we had presented three very solid eyewitnesses, in contrast to the damaged credibility of the prosecution's eyewitnesses and the ballistics expert. The jury seemed to pay close attention to both sides of the case during the few weeks of the trial. At this point, we considered whether we should rest our case instead of calling me and Steve Morris to the stand. Steve Morris was an eyewitness whose testimony, suppressed by the police and prosecutor in June 1973, eventually led to the writ of habeas corpus and granting of the retrial. Steve Morris was a gay white man, and it appeared the prosecutor would try to use Morris' homosexuality to discredit his testimony. Since the defense had already presented three strong eyewitnesses, we decided it wasn't necessary to put Morris on the stand and let the prosecutor cross-examine his personal life.

Much to the disappointment of the prosecution, the defense went ahead and rested our case. This appeared to shock the prosecution. The prosecutor was so outraged that he almost demanded that the defense put Morris on the stand. As it was, the prosecutor never got the chance to question Steve Morris. Later, we learned the prosecution had hoped to discredit all the defense witnesses and the entire defense case by attacking Steve Morris for being gay.

Throughout sessions of the three-week trial, I sat at the defense table, taking notes on a writing pad occasionally as if I were helping out my attorneys. My hopes were high of being found not guilty. Both Stuart and Tony had prepared each witness thoroughly. They knew that not only was my life on the line, but that I had waited for nine years to receive a fair trial for a murder I didn't commit, with most of those years spent in lockup units in Tracy and San Quentin.

Now let me tell you how low the prosecutor and Falzon got near the trial's end. When I entered the courtroom with the jury seated, I sat at the right side of the defense table, with the prosecution table four or five feet to my right. When I glanced over, I saw both Falzon and the prosecutor staring at me with their necks sticking out as if to provoke my temper in front of the jury. I looked at them glaring at me in this silly way. In case I might fall into their trap and lose my temper in front of the jury, which I had no intention of doing, Stuart Hanlon put his hand on my shoulder and said, "Pay them no attention." I nodded at Stuart and looked down at my notepad. I ignored those two grown men scowling at me like two bullies, but I think the jury noticed them.

In the San Francisco County Jail, I could meet in person, for the first time, a great number of people whose efforts had made the retrial possible. Their volunteer work had raised over $120,000 in $10 or $20 donations through churches, hotlink sales in San Francisco's Japantown

street fairs, and many more such events organized by the defense committees. During the weekends, I received visits from Doris Yamasaki,
Buddhist monks and other temple members, and Reverend Cha and
other Korean pastors and church people. We prayed together to keep
my morale and spirits high, and I was very grateful for these visits. At
the time of the retrial, all I knew was the convict's way of thinking and
my visitors had a totally different lifestyle, but I did my best to thank
them all.

The truth is, I will never be able to thank all the CSLDC supporters
enough in my lifetime for giving their hearts and souls for justice. I was
just a single Korean state prisoner on San Quentin's Death Row, but all
those supporters bound their hearts there with me, longing for me to be
free. Their sincerity gave me my deepest sense of comfort and light in the
dark world of prison.

Punish the Prosecution!

Now that both the prosecution and defense had presented their cases to
the jury, both sides were ready for closing arguments. The prosecutor
went first, outlining the case against me and summarizing the evidence
presented by the eyewitnesses and Serrato. After that, Stuart Hanlon
summarized the defense's case, and then Tony Serra gave a final closing
argument, the strongest I had ever heard. At first, he stood before the
jury very tall with his long hair combed back, but as his argument started
to heat up, his hair started flying about. With emotion in his voice, he
discredited all of the prosecution's witnesses and emphasized the difficulty of cross-racial suspect identification. As he spoke, he hammered
his right arm down again and again as if striking with an imaginary
sword at the miscarriage of justice. He said, "Punish the prosecution!"
He repeated "Punish the prosecution!" throughout his hour-long, powerful closing argument. Each juror appeared to be paying attention to his
every word. I sat and listened. Each time Tony lowered the sword of justice and asked the jury to punish the prosecution, I felt the impact of his
words. Stuart and Tony were finally bringing the truth of my case out
in the open—that the San Francisco prosecutor had wronged me for all
these years. For me, Tony Serra's closing argument was the highlight of
the retrial, and I felt in the highest spirits to hear Tony say, "Punish the
prosecution!" as if those righteous words might wash away all the pain
I had suffered.

The law allowed the prosecutor to have the first and last say. In his closing argument, the San Francisco prosecutor tried to strengthen his case, but his arguments sounded weak, hollow, and unconvincing. The next day, the judge instructed the jury, after which the jury retired to the deliberating room to decide on their verdict. While the jury deliberated, I was held in my jail cell on the seventh floor of the Hall of Justice, where I received a number of well-wishing visitors. I tried to smile and relate to them as best as I could, but years of solitary confinement and prison life had taken a toll on me. All the visitors were people who lived a normal life on the outside, with the freedom to support me, but only a few understood how difficult it was living the life of a convict—whether falsely imprisoned or not.

One person who had some understanding of my struggle was Raul Ramirez. While the jury was out, Raul Ramirez started visiting me every night. Because he wrote for the *Oakland Tribune,* we were allowed to meet in the attorney visiting rooms. But Raul visited as a friend. He had a very likeable personality, and I felt at ease with him and looked forward to his visits and personal support while we waited for the jury's decision. A man of high integrity, Raul gave me his personal friendship, which I will never forget.

Verdict

The jury took three days to deliberate. A jury, made up of both men and women, and mixed races but no Asians, elected Scott Johnson as foreman. I heard later that on their very first vote taken, six voted not guilty, three voted guilty, and three were undecided. The jury then reexamined the evidence against me. The foreman explained how difficult it was for most whites to identify Asians. They reviewed the eyewitness testimony by the woman who stood ten feet from the crime and had already encountered the real killer, and by the young Chinese man who had seen both me and the real killer before. On the third day, as the jury neared their verdict, the judge let them continue deliberating after 5 p.m. That evening, at 7:30 or 8, I was in my jail cell when the deputy informed me a verdict had been reached.

I was led downstairs back to the courtroom. The courtroom was packed full, mostly with elderly Koreans, young Asian Americans, and news media who had found out earlier in the day that the jury was nearing their verdict. As I walked into the courtroom, I felt confident the jury would not find me guilty. Through the bulletproof glass, I waved at all the supporters, who also seemed confident of the jury's decision. But all of us felt serious as the trial judge ordered the assembly to be quiet, and the jury filed into the courtroom.

Along with Stuart, Tony, and Tink, I remained standing, as did the prosecutor and Falzon at their table. The jury took their seats. Each juror looked totally serious and expressionless. Seeing this, I wondered if the jury might have turned against me in their verdict. Looking at them, the thought entered my mind, "What if I have lost the trial?" Then the judge said, "Have you reached a verdict?"

"Yes," said jury foreman Scott Johnson.

The judge asked the foreman to hand the jury verdict paper to the court clerk. As the foreman handed over the verdict, all the jurors still looked expressionless and serious. I too felt emotionless and remained calm, ready for the reading of the verdict. Stuart and Tony both put their hands over my shoulders as if to comfort me as the court clerk read: "We the jury of *Chol Soo Lee v. People of California* find the defendant— not guilty."

The whole courtroom went wild.

The judge banged his wooden hammer. "Order in court, order in court!"

I felt numb hearing the words "not guilty" read by the court clerk. As people calmed down, I started seeing the jurors' smiles and a smile broke through my nervousness. I turned around to wave thanks to my supporters, especially to Doris, my mother, K. W. Lee, Jay Yoo, the elderly Koreans, and the Asian American young people, who all returned heartfelt "you're welcome" gestures to my thanks.

The prosecutor and Falzon stood with their heads a bit down.

"Is this your true verdict?" asked the judge.

"Yes, Your Honor," Johnson replied with a tired smile.

The judge thanked the jury and said, "The jury is dismissed."

As the jury came down from their seats and moved toward the bulletproof glass door to leave, I stood between the defense and prosecution tables and reached out to shake the hand of each juror passing by. With each handshake, I said, "Thank you." Each juror shook my hand firmly and returned my heartfelt smile. As the jury filed out, the news media people started rushing toward the exits to go make phone calls. At this moment, I turned to the judge and requested permission to speak, which he granted. I turned to face all the CSLDC supporters. All the news media people stopped in their tracks at the door. With utmost sincerity I said, "Thank you for everything you have done for me. This is not my victory, but yours."

After saying these few words, a fury deep within me started to rise. I felt like a dam about to bust with the emotion and pain I'd pent up for years. I hadn't planned to speak to Falzon or the prosecutor, but suddenly I wanted them to hear about the hell they had put me through. I turned and almost shouting at them, I said, "It's people like you who make justice impossible!"

Hearing the anger in my voice, the judge said, "That's enough, Mr. Lee."

At this, I turned to talk with Stuart, Tony, and Tink. The judge dismissed the court. As I left the courtroom, I continued to wave my thank-yous to all the supporters in the courtroom.

I later learned from my attorneys that the SFPD had surrounded the courtroom with officers in riot gear armed with shotguns in case the verdict went against me and my supporters caused any problem. I was stunned to hear this. My supporters had always kept order in the courtroom, yet police were ready to use this kind of force on elderly people and young Asian Americans. This plan seemed almost like the San Francisco police wanted to punish those who joined the cause of justice on my behalf. On a brighter note, the jury foreman, Scott Johnson, learned more about my case by speaking with CSLDC members after the trial. As a result, he felt compelled to join the CSLDC and gave his support to my remaining prison case, which was still pending in the appeals court as undecided.

Victory Party

After leaving the courtroom, I was escorted back to my cell by a deputy. Even the deputy seemed relieved to hear that I was found not guilty. I walked through the mainline in my usual way looking serious and expressionless as I was returned to the maximum-security block with its five single cells. The max cell block in county jail was kind of a joke to me after years spent in the "Hole" of state prisons. I didn't say anything about the verdict to the two other prisoners in the max block. A short time later, the deputy informed me that I had an attorney visit. As I walked through the mainline corridor, I heard an inmate say, "That's him. He was just on the news." He sounded surprised to see me.

Passing through the mainline gates toward the visiting rooms, I was taken to a large conference room where the legal team was waiting—

Stuart, Tony, Tink, Sooknam, even Ranko, and a few others. They had brought in cake, a few other snack items, and bottles of sodas, which surprised me. Jail deputies do not normally allow attorneys to bring in such items, much less party items for a celebration. In my case, I think the attorneys could have brought in alcohol and the deputies would have looked the other way. The fact that San Francisco deputies allowed cake and use of the conference room for a party must have been an extremely rare event. It went to show that the deputies, especially the Chinese Americans, were glad that after over nine years of struggle, I was finally found not guilty for a crime I never committed. By then in 1982, many Chinese Americans worked as San Francisco County Jail deputies, and I'm sure they all knew from growing up in Chinatown or from their friends that I did not kill Yip Yee Tak.

It was smiles all around for everyone at the so-called victory party as each person shared some thoughts about the Free Chol Soo Lee Defense Committee, how it was formed in 1978, the four long years of hard work raising funds, uniting Asian people across America and overseas in Korea and Japan, and mounting the legal struggle. All of us could see in each other's eyes a great celebration for the cause of justice. In addition to everyone in the conference room, many of the elderly Koreans and Asian Americans who had witnessed the trial were out celebrating the not-guilty verdict at Hwan Il Kwan, a Korean restaurant in the San Francisco Richmond district. It was Friday night, September 3, 1982, a great night for enjoying victory over injustice. We had reached the top of the mountain. I am sure phone calls were made across America that day as supporters joined in celebration of the CSLDC's spectacular achievement. After years of extensive volunteer work, the defense committee members saw their total commitment to the ideal of justice become a reality. Starting with K. W. Lee's newspaper articles in 1978, it was the efforts of good people that had made this day possible.

After about forty-five minutes of celebrating and exchanging our good feelings, the party came to an end. But before I could be released from prison, there still remained one strong link—the prison case that needed to be broken in the chain of injustice that bound me.

With an expressionless face, I was escorted back to my cell. After returning to my cell, I was unable to fall asleep. I paced in my cell. A great burden was lifted off my shoulders, but I was still in jail. My thoughts were going everywhere. I wasn't really thinking about anything as if my mind was empty, but I kept hearing the words, "We the jury find the defendant, not guilty."

"Then why am I still in a jail cell?" I thought. My thoughts filled up, then emptied, then filled and emptied again and again throughout the long night. I finally fell asleep in the early morning hours, only to be awakened soon for county jail breakfast. It was as if yesterday was just another day in my ongoing struggle. Bitterness filled my soul with the awareness that I would soon be returning to "Bastille by the Bay."

My first visitor on Saturday was a newspaper reporter named Mr. Wood, whom I had consented to an interview for the *Sunday San Francisco Chronicle and Examiner.* Looking serious, Mr. Wood interviewed me for two hours. I thought it went well. Later, in the lonely evening hours, Raul Ramirez came to visit me. I was glad to see him again, and we talked happily for an hour. On Sunday, Mr. Wood's interview appeared on the lower half of the front page. After I read the article, I phoned my sister Margie, who was very happy to hear from me. I said, "There's a story about me in today's newspaper."

Through the phone I overheard Margie say happily to her daughter, "Mary, go to the store and get the Sunday paper for me!"

"Margie," I said, "I'll be transferred back to San Quentin Monday, but I'm hopeful of winning my appeal on the prison case, so I look forward to seeing you and your family soon."

We talked for about an hour. Just talking to Margie made me feel happy. Only with Margie did I feel free to talk about anything. As I hung up the phone, I promised myself to give her all the support I could once I was free.

September 5, 1982, was my last day in the San Francisco County Jail before returning to San Quentin. In the early evening, Raul showed up for a happy last visit in the San Francisco County Jail. In such a short time, I found in Raul the best friendship a human being can offer to another, and there was no low feeling during that visit, for I felt in my heart we would continue to be close friends for many years, if not the rest of our lives. Doris Yamasaki and a Buddhist monk also came to visit me. Doris had known me since the day I arrived in America and all through the years she cared for me like a younger brother, and still shares her care for me even to this day. In the early days, she owned a small beauty shop near Japantown where she would cut my hair for free. When I lived in Chinatown, she owned a Korean restaurant, and whenever I stopped by, she would tell me to come into the kitchen to eat. In over forty years, Doris has given and given without a thought of asking for anything in return. In her eyes, I see deep humanity in her wish for me to live a normal life in free society. I still hope that day will come when, for all her thoughtfulness toward me, Doris will have peace in her heart regarding my life.

As I reflect on people who had the greatest impact on my life, for whatever unexplained reason, I feel no hatred toward the man who tormented me the most, Frank Falzon. Maybe in the beginning Falzon really believed he'd caught Yip Yee Tak's killer. But with all the rumors in Chinatown after my arrest that I was innocent, followed by years when Tink Thompson found so much new evidence, Falzon refused to reconsider his mistake, with total disregard for my life in prison and on Death Row. As a lone Korean in Chinatown—a nobody with a criminal record since age fifteen—I was easy to frame. I couldn't hire or have an attorney appointed who believed I was innocent. I believe Falzon and Lassart compromised their duty and integrity, and caused me to suffer nine years of false imprisonment. Yet at the same time, my story ignited a desire within Asian communities in the United States and abroad to unite for the cause of justice on my behalf. They gained a greater understanding of racial injustice in America, a land where new Asian immigrants dream of success, but need to wake up to a new Asian American consciousness—because what happened to me could happen to them or their children.

"Treacherous" and "Evil" Crips

On Monday, I was transferred back to San Quentin's AC Hole on the east second tier where "B" group Death Row convicts were held. By this time, the convicts in my yard group were all new faces, except for Rudy. In particular, there were two newly arrived Crips—a tall guy, over 6', named Treacherous, or "Treach," and a small guy about 5'6" called Evil. Their nicknames suited them, as both were tough convicts. I was also surprised to learn that a psychopath name Coleman was allowed into our yard. Coleman was convicted for the rape and murder of a young teenager and fit the convicts' category of child killer. Since Coleman was African American, I left it up to the Crips to keep him under control.

On my first day back, they all came up to me, even Coleman, and said, "Man, Lee. Man, we're glad for you. We're happy. Man, you finally got them! You know, they fuck you over, they frame you like that. Now you got found not guilty." Here I'd been telling these guys I was not guilty, but not one had believed me. Yet when the system said I was not guilty, all the prisoners believed I was not guilty. Even the BGF members waved toward me through the fence, saluting with their fists in the air. I had always said I was innocent, but no one believed me since most convicts said they were innocent. Now they all expressed how fucked-up it was for me to be framed and spend all those years in prison.

I returned to my normal routine of lifting weights, but kept close eyes on both Treach and Evil, as they were as mean and hard as any convicts can be. However, as I got to know Treach and Evil, we got along well without friction in the yard. I especially kept close watch on Coleman, for I knew he was a psychopath, and sooner or later, he would act up. Fortunately, Rudy was on my side, so I told Rudy to keep watch on Coleman at all times. During nonyard days, we carried out a routine of doing sit-ups and push-ups in our cells, starting with 1,000 sit-ups and 1,000 push-ups. Within few weeks, we increased the push-ups to 2,000, but kept the sit-ups at 1,000. When one of us finished a set, the other would holler, "Go!" to the next guy. We could have done even more push-ups, but this was enough to keep us in shape and release the tension of being in our cells. All five of us in the yard group joined in this routine, each taking turns.

The 20/20 Feature

For the past few years I had been corresponding with a Japanese American woman, Michi Nishiura Weglyn, who was married to a Jewish man who had survived the Nazi concentration camps. Michi Weglyn herself had been interned during World War II and ended up writing one of the best-known books about the Japanese internment camps called *Years of Infamy*. In one of my letters to Mrs. Weglyn, I asked if she knew anyone from *60 Minutes* who could publicize my case to the American public. One day, I received a letter from the producer of ABC's *20/20*, asking for an interview, which Mrs. Weglyn had helped to arrange. I consented, and in late 1982, the *20/20* producer and her interviewer, Bob Brown, arrived at San Quentin, along with a camera and lighting crew. Before the interview, I went through the routine strip searches, after which I was taken to a holding cell, where I remained for almost an hour. Then I was led to a large room in waist chains, where people from *20/20* were waiting for me.

I met the producer for the interview, who probably felt it was safe for *20/20* to cover my case because I was found "not guilty" on the Chinatown case retrial. However, she clearly looked uncomfortable. Maybe it was her first time inside a state prison, and she'd never seen a convict in prison blue clothing with both hands chained to his waist. She sat nearby to one side while Bob Brown interviewed me. Two guards stood about ten feet back in the dark. I had felt a bit nervous while waiting in the holding cell, but I felt comfortable once the hour-long interview started. The questions Mr. Brown asked were easy questions about the case; he never asked any tough questions. After the interview, I thanked both the producer and Mr. Brown. Then I was escorted back to my cell. I thought the interview with *20/20* went well, and I wrote a thank-you letter to Mrs. Michi Nishiura Weglyn.

In late 1982, soon after the *20/20* interview, I received another interview request from Ms. Sandra Gin of *Asian Perceptions Now,* a Sacramento TV program about Asian Americans in California. I wrote back consenting to the interview. Within a few weeks, the *Asian Perceptions Now* crew came to San Quentin. I went through the usual strip search routine before meeting Ms. Gin and co-producer Tom Nakashima. I saw in their eyes that they were upset to see me in chains, but they were friendly and greeted both me and the prison guards warmly. As before, two guards stood ten feet behind me. Ms. Gin's questions were a bit more complex and detailed than Bob Brown's were from *20/20*. The interview lasted ninety minutes. As we parted, I thought it went well, but really, I had no idea how it went.

Looking back many years later, Warren Furutani told me the defense committee had thought my cause for justice would continue for years; they didn't expect I would be free anytime soon. The *20/20* ABC program focused more on how private investigator Tink Thompson solved the case. They also interviewed Ranko, Stuart Hanlon, and Frank Falzon, but seemed to make Tink Thompson the hero for winning the retrial, instead of showing the collective efforts of Asian American communities to build the support movement that made it possible to hire Tink Thompson as well as lawyers like Leonard Weinglass, Stuart Hanlon, and Tony Serra. Years later in 1989, Hollywood produced *True Believer,* a movie starring actor James Woods as a character based on Tony Serra. I was not even aware of the movie until it came out. Typical of Hollywood, 99 percent of *True Believer* was fiction rather than facts.

Waiting Game and Parting Shots

After returning to San Quentin, I waited for the outcome on my prison case. I wrote to Mr. Weinglass to ask when the appeals court would make a decision, feeling confident I would win my appeal. Meanwhile in the yard, I was building good rapport with Treach and Evil, who were hard-core Crips who refused the BGF's friendly gestures. Treach and Evil knew of my reputation as a hard-core convict who was not to be messed with. As for Rudy, he stuck by me like a true warrior. I day-dreamed with Rudy about all the things I wanted to do when I got out. But then Coleman, the sick child rapist and murder, started showing signs of his craziness. Instead of letting him agitate me, I decided to ignore him.

On January 14, 1983, the California Third District Court of Appeals overturned the death-sentence ruling in my prison case, mainly because Judge Chris Papas had allowed hearsay testimony from prison snitches. Judge Papas was so biased against me and broke so many rules that the appeals court had no choice but to overturn the ruling in the case, but they had to wait until after the retrial on the Chinatown case before they made their decision. The prosecutor then appealed the court of appeals decision to overturn my case, which caused another delay and more waiting.

While waiting for the result of the prosecution's latest appeal, I just needed to be extra cautious about Coleman. But I could see Treach and Evil watching for some sort of drama to unfold between me and Coleman. They didn't know me well and wanted to see how I'd react to Coleman's agitations. His behavior got worse. He started talking shit to me. I got sick of it and started thinking about making a move on him. Then one day in the yard in March, Rudy came over to me and said, "Hey Lee, you want to move on him together?"

"No, man," I said. Then Rudy and I both glanced over at Coleman, who was working out in the weight area. Stupid as he was, Coleman called out, "Hey Lee, can you give me a hand?"

I walked over to him. Now Coleman was right underneath the 160-pound bar, and I was standing over him. I saw Rudy sweeping the area nearby with a broom and coming closer. Rudy was obviously waiting for me to drop the weight on Coleman. Then he would swing the broom at Coleman's head. I saw Treach and Evil nearby, just watching. At that moment, I felt like dropping that weight and breaking Coleman's neck, but I held back. I said to myself, "I'm too close to getting out. Don't let go of the weight." Just then, Coleman realized the danger he was in. He quickly got up from the bench and acting very agitated, he began to talk shit at me. I started going toward him when I heard an unusual click. It was not the click of a shotgun but the click of a Mini-14 rifle. And then I heard the gun tower guard say, "Lee, stop!" I looked up. The gun tower guard usually had a shotgun in his hands, but this time he aimed his Mini-14 right at me. He could see I was about to go after Coleman, and he repeated, "Lee, stop right there."

Coleman stood no chance against me, so what saved Coleman was the fact that the gunman aimed the Mini-14 at me and not the shotgun. Before the guards came to take me off the yard, I said to Rudy, "Rudy, down Coleman."

"All right," Rudy nodded.

A sergeant escorted me back inside the unit to my cell. On the way, he said, "Lee, you only have a short time left. Your final appeal decision should come through any day now. Why don't you just ride out the time until you return to court? You don't need to get another case against you now. Just calm down and wait." I looked at the sergeant and knew he was making sense. But in another way, he was asking me to PC, which I just couldn't accept after so many years of standing up for myself.

"I will keep cool. But if any trouble comes my way, I will defend myself," I said.

Locked back in my cell, I still felt agitated. My thoughts turned over and over. I knew it was the right move not to kill Coleman, yet I had the perfect chance to kill him. I still regret to this day that by all rights I should have killed him. Was my freedom more important than upholding the convicts' code? That question remains unanswered, for I am free now, and Coleman the psychopath is still in prison. If he is still on Death Row, I do not know or care.

As I waited for yard recall to see if Rudy made a move on Coleman, I heard shotgun fire in the AC yard, which answered my question. Rudy's cell was further up the tier than mine, so I was unable to see him when the guards locked him back in his cell. Then Coleman passed by my cell handcuffed in the back. Back in his cell, he cried like a baby and screamed like a madman. After dinner, I received a note from Rudy: "Lee, after you were taken off the yard, Coleman got near me as if wanting to fight during yard recall, so I knocked him to the ground on the first punch. Before I could do more, the guard got us with the shotgun. Little Evil was nearby, and we both got shot badly, but Coleman escaped getting shot because he was on his ass. See you tomorrow during shower time."

So Rudy did what was expected of him. Next day on my way to shower, I saw little Evil lying on his stomach with his shirt off. Most of his back was shot up with birdshot, and he had a sad grin on his face and shook his head as he saw me. Rudy also got shot all over. When I saw Rudy lying there on his bed grinning, I gave him a smiling nod. Only Treach escaped getting shot because he wasn't nearby. My trouble with Coleman was over.

However, our victory over Coleman was short lived. The next day, the prison administrator sent Billy Ray back to the AC and placed him in a cell in back. From a cell way in back, he could see who was going to the yard and could smuggle a piece out to make a hit. There could be only one reason they brought Billy Ray back—to make a hit on me before I made it out to court. As it was, I had no idea what day I'd be going to court. I saw the setup, as did Rudy, Treach, Evil, and all the other convicts in my yard. At this point, we were all on ten-day lockdown due to the shooting in the yard, with eight more days before returning to the yard, but Rudy and Evil were in too much pain and wouldn't be going out.

Tension and anger filled me to no limits to see this last setup by the guards and administration to have me killed. They brought Billy Ray, a known member of the Aryan Brotherhood, back to the AC to make one last attempt on my life. Having gone through so many struggles to survive, I had to face yet one more life-and-death setup. I readied myself for the day our yard opened back up again. Last time Billy Ray was in the AC Death Row yard, he had said not one word to me or me to him. This time, he called out my name in a friendly tone. I knew he was using the old routine of acting friendly to get closer to make the hit.

These back-to-back setups were tiresome. First, Coleman, a sick coward, and now this—a far more powerful enemy, who knew all the ins and outs of prison life. Billy Ray was not to be underestimated, and I'm sure he had already proven himself, in some way, for the guards to put him in the yard with me, hoping I stood no chance of survival against him.

Thinking about setups, I wondered if putting me in Hisi's BGF yard on Death Row might also have been setting me up to be hit by Big Red, who didn't care too much for me since I was a friend of Jo-Mo, who had stabbed Big Red in Tracy in 1977. After one day in Hisi's BGF yard, I hadn't felt right about returning to his yard.

My thoughts refocused on getting out of prison alive, especially when freedom was within such short reach. Having experienced life in the Hole for close to six years, with only a few breaks to go out to court, I had met all challenges and survived many near-hits against me. In my mind and soul, I had no desire for another life-or-death confrontation with another convict. Still, there was no other stand I could take to avoid a confrontation with AB Billy Ray. The demands of prison life gave me no other choice as a convict but to accept this final challenge by the California guards and prison administration. They placed me in that position whether I wanted it or not. Billy Ray and I were being used for a racial payback scenario because I defended myself against Needham and the white bikers in Tracy's L wing in 1977. The racist San Quentin administration had a score to settle with me.

It was one day before we'd be taken off lockdown. Only Treach, Billy Ray, and I would be going to the yard since Evil and Rudy were still recovering from their shotgun wounds. I wrote a short note to Treach: "I plan to go off on AB Billy Ray once we are in yard, so be careful."

I received a note back from Treach that said, "Lee, just duck back. This one is on me." The note surprised me greatly since I was not as tightly connected with Treach and Evil as I was with Tookie. In the five months since returning from my retrial in San Francisco, I got along well with Treach and Evil, but in a distant way. They kept mostly to themselves, but maybe I gained their respect when I went after Coleman even with a very short time left to serve.

Treach's note was saying that once we were in the yard, he would move on Billy Ray. He wanted me to avoid further violent confrontations set up by the racist prison administration, so I could be transferred out of San Quentin. Billy Ray might not be taking a piece out to the yard, but it was possible prison guards had planted a knife in the yard. Once a confrontation between me and Billy Ray started, the gun rail guard would use his shotgun, or most likely the Mini-14, rifle to shoot me dead. The prison administration would justify their use of force as necessary to break up the confrontation.

Treach, who understood the prison administration's politics, was willing to put his life on the line on my behalf, even though there was no war between the Crips and the ABs. As African Americans, the Crips naturally had an undeclared war against the racist white AB, but Treach was going out of his way to make a move on Billy Ray and stand solidly with me. The next day, the AC prison guards let Treach out first and then Billy Ray. As I waited for the guards to escort me to the yard, I heard shotgun fire in the AC yard, which was a sign that Treach moved on Billy Ray and also canceled my yard time. A little later, I saw Treach and Billy Ray getting escorted back to their cells. I received a note that said, "Billy Ray said to Treach, 'I got no beef with you,' and tried to walk away, but Treach went after Billy Ray and made a move against him. Both were shotgunned from the gun tower."

About an hour later, the guards let us out to shower. I was one of the first to be escorted, and as I neared Treach's cell, I stopped to check up on him. Treach was shot up bad, but able to get off his bed. He gave me a wide happy smile—his way of saying he took care of business. I nodded to him in appreciation. It occurred to me that within the past ten days, three of the convicts in my yard group of five were shot by prison guards, and two of the three volunteered to get shot on my behalf. As Death Row convicts, Rudy and Treach both put their lives on the line just to make sure I would leave San Quentin alive.

That same day, another big surprise awaited me.

Transfer

At about noon, my name was called out for transfer to court. I was surprised and relieved. Within the past ten days, two attempts had been made on my life. I hadn't been told of my upcoming transfer, even though the San Quentin prison officials already had the paperwork ready weeks before I left San Quentin. And now the transfer to court was finally coming through, the same day I could have been stabbed or shot to death. I was getting out of San Quentin unhurt. I was in a state of disbelief, as a convict's life is thinner than a razor's edge.

I was strip-searched for the last time by San Quentin guards and handed over to waiting deputies from Stockton. The only things I took with me were a piece of paper with names, addresses, and phone numbers of people I kept in touch with, and a poster of a dragon that I had made in San Quentin's AC. All the rest of my personal property I gave away to many different convicts I knew from the Death Row AC or the BGF yard. Calmly, I got into the backseat of a waiting car. The two-hour ride to San Joaquin County Jail in Stockton was quiet, with no conversation between me and the deputies.

During the ride, my mind kept reflecting on that morning's confrontation with Billy Ray. Thanks to Treach's "this one is on me," I survived when I might not have. This kept going through my thoughts. Then I thought of my near-confrontation with Coleman, which could have gotten me shot, if Rudy had not downed Coleman and gotten himself and Evil shot instead. I found myself reviewing the near-hits and misses during my years in Tracy, and especially in San Quentin, where I almost got stabbed on my second day there.

I was very fortunate to have some good allies on Death Row and to escape all the attempts on my life in San Quentin, where the AB and La Eme rule. I was very fortunate to have gotten out of Tracy's L yard alive, where I was outnumbered twenty-five to one by the white enemies of the NF, with only Johnny Spain to sit with me in the middle of the yard and watch my back. As all these near-death situations flashed through my mind, I thought it was truly a miracle that I was leaving after ten years of imprisonment and was only shot once during the confrontation with Harris. I looked out the car window. Freedom might be just a few days ahead of me if the San Joaquin Superior Court granted bail. Leaving San Quentin, I felt like I was coming out of the very depths of death itself.

As before, the car escorting me to the Stockton County jail took back roads, which allowed me to see the people, trees, houses, and ordinary things in free society that I was unable to see or feel while imprisoned. I felt calm and safe from the living hell of state prison. Then we arrived at the San Joaquin County Jail in Stockton. After the routine strip search, I was booked on a first-degree murder charge. The jail administration saw me as a high-security risk, so I was handcuffed in the back as the deputies escorted me to a small max cell block with no other prisoners. The cement walls were thick with bars on the cell door, almost like the strip solitary cells of state prison.

The San Joaquin County Jail seemed old. The walls were much thicker than the state prison's were. The cell block was unpainted, with blackish-gray cement, which made the max cell block feel like a dark and forbidding place. I felt very alone, as if I were the only prisoner in the jail. I could not hear any sounds—no people, no TV, or anything. After the booking, I was allowed two collect phone calls, so I called Jay Yoo and Doris Yamasaki to tell them where I was. First, I asked Jay Yoo, who was still national coordinator of the CSLDC, about the people whose house would be used as collateral to cover my bail in case the court granted bail. I asked that he try to set up the property bond, which had to be double the bail amount.

"I will arrange everything as soon as possible and visit you soon at the jail," he said.

When I talked to Doris Yamasaki, it was so comforting to hear her reassuring voice on the phone. She was very glad to hear I was in the county jail and out of the dangers of San Quentin. It seemed Doris' awareness of any situation was very high even though she had never experienced the situations I did. I always valued her thoughtfulness, and she always seemed to know exactly what to do.

I spent a quiet but restless first night in San Joaquin County Jail. I had some smokes and coffee but nothing to read. I exercised to pass the time. I felt time was moving so slowly. Next morning after breakfast, I heard the Latino voice of another prisoner who must have heard I was there and knew which cell I was in. He hollered through the front gate of the max cell block, "Hey Lee, what's happening? Do you need anything?"

"Hey, what's going on? Can you send me some books? Everything else is cool."

"All right, I will try to get some books to you."

I had no idea who he was, but there were some NFs and other Latino convicts I knew in Tracy who came from Stockton. The books never arrived, which probably meant the deputy guards were not allowing anything to be passed between me and other prisoners at the jail. After lunch, two county jail guards came to my cell and asked me politely, "Do you want to shower and get some exercise in the yard?"

"Yes," I replied.

I was placed in waist and leg chains before being allowed out of my cell to an open shower area, where the chains were removed. Both guards stood around while I showered. Without saying so, the county jail administration considered me a very high-security risk prisoner. After the shower, I was escorted to a door leading to a yard with only a cement floor and walls, and a basketball on the ground. I ran around the small yard a few times, did a few hundred push-ups, and played with the basketball, while both guards watched me inside the yard. After about forty-five minutes, they told me yard time was over and put the waist and leg chains back on to escort me back to my cell.

Next, I received a visit from Jay Yoo. We were both happy to see each other. He explained that the CSLDC planned to put up a property bond and were ready for the possibility that the judge might grant me bail. "Also, three different Korean newspapers wish to interview you," he said.

"That's fine with me," I said. On three consecutive nights, I gave interviews to three different Korean newspapers, including a reporter who came from Korea.

During this time, I was held in the max cell block of San Joaquin County Jail for ten days without ever seeing any other county jail prisoners. This was one of the hardest times I did in all the nine years and nine months of my imprisonment. Finally, one morning I was informed it was time for the arraignment. Once again, I was chained to my waist with leg irons. Wearing county jail clothes, I was placed in the backseat of a car with two county jail deputies in front. After a short ride, I entered the courtroom still in chains and saw Stuart Hanlon and some supporters there. After I pled not guilty to the charge of first-degree murder, Stuart asked for bail, and I was surprised to hear the San Joaquin Superior Court judge grant me bail of $250,000. I thought the amount would be much higher. Surprisingly, the prosecutor did not challenge the amount or seek no bail on my case. I met briefly with Stuart, who assured me my supporters would use their properties to get me out on bail. Then I was taken back to county jail.

That afternoon on the same day of March 28, 1983, I was taken back before the same judge I had seen earlier. Stuart informed him that three properties had been put up for my bail—Ranko's parents' house in Stockton, the Buddhist temple in San Francisco, and Jay Yoo's house in Sacramento. Their combined value fell just short of the required double amount of bail. However, the judge seemed impressed that people were willing to put up their properties as bond, and so he reduced the bail to allow me to be released from prison based on the actual value of property bond raised by my supporters.

By then, more people were arriving in Stockton from the Bay and Sacramento areas. Word got out that I would soon be free on bail. I was taken back to the county jail to wait for the paperwork to be finished. Even though I had waited for this day for so long, during the two-hour wait I was in a state of disbelief. Just that morning, I was led into a courtroom in leg and waist chains. Now I was wearing prison blue clothing, waiting to be free. After all the paperwork was done, Stuart Hanlon waited alone for me at the booking desk. Before he led me outside, he said, "There are a lot of news media people and supporters waiting for you. If you're not ready to face them, we could go out through the back door."

I felt numb. To be a free man all I had to do was walk a few steps out the door.

"I will walk through the front door," I said.

Stuart smiled. With controlled emotion, I followed him out of the Stockton County jail in the late afternoon into a group of about twenty-five or thirty supporters waiting along with news media. I approached the news microphone to thank all the supporters and allowed myself to be congratulated with hugs and pats. The last to give me a freedom hug was my strongest supporter, Ranko Yamada. As she gave me a friendly hug, Ranko whispered to me, "This is your life now."

*　　　*　　　*

Editorial note: On February 28, 1983, the California State Supreme Court rejected the prosecution's appeal to overturn the nullification of the Tracy murder conviction. The prosecution then moved to retry Lee on the Tracy prison killing charge. Chol Soo Lee's cocounsels reached a plea bargain in which Lee agreed to a lesser second-degree murder charge without admission of guilt. Lee, who had served nearly ten years in prison, was given the credit for his time served and released from prison on bail by California Superior Court judge K. Peter Saiers on March 28, 1983.

Postscript

During the decades since the retrial in San Francisco, I was very lucky to be befriended by many of the people who were involved in the movement to free me. I know there could never be better friends than these individuals. Every day, I am very grateful for all their efforts to help me live a normal life after prison. Without them, it is very possible I would have returned back to the only life I knew since my youth and could be back in prison today.

Long after the Chinatown murder retrial ended, Stuart Hanlon became one of my closest friends. He seemed to understand far better than I, and with great compassion, how I lacked the mind-set to function in a free society, and how difficult that adjustment might be. He never gave up on me.

After my release, journalist Raul Ramirez also spent a lot of time with me, trying to show me how normal people live. But I think he went through great anguish in the process. I realize now that after existing on a razor's edge between life and death during my ten years in prison, I walked into freedom like a baby who had to relearn how to think, act, have normal relationships, and learn the responsibilities of being a free man. I also believe I was suffering from posttraumatic stress disorder, so I might have been physically free, but mentally I continued to think like a convict. My self-destructive behavior, unfortunately, took a toll on Raul, and eventually the task of helping me readjust proved too great for him to handle alone. He realized I had to find my own path up the mountain of freedom. But I will never forget how Raul stood by me, even during some of my darkest hours as a free man. He tried his best to be a true friend while I went through madness. *[Editorial note: Raul Ramirez passed away at age 67 on November 15, 2013, in Berkeley, California, after a brief battle with esophageal cancer.]*

I must mention the one person who did the most to keep my spirits up through all my years of imprisonment—Ranko. I never discussed with

Ranko, in all the years I knew her, why she decided to help me when no one else seemed to care. Maybe it was her greater sense of justice prevailing, or her sense of loyalty to a friend of her elder sister, or maybe it was both. It's a question I need to ask her someday. I know now the reason was not her personal feelings.

But this was something that was hard to accept thirty years ago. The day of my release in 1983, I headed to Ranko's parents' house in Stockton, where they were hosting a party to celebrate my freedom. Greeting me there was an excited crowd of about thirty-five of my supporters, mostly from the San Francisco Bay and Sacramento areas. During the celebration, I just wanted a few minutes alone with Ranko, but I noticed she kept her distance from me. Still, I kept looking for her, and finally asked someone, "Where's Ranko?"

"She left the party to attend a meeting," someone replied.

I couldn't help but feel great emptiness within me. It was too difficult for me to accept. Amid all the smiles and happiness people showed during the two hours of the party, I felt only sadness when this day should have been the happiest day of my life. After the party, I kept my distance from Ranko. I showed her only coldness and didn't speak to her. Since my release, there was only one occasion when we met for dinner to discuss nonpersonal matters she wanted to clear up with me.

All these years later, I see Ranko in a different way. I think about how, at age twenty-one, this woman committed herself to helping someone she barely knew—a very noble commitment. After I expressed my love for her, that could have turned her off completely and caused her to cut off all ties with me. But she didn't. Ranko's response, all through the years, expressed an unwavering struggle for justice as her main inspiration. To this day, I still feel a special friendship toward Ranko. It is not a personal friendship I feel now, but a spiritual one.

Looking back on my life, I see that even when I was a Death Row inmate, I was far more alive than many other convicts. To truly kill a person, one must rob him of his will to live. As for myself, I could never accept a scenario where I just lay down and died, for my whole existence was about survival since my birth. I had gone through so many hardships that I'd lost track of how many times I faced death. Now, during the writing of this memoir, I feel this is my last journey of my life. Or maybe it could be the start of a new life.

Glossary of Prison Terms

AB	Aryan Brotherhood: a white supremacist prison gang.
AC	adjustment center: a "prison within a prison"; high-security area for convicts viewed as troublemakers by prison administration. Also known as the Hole.
BGF	Black Guerilla Family: a black California prison gang founded by George Jackson, rooted in the Black Power movement.
Bikers	Motorcycle gang whose members are predominantly white supremacist.
canteen	See *commissary*.
CDC	California Department of Corrections.
CDC 115	Prison disciplinary report of a serious violation of law or prison rules, usually accompanied by legal or disciplinary penalties, or both.
CDC 128	Prison information write-up of misconduct that is usually minor but is nonetheless permanently entered into a prisoner's central file.
cell	Small locked holding space where a prisoner lives and sleeps.
cell block	Two or more cells located in one section of a prison facility.
central file	File documenting each prisoner's lifelong record of conduct.
chow hall	Dining room for prisoners.
classification	Committee for profiling prisoners and assigning them to housing units.
commissary store	Prisoner store or system in prison for purchasing items for personal use.
convict	An inmate who is generally respected by other inmates.
convicts' code	Unwritten set of rules of conduct among convicts.
CYA	California Youth Authority.

Death Row	Prison unit for prisoners with death penalty sentences.
docket	Written note from administration directing prisoner to appear somewhere.
dockets	Scrip money used in the prison commissary.
DVI	Deuel Vocational Institution in Tracy, California. Often referred to as "Tracy" by inmates.
fish	A new prisoner who does not yet know the ways and rules of prison life.
free men	Prison employees who are not guards or inmates.
gladiator school	Nickname used by inmates and staff to refer to prison facilities, such as DVI, for their reputation in fostering a culture of rampant violence among inmates.
gun tower	Surveillance station with guards armed with shotguns and Mini-14 rifles.
hit	Planned assassination.
Hole	Isolated disciplinary unit for segregation of violent prisoners.
La Eme	Mexican Mafia: California prison gang of mostly Southern California Latinos. The name, La Eme, refers to the letter "M" in Spanish.
leg irons	Restraints often used during off-site transport of prisoners.
lockdown	Security measure requiring that mainline prisoners stay in their cells.
lockup unit	Housing subsection of the adjustment center.
mainline	General housing units and facilities for the "well-behaved" convict population who are not placed into isolation or protective custody. Also known as general population.
Mini-14	Lethal automatic rifle used by gun tower guards.
move	A planned maneuver or attack against an enemy.
NF	Nuestra Familia: California prison gang of mostly Northern California Latinos.
PA	Prison administrator
PC	Protective Custody: the segregation of certain prisoners to protect them from other prisoners while in custody.
piece	A prison-made weapon, usually a knife.
prison industries	Section where prisoners work manufacturing jobs.
punk	A derogatory term for a weaker male inmate who is used for sex.
R&R	Receiving and Releasing.

rat	An informer or inmate who cooperates with authorities to report on convicts.
sally port	High-security corridor in prison with locked doors on each end. Only one door can open at a time.
setup	Planned victimization of a specific target.
shank	Prison-made knife used to stab someone.
shotgun	Intentionally nonlethal weapon used by tower guards to stop fighting among convicts.
snitch	See *rat*.
spear	Prison-made weapon.
strip search	Routine full-body search of prisoners coming and going within and out of prison facilities.
tiers	Floor levels on the cell block, which often serve as territorial units.
trustee	Prisoner trusted to do work outside his cell, such as sweeping up or food service.
TS	Texas Syndicate: A Latino prison gang founded at Folsom State Prison in the early 1970s in response to other prison gangs, especially the Aryan Brotherhood and La Eme, that victimized native Texan inmates.
waist chain	Bodily restraint.
welfare package	Personal need items (e.g., soap, toothpaste, tobacco) given to new inmates by fellow gang members or racial group members.
yard	Fenced outdoor exercise area for prisoners.
zip gun	Prison-made hand gun.

About the Editor

RICHARD S. KIM is associate professor of Asian American studies at the University of California, Davis. He received his PhD in US history from the Department of History at the University of Michigan. He also obtained an MA in Asian American studies from UCLA. He is the author of *The Quest for Statehood: Korean Immigrant Nationalism and U.S. Sovereignty, 1905–1945* (Oxford University Press, 2011). His research and teaching interests include Asian American history, transnationalism and diaspora, race and ethnicity, and social and political movements.

INTERSECTIONS

Asian and Pacific American Transcultural Studies

What Is Asian American Biblical Hermeneutics? Reading the New Testament
TAT-SIONG BENNY LIEW

The New Sun
TARO YASHIMA

Hakka Soul: Memories, Migrations, Meals
CHIN WOON PING

A Japanese Robinson Crusoe
JENICHIRO OYABE

Rosebud and Other Stories
WAKAKO YAMAUCHI
LILLIAN HOWAN, ED.

The Dance of Identities: Korean Adoptees and Their Journey toward Empowerment
JOHN D. PALMER

From Okinawa to the Americas: Hana Yamagawa and Her Reminiscences of a Century
AKIKO YAMAGAWA HIBBETT, ED.

Ancestry of Experience: A Journey into Hawaiian Ways of Knowing
LEILANI HOLMES

Scrutinized! Surveillance in Asian North American Literature
MONICA CHIU

Encountering Modernity: Christianity in East Asia and Asian America
ALBERT L. PARK AND DAVID K. YOO, EDS.

Transpacific Studies: Framing an Emerging Field
JANET HOSKINS AND VIET THANH NGUYEN, EDS.

Out of the Dust: New and Selected Poems
JANICE MIRIKITANI

Romancing Human Rights: Gender, Intimacy, and Power between Burma and the West
TAMARA C. HO

The Blind Writer: Stories and a Novella
SAMEER PANDYA

Ship of Fate: Memoir of a Vietnamese Repatriate
TRẦN ĐÌNH TRỤ
BAC HOAI TRAN AND JANA K. LIPMAN, TRANS.

Printed in the United States
By Bookmasters